JACKSON SCHOOL PUBLICATIONS IN INTERNATIONAL STUDIES

JACKSON SCHOOL PUBLICATIONS IN INTERNATIONAL STUDIES

Senator Henry M. Jackson was convinced that the study of the history, cultures, political systems, and languages of the world's major regions was an essential prerequisite for wise decision-making in international relations. In recognition of his deep commitment to higher education and advanced scholarship, this series of publications has been established through the generous support of the Henry M. Jackson Foundation, in cooperation with the Henry M. Jackson School of International Studies and the University of Washington Press.

The Crisis of Leninism and the Decline of the Left:
The Revolutions of 1989, edited by Daniel Chirot

Sino-Soviet Normalization and Its International Implications,
1945–1990,
by Lowell Dittmer

The Crisis
of
Leninism
and the
Decline of the Left

The Revolutions of 1989

Edited by DANIEL CHIROT

UNIVERSITY OF WASHINGTON PRESS
Seattle and London

LIBRARY OF CONGRESS CATALOGING-IN-PUBLICATION DATA

The Crisis of Leninism and the decline of the Left : the revolutions
  of 1989 / edited by Daniel Chirot.
      p.   cm. — (Jackson School publications in international studies)
      Papers from a conference held at the Henry M. Jackson School of International
  Studies.
      Includes index.
      ISBN 0-295-97110-X (alk. paper). — ISBN 0-295-97111-8 (pbk. : alk. paper)
      1. Soviet Union—Politics and government—1985- —Congresses.   2. China—
  Politics and government—1976- —Congresses.   3. Europe, Eastern—Politics and
  government—1989- —Congresses.   I. Chirot, Daniel.   II. Henry M. Jackson School of
  International Studies.   III. Series.
  DK288.C74   1991   91-11289
  909.82'9—dc20   CIP

Contents

Acknowledgments

This conference and book were made possible by a grant from the Henry M. Jackson Foundation. I would like to thank Robin Pasquarella, Lisa Napoli, and Susan Gould of the Foundation for their help and advice. Also, I thank Mary Bernson, Betsy Goolian, Laurie Pollack, and Karen Walton of the Henry M. Jackson School of International Studies at the University of Washington who helped me organize the conference and prepare some of its papers for publication. Finally, my able research assistant, Betsy Amsden, helped me greatly, and I thank her, too.

DANIEL CHIROT
December 1990
Seattle

Introduction

DANIEL CHIROT

NO POLITICALLY literate person in the world can doubt that 1989, like 1789, will be remembered as one of those decisive years in which decades of slow political and economic change and development culminated in a series of unexpected, dramatic events that suddenly redefined the world. But this does not mean that there is anything close to universal agreement, even among the most expert analysts, about the full meaning and consequences of what happened. That communism collapsed in Eastern Europe is obvious. But will it therefore disappear entirely in the Soviet Union, too? And what about China, North Korea, Vietnam, and Cuba? Is this the end of socialism, or just of its Marxist-Leninist version? Or, as some on the left believe, is what happened merely the death of a Stalinist deviation that distorted and postponed the true historical mission of Marxism? Will liberal democratic capitalism in its Anglo-American form, which fifty years ago seemed on the verge of extinction at the hands of a combined fascist-communist, totalitarian alliance, now sweep to global triumph and end the debates about what is the best model of society? Or is America also on a downward path, like its former enemy, the Soviet Union, and will the world of the near future be even more full of conflict and danger than the past few decades of stable cold war?

To answer all these questions it is necessary to know the future, not just for one or two years, but for many decades, or perhaps a century or two. After all, without stretching historical analogies too far, it is worth remembering that those who may have tried to judge the consequences of the American Revolution in 1777, one year after the Declaration of Independence, or of the French Revolution in 1790, one year after the fall of the Bastille and the sweeping reforms of the early revolutionary days, or of Russian Bolshevism in 1918, would have missed most of the significant consequences of what was going on under their very eyes. No matter how historians may argue, often with great insight, that the American Constitution, the emergence of Bonapartism, and the triumph of Stalinism were inherent in the developments of the very early revolutionary years in the United States, France, and Russia, these developments hardly seemed inevitable to those who lived through them. Nor is the ultimate triumph of capitalist liberalism inevitable today, though it now seems more likely than it did a few years ago. At the same time, the defeat of Soviet communism and its disintegration in the most advanced part of the former communist world, namely Eastern Europe, may not spell the end of all totalitarian utopias for the rest of human history. Our happiness about what happened must be tempered by the memory of all that preceded 1989 in the twentieth century.

Our inability to predict the future necessarily impedes our interpretative powers. It would be nice to know how the drama of the revolutions of 1989 will end; then the history of these events could be written as a coherent play, with a beginning in the first half of the twentieth century, a development during the cold war, a climax in the late 1980s, an unfolding of the consequences of the climax in the 1990s, and a logically satisfying end at the start of the twenty-first century. But our failure to see the future does not excuse us from trying to explain these great events, nor from trying to interpret them in a way that can help us make reasonable estimates about possible future lines of change that will flow from the extraordinarily climactic year of 1989.

Knowing very well that any final judgment is premature, but that 1989 was far too consequential and interesting a year to let it lie unexamined for a few decades, the Henry M. Jackson Foundation funded a gathering for a few days in Seattle in late October 1990, so that a small number of major scholars could discuss some of the most critical questions posed by the events of the past year. We tried to avoid punditry, leaving that to those who know less but are much surer of their infallibility than most of us. Instead, we concentrated on recent history, on the examination of the ideological conflicts that have shaped the twentieth century, and on an evaluation of the social, political, and economic forces unleashed by the revolutions of 1989. The nine essays that make up this book were presented at that conference.

We seemed to disagree about two important issues. One key disagreement was between the "Asianists" and those of us who have specialized in studying European societies (including the United States and Canada, of course). Elizabeth Perry, Nicholas Lardy, and Bruce Cumings presented papers that emphasized the survival of communism in Asia despite the trauma of Tiananmen Square in China, the economic difficulties in China, Vietnam, and North Korea, and the loss of almost all hope of future political, military, and economic aid from their former European allies in the last two of these countries. On the other hand, Ken Jowitt strongly stated his position that Leninism—that is, rigorous one-party rule guided by the vision of a future classless socialist utopia, and characterized by harsh economic central planning as the only road to rapid modernization and industrialization—died once and for all in 1989. He ascribed the ostensible survival of Leninist regimes in East Asia and Cuba to the simple fact that tough old leaders from the original revolutionary generation are still alive. These leaders have devoted their lives to unending war and struggle and cannot renounce their dreams, or admit that their goals cannot be realized. But in all cases, these are old men, especially in China; after they die, Jowitt claims, Leninism, which has been morally disgraced and shown to be an inferior economic model, will collapse as quickly as in Eastern Europe. Stephen Hanson's exceptionally original analysis of how Gorbachev tried to revive Marxism-

Leninism, and how he failed, concurs with Jowitt's judgment, as does my essay on Eastern Europe. Seymour Martin Lipset's detailed exposition of how the left has been failing throughout the noncommunist world for over a decade also supports implicitly the notion that the remaining communist dinosaurs may be walking corpses rather than the living, growing embodiments of a future they once claimed to herald.

But on closer inspection, the disagreement between these two sets of views is not that large. Nicholas Lardy explains that communist China's economic reforms have succeeded far better than those tried in European communist countries, but that has been done by allowing the private sector to grow so quickly that it now represents over half of all production in China. It can be argued that if the Soviet Union or any East European country had managed such a feat during the 1980s, it would not have been reduced to such dire straits by the end of the decade. Elizabeth Perry, by also mentioning Taiwan, emphasizes the very important fact that there is nothing inherent in Chinese culture that will always block democracy and capitalism. On the contrary, the reason the demonstrations during the spring of 1989 failed to revolutionize China was that their student leaders did not make enough of an effort to mobilize the broad popular support that might have been forthcoming. The scope of the demonstrations suggests that the student leaders, who played out the role of traditional Confucian literati more than of popular leaders, could have done much better, and that there exists the moral basis for a future overthrow of communism. Bruce Cumings, in the part of his essay that discusses North Korea, reminds us that Kim Il Sung may be a living anachronism but he is also the product of a long history of internal civil conflict in Korea and intense international rivalries around Korea. The events behind these internal and external conflicts have not been forgotten, even if conditions have changed. Thus, unlike the rapid reunion of West and East Germany, the easy dismantling of the border between North and South Korea is unlikely even after Kim's death. In all, then, the articles of the "Asianists" remind us of something we all know, but too often forget. Each country is distinctive, and efforts to understand the general forces at work throughout the world should not overlook the specific historical and cultural influences that make seemingly similar global forces have such different effects in various parts of the world.

The other major disagreement that appeared was between the liberal optimists and those who see a problematic future for the liberal capitalist model. Not all papers discussed this dichotomy, but the important program set forth by Walt Rostow made his faith in the power of liberalism evident. His suggestions amount to nothing less than a call for the United States, in conjunction with Western Europe and Japan, to set out on the path originally envisioned by a confident, rich, powerful America at the time of the Marshall Plan in the late 1940s. It is a welcome reminder to think broadly about the immense forces for good that can be unleashed by combining capitalist dynamism with reasonable government planning and help. Seymour Martin

Lipset's argument about the global decline of the left indicates his broad agreement with Rostow's faith in the power of liberal capitalist democracy to solve the major problems facing modern societies. If the socialist model has failed so badly, what is left but the liberal model? In fact, as Lipset points out, that is the direction in which the democratic parts of the world have moved in the past two decades, and with good reason. But Ken Jowitt, whose admiration for liberalism is evident, is much more pessimistic. In much of the world, including the Soviet Union and Eastern Europe, he fears the rise of hysterical nationalism, anti-Westernism, and a turning toward religious rejections of modernity. Bruce Cumings reminds us that liberalism's limitations viewed from both the left and the right have been the basis of the most disturbing ideological movements in the twentieth century. Not all economic modernization is liberal, and the obvious failure of an antiquated Stalinist model does not mean that the only alternative is the American way. David Calleo, whose essay explores relations between the United States and Western Europe, points out that great tensions remain, and that there is now less basis for agreement than when there was a powerful external enemy. Unless we develop more imaginative ways of understanding the world, we risk seeing the growth of very serious divisions within the advanced capitalist democracies. Calleo, in fact, views the United States as a country as bereft of a viable world vision as the Soviet Union, and implies that both superpowers, not just the Soviets, have failed. To hold on to the fossilized doctrines of the cold war can lead only to disaster.

Again, however, the differences are not as great as they might seem to be. Rostow subtly includes an attack against the Anglo-American conservative ideologues of the 1980s by insisting that government involvement is crucial if economic development is to occur. Nor did the Marshall Plan succeed just because a free market existed. There had to be a vision, a belief that great accomplishments were possible. American aid was certainly important for its own sake, but even more, it provided a "jump start" and the confidence that recovery and growth were possible. To promote economic development in the former communist countries devastated by decades of technological backwardness and mismanagement, there has to be faith that it is possible, and this is something that only capital and aid from the West can provide. Someone must now provide vision like that offered by the United States to Western Europe in the late 1940s, otherwise the immense problems that beset the former communist countries will prove insurmountable. Calleo, whose skepticism about the United States seems to be in opposition to Rostow's optimism, is really calling for the same thing in defining American foreign policy, a new and viable vision. And ultimately, Calleo believes that the main barrier to a successful American policy is the mistaken domestic policies of the 1970s and 1980s, which have led to a stagnant American economy, an unworkable deficit, a narrow, pinched view of the role of government, and a loss of faith in our ability to solve our own problems. If we fail to solve those problems, how can we impart any vision to a doubting world?

Both Jowitt and Cumings agree that the problem with the emerging ideological smugness in the United States is that it fails to examine why, despite
the evident material successes of liberal capitalism in the twentieth century,
most of the last eight decades have been occupied by struggles between that
order and its fascist, communist, and anti-Western opponents. In other
words, if we're so good, why has it taken so much violence and suffering in
the twentieth century to prove it? To ask the question is not to be antiliberal,
antidemocratic, or anticapitalist; it is, however, to recognize history. Why,
after all, did most of the intellectuals in most of the world remain antiliberal,
antidemocratic, and anticapitalist until they were forced by war or catastrophic political and economic failures to recognize that they had been
wrong? And what makes us think that the lesson has been learned? Americans thought theirs was the natural order for the whole world in 1918 at the
end of World War I, and again in 1945 after World War II. Should we be
confident now in 1990, after the cold war? Or are the events in the Near East
merely the prelude to another set of desperate struggles that will again test
liberal democracy? Is there any proof that the virtues of the eighteenth-
century European Enlightenment are now all that obvious to the majority of
the world? Even Lipset's paper, which celebrates the triumph of liberal democracy, ends with the reminder that it would be an error to project an eternal future from a trend that has taken hold only in the last couple of decades,
and that could be reversed once more in the future.

Despite ostensible disagreements on some important points, on others
there are obvious agreement. We could have found some scholars who still
believe that the failure of Leninism in Europe was not a serious blow against
socialism, and even some to defend the systems that fell, but these days such
arguments are a combination of wishful thinking and willful ideological men-
dacity. None of the papers in this book take such views. We could have
found scholars who really believe that this is the "end of history," and that
the triumph of American liberalism is assured once and for all. Although
some—probably most—of the authors of the articles in this book may wish
that this were so, none are able to dismiss their well-developed historical
skepticism quite so easily.

Along with the general issues about which we could agree or disagree,
each of these papers contains much that is unique. In particular, Stephen
Hanson makes a point that most Soviet specialists might deny. Gorbachev,
whose drive for internal Soviet reform and whose unwillingness to accept
continued Soviet military intervention abroad made the revolutions of 1989
possible, was not only a committed modernizer but a believing Marxist-
Leninist who was led into error precisely for that reason. He believed that to
save the Soviet system he had to free the natural inclination of the Soviet
masses to be active, dedicated communists, and thus their innate desire to
work harder to increase their productivity. He believed that he had to liberate his people from the artificial constraints of repressive Stalinism. How it
was possible for Gorbachev and those immediately around him to believe

that the liberated masses would turn out to be enthusiastic communists needs to be explained. Doing that, Hanson suddenly unlocks the key mystery about Gorbachev: how he could make the enormous errors that have virtually destroyed the system in which he believed, even as he remained so confident in his ability to solve his country's problems. Only in 1990 did it begin to dawn on him that he had misjudged the situation. Yet he could not have chosen a different path, because he had run up against contradictions in Marxism that had almost destroyed it before, but were now too great to overcome.

Elizabeth Perry's essay and mine have much to say about another crucial topic, the loss of moral legitimacy in communist systems. Most social scientists, even as they meticulously catalogued all the economic failures, social problems, and political contradictions of communism, failed to foresee what was to happen in 1989. In the end, whether in China, the Soviet Union, or the six different countries of Eastern Europe that experienced revolutions, the ruling parties had lost their moral legitimacy. That did not happen just in 1989 (Nicholas Lardy suggests that in China, at least, it was a much older problem), but it took place gradually, undermining the moral basis of the party-states so that in Europe they were left without any residue of support in a time of sudden crisis. Even the elites, with a few exceptions, such as Gorbachev, had ceased to believe. But social scientists, who have become quite good at measuring economic, demographic, or other social trends, remain uncomfortable dealing with such vague concepts as "legitimacy," "faith," and "morality." It may be that this is what was missing in the work about communist societies before 1989: a precise awareness of how vulnerable social systems had become when no longer supported by any faith. That should be a lesson to those who study other societies, for the twenty-first century will almost certainly be filled with many examples of societies that will collapse because of moral failure and lack of legitimacy.

One of the most astonishing insights to be gained by studying the events of 1989 is that George Orwell's brilliant understanding of modern totalitarianism, and Hannah Arendt's equally persuasive and penetrating discussion of that phenomenon, were wrong. The more modern a society, the more educated, the more literate, the more difficult it becomes to maintain the web of lies on which communist regimes came to depend. It is simply not true that the modern state can monopolize forever the means of communication and so atomize a society that resistance, or even deviant thinking, becomes impossible. On the contrary, such strategies of falsification work only for a time, but gradually fail as societies modernize and become more literate and aware. Yet it took so long for this to become apparent—almost sixty years in the Soviet Union (since the start of Stalinist collectivization) and over forty in Eastern Europe—that Orwell and Arendt remain useful. No doubt if a brilliant new utopian theory were to appear, promising salvation at the cost of enslavement, countless intellectuals would rush to accept it all over the world, and new revolutions would come to recreate revived forms of totalitarianism that would themselves take decades to erode. After all, what are the Iranian and Ba'thist tyrannies in the Near East if not a proof that this is possible, even in the very late twentieth century?

Such grand conclusions, which have a way of turning into boring superficiality if they are treated too ponderously, are ably discussed by Ken Jowitt, and especially by Bruce Cumings with a fine sense of irony that allows readers to think about the most important ideological questions of our day without sinking into pompous platitudes. These two essays are reminders that it remains extremely important to analyze the abstract thoughts of political intellectuals very carefully. It is from them that the biggest and most awful ideas of our century have come.

The contributors to this volume have not made many specific predictions. But by explaining what happened, what forces have been at work in the great struggles that led to 1989, and how these forces continue to operate, we hope to have made it clear that there continues to be a future over which to struggle, and that no outcome is predetermined.

The Crisis

of

Leninism

and the

Decline of the Left

The Revolutions of 1989

What Happened in Eastern Europe in 1989?

DANIEL CHIROT

THE WORLD KNOWS that in Eastern Europe communism collapsed in 1989, and that the USSR set out on a path that not only promises the end of socialism but threatens its very territorial integrity. But knowing this does not explain why it all happened. Nor are the implications of all these revolutionary events as clear as the immediate, short-run strategic effects that follow from the dissolution of the Warsaw Pact and the Council for Mutual Economic Assistance.

There are many ways of looking at the "Revolution of 1989." As with other great revolutionary events—the French Revolution of 1789, the European revolutions of 1848, the Bolshevik Revolution of 1917, or the Chinese Revolution of 1949—economic, political, cultural, and social analyses offer only partial insights. Everything was interconnected, yet no single analysis can entirely absorb all aspects of such cataclysmic events. Even after two hundred years, the French Revolution is still a subject for debate, and novel interpretations remain possible; and if the political controversy generated by that revolution two centuries ago has cooled somewhat, for well over a century and a half it remained a burning issue at the center of European and world politics. [1]

We should not be surprised, then, if over the next several decades the events of 1989 form the basis of much passionate political and scholarly debate. Having said this, I should add that for those of us interested in social change, revolutionary periods offer the most important fields of observation. We cannot, of course, conduct controlled laboratory experiments that suit the needs of our research. But, in fact, revolutions are large-scale social experiments. Although they are not tailored to scholarly ends, or by any stretch of the imagination controllable, they are the closest thing we have to those major scientific experiments that have shaped our understanding of the physical world. Great revolutions, then, are better windows into how societies operate in the long run than almost any other type of historical event. Therefore, aside from being immediately and keenly interested in the events that took place in Eastern Europe in 1989 because they are reshaping the international political order, we also have a fascinating, unexpected, revealing glimpse into how seemingly stable, enduring social systems fail and collapse.

THE UNDERLYING CAUSES

Economic Problems

There is no question that the most visible, though certainly not the only reason for the collapse of East European communism has been economic. It is not that these systems failed in an absolute sense. No East European country, not even Romania, was an Ethiopia or a Burma, with famine and a reversion to primitive, local subsistence economies. Perhaps several of these economies, particularly Romania's, and to a more limited extent Poland's, were headed in that direction, but they had very far to fall before reaching such low levels. Other economies—in Hungary, but even more so in Czechoslovakia and East Germany—were failures only by the standards of the most advanced capitalist economies. On a world scale these were rich, well-developed economies, not poor ones. The Soviet Union, too, was still a world economic and technological power, despite deep pockets of regional poverty and a standard of living much lower than its per capita production figures would indicate.[2]

There is no need to go over the defects of socialist economies in detail. These have been explained by the many excellent economists from those countries, particularly the Poles and Hungarians—the two most famous of whom are Wlodzimierz Brus and János Kornai.[3]

The main problem is that investment and production decisions were based largely, though not entirely, on political will rather than domestic or international market pressures. To overcome the force of the domestic market, which ultimately meant consumer and producer wishes and decisions, the quantities and prices of goods and services were fixed by administrative order. And to exclude external market forces, which might have weakened domestic guidance of the economy, foreign trade with the advanced capitalist world was curtailed and strictly controlled, partly by fiat but also by maintaining nonconvertible currencies. The aim of curtailing the power of market forces was achieved, but an inevitable side effect was that under these conditions it became impossible to measure what firms were profitable and what production processes were more or less efficient. There were no real prices.

As the inefficiencies of socialist economies became evident, it proved impossible to reform them, largely because the managers were so closely tied to the ruling political machinery. They were able to lobby effectively to steer investments in their direction, regardless of the efficiency of their enterprises. Success as a manager was measured by the ability to produce more, maintain high employment, and attract politically directed investment, not by producing marketable goods more efficiently. Equally important, the very concept of profit as a measure of efficiency was foreign to these managers.[4]

Such systems developed inevitable shortages of desired goods. This was partly because production was so inefficient that it kept the final output of consumer goods lower than it should have been at such high levels of industrialization. And the very crude ways of measuring success, in terms of gross output, slighted essential services and spare parts, so that the very production process was damaged by shortages of key producer goods and services.

But whereas in some cases it was possible to carry out reform, most notably in agriculture and some services (the outstanding successes were the Chinese decollectivization of agriculture after 1976 and the Hungarians' ability to privatize some services and small-scale agricultural production), in industries the power of the communist party and its managers was simply too strong to carry out real change. Furthermore, the sincere commitment to full employment and the maintenance of low food prices further damaged efficiency.[5]

But none of this would have made the slightest sense without the ideological base of communism. Some critics of communist economic arrangements have argued that the system was simply irrational. In strict economic terms, it may have been, but that hardly explains its long life. The key is that political will was ultimately the primary determinant of economic action, and this will was based on a very coherent world view developed by Lenin, Stalin, and the other Bolshevik leaders. This view then spread to other communist leaders, and was imposed on about one-third of the world's population.

Lenin was born in 1870, and Stalin in 1878 or 1879. They matured as political beings in their teens and early twenties when the most advanced areas of the world were in the industrial heartland of Western Europe and the United States, in the Ruhr, or in the emerging miracles of modern technology being constructed in the American Middle West, from Pittsburgh and Buffalo to Chicago. It is not mere coincidence that these areas, and others like them (including the major steel and shipbuilding centers of Britain, or the coal and steel centers of northern France and Belgium), became, one hundred years later, giant rust belts with antiquated industries, overly powerful trade unions, and unimaginative, conservative, and bureaucratic managers. It has been in such areas, too, that industrial pollution has most ravaged the environment, and where political pressures resistant to free trade and the imposition of external market forces were the fiercest in the advanced countries. But in 1900 these areas were progressive, and for ambitious leaders from a relatively backward country like Russia, they were viable models.

Lenin, Stalin, and all the other Bolshevik intellectuals and leaders— Trotsky, Kamenev, Zinoviev, Bukharin, and so many others—knew that this was what they ultimately had to emulate. They felt, however, that they would make it all happen more quickly and more efficiently by socialist planning than by the random and cruel play of market forces. Despite the inherent inefficiencies of socialism, these astonishing, visionary men— particularly Stalin—actually succeeded. The tragedy of communism was not its failure, but its success. Stalin built the institutional framework that, against all logic, forced the Soviet Union into success.[6] By the 1970s the USSR had the world's most advanced late nineteenth-century economy, the world's biggest and best, most inflexible rust belt. It is as if Andrew Carnegie had taken over the entire United States, forced it into becoming a giant copy of U.S. Steel, and the executives of the same U.S. Steel had continued to run the country into the 1970s and 1980s!

To understand the absurdity of this situation, it is necessary to go back and take a historical look at the development of capitalism. There have been five industrial ages so far. Each was dominated by a small set of "high technology" industries located in the most advanced parts of the industrial world. Each has been characterized by rapid, extraordinary growth and innovation in the leading sectors, followed by slower growth, and finally relative stagnation, overproduction, increasing competition, declining profits, and crisis in the now aging leading sectors. It was precisely on his observations about the rise and fall of the first industrial age that Karl Marx based his conclusions about the eventual collapse of capitalism. But each age has been followed by another, as unexpected new technologies have negated all the predictions about the inevitable fall of profits and the polarization of capitalist societies into a tiny number of rich owners and masses of impoverished producers.

The ages, with their approximate dates, have been: (1) the cotton-textile age dominated by Great Britain, which lasted from about the 1780s into the 1830s; (2) the rail and iron age, also dominated by Britain, which went from the 1840s into the early 1870s; (3) the steel and organic chemistry age, one that also saw the development of new industries based on the production and utilization of electrical machinery, which ran from the 1870s to World War I, and in which the American and German economies became dominant; (4) the age of automobiles and petrochemicals, from the 1910s to the 1970s, in which the United States became the overwhelmingly hegemonic economy; and (5) the age of electronics, information, and biotechnology, which began in the 1970s and will certainly run well into the first half of the next century. In this last age, it is not yet certain which economies will dominate, though certainly the Japanese and West Europeans are well on their way to replacing the Americans.[7]

Transitions have been difficult. Depressions and political turmoil from the 1820s to the 1840s, in the 1870s and 1880s, and in the 1920s and 1930s can be explained, in good part, by the complications of passing from one age to another. World War I—or more particularly the mad race for colonies in the late nineteenth century and the European arms race, especially the naval one between Germany and Britain—was certainly a function of the shifting economic balance in Europe. World War II resulted from the unsatisfactory outcome of the First World War, and from the Great Depression of the 1930s. The shocks from the latest transition to the fifth industrial age have been mild by comparison, but the difficulties that attended past transitions produced many predictions about the imminent collapse of capitalism that seemed reasonable at the time.[8] This brief bit of economic history has to be connected to the events of 1989.

The Soviet model—the Leninist-Stalinist model—was based on the third industrial age, the one whose gleaming promises of mighty, smoke-filled concentrations of chemical and steel mills, huge electric generating plants, and hordes of peasants migrating into new factory boomtowns mesmerized the Bolshevik leadership. The Communist Party of the Soviet Union found out that creating such a world was not easy, especially in the face of stubborn peasant and worker refusal to accept present hardships as the price for eventual industrial utopia. But Stalin persuaded the CPSU that the vision was so correct that it was worth paying a very high price to attain it. The price was paid, and the model turned into reality.[9]

Later, the same model was imposed on Eastern Europe. Aside from the sheer force used to ensure that the East Europeans complied, it must also be said that the local communists, many of whom were only a generation younger than Stalin, accepted the model. Those who came from more backward countries particularly shared Stalin's vision. In Romania, Nicolae Ceausescu held on to it until his last day in power. It was based on his interpretation of his country's partial, uneven, and highly unsatisfactory drive for industrialization in the 1930s, when he was a young man just becoming an active communist.[10] To a degree we usually do not realize, because China remained so heavily agricultural, this was Mao's vision too.[11] Today its last practitioner is Ceausescu's contemporary and close ideological ally, Kim Il Sung.

In the Soviet Union, in the more backward areas of Eastern Europe, in the already partly industrial areas of China (especially on the coast and in Manchuria), and in North Korea, the model worked because there were a lot of peasants to bring into the labor force, because this type of economy required massive concentrations of investments into huge, centralized firms, and because, after all, the technology for all this was pretty well worked out. Also, producer goods were more important than consumer goods at this stage. (It is worth remembering, too, that these were all areas where industrialization had begun *before* communism, either because of local initiatives, as in Russia or most of Eastern Europe, or because of Japanese colonial investments, as in North Korea and Manchuria.)

I should note, in passing, that the model is particularly disastrous for very backward economies that have no industrial base to begin with. Thus, whatever successes it may have had in East Asia and Europe, it has produced nothing but disaster when tried in Africa or Indochina.

But if the Stalinist model may be said to have had some success in creating "third age" industrial economies, it never adapted well to the fourth age of automobiles, consumer electrical goods, and the growth of services to pamper a large proportion of the general population. This is why we were able to make fun of the Soviet model, even in the 1950s and 1960s, because it offered so few luxuries and services. But the Soviets and those who believed in the Stalinist-Leninist model could reply that yes, they did not cater to spoiled consumers, but the basic sinews of industrial and military power, the giant steel mills and power generating plants, had been built well enough to create an economy almost as powerful as that of the United States.

Alas for the Soviet model, the fifth age turned out to be even more different. Small firms, very rapid change, extreme attention to consumer needs,
reliance on innovative thinking—all were exactly what the Stalinist model
lacked. Of course, so did much of America's and Western Europe's "rust
belt" industry—chemicals, steel, autos. But even as they fought rearguard
actions to protect themselves against growing foreign competition and technological change, these sectors had to adapt because market pressures were
too intense to resist. Their political power was great, but in capitalist societies open to international trade it was not sufficient to overcome the world
market. In the Soviet case, such industries, protected by the party and
viewed as the very foundation of everything that communism had built,
were able to resist change, at least for another twenty years. That was what
the Brezhnev years were—a determined effort to hold on to the late
nineteenth-century model the Bolsheviks had worked so hard to emulate.
So, from being just amusing, their relative backwardness in the 1970s and
1980s became dangerous. The Soviets and East Europeans (including the
Czechs and East Germans) found themselves in the 1980s with the most advanced industries of the late nineteenth and early twentieth centuries—
polluting, wasteful, energy intensive, massive, inflexible—in short, with
giant rust belts.[12]

Of course, it was worse than this. It was not just the adherence to an outdated, inflexible model that prevented adequate progress, but all of the well-
known failures of socialism. The point is that the struggle to keep out the
world market, to exclude knowledge about what was going on in the more
successful capitalist world, became more and more difficult. It also became
more dangerous because it threatened to deepen backwardness. Finally,
what had been possible in the early stages of communism, when the leadership was fresh and idealistic about creating a more perfect world, no longer
succeeded in the face of the growing awareness and cynicism about the
model's failure.

But the Soviet and East European leaders in the Brezhnev years were
very aware of their growing problems. Much of their time was spent trying
to come up with solutions that would nevertheless preserve the key elements of party rule, Soviet power, and the new ruling class's power and privilege. The Soviets urged their East European dependencies to overcome
their problems by plunging into Western markets. That was the aim of
détente. China, of course, followed the same path after 1978. This meant
borrowing to buy advanced technology, and then trying to sell to the West to
repay the debts. But as we now know, the plan did not work. The Stalinist
systems were too rigid. Managers resisted change. They used their political
clout to force ever greater investments in obsolete firms and production processes. Also, in some cases, most notably in Poland and Hungary, foreign
loans started to be used simply to purchase consumer goods to make people
happier, to shore up the crumbling legitimacy of regimes that had lost what
youthful vigor they had once possessed and were now viewed simply as tools

of a backward occupying power. This worked until the bills came due, and prices had to be raised. Societies with little or no experience with free markets responded to price increases with political instability. This was especially true in Poland, but it became a potential problem in Hungary (and China) because it created growing and very visible social inequities between the small class of new petty entrepreneurs and the large portion of the urban population still dependent on the socialist sector.[13] (Kornai and others have explained why the partial freeing of the market in economies of shortage create ate quasi-monopolistic situations favoring the rapid accumulation of profits by those entrepreneurs able to satisfy long repressed, immense demand.)[14]

What had seemed at first to be a series of sensible reforms proved to be the last gasp of European communism. The reforms did not eliminate the rigidities of Stalinism, but they spread further cynicism and disillusionment, exacerbated corruption, and opened the communist world to a vastly increased flow of Western capitalist ideas and standards of consumerism. They also created a major debt problem. In this situation, the only East European leader who responded with perfect consistency was Ceausescu. He reimposed strict Stalinism. But neither Romania's principled Stalinism, Hungarian semireformism, nor Polish inconsistency and hesitation worked.[15]

Political and Moral Causes of Change

If understanding economic problems is fundamental, it is nevertheless the changing moral and political climate of Eastern Europe that really destroyed communism there. There is no better way to approach this topic than by using the old concept of legitimacy. Revolutions occur only when elites and some significant portion of the general population—particularly intellectuals, but also ordinary people—have lost confidence in the moral validity of their social and political system.

There have never been advanced industrial countries, except at the end of major, catastrophic wars, in which the basic legitimacy of the system collapsed. And if some serious questions were raised in Germany after World War I, France in 1940, or Germany and Japan in 1945, there were no successful revolutions there. It would be laughable to claim that Eastern Europe's economic problems in the 1980s approached such levels of massive crisis as those brought about by utter defeat in international war. To have had such revolutionary situations developing in times of peace and relative stability, in societies with a strong sense of their nationhood, with functioning infrastructures, police forces, armies, and governments, in the absence of foreign invaders or international crises, without precipitating civil wars, famines, or even depressions, is unprecedented. No mere recitation of economic problems can provide sufficient explanation.

To see how this loss of legitimacy occurred, it is necessary to go back to the beginning. In the mid to late 1940s, at least among cadres and a substantial number of young idealists, communism had a considerable degree of legitimacy, even where it had been imposed by force, as in all of Eastern Europe. After all, capitalism seemed to have performed poorly in the 1930s, the liberal European democracies had done little to stop Hitler until it was too late, and Stalin appeared to be a leader who had saved the Soviet Union. The claim that Marxism-Leninism was the "progressive," inevitable wave of the future was not so farfetched. In fact, many intellectuals throughout Europe, East and West, were seduced by these promises.[16]

In the Soviet Union itself, as in China after 1949, communism benefited from the substantial nationalist accomplishments it had to its credit. Foreigners had been defeated and national greatness reasserted. For all of the problems faced by these regimes, there was clear economic growth and extraordinary progress.[17]

The repressions, terror, and misery of life in the early 1950s soured some believers, but after Stalin's death, reform seemed possible. And after all, the claims made about rapid urbanization, industrialization, and the spread of modern health and educational benefits to the population were true. Not 1956, when the Hungarian revolution was crushed, but 1968 was the decisive turning point. That was when the implications of the Brezhnev policy became clear. Fundamental political reform was not going to be allowed. It must be said in Brezhnev's defense that what happened in 1989, in both Eastern Europe and China, has proved that in a sense his policy of freezing reform was perfectly correct. To have done otherwise would have brought about an earlier demise of communism. Economic liberalization gives new hope for political liberalization to the growing professional and bureaucratic middle classes and to the intelligentsia. It further increases the appeal of liberal economic ideas as well as of democracy. The demand for less rigid central control obviously threatens the party's monopoly of power.

Whatever potential communist liberalism may have had in the Prague Spring of 1968, the way in which it was crushed, and the subsequent gradual disillusion with strictly economic reform in Hungary and Poland in the 1970s, brought to an end the period in which intellectuals could continue to hope about the future of communism.

But this was not all. The very inflexibility of communist economies, the unending shortages, and the overwhelming bureaucratization of every aspect of life created a general malaise. The only way to survive in such systems was through corruption, the formal violation of the rules. That, in turn, left many, perhaps almost all of the managerial and professional class, open to the possibility of blackmail, and to a pervasive sense that they were living a perpetual lie.[18]

Then, too, there was the fact that the original imposition of the Stalinist model had created tyranny, the arbitrary rule of the few. One of the characteristics of all tyranny, whether ideological and visionary, as in this case, or merely self-serving and corrupt, is that it creates the possibility for the dissemination and reproduction of petty tyranny. With tyrants at the top, entire bureaucracies become filled with tyrants at every level, behaving arbitrarily and out of narrow self-interest. The tyrants at the top cannot hope to enforce their will unless they have subservient officials, and to buy that subservience they have to allow their underlings to enjoy the fruits of arbitrary power. In any case, arbitrary, petty tyranny becomes the only model of proper, authoritative behavior.

This is one of the explanations given in recent attempts to explain the almost uncontrolled spread of purges in the USSR in the 1930s, and of course the ravages of the Chinese Cultural Revolution from 1966 to 1976. Once the model is set from the top, imitating that behavior becomes a way of ensuring survival for officials. But even beyond that, a tyrannical system gives opportunities for abuse that do not otherwise exist, and lower level officials use this to further their own narrow ends. (This is not meant to suggest that in some way the tyrants who ruled such systems, and their immediate followers, can be absolved of responsibility for the abuses; it does imply that the way tyrannies exercise power is necessarily deeply corrupt.)[19]

Daily exposure to petty tyranny, which at the local level rarely maintains the ideological high ground that may have inspired a Lenin, Stalin, Mao, or even a Ceausescu, also breeds gradual disgust with corruption and the dishonesty of the whole system. In the past, peasants subjected to such petty tyranny may have borne it more or less stoically (unless it went too far), but educated urbanites living in a highly politicized atmosphere where there are constant pronouncements about the guiding ideological vision of fairness, equality, and progress could not help but react with growing disgust.[20]

In that sense, the very success of communism in creating a more urban, more educated, more aware population also created the potential for disintegration. The endless corruption, the lies, the collapse of elementary social trust, the petty tyranny at every level—these were aspects of life less easily tolerated by the new working and professional classes than they might have been by peasants. (This remains, of course, the advantage of the Chinese communists; they can still rely on a vast reservoir of peasant indifference and respect for authority as long as agriculture is not resocialized.)[21]

The whole movement to create alternate social institutions, free of the corruption and dishonesty of the official structures, was the great ideological innovation that began to emerge in Poland in the 1970s and 1980s in the efforts to establish a "civil society." Traditional revolutionary resistance, taking to the streets, covert military actions, and assassinations were all generally fruitless because they provoked heavy military intervention by the Soviets. But by simply beginning to turn away from the state, by refusing to take it seriously, Polish and then other Central European intellectuals exposed the shallowness of communism's claims, and broke what little legitimacy communist regimes still had. Because of his early understanding of this fact, and his excellent descriptions of how this new ideology grew in Central Europe, Timothy Garton Ash has earned his justly deserved fame.[22]

Certainly, in the Soviet Union all these forces were at work, too, but the patriotism engendered by superpower status (though it has turned out that this was largely Russian, not "Soviet" pride and patriotism), the sheer size of the military, and the long history of successful police terror and repression kept the situation under better control than in much of Central Europe. Yet, combined with the slow erosion of legitimacy was the fundamental economic problem of failure to keep up with the rapidly emerging fifth industrial age in Western Europe, in the United States, and—most astonishingly for the Soviets—in East Asia.[23]

There is no doubt that in the mid-1980s, after Solidarity had apparently been crushed in Poland, with the Soviets massacring Afghan resistance fighters, with Cuban troops successfully defending Angola, and with Vietnam controlling all of Indochina, it seemed to the rest of the world that Soviet military might was insurmountable in countries where the Soviet system had been imposed. But underneath, the rot was spreading. So the question is not "What was wrong with Eastern Europe" or "Why was communism so weak?" Every specialist and many casual observers knew perfectly well what was wrong. But almost none guessed that what had been a slowly developing situation for several decades might take such a sudden turn for the worse. After all, the flaws of socialist economic planning had been known for a long time. Endemic corruption, tyranny, arbitrary brutality, and the use of sheer police force to maintain communist parties in power were hardly new occurrences. None of them answer the question, "Why 1989?" Almost all analysts thought the Soviet system would remain more or less intact in the USSR and in Eastern Europe for decades.

To understand why this did not happen requires a shift in analysis from a discussion of general trends to a review of some specific events in the 1980s.

THE EVENTS OF THE 1980S

If there was a central, key series of developments that began to unravel the entire system, it has to be in the interaction between events in Poland in the early 1980s and a growing perception by the Soviet leadership that their own problems were becoming very serious.

As late as 1987, and throughout most of 1988, most specialists felt that the Soviet elite did not understand the severity of their economic situation. Gorbachev almost certainly did, as did many of the Moscow intellectuals. But there was some question about the lesser cadres, and even many of the top people of the government. But as Gorbachev's mild reforms failed to have a beneficial impact, as the original impact of his policy of openness, encouragement, and antialcoholism ran into sharply diminishing returns, the Soviet economy began to slip back into the stagnation of the late Brezhnev years.[24]

Serious as rising discontent in the Soviet Union might have seemed to Gorbachev, of more immediate concern was the direct military threat of the Soviet's inability to keep up with the developments of the fifth industrial age. While the Soviet nuclear deterrent was unquestionably safe and effective in preventing a frontal attack by the United States, the growing gap between Western and Soviet computer and electronic technology threatened to give NATO (and ultimately Japan) a striking advantage in conventional weapons. This is almost certainly why the Soviets were so worried about "Star Wars," not simply because the illusion of an effective antiballistic missile defense was likely to unbalance the nuclear arms race. Pouring billions into this kind of research was likely to yield important new advantages in lesser types of electronic warfare that could be applied to conventional air and tank battles. This would nullify the Soviet's numerical advantage in men and machines, and threaten Soviet military investments throughout the world.[25]

Given the long-standing recognition by the major powers that nuclear war was out of the question, a growing advantage by the capitalist powers in electronic warfare threatened to turn any future local confrontation between Western and Soviet allies into a repetition of the Syrian-Israeli air war of 1982. From the Soviet point of view, the unbelievable totality of Israel's success was a warning of future catastrophes, even if Israel's land war in Lebanon turned out to be a major failure.[26]

There was one other, chance event that precipitated change in the Soviet Union by revealing to the leadership the extent of the country's industrial ineptitude. This was the Chernobyl catastrophe. But unlucky as it may have been, it served more to confirm what was already suspected than to initiate any changes. The fact is that many such massive industrial and environmental accidents have happened in the Soviet Union. When they occurred in the past, they had little effect, though throughout the 1970s and 1980s there was a growing environmental movement. But on top of everything else, the 1986 nuclear plant accident seemed to galvanize Gorbachev and his advisers.[27]

Meanwhile, in Eastern Europe, the communist orthodoxy imposed under Brezhnev was seriously threatened in Poland. Rising discontent there had made Poland ungovernable by the mid-1980s. It seemed that Hungary was going to follow soon. Economic reforms were not working, the population was increasingly alienated, and while there was no outward sign of immediate revolt, the Jaruzelski regime had no idea how to bring the situation under sufficient control to carry out any measures that might reverse the economic decline and help regain the trust (rather than the mere grudging and cynical acceptance) of the population.[28]

In retrospect, then, the events in Poland in the late 1970s, from the election of a Polish pope, which galvanized the Poles and created the massive popular demonstrations that led to the creation of Solidarity, to the military coup that seemed to destroy Solidarity, had set the stage for what was to happen. But the slow degeneration of the situation in Poland, or in all of Eastern Europe, would not have been enough to produce the events of 1989 had it not been for the Soviet crisis. On the other hand, had there been no breakdown of authority in Poland, and a looming, frightening sense of economic crisis and popular discontent in Hungary, and probably in the other East European countries as well, the Soviets would certainly have tried to carry out some reforms without giving up their European empire. The two aspects of the crisis came together, and this is why everything unraveled so quickly in the late 1980s.[29]

Gorbachev must have realized that it was only a matter of time until there was an explosion—a bread riot leading to a revolution in Poland, or a major strike in Hungary—which would oblige the government to call out the army. The problem was that neither the Polish nor the Hungarian army was particularly reliable. The special police could always be counted on, but if they were overwhelmed, it would be necessary to call in Soviet troops. This the Soviet economy could not bear if it was also to reform itself enough to begin to meet the challenges of the fifth industrial age, especially if this involved increased trade and other contacts with the advanced capitalist countries.

I believe that sometime in 1988 Gorbachev decided he must head off the danger before it was too late to prevent a catastrophic crisis.[30] I cannot prove this, because the documentation is not available, but I am almost certain that because of this decision, in discussions with the Poles there emerged the plan to allow partly free elections and the reopening of talks with Solidarity. The aim would be to relegitimize the regime, and give it enough breathing room to carry out economic reforms without risking strikes and massive civil disobedience. The idea of "roundtable" talks between Solidarity and the regime was proposed in a televised debate between Lech Walesa and a regime representative on November 30, 1988. The talks themselves began February 6, 1989.[31]

It did not work. The reason is that everyone—Gorbachev, the communist parties of Eastern Europe, foreign specialists, and intelligence services in NATO and the Warsaw Pact—vastly underestimated the degree to which the moral bankruptcy of communism had destroyed any possibility of relegitimizing it.

There was something else, too—an event whose import was not fully appreciated in the West, and which remains almost unmentioned. In January 1989, Gorbachev tried an experiment. He pulled almost all of the Soviet army out of Afghanistan. The United States and the Pakistani army expected this to result in the rapid demise of the communist regime there. To everyone's surprise, it did not. I think this might have been an important card for Gorbachev. He could point to Afghanistan when his conservative opponents, and especially his military, questioned his judgment. Afghanistan was proof that the Soviets could partly disengage without suffering catastrophe, and that in some cases it might even be better to let local communists handle their own problems. I suspect that a rapid victory by the anticommunist guerrillas in Afghanistan would have slowed progress in Eastern Europe, if not ending it entirely.[32]

We know how rapidly event followed event. Despite the patently unfair arrangements for the Polish election designed to keep the communist party in power, the electorate refused, and party rule collapsed. Since the Soviets had agreed to the process, and wanted to avoid, at almost any cost, a war of invasion, they let Poland go. Once it became obvious that this was happening, the Hungarians set out on the same path.[33]

Then, partly out of a well-timed sense of public relations, just before George Bush's visit, the Hungarians officially opened their border with Austria. In fact, the border had no longer been part of any "iron curtain" for a long time, but this move gave thousands of vacationing East Germans the idea that they could escape to the West. We know that this set off a mass hysteria among East Germans, who had given up hope of reform, and whose demoralization and disgust with their system led hundreds of thousands to want to flee. They rushed to West German embassies in Budapest and Prague, and began demonstrating in East Germany, particularly in Leipzig and Dresden.[34]

The failure of communism in East Germany in many ways represents the ultimate failure. Here was a country that was not poor, where there were two hundred automobiles for every thousand inhabitants, and where for years Western, particularly West German, sympathizers had said that communism was working by producing a more communal, more kindly Germany than the harsh, market driven, materialistic West German Federal Republic. It was another misconception born of wishful thinking.[35]

It is known that Honecker ordered repressive measures. Earlier, during the summer, Chinese officials had visited East Berlin to brief the East Germans on how to crush prodemocracy movements. But during his early October visit to East Germany, Gorbachev had publicly called for change and let it be known that the Soviets would not intervene to stop reform.[36]

Now, in October, ambulances were readied to cart away the thousands of dead and injured bodies in Leipzig and perhaps Dresden that were sure to be produced by the crackdown. This was prevented. Most accounts credit a local initiative in Leipzig led by the conductor Kurt Mazur, although the central party machinery, taken in hand by Egon Krenz, also played a pacifying role. It is likely that an appeal was made to the Soviets, and that the local Soviet military commander said he would not intervene. Knowing this, the East German Communist Party simply overthrew Honecker rather than risk physical annihilation.[37]

East Germany was no China, despite Honecker's claim that it would be. It had no reserve of ignorant, barely literate peasant boys to bring into the breach; and its economy was far too dependent on the West German connection to risk a break. So, once repression was abandoned, the system collapsed in a few weeks. With East Germany crumbling, the whole edifice of communist rule in Eastern Europe simply collapsed. On November 9 the Berlin Wall was opened. It was no longer possible to maintain it when the government of East Germany was losing control over its population, and the rate of flight was increasing at such a rapid rate.

East Germany was always the key Soviet position in Europe.[38] It was on the internal German border that the cold war began, and it was there that

the military might of the two superpowers was concentrated. When the Soviets abandoned the East German hard-liners, there was no hope anywhere
else in Eastern Europe. The Bulgarians followed in order to preserve what
they could of the party, and Todor Zhivkov resigned after thirty-five years in
power on the day after the Berlin Wall was opened (November 10). This was
surely no coincidence. A week later demonstrations began in Prague, and
within ten days it was over. Only Ceausescu of Romania resisted.[39]

Enough is now known about Ceausescu's Romania that it is unnecessary to
give much background. Only three points must be made.

First, Ceausescu himself still held on to the Stalinist vision. Aside from
the possible exception of Albania (which began to change in the spring of
1990),[40] there was only one other communist country where the model was so
unquestioned—North Korea. In fact, Ceausescu and Kim Il Sung long considered themselves close allies and friends, and their style of rule had many
similarities. Yet in Romania, and probably in North Korea, this model
turned sour about two decades ago, and pursuing it meant economic stagnation, a growing gap between reality and ideology, and the progressive alienation of even the most loyal cadres.[41]

Second, Romania was the most independent of the Warsaw Pact European countries, and so felt itself less dependent on Soviet support. But
though this brought considerable legitimacy to the Romanian regime in the
1970s, when partial independence was thought to be grounds for hope, by
the late 1980s that hope had failed, and the intellectuals, as well as a growing
number of ordinary urban people, had noticed that the Soviet Union had become more progressive than Romania.[42] In southern Romania they listened
to Bulgarian television and radio, and when they heard that even there (for
the Romanians Bulgaria has always been a butt of jokes as a backward, thick-
headed, peasant nation) there were reforms, it must have had a considerable
impact. In the north and west, Romanians could pick up the Hungarian and
Yugoslav media, and so be informed about what was going on elsewhere. In
the east, of course, they had the example of the Soviet Union, and of
Romanian-speaking Soviet Moldavia, where, for the first time since the
1940s, people were freer to demonstrate than in Romania itself. I should add
that aside from broadcasts from these neighboring countries, Radio Free Europe also played a major role in educating Romanians about what was going
on elsewhere in Eastern Europe. The point is that, again unlike China, it
proved impossible to keep news about the world out of the reach of the inte-
rior.

Finally, and this is much less known than other aspects of Romania's recent history, even at its height the Ceausescu regime relied heavily on the
fear of Soviet invasion to legitimize itself. There was always the underlying
assumption that if there was too much trouble, Soviet tanks would come in.
Was it not better to suffer a patriotic Romanian tyrant than another episode
of Soviet occupation? Once it became clear, in 1989, that the Soviets were
not going to march, the end was in sight. It was only because Ceausescu

himself was so out of touch with reality, and because he had so successfully destroyed his communist party by packing it with relatives and sycophants (like Kim Il Sung), that no one told him the truth, and he was thus unable to manage the more peaceful, gradual, and dignified exit of his Bulgarian colleague Todor Zhivkov.[43]

So, in the end, communism collapsed. The ramifications are far from clear, and there is no way of knowing how things will develop in the Soviet Union. But come what may in the USSR, it is certain that the Soviet empire in Eastern Europe is dead, and that there are almost no foreseeable circumstances that would make the Soviet army invade any of its former dependencies. We cannot be sure what directions the various revolutions of Eastern Europe will take, though it is safe to predict that there will be important differences from country to country. On the whole, it is also possible to be somewhat optimistic about the future of Eastern Europe, or at least its northern "Central European" parts, if not necessarily the Balkans and the Soviet Union. Why this is so I shall leave to my concluding remarks, in which I will try to draw together some of the lessons Eastern Europe has taught us about revolution and social change in general.

THE CAUSES OF REVOLUTION IN ADVANCED SOCIETIES

Eastern Europe and the Traditional Causes

Most widely accepted sociological models of revolution are of limited help in explaining what happened in Eastern Europe in 1989. There was no sudden fall in well-being after a long period of improvement. If the Polish, Hungarian, and Romanian economies were deteriorating (at very different rates), those of East Germany and Czechoslovakia were not causing immediate problems. People felt deprived when they compared themselves with West Europeans, but this had been true for well over three decades. In Poland, as a matter of fact, the sharpest period of economic deterioration was in the early 1980s, and though the situation had not improved much since then, it could be assumed that people were getting used to it.[44]

In Poland, a prolonged period of protest was marked by open explosions in 1956, 1968, 1970, 1976, and of course 1980–81. As time advanced, Poles learned to organize better and more effectively. But this gradual mobilization and organization seemed to have been decisively broken by the military seizure of power. In fact, there is good evidence that the party and police had learned even more from the long series of protests than the protesters themselves, and had become adept at handling trouble with just the right level of violence. Certainly, in the early 1980s the Jaruzelski regime was able to impose peacefully a whole series of price increases that in the past had provoked massive, violent uprisings.[45]

Only in Hungary was there much open mobilization of protest in the late 1980s, and that only in the last couple of years. Much of it was over ecological and nationalist issues that did not take the form of direct antiregime activity. In fact, the communists even supported some of this activity.[46]

None of the other countries had much open dissent. At most, in Czechoslovakia a few, seemingly isolated intellectuals had organized themselves, but they had no followers. In East Germany the Protestant churches had supported some limited draft protests and a small peace movement, but the regime had never been directly threatened. In Bulgaria only a handful of intellectuals ever made any claims to protest. In Romania, there had been some isolated outbreaks of strikes in the late 1970s, and a major riot in Brasov, in 1987, but there even intellectual protest was muted, rarely going beyond very limited literary activities.[47]

Nor was the international position of the East European countries at stake. Whereas in the Soviet Union, key elites, particularly in the KGB, saw the impending danger to the USSR's international strength, in Eastern Europe no one cared about this kind of issue. None of the East European elites saw their countries as potentially powerful nations, nor was their national existence threatened by any outsiders except the Soviets. And that threat, present since 1945, was now so highly attenuated as to be almost absent. That the Soviets were unpopular in Eastern Europe was a given, and a very old one, but there was no new risk of further intervention or damage because of these countries' weakness.[48]

Perhaps, however, the debt crisis in Poland and Hungary (and in Romania, because it had provoked such harsh and damaging countermeasures by Ceausescu) was the equivalent of visible international failure that exposed the incapacity of the regimes. But though this remained severe in Poland and Hungary in the late 1980s, elsewhere the problem was not acute.[49]

Nor can a very strong case be made for the rise of an economically powerful new class fighting for political power. Political and economic power was firmly in the hands of what Djilas had called the New Class. But that class, the professional party cadres, had been in charge for four decades, and it seemed neither highly dissatisfied nor in any way revolutionary. The leadership of the revolutions, if there was any, was in the hands of a few intellectuals who represented no particular class.[50]

Poland, of course, was different. There, an alliance between the Catholic Church, the unionized working class, and dissident intellectuals was very well organized, and it had almost taken power in 1980. But the days of Solidarity seemed to have passed, and the regime reasserted visible control. Virtually none of the Polish opposition thought there was much chance of success in an open, violent confrontation. So even in Poland, this was not a traditional revolution. The opportunity for that had passed with the successful imposition of martial law.[51]

What happened was that the moral base of communism had vanished. The elites had lost confidence in their legitimacy. The intellectuals, powerless as they seemed to be, disseminated this sense of moral despair and corruption to the public by their occasional protests and veiled commentaries, and the urban public was sufficiently well educated and aware to understand what was going on. The cumulative effect of such a situation, over decades, cannot be underestimated. Those who had had hope, during the 1940s and 1950s, were replaced by those who had never had hope and who had grown up knowing that everything was a lie. Educated youths, not just university students but high school students as well, knew enough about the rest of the world to realize that they had been lied to, that they had been cheated, and that their own leaders did not believe the lies.[52]

What took everyone by surprise was the discovery that the situation was not all that different in the Soviet Union. Nor could anyone foresee the kind of panicked realism, combined with astounding flexibility and willingness to compromise, shown by Gorbachev. In the end, this was the reason revolution came in 1989 rather than in the 1990s. But sooner or later, it would have happened.

Eastern Europe and Other Modern Revolutions

This brings up a serious issue. It has long been assumed that modern methods of communication and the awesome power of tanks, artillery, and air power would prevent the kind of classical revolution that has shaken the world so many times since 1789.

Even relatively inefficient regimes, such as the Russian autocracy, or the Kuomintang (KMT) in China, fought successfully against revolution until their armies were decisively weakened by outside invaders. In China's case, it took the communists two decades to build the strong army that finally won power for them, and they probably would have failed had it not been for the Japanese invasion.[53]

Many utterly corrupt, weak African, Asian, and Latin American regimes have held on to power for a long time with little more than mercenary armies whose loyalties were purchased by allowing them to loot their own countries. This is what goes on, for example, in Burma, Guatemala, and Zaire. Cases where such regimes were overthrown show that it takes long years of guerrilla organization and warfare to carry out revolutions, and then the chances of success are slim. If revolutions occurred in Batista's Cuba and Somoza's Nicaragua, in Uganda Idi Amin held on until he foolishly provoked Tanzania into attacking him. If Baby Doc Duvalier was frightened into leaving office in Haiti, it is not clear, even today, that the Duvalier system has been removed fully.[54]

Finally even anticolonial wars, in which the overwhelming majority of populations have sympathized with revolutionary movements, have been long, bloody events when the colonizers have chosen to fight back, as the Dutch did in Indonesia, the French in Indochina and Algeria, and the British in Kenya and Malaya (where, however, the Malay population rallied to the British side against the Chinese revolutionaries). A particularly startling case was the Bangladesh war, when massive popular opposition to Pakistani rule still needed help from an Indian military invasion to get rid of the Pakistani army.[55]

Only internal military coups, as when the Ethiopian or—much earlier—the Egyptian monarchies were removed, seem to make for relatively easy revolutions.[56]

But none of these types of revolutions fit what happened in Eastern Europe. There, even if the Romanian case is included, the total level of bloodshed was minuscule compared with other revolutions. There were no military coups. In Romania there was almost certainly cooperation between the army and the population, but no direct coup, and that was the only case where the army was involved at all. But compared with any African, Latin American, or almost any noncommunist Asian dictatorship, the East European communist regimes were overwhelmingly strong. They had large, effective, loyal secret police forces, an abundance of tanks and soldiers led by well-trained (though not necessarily enthusiastic) officers, excellent internal communications, and no threat of external, hostile invasion. Only in Romania was the army thoroughly alienated.

Again, we are left with the same explanation: utter moral rot.

Few observers have noticed a startling parallel between events in Eastern Europe in 1989 and in Iran in 1979. There, too, the shah should have been stronger. But even though there were a lot of deaths in the final days, and months of rioting before the shah's departure in January, many were taken by surprise by the overwhelming lack of legitimacy of the regime. Even the newly prosperous middle classes and the young professionals, who had much to lose if the shah was overthrown, failed to back him.[57]

While this is not a suitable place to discuss Iranian society and politics in the 1960s and 1970s, it is evident that the rapid modernization and urbanization of the society helped its intellectuals disseminate their feelings of disgust about the shah's regime, with its empty posturing, its lies, its torturers, its corruption, and its lack of redeeming moral values.

We can wonder, of course, to what extent the rising intellectual and professional classes in urban France in 1787 to 1789 felt the same way about the French monarchy, church, and aristocracy, and the extent to which such feelings played a decisive role in unleashing that revolution. We know that in Petrograd and Moscow from 1915 to 1917, whatever the level of popular misery, the professional and middle classes felt a good bit of disgust at the corruption and lack of morality at the imperial court.

The lesson may be that in fact we need to combine some Marxist notions of class with an understanding of John Rawls's theory of justice as fairness to understand what happened in Eastern Europe.[58] Economic modernization did, indeed, produce a larger middle class (not in the sense of bourgeois ownership, of course, but in the cultural and educational sense, as well as in its style of life). That class was in some ways quite favored in communist regimes. But because of the flaws of the socialist system of economic management, it remained poorer than its West European counterpart, and even seemed to be falling further behind by the 1980s. That is the Marxist, or class and material, basis of what happened.

But more important, the educated middle classes in a modern society are well informed, and can base their judgments about morality on a wider set of observations than those with very limited educations. The artistic and literary intellectuals who addressed their work to these middle classes helped them understand and interpret the immorality of the system, and so played a major role. They needed receptive audiences, but it was their work that undid East European communism.

Without the social changes associated with the economic transformations that took place in Eastern Europe from 1948 to 1988, these revolutions would not have taken place. But it was not so much that new classes were striving for power as that a growing number saw through the lies on which the whole system was based. That is what utterly destroyed the will of those in power to resist.

Once these conditions were set, the massive popular discontent with material conditions, particularly on the part of the working classes in the giant but stagnating industries that dominated communist economies, could come out into the streets and push these regimes over.

Models and Morals

That raises three final points. First, the fundamental reason for the failure of communism was that the utopian model it proposed was obviously not going to come into being. Almost everything else could have been tolerated if the essential promise was on its way to fulfillment. But once it was clear that the model was out of date, and its promise increasingly based on lies, its immorality became unbearable. Perhaps, in the past, when other ideologically based models failed to deliver their promises, systems could still survive because the middle classes and intellectuals were present in smaller numbers. But in an advanced society the absurdity of basing a whole social system on an outdated industrial age was more than an economic mistake. It undermined the whole claim to scientific validity which lay at the heart of Marxism-Leninism.

Second, much of the standard of morality that created such a revolutionary situation in Eastern Europe was based on the middle classes' interpretation of what was going on in other countries, namely in Western Europe. This is one reason why, despite all the economic and political troubles that are sure to accumulate in the near future in Eastern Europe, there is some reason for optimism. Western Europe is no longer the warlike set of competing imperialistic powers it was when the East Europeans first began to look to the West as their model in the nineteenth century, and through 1939. All of Western Europe is democratic, its various countries cooperate very well with each

other, and on the whole they have abandoned their imperialistic pretensions. This means that as a model, Western Europe is a far healthier place
than it was in the past.

This does not mean that all future revolutionary intellectuals and scandalized middle classes will look to Western Europe, or the United States, as
their model. After all, the Iranians looked to Islam, and it is only because
Eastern Europe has long been so close to Western Europe that it automatically looks in that direction.

Third, we must come to realize that in the twenty-first century there will
still be economic problems, political instability, and revolutions. But more
than ever, the fundamental causes of revolutionary instability will be moral.
The urban middle and professional classes, the intellectuals and those to
whom they most directly appeal, will set the tone of political change. Regimes to which they do not accord legitimacy because these regimes are seen
as unfair and dishonest will be shaky. When these classes can be persuaded
to defend their own narrow material interests, when they accept immoral
and unfair behavior, then regimes, no matter how corrupt, will be safe. But
it would be foolish for regimes that are defending essentially unjust social
systems to rely too much on the continued acquiescence of their middle
classes and intellectuals.

But many of us who study social change must be reminded that we barely
know how to study moral perceptions and legitimacy. We have been so busy
studying material changes, which are, after all, more easily measured and
perceived, that we do not know where to look to sense the moral pulse of key
classes and intellectuals. In some ways, the lesson of Eastern Europe has this
to offer, too. Sometimes literature written for what seems to be a handful of
people is a better measure of the true state of mind of a society than public
opinion polls, economic statistics, or overt political behavior.

An alternative "civil society"—places where people could interact freely
and without government interference, where they could turn their backs on
the party-state's corruption—was in creation in Eastern Europe before 1989.
This alternative civil society was the creation of intellectuals, novelists, playwrights, poets, historians, and philosophers like Václav Havel, Miklós
Haraszti, Adam Michnik, George Konrád, and hundreds of other, less famous ones. In a sense, in their literature and pamphlets, in their small discussion circles, they imagined a future that most of their people could only
dimly perceive, and which hardly anyone believed possible.

Vladimir Tismaneanu, in an article entitled "Eastern Europe: The Story
the Media Missed," correctly pointed out that most Western observers
never grasped the significance of this creation of an alternative "civil society."[59] That is, almost correctly, because even before 1989 those most closely
following the intellectual life of East Central Europe were aware of what was
going on, and were writing about it. Garton Ash was the best known, but a
few other scholars saw it too.[60] On the whole, however, most of the specialists
on communism were too hard-headed, too realistic, and even too dependent

on social science models to take such highly intellectualized discussions seriously.

After the fact, it is easy for us to say this. Before the fact, almost none of us saw it.

NOTES

I would like to thank Tim McDaniel for his helpful comments on my paper.

1. Because of the second centennial anniversary in 1989, this has been a particularly busy period for the publication of new works on the French Revolution. That the event still generates considerable excitement is shown by the controversies about Simon Schama's hostile critique of the Revolution, *Citizens: A Chronicle of the French Revolution* (New York: Knopf, 1988). A more positive evaluation is Eric J. Hobsbawm's *Echoes of the Marseillaise: Two Centuries Look Back on the French Revolution* (New Brunswick: Rutgers University Press, 1990). A lively review essay about recent books on the Revolution is Benjamin R. Barber's "The Most Sublime Event," *The Nation*, March 12, 1990, pp. 351–60.

2. A review of the condition and prospects for the East European economies can be found in *Eastern European Politics and Societies* 2:3 (Fall 1988), "Special Issue on Economic Reform," edited by John R. Lampe. Although the articles in this issue emphasize the region's economic problems, not all are pessimistic, and none predicted the astounding political changes that were to begin within months of publication. The same is true of a slightly older, but still recent, review of Eastern Europe's economies, with some comparative chapters on other socialist economies in Ellen Comisso and Laura Tyson, eds., *Power, Purpose, and Collective Choice: Economic Strategy in the Socialist States* (Ithaca: Cornell University Press, 1986). A surprisingly positive account of the Soviet economy published a few years ago by Ed A. Hewett also seemed to soften the nature of the crisis, even though Hewett gave an excellent account of the many problems facing the Soviets. See his *Reforming the Soviet Economy: Equality Versus Efficiency* (Washington, D.C.: Brookings Institution, 1988).

3. János Kornai, *Economics of Shortage*, 2 vols. (Amsterdam: North Holland, 1980), and Wlodzimierz Brus, *Socialist Ownership and Political Systems* (London: Allen and Unwin, 1977).

4. The popular resistance to accepting capitalist profits should not, after all, be surprising. Karl Polanyi's seminal work, *The Great Transformation* (Boston: Beacon, 1957), showed how difficult it was for the English to accept the notion that market forces should regulate the economy in the early nineteenth century. By now, the capitalist West has had almost two centuries to get used to this dramatic change in the organizing principles of society, but only in the last few decades has resistance to the market waned in Western Europe. That Eastern Europeans, and even more the Russians, should view markets with suspicion is understandable. Among the many discussions of this, Geoffrey Hosking's new book, *The Awakening of the Soviet Union* (Cambridge: Harvard University Press, 1990), is particularly good. He writes: "How many times over the last year or two have I heard Soviet citizens use the word 'speculator' to disparage private traders or co-operatives providing at high prices goods and services seldom available at all in the state sector? This sullen egalitarianism dovetails neatly with the interest of the party-state apparatus in retaining their network of controls and hence their grip on the economy" (p. 132).

5. On China, see Nicholas Lardy, *Agriculture in China's Modern Economic Development* (Cambridge: Cambridge University Press, 1983), pp. 190–221. On Hungary see Tamás Bauer, "The Hungarian Alternative to Soviet-Type Planning," *Journal of Comparative Economics* 7:3 (1983), pp. 304–16. See also Ellen Comisso and Paul Marer, "The Economics and Politics of Reform in Hungary," in Comisso and Tyson, eds., *Power, Purpose, and Collective Choice*, pp. 245–78.

6. Although the story is now well known, it is worth reviewing the nightmarish quality of this success. For a good account, see the essays in Moshe Lewin, *The Making of the Soviet System* (New York: Pantheon, 1985).

7. The attempt to fit the industrial era into such simple stages oversimplifies its economic history. Walt W. Rostow identifies nine "trend periods" in *The World Economy: History and Prospect* (Austin: University of Texas Press, 1978), pp. 298–348. My industrial ages group together his first and second periods (1790–1848), take his third period (1848–73) as a distinct age, group together his fourth and fifth periods (1873–1920), his sixth, seventh, and eighth periods (1920–72), and consider his ninth (starting in 1972) as the beginning of a new industrial age. I rely more on the history of technology provided by David S. Landes in *The Unbound Prometheus: Technological Change and Industrial Development in Western Europe from 1750 to the Present* (Cambridge: Cambridge University Press, 1969) and by the various authors in Carlo M. Cipolla's edited series, *The Fontana Economic History of Europe* (Glasgow: Fontana/Collins, vols. 4–6, 1973–76), than on price data and business cycles. I explain my reasoning more fully in Daniel Chirot, *Social Change in the Modern Era* (San Diego: Harcourt Brace Jovanovich, 1986), pp. 223–30. The point, however, is not to argue about precise periodization, but to recognize that there are different technologies, different types of social organization, and different models of behavior at different stages of the industrial era. The forceful maintenance of an outdated model is one of the main reasons for the backwardness of Soviet type economies.

8. Karl Polanyi's *The Great Transformation* was one such prediction. So was Lenin's in *Imperialism: The Highest Stage of Capitalism* (New York: International Publishers, 1939). For an account of the ideological effects of the Great Depression of the 1930s on Eastern Europe, see Daniel Chirot, "Ideology, Reality, and Competing Models of Development in Eastern Europe Between the Two World Wars," *Eastern European Politics and Societies* 3:3 (1989), pp. 378–411.

9. Alexander Erlich, *The Soviet Industrialization Debate* (Cambridge: Harvard University Press, 1960). Whether or not this strategy was necessary remains a subject of debate in the Soviet Union, where Stephen F. Cohen's book on Bukharin has been greatly appreciated by the Gorbachev reformers, because Bukharin was the most important ideological opponent of the Stalin line. See Cohen's *Bukharin and the Bolshevik Revolution: A Political Biography, 1888–1938* (Oxford: Oxford University Press, 1980). For Eastern Europe, however, the issue is moot.

10. Vladimir Tismaneanu, "The Tragicomedy of Romanian Communism," *Eastern European Politics and Societies* 3:2 (1989), pp. 329–76, gives the most recent and best short account of the origins and development of the Romanian Communist Party from the prewar period until 1989, and explains Ceausescu's role in determining its fate.

11. Lardy, *Agriculture in China's Modern Economic Development*, pp. 130, 155, 158, 165.

12. Geoffrey Hosking quotes the Soviet reform economist Otto Latsis, who put it

this way: "They build irrigation channels which bring no increase in agricultural production. They produce machine tools for which there are no operators, tractors for which there are no drivers, and threshing machines which they know will not work. Further millions of people supply these superfluous products with electricity, ore, oil, and coal. In return they receive their wages like everyone else, and take them to the shops. There, however, they find no goods to buy, because their work has not produced any." And Hosking also quotes Soviet Premier Ryzhkov: "We produce more tractors in this country than all the capitalist countries put together. And yet we don't have enough tractors." *The Awakening of the Soviet Union*, p. 134.

13. Kazimierz Poznanski ascribes the failure of the Polish reforms in the second half of the 1970s to political pressure rather than to economic mismanagement, but it would be fruitless to argue about which came first. See his "Economic Adjustment and Political Forces: Poland since 1970," in Comisso and Tyson, eds., *Power, Purpose, and Collective Choice*, pp. 279–312.

14. Comisso and Marer, in their article "The Economics and Politics of Reform in Hungary," cover this and the other major contradictions in the Hungarian economic reforms, pp. 267–78.

15. On the debt crisis and Eastern Europe, see Laura D'Andrea Tyson, "The Debt Crisis and Adjustment Responses in Eastern Europe: A Comparative Perspective," in Comisso and Tyson, eds., *Power, Purpose, and Collective Choice*, pp. 63–110. On Romania, see Ronald H. Linden, "Socialist Patrimonialism and the Global Economy: The Case of Romania," in the same volume, pp. 171–204.

16. Jan Gross stresses this in "Social Consequences of War: Preliminaries to the Study of Imposition of Communist Regimes in East Central Europe," *Eastern European Politics and Societies* 3:2 (1989), pp. 213–14. There is no way of quantifying the extent to which youthful enthusiasm helped communist cadres take power and effectively transform their societies in the late 1940s and early 1950s, but the phenomenon is attested to by numerous literary sources describing the period. Even such bitter anticommunists as Milan Kundera, in *The Joke* (New York: Harper and Row, 1982), verify this. Had there never been a substantial body of energized believers, it is unlikely that the sheer force of Soviet military might could have held all of Eastern Europe in its grip. On the other hand, as Gross and others, for example Elemér Hankiss in "Demobilization, Self-Mobilization, and Quasi-Mobilization in Hungary, 1948–1987," *Eastern European Politics and Societies* 3:1 (1989), pp. 105–51, have pointed out, communist regimes worked hard to destroy social cohesion and any type of genuine solidarity, so that in the long run it was inevitable that the enthusiasm of the early intellectual believers would be curbed and debased. As for Western— particularly French—Marxism, Tony Judt believes that it also contributed to the legitimacy of East European communist regimes. See his *Marxism and the French Left* (Oxford: Oxford University Press, 1986), pp. 236–38. Thus the rise and demise of Marxism in Eastern and Western Europe are not wholly separate phenomena, but fed on each other.

17. The best known explanation of communism as nationalism is Chalmers Johnson, *Peasant Nationalism and Communist Power: The Emergence of Revolutionary China, 1937–1945* (Stanford: Stanford University Press, 1962), especially pp. 176–87. Johnson explicitly compares Yugoslavia with China. To varying degrees, but most strongly in Poland, Czechoslovakia, and Albania, the communists were able to make similar claims as national saviors after 1945 elsewhere in Eastern Europe. In East Germany, Hungary, Bulgaria, and Romania, they could at least claim to repre-

sent the substantial leftist nationalist sentiments that had been silenced during the period of nazism or the German alliance.

18. Again, it is difficult to quantify feelings of moral revulsion. But the sense of all-pervasive corruption and self-disgust can be grasped in most literature of Eastern Europe, starting in the 1950s and becoming ever more obvious with time. A particularly somber view is given by Petru Dumitriu's *Incognito* (New York: Macmillan, 1964).

19. Although he certainly exaggerates the role of local officials, this is a central theme in J. Arch Getty's revisionist view of the Stalinist purges in *Origins of the Great Purges: The Soviet Communist Party Reconsidered, 1933–1938* (Cambridge: Cambridge University Press, 1985). On the Chinese Cultural Revolution, see Hong Yung Lee, *The Politics of the Chinese Cultural Revolution* (Berkeley and Los Angeles: University of California Press, 1976). While such events could not have begun without central direction, they could not have been carried out without local officials trying to ingratiate themselves by imitating the top. But this very process led to widespread cynicism and corruption, and so had to undermine the long-term legitimacy of communism.

20. James C. Scott's argument about how the violation of a "moral economy's" sense of justice leads to revolts is based on observations of peasants, but it applies even more to urban intellectuals and professionals. It is now evident that they also have a "moral economy," though one tied to their own sense of self-worth rather than to their subsistence. See *The Moral Economy of the Peasant: Rebellion and Subsistence in Southeast Asia* (New Haven: Yale University Press, 1976), particularly pp. 157–92.

21. Yet it is difficult to believe that China will not follow the same course as Eastern Europe in future years. The crisis of the Democracy Movement in the spring of 1989 was caused by all the same conditions that led to the collapse of communism in Eastern Europe: the contradictions of economic reform in a system still run by communist officials, growing corruption, loss of faith in the official ideology, and increasing disgust with the endless hypocrisy of those in power. The main difference, of course, was that China in 1989 was much less developed, much less urbanized than the East European countries, and also much more insulated from the effects of the economic and political crisis in the Soviet Union. For a brief review of the events in China and their causes, see Jonathan D. Spence's new book, *The Search for Modern China* (New York: Norton, 1990), pp. 712–47.

22. His major essays from the late 1980s have been collected in Timothy Garton Ash, *The Uses of Adversity* (New York: Random House, 1989).

23. Kazimierz Poznanski, *Technology, Competition and the Soviet Bloc in the World Market* (Berkeley: Institute of International Studies, University of California, 1987).

24. Each new report from the Soviet Union makes the Brezhnev years and the prognosis for the future seem bleaker. For years the CIA reports painted a more pessimistic economic picture than the official Soviet reports, but recently Soviet economists have said that even the CIA reports were too optimistic. As an example of what is now known about the state of the Soviet economy, and how it got to its present crisis, see Bill Keller, "Gorbachev's Need: To Still Matter," *New York Times*, May 27, 1990, pp. 1, 6. None of this is new to the academic specialists; see, for example, Marshall Goldman, *USSR in Crisis: The Failure of an Economic System* (New York: Norton, 1983).

25. That scientists did not believe the extravagant claims made by the proponents

of the Strategic Defense Initiative is clear. See, for example, Franklin A. Long, Donald Hafner, and Jeffrey Boutwell, eds., *Weapons in Space* (New York: Norton, 1986), particularly the essay by Hans Bethe, Jeffrey Boutwell, and Richard Garwin, "BMD Technologies and Concepts in the 1980s," pp. 53–71. Yet the Soviets were very troubled by it, and it was Gorbachev's political genius that figured out that American funding for military research could be reduced only in the context of a general move toward disarmament, and this necessitated a reversal of traditional Soviet foreign policy that would reassure the West. For an appreciation of Gorbachev's policy in an otherwise harshly critical article, see Elena Bonner, "On Gorbachev," *New York Review of Books*, May 17, 1990, p. 14. In general, it seems to me that the Soviets' fear that their conventional warfare capabilities would be undermined by the West's technological superiority has been relatively neglected in most of the discussion about arms control. It has, however, been noted by experts. See Alan B. Sherr, *The Other Side of Arms Control: Soviet Objectives in the Gorbachev Era* (Boston: Unwin Hyman, 1988), pp. 38 and 63.

26. Chaim Herzog, *The Arab-Israeli Wars* (New York: Random House, 1982), pp. 347–48. That the Soviets remained very concerned by this is shown by statements in Alexei Arbatov, Oleg Amirov, and Nikolai Kishilov, "Assessing the NATO-WTO Military Balance in Europe," in Robert D. Blackwell and F. Stephen Larrabee, eds., *Conventional Arms Control and East-West Security* (Durham: Duke University Press, 1989), pp. 78–79.

27. Hosking, *The Awakening of the Soviet Union*, pp. 56–60.

28. The desperate, almost comical attempts made by the Jaruzelski regime to create new organizations and institutions that would reimpose some sort of political and social coherence, and bring society back into the system, are explored very well by George Kolankiewicz in "Poland, and the Politics of Permissible Pluralism," *Eastern European Politics and Societies* 2:1 (1988), pp. 152–83. But even Kolankiewicz thought that the attempt to include broader segments of the population, particularly the intellectuals, in officially defined institutions might meet with partial success. In the event, it turned out that these desperate inclusionary policies also failed.

29. Timothy Garton Ash, "Eastern Europe: The Year of Truth," *New York Review of Books*, February 15, 1990, pp. 17–22. A collection of Garton Ash's new essays on 1989 appears in *We the People: The Revolution of '89. Witnessed in Warsaw, Budapest, Berlin and Prague* (Cambridge: Granta/Penguin, 1990).

30. The summer of 1988 was certainly a time when it became obvious that the forces of political and social disintegration in the Soviet Union were starting to get out of hand, too, and this no doubt influenced Gorbachev greatly. See the essays of Boris Kagarlitsky in *Farewell Perestroika: A Soviet Chronicle* (London: Verso, 1990), particularly "The Hot Summer of 1988," pp. 1–29.

31. The whole process is well documented by Polish publications, particularly issues of *Rzeczpospolita*, *Polityka*, and *Trybuna Ludu*. I thank Dieter Bingen of Cologne's Bundesinstitut für ostwissenschaftliche und internationale Studien for helping me understand the sequence of events in Poland during this period.

32. Bill Keller, "Getting Out with Honor" (February 2, 1989), in Bernard Gwertzman and Michael T. Kaufman, eds., *The Collapse of Communism* (New York: The New York Times, 1990), pp. 10–12. This book is a collection of relevant articles published in the *Times* during 1989.

33. John Tagliabue, "Solidarity May Win 40 Percent of Parliament" (February 19, 1989), *The Collapse of Communism*, pp. 20–21; "Stunning Vote Casts Poles into Un-

charted Waters" (June 5, 1989), p. 121; "Warsaw Accepts Solidarity Sweep and Humiliating Losses by Party" (June 8, 1989), pp. 121–23; and "Jaruzelski, Moved by 'Needs and Aspirations' of Poland Names Walesa Aide Premier" (August 19, 1989), pp. 130–32. To this must be added the August 17, 1989, article from Moscow by Bill Keller, "In Moscow, Tone Is Studied Calm," pp. 132–33.

34. Henry Kamm, "East Germans Put Hungary in a Bind" (September 1, 1989), *The Collapse of Communism,* pp. 154–56; and Serge Schmemann, "East Germans Line Émigré Routes, Some in Hope of Their Own Exit" (October 4, 1989), p. 158, and "Security Forces Storm Protesters in East Germany" (sent from Dresden, October 8, 1989), p. 159.

35. Thomas A. Baylis, "Explaining the GDR's Economic Strategy," in Comisso and Tyson, eds., *Power, Purpose, and Collective Choice,* especially the optimistic conclusion, pp. 242–44. A conventionally favorable summary of how East German communist labor relations worked is found in Marilyn Rueschemeyer and C. Bradley Scharf, "Labor Unions in the German Democratic Republic," in Alex Pravda and Blair A. Ruble, eds., *Trade Unions in Communist States* (Boston: Allen and Unwin, 1986). Judging by the comments from these and similar studies, East Germans should not have behaved the way they did in 1989.

36. In a speech on October 7 in the GDR, Gorbachev said, "life itself punishes those who delay." Timothy Garton Ash, "The German Revolution," *New York Review of Books,* December 21, 1989, p. 14. Then, on October 25 in Helsinki, he said that the Soviet Union did not have the moral or political right to intervene in the affairs of Eastern Europe. This was interpreted by his spokesman, Gennadi I. Gerasimov, as the replacement of the Breshnev Doctrine by the "Sinatra Doctrine" (after the song "I Did It My Way"). Bill Keller, "Gorbachev in Finland, Disavows Any Right of Regional Intervention," in *The Collapse of Communism* (October 25, 1989), pp. 163–66.

37. Garton Ash, "The German Revolution," p. 16.

38. Christopher Jones, "Gorbachev and the Warsaw Pact," *Eastern European Politics and Societies* 3:2 (1989), pp. 215–34.

39. Serge Schmemann, "East Germany Opens Frontier to the West for Migration or Travel: Thousands Cross," *New York Times,* November 10, 1989, p. 1. Clyde Haberman, "Bulgarian Chief Quits After 35 Years of Rigid Rule," same issue of the *Times,* p. 1. Timothy Garton Ash, "The Revolution of the Magic Lantern," *New York Review of Books,* January 18, 1990, pp. 42–51. The Czech communist regime fell on November 24.

40. Louis Zanga, "Albania Decides to End Its Isolation," *Soviet/East European Report,* Radio Free Europe/Radio Liberty, May 1, 1990, p. 4; Zanga, "Even in Albania Economic Reforms and a Multiparty System," *Soviet/East European Report,* RFE/RL, January 10, 1991, pp. 1, 4.

41. The Ceausescu regime began to move in this direction in the early 1970s, though the full ramifications of the return to autarkic Stalinism did not become entirely obvious until the early 1980s. For an explanation of the changes in the early 1970s, see Ken Jowitt, "Political Innovation in Rumania," *Survey* 4 (Autumn 1974), pp. 132–51, and Daniel Chirot, "Social Change in Communist Romania," *Social Forces* 57:2 (1978), pp. 495–97. Jowitt noted Ceausescu's references to his "beloved friend" Kim Il Sung and to the fact that a young reform communist who had built up well-educated, technocratic cadres, and who was expected to become increasingly important, was suddenly demoted. That was Ion Iliescu, the man who was to become

the first postcommunist president of Romania! Jowitt again emphasized the similarity of the North Korean and Romanian regimes in "Moscow 'Centre,'" *Eastern European Politics and Societies* 1:3 (Fall 1987), p. 320. For a brief description of what Romania was like by 1988, see Daniel Chirot, "Ceausescu's Last Folly," *Dissent*, Summer 1988, pp. 271–75. In North Korea, despite the many similarities with Romania, decay was not as advanced in the late 1980s, perhaps because, as Bruce Cumings has suggested, Kim's autarkic Marxist patrimonialism was more in tune with Korean historical and cultural tradition than Ceausescu's was with Romania's past. See Bruce Cumings, "Corporatism in North Korea," *Journal of Korean Studies* 4 (1982–83), particularly p. 277, where he quotes Ken Jowitt's quip about Romania and North Korea being examples of "socialism in one family." Since then, that quote has been widely repeated without being attributed.

42. One of the best accounts of what was going on in Romania was written by the Romanian dissident Pavel Campeanu: "Birth and Death in Romania," *New York Review of Books*, October 23, 1986. That article was written anonymously. His "The Revolt of the Romanians," *New York Review of Books*, February 1, 1990, was signed. See also Daniel N. Nelson, *Romanian Politics in the Ceausescu Era* (New York: Gordon and Beach, 1988), pp. 213–17.

43. There could hardly be a better demonstration of how removed Ceausescu had become from reality than the way in which he was overthrown. The shock on his face as the crowd he was addressing began to jeer him, December 21, 1989, was captured on television. More than this was the unbelievable ineptitude of his attempt to escape, even though, in fact, his security forces had the capacity to resist. Some highly placed Romanians have told me that Ceausescu realized in the last few days that changes had to be made, and that he was hoping to reassert his full control before starting to reform. But it is quite clear that despite the years of growing misery and the alienation of all Romanians outside the Ceausescu family, he still believed he had enough legitimacy to carry on. His surprise may have been due to the fact that the demonstration against him was probably instigated by elements in the army and from within the Securitate itself. The reports in the *New York Times* on Romania from December 22 to December 25, 1989, give the essence of the story without, however, clarifying what still remains, much later, a murky sequence of events.

44. The famous J-Curve theory of James Davies predicted that a growing gap between rewards and expectations would lead to revolutions; see his article, "Toward a Theory of Revolution," *American Sociological Review* 27:1 (1962), pp. 5–19. Ted Gurr expanded on this and other "psychological explanations" of revolution in *Why Men Rebel* (Princeton: Princeton University Press, 1970). These would be, at best, weak explanations of what happened, except for the obvious point that many people must have been dissatisfied for regimes that were essentially intact to fall so quickly. There is no obvious reason why discontent should have been any higher in 1989 than five, ten, or twenty years earlier.

45. Michael Bernhard has shown that in fact the party-state machine in Poland learned from the events of the 1970s and of 1980, and that Jaruzelski was able to impose martial law, raise prices repeatedly, and avoid the political turmoil that had occurred earlier. "The Strikes of June 1976 in Poland," *Eastern European Politics and Societies* 1:3 (1987), pp. 390–91. Both the opposition and the regime became more sophisticated with time, but by the mid-1980s, the regime had won. The prevailing political attitude, according to many, and on the whole fairly reliable surveys done in Poland, was growing apathy toward all political issues. See Jane L. Curry, "The Psy-

chological Barriers to Reform in Poland," *Eastern European Politics and Societies* 2:3 (1988), particularly p. 494. David S. Mason's *Public Opinion and Political Change in Poland, 1980–1982* (Cambridge: Cambridge University Press, 1984) consistently shows this, but also that the turn in the "J," that is, the growing gap between a deteriorating reality and high expectations created by the growth of the early 1970s, took place in the late 1970s and in 1980. As the 1980s unfolded, peoples' expectations fell into line with reality as the excitement of 1980–81 was replaced by the apathy and hopelessness of martial law. See particularly pp. 42–53 and 222–32.

46. Elemér Hankiss in "Demobilization, Self-Mobilization, and Quasi-Mobilization in Hungary, 1948–1987," pp. 131–39.

47. Vladimir Tismaneanu, quoting Václav Havel, points out that the dissidents in these countries made up a "minuscule and rather singular enclave." *The Crisis of Marxist Ideology in Eastern Europe: The Poverty of Utopia* (London: Routledge, 1988), p. 166. In his chapter on intellectual dissidents (pp. 160–82), however, Tismaneanu is prophetic in noting that the refusal of the intellectuals to accept the lies of communism can destroy these systems precisely because they are ultimately based on ideas. This, in fact, was the entire premise of the dissident intellectuals, particularly in Poland, Czechoslovakia, and Hungary.

48. The analysis of conflicts between states trying to reform, in order to keep up their power in the international arena, and obstructionist traditional elites makes up an important part of Theda Skocpol's theory of revolution in *States and Social Revolutions* (Cambridge: Cambridge University Press, 1979). Classes more committed to reform, then, play an important role in conducting revolutions. But however much merit this argument has in explaining the classical French, Russian, and Chinese revolutions, it seems to have little bearing on what happened in Eastern Europe in 1989. It may, however, have considerable bearing on the future of politics in Russia.

49. Przemyslaw T. Gajdeczka of the World Bank claimed in 1988 that the debt problem was more or less under control, and that international lenders rated only three countries poorly: Poland, Romania, and Yugoslavia. "International Market Perceptions and Economic Performance: Lending to Eastern Europe," *Eastern European Politics and Societies* 2:3 (1988), pp. 558–76.

50. That rising classes cause revolutions is at the heart of the Marxist theory of revolution. An interesting twist to this was suggested by George Konrád and Iván Szelényi in *The Intellectuals on the Road to Class Power* (Brighton: Harvester Press, 1979). Intellectuals were identified as the rising class that helped put the communists into power and were becoming the ruling class. But intellectual dissidents in Eastern Europe represented no class, were not numerically large, and were held together by a common moral position, not their position in the economic structure. Zygmunt Bauman identified their role more correctly by pointing out that they were more the carriers of national consciousness and morality than a class as such. "Intellectuals in East-Central Europe: Continuity and Change," *Eastern European Politics and Societies* 1:2 (1987), pp. 162–86.

51. Only in Poland could it be said that Charles Tilly's theory about revolutions—that it is organization of the revolutionary groups that counts most—works at all. But even in Poland, the height of organizational coherence in Solidarity was reached in 1980. To the limited extent that Poland fits Tilly's theories about mobilization, this cannot explain the loss of nerve and collapse in the other communist regimes. See Tilly's *From Mobilization to Revolution* (Reading: Addison-Wesley, 1978).

52. Thus the first step of what Jack A. Goldstone has called the "natural history"

approach to the study of revolutions, based largely on the 1938 work of Crane Brinton, turns out to describe some of what happened in Eastern Europe too: "Prior to a great revolution, the bulk of the 'intellectuals'—journalists, poets, playwrights, essayists, teachers, members of the clergy, lawyers, and trained members of the bureaucracy—cease to support the regime, writing condemnations and demanding major reforms." Goldstone, "The Comparative and Historical Study of Revolutions," *Annual Review of Sociology* 8 (1982), pp. 189–90. See also Crane Brinton, *The Anatomy of Revolution* (New York: Vintage, 1965). But most recent theorists of revolution have not taken this observation as anything more than a symptom of deeper class and structural conflicts, and none seem to have believed it could be the prime cause of revolutions. Goldstone's own theory that rapidly rising demographic pressures explain revolutions has much validity in premodern history (pp. 204–5); it has no bearing on Eastern Europe.

53. See Johnson, *Peasant Nationalism*, pp. 31–70.

54. It would be pointless to extend the number of examples, because there are so many. For some African cases, see Robert H. Jackson and Carl G. Rosberg, *Personal Rule in Black Africa: Prince, Autocrat, Prophet, Tyrant* (Berkeley and Los Angeles: University of California Press, 1982), particularly chapter 6, "Tyrants and Abusive Rule" (about the incredible misrule of Idi Amin of Uganda and Macias Nguema of Equatorial Guinea). For Haiti, Robert I. Rotberg's classic study, *Haiti: The Politics of Squalor* (Boston: Houghton Mifflin, 1971), remains excellent. The tyranny in Burma and the revolution of 1988 (whose ultimate effects are still pending, despite the effective repression that took place during that year) are discussed by Bertil Lintner in *Outrage: Burma's Struggle for Democracy* (Hong Kong: Review Publishing, 1989).

55. Leo Kuper, in *Genocide* (New Haven: Yale University Press, 1981), estimates that up to three million Bengalis were killed as the Pakistani Army tried to reverse the overwhelming electoral victory of the independence-minded Awami League (pp. 78–80). Of course, it was not just the army, but a general collapse into anarchy and interethnic warfare, that contributed to the high death toll. The point is that despite all this, as in Cambodia in 1979, or Uganda, also in 1979, the nightmare perpetrated by the government in control against the wishes of the large majority of the population could be overthrown only by outside military intervention (p. 173). By these standards, the European colonial powers, however brutal they may have been, seem to have been more prone to give in to a combination of moral arguments against what they were doing and simple calculations of the costs and benefits of their colonial wars. None of these cases shed much light on what happened in Eastern Europe, either internally or because of any Soviet actions. After all, the last case of large-scale killing by the Soviets in Eastern Europe was in Hungary in 1956.

56. Ryszard Kapuscinski's *The Emperor* (London: Picador/Pan, 1984), about the fall of Haile Selassie, makes that emperor seem very much of a Ceausescu-like figure—out of touch with his population and with his own elite. But some have pointed out that Kapuscinski's book may have been as much about his native Poland under Gierek as about Ethiopia. The violence that followed the first, peaceful stage of the Ethiopian Revolution, however, is unlikely to be repeated in Eastern Europe, though it is a chilling reminder of what happens when a disintegrating multiethnic empire tries to hold itself together at any cost.

57. Tim McDaniel has pointed out the extraordinary analogy between the Russian Revolution of 1917 and the Iranian one of 1978–79. In both cases, autocratic modernizing regimes, despite some real successes, managed to alienate almost all elements

in the society. In the case of Iran, this was even more startling because, as in Eastern Europe, there was no major defeat, just a collapse. *A Modern Mirror for Princes: Autocratic Modernization and Revolution in Russia and Iran* (Princeton: Princeton University Press, 1991).

58. John Rawls, *A Theory of Justice* (Cambridge: Harvard University Press, 1971).

59. *Bulletin of the Atomic Scientists*, March 1990, pp. 17–21.

60. For example, Tony R. Judt in a paper delivered at the Woodrow Wilson Center in Washington during the summer of 1987 and published as "The Dilemmas of Dissidence: The Politics of Opposition in East-Central Europe," *Eastern European Politics and Societies* 2:2 (1988), pp. 185–240. The journals *Telos* and *Cross-currents*, run by scholars from Central Europe, were aware of what was going on, as were some other equally specialized publications in Europe. But before the events of 1989, very few scholars or intellectuals paid much attention to such publications, and even most specialists, especially those in the policy-related fields, hardly took them seriously.

2

Gorbachev:
The Last True Leninist Believer?

STEPHEN E. HANSON

MIKHAIL GORBACHEV, in his tenure as general secretary of the CPSU from 1985 to the present, has irreversibly changed the nature of Soviet politics and society. However, the problem of how to conceptualize the precise nature of this change has proved to be a thorny one for contemporary Soviet studies. The two paradigms that have dominated scholarly analysis of the Soviet Union to date—the totalitarian model and modernization theory—have each been faced with enormous difficulties in making sense of the Gorbachev *perestroika* reforms. The totalitarian model, which in its original form insisted that the Soviet system was inherently immutable and driven toward absolute power,[1] simply proved incapable of accommodating the mounting evidence that Gorbachev was not a "refined Stalinist,"[2] but a man committed to changing the very nature of party rule in the USSR. The destruction of the Stalinist system, which the totalitarian model insisted could occur only after power was wrenched from it, had contrary to all expectations been initiated by the party elite itself. Although the collapse of communism in 1989–90 had in a sense vindicated the totalitarian assumption that a "reformed Leninism" was essentially an impossibility, the model had failed to provide any satisfactory explanation why the Gorbachev Politburo had led the headlong rush toward Leninism's worldwide dismantling.

Modernization theory, on the other hand, readily explained why Gorbachev had initiated "radical reform" in the USSR: he was responding to the political "imperative" in an industrialized society to introduce norms of political democracy and market efficiency.[3] Gorbachev's ascendance could be seen as the final victory of the "reformers" in the Soviet elite in their long battle with ideological "conservatives,"[4] and the long-awaited emergence of a fully "modern" leader in a "deideologized" CPSU.[5] Gorbachev's constant use of Leninist phraseology in his advocacy of *perestroika* could be explained as a necessary concession to the old norms of party rule—a concession that would become unnecessary once the power of the apparat had been broken. But modernization theory, having identified Gorbachev's *perestroika* with the cause of modernity in the Soviet Union,[6] was subsequently unable to make sense of the increasing marginalization of perestroika and, by 1990, the near disintegration of the Soviet Union itself. If Gorbachev represented the triumph of modernity and rationality in Soviet politics, why was he at the last moment recoiling from the implications of the plan for full marketization of the Soviet economy advocated by Boris Yeltsin and his own economic adviser, Stanislav S. Shatalin? Why, as late as the summer of 1990, was he still insisting on preserving the essential elements of the "socialist choice" in a reformed USSR? And if Soviet society had become essentially "modern" through industrialization, urbanization, and education,[7] why did the collapse of Leninism seem to be leading to social anarchy and perhaps civil war, rather than allowing for a peaceful evolution toward Western norms of liberalism and capitalism?

Both paradigms, then, explained at best only part of the Gorbachev story. Modernization theory had predicted the eventual emergence of a Leninist reformer who would attack the Stalinist system, and thus it was plausible as an explanation for Gorbachev's initial reformism. But it had trouble explaining why that reformer would cling to his outmoded ideology long after it was politically expedient to do so. Totalitarian theory had argued that no reform remaining within the ideological confines of Leninism could succeed; thus the ultimate collapse of *perestroika* made sense. But it had trouble explaining how *perestroika* could have been launched by the party elite in the first place, given Gorbachev's apparent continuing ideological commitment to Marxism-Leninism. As had been the case with scholarly analysis of the historical link between Leninism and Stalinism, and of that between Stalinism and the post-Stalin era, analysis of the Gorbachev period tended either to insist on the essential immutability of the communist system or to overemphasize the elements of change in Soviet society, in both cases presenting a one-sided picture of the Gorbachev phenomenon. Gorbachev, who was simultaneously a committed Leninist *and* the major force behind policies that destroyed the existing system of party rule in the USSR, was inexplicable from either point of view.[8]

THE WEBERIAN PARADIGM

In this essay I will attempt to analyze the Gorbachev era from a somewhat different theoretical perspective, applying to the study of contemporary Soviet politics the comparative sociological framework developed by Max Weber. A comprehensive overview of Weberian theory is, of course, beyond the scope of this paper; here I will merely summarize three major elements of Weber's original analytic framework that, when applied to the study of Leninism in the USSR, distinguish it decisively from both the totalitarian approach and modernization theory: (1) its methodological stress on "ideal types" of legitimate domination, (2) its emphasis on the role of revolutionary charisma in bringing about social change, and (3) its rejection of historical teleology in evaluating political outcomes.

Weberian comparative analysis of political regimes begins with the assumption that all political institutions rest on some form of domination *(herrschaft).*[9] To acquire any degree of social stability, however, political domination must be perceived as legitimate by at least a certain segment of society. Weber argues that historically there have been three major types of legitimate domination: the traditional, the rational-legal, and the charismatic. Traditional domination rests on a belief in the sanctity of age-old customs governing politics; rational-legal domination rests on a belief in the legitimacy of the impersonal "rules of the game" according to which political life is conducted; and charismatic domination rests on a belief in the extraordinary abilities of the leader or institution to bring about "political miracles" on a fairly continuous basis. But these three analytic categories are to be understood only as "ideal types" for the classification of different empirical political and social institutions; no *purely* traditional, rational-legal, or charismatic order can be found anywhere in reality.

Weberian analysis then makes a further distinction between the "routinized" forms of social life—the traditional and rational-legal types of domination—and the extraordinary, revolutionary force of charisma, which works to undermine all existing institutional routines. This distinction is manifested in the fundamental political problem of how to organize economic activity on a society wide basis. While both traditional domination and rational-legal forms of political domination can sustain themselves on the basis of stable routines governing economic activity (the former by relying on the maintenance of the natural, cyclical rhythms of village agriculture; the latter by presiding over the introduction of "rational" time-discipline in economic life within the framework of modern capitalism), charismatic domination in its pure form appears to be fundamentally incompatible with the observance of any sort of economic routine. As a result, charismatic orders will tend to support themselves materially through plunder, donations, or booty; at some point, there is a tendency for charisma to undergo "routinization," as mundane economic demands reassert themselves. In periods of social dislocation and economic collapse, however, the "specifically revolutionary" force of charisma is decisive in determining which new political and economic institutions are likely to be established in place of those that fail.

Because Weber insisted that traditional, rational-legal, and charismatic forms of domination were to be thought of as "ideal types" rather than actual social "systems," and because he saw the inherently unpredictable force of charisma as playing a crucial role in shaping human history, there is no implicit historical teleology underlying the Weberian framework. Thus, unlike modernization theory, Weberian analysis does not assume the eventual historical triumph of "modernity" in all social systems. To be sure, Weber appreciated the immense power of rational-legal forms of domination—in particular, the institutions of rationalized modern capitalism—but did not conclude that traditional and charismatic forms of social life would eventually be completely displaced. On the contrary, he argued that political and economic bureaucratic proceduralism might increasingly be perceived as a sort of "iron cage" by those subjected to it; this could ultimately lead to the emergence of new charismatic prophets, or to the rebirth of traditional ideals, which might promise an escape from the rational-legal domination.[10]

How might the Weberian framework for comparative analysis be applied to the study of the Soviet Union? For the Weberian, the establishment of the Bolshevik regime in the USSR can itself be seen as an attempt by Marxist revolutionaries to escape the iron cage of modern capitalism while still achieving the economic power of rational-legal modes of social organization. Here I follow the pathbreaking work of Ken Jowitt, who has argued that Leninist institutions in the USSR and elsewhere can be understood, in ideal-typical terms, as representing a novel form of domination that *combines* charismatic and rational-legal elements. Leninism, according to Jowitt, is neither wholly revolutionary and geared to the destruction of Western norms of political and economic life, as the totalitarian paradigm implies, nor fully "modern," as modernization theory suggests it has become in the post-Stalin era. Political domination by the party-state in the USSR is organized around principles of "charismatic impersonalism"—an *amalgam* of rational-legal norms of impersonal procedure with a charismatic, revolutionary emphasis on transcending the existing mundane order. It is precisely in its historically unprecedented attempt to combine these seemingly incompatible elements in political and economic practice that the true uniqueness of Leninism as a form of domination is revealed.[11]

I believe that Jowitt's conception of "charismatic impersonalism" can be extended to an analysis of the entire historical period connecting the original theoretical works of Marx to the "radical reforms" of Gorbachev, focusing on one key aspect of this ideological lineage: the specifically Marxist-Leninist conception of time.[12] Just as liberal capitalist industrialization in the West depended on a prior religious rejection of traditional modes of organizing economic time—according to the natural cycles of the sun, the moon, and the seasons—in favor of abstract rational-legal time discipline regulated by the mechanical clock,[13] industrialization in the Soviet Union was based on an ideology that similarly provided a rationale for the political destruction of traditional agrarian rhythms of economic life. But while the ideology of Western industrialization was based on a secularized Calvinism accepting the inexorable nature of time's dominion over human action, and arguing for time discipline in daily life as a sober adjustment to this fact, Marxism-Leninism argued that time discipline was necessary for a quite different reason: exercising time discipline in the present, in the service of the revolutionary movement, would lead to the ultimate establishment of a communist society *beyond time constraints altogether.* Thus the Leninist conception of time can itself be seen as "charismatically impersonal"—an amalgam of rational-legal norms of time discipline with a charismatic emphasis on the miraculous transcendence of time through revolutionary activity. In examining the history of this "charismatically impersonal" conception of time, one discerns three distinct cycles of development—cycles that parallel similar stages of development in Western industrialization. Just as the diffusion of a modern time sense in Western Europe presupposed first the theoretical innovations of Protestant religious doctrine, then the conquest of political power by an elite substantially committed to this doctrine, and then the widespread imposition of abstract time constraints in everyday life through socioeconomic institutions such as the factory and the school, the development of the Leninist view of time has gone through theoretical, political, and socioeconomic cycles.[14] Indeed, these cycles in the history of the Marxist-Leninist revolutionary movement have unfolded according to a remarkably consistent pattern. In each cycle, a striking innovation in the theory and practice of charismatically impersonal time by a founder or set of founders—Marx and Engels in the theoretical cycle, Lenin in the political cycle, and Stalin in the socioeconomic cycle—has been followed, after the founders' deaths, by a loss of revolutionary momentum and a split of the movement into three groups: a "left" group stressing a more fully charismatic interpretation of Marxism; a "right" group adopting a more fully rational-legal, procedural Marxism; and a "center" group more dedicated to attacking left and right "deviations" from orthodoxy than to fighting for further revolutionary advance. If left-wing Marxism is analytically charismatic in stressing the miraculous achievement of revolutionary goals in a short period, and right-wing Marxism is analytically rational-legal in stressing the empirical laws governing social evolution, then centrist Marxism can best be described as "neotraditional"—based on a quasi-theological understanding of Marxist ideology as infallible dogma, with the "orthodox" leadership seen as the sole legitimate interpreter of that dogma.[15]

It is only with an ideal-typical understanding of Marxist theory, Leninist politics, and Stalinist economics as essentially "charismatically impersonal" and with a sense for the cyclical dynamic of development within this ideological lineage over time that Gorbachev's *perestroika* can be approached theoretically. With this in mind, I will turn to a more detailed summary of the three cycles of innovation and breakdown in the history of "charismatically impersonal" time in the development of Marxism and of the Soviet Marxist state, and then examine how Gorbachev's *perestroika* emerges from that history.

CHARISMATICALLY IMPERSONAL TIME FROM MARX TO GORBACHEV

The theoretical work of Karl Marx can be seen as the creation of an entirely unprecedented way of conceiving of the relation between the force of time and human activity. Specifically, Marx combined in a novel way an empirical analysis of linear history as subject to scientific, temporal laws with a revolutionary call to establish a new social order where those laws would no longer apply. Marx contrasted this conception of "historical materialism," whose workings would eventually result in the establishment of communist society, with both anarchism and utopian socialism.[16] Anarchism, Marx argued, was based on the idea that one could break with all past history simply through revolutionary action without any prior analysis of when conditions for revolution might be ripe; this led anarchists to continual revolutionary failure. Utopian socialism was based on the idea that one could achieve a qualitatively better social order within the framework of bourgeois history, ignoring the need for a revolutionary break with time; this doomed it to remain subject to the economic laws inherent in bourgeois society. Marxism, by contrast, was simultaneously *scientific* and *revolutionary*. By combining the disciplined analysis of empirical conditions with revolutionary action to overthrow the capitalist order, Marxism would provide a theoretical tool for the practical realization of communism as "the *real* movement which abolishes the present state of things."[17]

But after Marx's death and the death of his close collaborator Engels, the Marxist movement during the period of the Second International split into right, left, and center wings. The right wing proclaimed an ideal of gradual, evolutionary socialism within the framework of capitalism, rejecting the need for revolutionary action; this tendency best found expression in the work of Eduard Bernstein. The left wing stressed mass revolutionary action above all else, and castigated Marxists who seemed to have lost touch with this aspect of the doctrine; this tendency was represented most ably by Rosa Luxemburg. Finally, there emerged a center group, which focused primarily on the need to preserve Marxist orthodoxy against attacks from the left and right alike; its major spokesperson was Karl Kautsky. However, none of these three groups provided a workable balance of revolutionary enthusiasm with practical political effectiveness. With the advent of the First World War, and the disintegration of the Second International, it appeared that the collapse of Marxism as an effective revolutionary force was imminent.

Instead a new cycle of development began, with the success of Lenin's "party of a new type" in coming to power in Russia. Lenin's innovation was to combine the elements of charisma and modernity in Marx's conception of time in the structure of a practical political institution, a party of "professional revolutionaries."[18] In being both "professional" (subject to time discipline) and "revolutionary" (ready for charismatic action twenty-four hours a day), the Bolshevik party member could act on both strands of the Marxist idea of charismatically impersonal time.

But this innovation on the political level left unanswered how this synthesis of revolution and discipline could extend to the sphere of everyday economic activity. After the Bolshevik victory in the Civil War, despite the unanimous view of the leadership that Leninist party discipline must be maintained at all costs, the party again split into left, center, and right wings in addressing the issue of "socialist construction." The left wing now favored party-directed charismatic activity in economic production through campaign style discipline such as was embodied in Trotsky's proposal for "labor armies"; the "militarization of labor" would tap into the same heroic energies that had won the Civil War for the Red Army, transforming the Soviet Union miraculously into an advanced industrial society. The center tendency, best represented in the writings and policies of Zinoviev, concentrated on criticizing Trotsky's and then Bukharin's deviations from orthodoxy while failing to provide any positive answers to the dilemmas of economic construction in the Soviet Union. Finally, the right wing, acting on Bukharin's assumption that the development of a socialist economy in the USSR would be a long-term, evolutionary process, favored the explicit adoption of impersonal Western notions of time discipline, both on the macroeconomic level, where slow growth was advocated over revolutionary economic campaigns, and on the microeconomic level, where Western ideas on the "rationalization" of labor became an entrenched part of Soviet economic thinking.[19] Once again, by the end of the period of the New Economic Policy, the loss of revolutionary momentum caused by these innerparty splits, and the party leadership's lack of any clear strategy for *combining* revolution and discipline in socialist economic life in order to regain that momentum, threatened the survival of the revolutionary movement.

In this context we must recognize that despite their extremely coercive nature, the primary economic institutions of Stalinist-forced industrialization of the USSR—the Five-Year Plan on the macroeconomic level and shock-work and Stakhanovism on the microeconomic level—were remarkable innovations making possible a third cycle of Marxist-Leninist development: the establishment of *socioeconomic* charismatic impersonalism in time use. The Soviet manager overfulfilling his formal plan targets, and the shock-worker or Stakhanovite breaking through the limits of "bourgeois" norms of production, were the economic equivalents of the "professional revolutionaries" of the Leninist party, rejecting neither the necessity of taking impersonal time constraints into account in economic activity nor the simultaneous revolutionary necessity of charismatically transcending these very constraints.

So far, in terms of the general sequence of these broad stages of development—from theoretical innovation to political institutionalization to socioeconomic institutionalization—the history of charismatically impersonal time under Leninism parallels closely the analogous history of the development of the patterns of rational-legal time use characteristic of Western industrialization. However, the essential difference between capitalist and Leninist development becomes clear when a fourth stage in the development of capitalist time discipline is examined—the period of the *cultural internalization* of modern time norms. The current period of Western development depends on a widespread legitimation of abstract time discipline that has taken place in Western societies; a crucial segment of both intellectual and manual laborers in capitalist societies can be expected to behave like classic Protestants even without external compulsion. This clearly lends much stability to the capitalist system; without this cultural internalization of modern time norms, capitalist activity might well continue, but with much more political coercion and labor strife. How does this situation compare with that in the Soviet Union?

In fact, the *issue* of the need for cultural internalization of Leninist time norms has been a paramount one in the USSR ever since the end of the harshest methods of coercion after Stalin's death in 1953. Without a reliance on police terror, a truly "revolutionary" attitude toward labor discipline on the part of Soviet workers could be guaranteed only through a decisive socialist cultural transformation—a mass internalization of charismatically impersonal norms of time use throughout the Soviet population. But none of the post-Stalin Soviet leaders have been successful in inculcating "heroic" self-discipline among workers in the context of Stalinist socioeconomic institutions. Again, there has been a split into left-wing, right-wing, and neo-traditional "center" strategies here. Malenkov, during the short period he directed Soviet economic policy in the year after Stalin's death, appeared to be moving the Soviet system toward "right-wing" acceptance of the liberal capitalist conception of how to produce a loyal work culture—that is, provide workers with more consumer goods and let things evolve naturally from there. Khrushchev, with his emphasis on voluntaristic mass economic campaigns to create a culture of time transcendence in the Soviet Union—which was expected to result in the achievement of full communism by 1980—represents the "left" strategy in the post-Stalin era. Brezhnev, with his uncritical acceptance of Stalinist economic orthodoxy and his basic lack of a strategy for revolutionary progress, represents the "neotraditional" center. As in the prewar period of the Second International, and in the period of the NEP, the left strategy proved unrealistic, the right strategy seemed unrevolutionary, and the center strategy resulted in a "period of stagnation" in which the loss of revolutionary momentum and the threat to the Leninist movement were quite evident.

Mikhail Gorbachev's professed desire for a "radical reform" of Soviet institutions during his tenure as general secretary of the CPSU was thus a response to the failure of right, left, and center strategies in the post-Stalin era in dealing with the problem of the evident lack of a cultural internalization of Leninist norms of time discipline in Soviet society. Gorbachev must be understood neither as a "refined Stalinist" nor a closet "modern" who disguised himself long enough to rise to the position of leader of the CPSU, but as a would-be innovator within the context of the charismatically impersonal conception of time in the mold of Marx, Lenin, and Stalin. Specifically, Gorbachev's *perestroika* was introduced as an attempt to bring about the rapid transformation of Soviet culture in a charismatic direction—to produce a culture, and not merely a socioeconomic structure, based on a mass internalization of norms of time transcendence in everyday life. I will analyze the three major stages of Gorbachev's efforts to move the Soviet Union in this direction—the period of "acceleration" *(uskorenie)*, the period of "restructuring" *(perestroika)*, and the final continuing period of the rejection of Leninist norms of party rule—as a logical policy sequence given Gorbachev's analysis of the nature of Soviet society and his professed desire to reinfuse the institutions of Soviet socialism with new revolutionary content. Finally, I will argue that unlike the innovations of Marx, Lenin, and Stalin, Gorbachev's mechanisms for achieving a charismatically impersonal attitude toward time in Soviet mass culture were doomed to failure—a failure that meant the destruction not only of Gorbachev's vision but of the economics of Stalinism and the politics of Leninism as well.

GORBACHEV'S EARLY CAREER

Before examining the three stages of Gorbachev's reform strategy, we must first address the question: how was it possible that a "true believer" in the Marxist ideal of charismatic impersonalism in time orientation, one who aimed to remake Soviet culture along charismatic lines, could emerge as leader of the CPSU after two decades of stagnation and corruption of the party-state under Brezhnev? To answer this question, it is necessary to emphasize the particular set of life experiences that uniquely shaped Gorbachev and his generation within the party.[20] Here, three factors are crucial to an explanation of the idealistic mindset of Gorbachev and his advisers: their teenage experience of Soviet victory in World War II and postwar reconstruction, an early adulthood in the heady days of Khrushchevian optimism about the Soviet future, and long and bitter years of marginalization from the center of party life under Brezhnev during the years of political maturity.

Stalin's victory in World War II, the emergence of the Soviet Union as a superpower, and the establishment of Leninist regimes in Eastern Europe were key elements in legitimizing Stalin's socioeconomic charismatic impersonalism on a mass level in Soviet society. Certainly, no generation felt this more keenly than Gorbachev's. Fourteen years old in 1945, Gorbachev came of age in an environment marked by heroic mass struggle and sacrifice under Leninist auspices. Unlike the generation of Khrushchev and Brezhnev, whose political outlook was shaped by the struggle to establish the socioeconomic institutions of Stalinism in a hostile social environment, and who therefore saw victory in the war mainly as a decisive legitimation of the Stalinist *socioeconomic* system, Gorbachev experienced the war years and the postwar reconstruction quite different—as a realization of the Leninist *cultural* ideal of complete heroic participation of the masses together with the party in a common cause.[21] The older generation of leaders had been promoted not only for their acceptance of norms of revolutionary time discipline in Soviet institutions, but for their ruthlessness in fighting kulaks, bourgeois wreckers, and enemies of the people; they were not likely to be persuaded that the cultural ideals of communism could be achieved in the absence of the central leadership of the party-state. Gorbachev, on the other hand, first experienced Leninism in a context of wartime unity between party and people, which made the vision of a rapid diffusion of the norms of disciplined time transcendence throughout Soviet culture seem not a vain dream but part of historical experience.[22]

The idealism of Gorbachev and his generation was solidified by the experience of party work under Khrushchev. Khrushchev's own charismatic solution to the problem of creating a cultural basis for communism in the USSR closely paralleled the vision of Leninism characteristic of the eager and idealistic Gorbachev, now in his midtwenties. Of course, Khrushchev himself never questioned the fundamentals of the Stalinist planning system; he was convinced that inspirational campaigns, and not Stalinist coercion, would allow cultural charismatic impersonalism to take root in the USSR within the context of Stalinist planning and norm setting. But in his call to establish "full communism" by 1980, Khrushchev validated on a political level the vision of unity between party and society that Gorbachev had experienced during and immediately following World War II.

Khrushchev's ouster by the Brezhnev oligarchy in 1964 could only have been seen, by Gorbachev and those like him, as a betrayal of a realizable and noble vision. Unlike the older generation of Brezhnev, Gorbachev had not personally witnessed the failure of similar promises of the rapid victory of communism in the early years of the revolution; he had no internalized appreciation of just how hard-fought the battle had been for the establishment of Stalinist economic institutions in the early 1930s. That Khrushchev's rule threatened the continuation of the established Soviet economic system therefore must have seemed less important to Gorbachev than it did to the older generation; what resonated for the Gorbachev cohort within the party was Khrushchev's vision of the achievability of communism—a vision on which Brezhnev had seemingly turned his back.

Such an impression could only have been strengthened by the years of party decay and loss of momentum under Brezhnev's leadership, which Gorbachev, like most of his future advisers, watched from the periphery of the Soviet Union, in places like Stavropol, Sverdlovsk, Siberia, and the Transcaucasus. With no opportunity to test their own ideas about furthering the revolutionary cause of Leninism, these men were left with an absolute hatred of ossified central control and the idealistic belief that its destruction would by itself lead to a rapid realization of the cultural ideals promulgated by Khrushchev.

Brezhnev's neotraditional rule from 1964 to 1982 therefore had a different effect on the Gorbachev generation than on the older generation of party members or on the younger generation born after Stalin's death. Brezhnev's stress on party and state orthodoxy led among the older generation to increasing corruption and a loss of interest in further revolutionary advance, as they began to identify the maintenance of their own power with the defense of Leninism itself. The younger generation born after World War II, who had seen nothing but the period of Leninism's decline, were not so much corrupted—since they had never internalized the values of revolutionary Leninism—as they were alienated from the regime over time. But for the small group who shared the political and life experiences of Gorbachev, Brezhnevism absolutized a particular type of Leninist idealism—an idealism based on a deeply held belief that mass, disciplined time transcendence was an achievable cultural goal and that Soviet society, like the Gorbachev generation itself, awaited only the destruction of Brezhnevism for its realization.

The Gorbachev cohort was thus, by the 1980s, the last substantial group in Soviet society both to believe in the original ideals of Marxism and Leninism *and* to remain substantially uncorrupted.[23] The idealism characteristic of party members of Gorbachev's generation had prevented them from using their party positions merely as tools for furthering personal power and privilege, and led them to despise the large number of cadres who did. This is what ultimately created a political opening for Gorbachev and those who shared his outlook. To understand how this marginal group of idealistic Leninists rose to positions of central power in the USSR, we must briefly examine the history of the immediate pre-Gorbachev period, the Andropov-Chernenko interregnum.

Yuri Andropov's background was quite different from Gorbachev's. Born in 1914, he had been old enough to appreciate the struggles of Stalinist industrialization and collectivization, and showed no inclination during his brief reign as general secretary to attack the fundamental institutions of the Soviet economy. But his position as KGB chief during the worst years of Brezhnevism's corruption gave him a unique appreciation of just how severe the situation within the party, and how frequent the "violations of labor discipline" by Soviet workers, had become by 1982. Determined to reverse these trends, Andropov began to attack party corruption and worker inefficiency alike under the auspices of an all-out "campaign for discipline."

How would Andropov's policies have progressed if he had lived? The idea of a mass "discipline campaign" to improve Soviet economic production was not new; it was merely a reiteration of faith in the Stalinist charismatically impersonal conception of time in socioeconomic affairs, stressing the need to combine campaign style enthusiasm with disciplined work. But Andropov provided no clear response to the cultural dilemmas that had made the Stalinist synthesis of discipline and enthusiasm increasingly unworkable in the post-Stalin era. The early successes of the antialcohol and anticorruption campaigns were bound to fade as the most egregious violation of party and work norms were eliminated; Andropovism would sooner or later have run up against the same difficulties that Gorbachev was to encounter in his second year in office, as cultural opposition to the further tightening of discipline and the stricter enforcement of sobriety began to manifest itself. Whether Andropov would have moved in a direction similar to Gorbachev's, slid back into Brezhnevian tolerance, or increased the use of secret police coercion in party and economic affairs—thus raising the specter of a return to Stalinism—is hard to say. Andropov did not live long enough to allow for an unambiguous interpretation of his leadership in terms of the theoretical framework set out here.

What is crucial to emphasize is the immediate political effect of Andropov's brief period of leadership: the promotion of the Gorbachev generation of "Leninist Romantics"[24] to top party posts. Striving to build a power base within the party that would be untainted by corruption, Andropov found allies in the one group who remained committed to the possibility of a cultural realization of the ideals of Marxism-Leninism. Andropov counted on the hatred of corruption, and faith in the revolution, of these younger party members. What he could not have foreseen was that the discipline and faith of Gorbachev and his cohort would later fuel a fanatical effort to reform Leninism along the lines of these cultural ideals even at the cost of party rule itself.

If Andropov's tenure as general secretary led to the promotion of Gorbachev and members his generation to key party positions, Konstantin U. Chernenko's even briefer reign put the finishing touches on the political discrediting of Brezhnevism. While Brezhnev could at least claim to be preserving political and socioeconomic orthodoxy while awaiting the revolution's ultimate international victory, Chernenko's *return* to Brezhnev's policies after Andropov's promised purification of the movement seemed a final repudiation of the party's claim to be revolutionary in its essence. The same old guard that had maintained a somewhat unexamined support for Brezhnevism as representing the triumph of "real socialism" were now forced to deny any such legitimacy to the ailing Chernenko's embarrassing (and embarrassingly brief) period of leadership. Looking within the existing party elite for a new source of inspiration and revolutionary rejuvenation, the CPSU leadership, still dominated by Brezhnev appointees, settled on one of Andropov's youngest and most prominent protégés, Mikhail Gorbachev. Humiliated by two decades of increasing corruption, declining Soviet international prestige, and finally the spectacle of three general secretaries dying within two and a half years, the old guard allowed political changes in Gorbachev's first few years in office that would formerly have been unacceptable to them. Within a few years, every member of the last Brezhnev Politburo had been ousted from the leadership, and Gorbachev had set out to remake the political and socioeconomic systems of the USSR according to an absolutized ideal of cultural charismatic impersonalism in time orientation.

FROM USKORENIE TO PERESTROIKA: GORBACHEV'S FIRST TWO YEARS

Gorbachev was named general secretary of the CPSU on March 11, 1985. From that point until the Twenty-seventh Party Congress of the CPSU in February 1986, he was mainly engaged in the struggle to consolidate his political authority, purging holdovers from the Brezhnev era in the party apparatus and promoting his own supporters. By the time the Congress met, nearly 40 percent of the Central Committee was newly elected.[25] In economic policy, Gorbachev pushed for a new attack on alcoholism among Soviet workers and for a strengthened enforcement of labor discipline. In short, the new general secretary made it clear that he was following his mentor Andropov in attacking the corrupt, neotraditional form of Leninism characteristic of the Brezhnev period. But there was little indication that Gorbachev would go beyond these policies and attack the institutional structure of Leninism itself.

By the time of the Party Congress, however, Gorbachev felt secure enough in his position to begin articulating a distinctive "Gorbachevian" interpretation of the current tasks of the party—an interpretation that broke more decisively with Brezhnevian Marxism-Leninism than anything put forth by Andropov. This new interpretation of party ideology had three major components: relativization of the international arena as a realm for the legitimation of Soviet rule and a corresponding reemphasis on domestic politics, an insistence that the Soviet Union was at a turning point (*perelom*) in its development, and a call for the acceleration (*uskorenie*) of socioeconomic development as the proper response to this challenge.

The downgrading of the importance of international socialism as a sphere for the legitimation of party rule had been an important aspect of the previous innovations within the framework of charismatic impersonalism in time orientation by Lenin and Stalin. Lenin, in his *Imperialism,* had broken with Kautsky's neotraditional form of internationalism, which was based on the preservation of Germany's superior standing within the Second International as a concretization of revolutionary orthodoxy, by establishing the rival doctrine that a proletarian revolution in backward Russia would break the structure of imperialism at its weakest point. Likewise, in 1924 Stalin had broken with Zinoviev's similar form of neotraditional internationalism, during the latter's period of leadership of the Comintern, with his development of the doctrine of "socialism in one country."

Gorbachev's break with Brezhnev's neotraditionalism, interestingly enough, closely paralleled these two earlier leaders' attempts to establish themselves as Marxist innovators on the Russian scene rather than orthodox "centrists" focusing their attention on international affairs. Thus Gorbachev's report to the Twenty-seventh Party Congress broke with the long-standing practice under Brezhnev of starting out each Congress address with a chronicle of recent socialist victories in the Third World. Gorbachev began his speech with an unprecedented portrayal of the "complex" state of affairs in the world, printed in official documents under the subheading "Tendencies and Contradictions." Despite Gorbachev's stern denunciations of the "imperialist system [which] is still living off the plunder of the developing countries, off their totally merciless exploitation," the major thrust of his analysis was the need for "constructive and creative interaction between states and peoples of the entire world."[26] The section of Gorbachev's speech dealing explicitly with international affairs—relegated to near the end of the general secretary's report—made it clear that he saw little hope of further socialist advance abroad without prior reform in the Soviet Union:

> Today the destinies of peace and social progress are tied up more closely than
> ever with the dynamism of the economic and political development of the so-
> cialist world system. . . . Both friends and enemies look upon us, the immense,
> many-faced world of the developing countries looks upon us, seeking its choice,
> its path. What this choice will be depends to a large extent on the successes of
> socialism, on the credibility of its responses to the challenge of the times.[27]

The message was clear: in an exceedingly complex world, the progress of socialism on a global scale depended on the Soviet Union's response to its own
internal problems.

If Gorbachev's reemphasis of Soviet domestic politics over international
affairs prepared the ground for his advocacy of change, his argument that the
Soviet Union had reached a turning point (*perelom*) in its development, one
analogous to earlier periods of revolutionary advance in Soviet history,
showed his desire to usher in a new cycle of Leninist development. Just as
Lenin had broken with the "left" anarchists, the "right" economists, and the
Kautskyan "center" in establishing a Marxist political regime, and just as Stalin had broken with Trotsky, Bukharin, and Zinoviev in establishing a Leninist socioeconomic regime, Gorbachev now explicitly broke with the
Brezhnevian status quo:

> For a number of years the deeds and actions of party and government bodies
> trailed behind the needs of the times and of life. . . . The problems in the coun-
> try's development built up more rapidly than they were being solved. The
> inertia and stiffness of the forms and methods of administration, the decline of
> dynamism in our work, and an escalation of bureaucracy—all this was doing no
> small damage. Signs of stagnation had begun to surface in the life of society. . . .
> The situation called for change, but a peculiar psychology—how to improve
> things without changing anything—took the upper hand. . . . But that cannot be
> done, comrades. Stop for an instant, as they say, and you will fall behind a
> mile.[28]

Gorbachev's insistence that 1986 marked a *perelom* in Soviet history therefore presented the party a stark choice: undertake "radical reform" of Soviet
institutions, or watch the party's last chance for revolutionary renewal slip
by.

In essence, Gorbachev's analysis paralleled Lenin's battle cry in *What Is
To Be Done?* to put an end to the stagnation of the Second International by
undertaking revolutionary action, as well as Stalin's famous call to "catch up
and overtake" the capitalist countries in ten years or be crushed by the international bourgeoisie. The difference was that with political and socioeconomic institutions already controlled by the Leninist party-state and
organized along charismatically impersonal lines, the only fortress left for the
Bolsheviks to storm was the fortress of time's dominion over Soviet culture
itself. Thus Gorbachev, from the outset, operated with an ideal of success for
his reform effort that was—from the Weberian perspective—unrealizable:

the realization of a mass cultural norm of permanent revolutionary time transcendence in Soviet society.

This vision was encapsulated in the early Gorbachev slogan *uskorenie,* or acceleration. As a criterion for economic progress, *uskorenie* differed from the typical liberal capitalist standard of success in crucial respects. Whereas elites in capitalist regimes tend to judge themselves by whether they can sustain a simple growth rate in GNP, assuring themselves that this means they are making "progress" in linear time, Gorbachev was calling for the creation of an economic mechanism which would, in principle, result in *continually increasing growth rates*—2 percent one year, 4 percent the next, 6 percent the next, and so on. If simple growth allowed capitalists to feel they were keeping pace with time, "acceleration" would guarantee to Leninism an eternal dynamism in Soviet life that would ultimately usher in a qualitatively different sort of social order. It was in this sense that Gorbachev could argue that while acceleration means "[f]irst and foremost, raising the economic growth rate," he continued on to say that it "does not amount only to a transformation in the economic field," but actually "holds the key to all our problems in the near and more distant future—economic and social, political and ideological, and internal and external ones."[29]

Very quickly, of course, such a standard of success would work to undermine Gorbachev's authority, as the promised renewal of socialism failed to take place. But it is crucial to realize that the charismatic component in Gorbachev's time orientation—his sense that a rapid overcoming of current time constraints was possible through correct revolutionary action—was from the outset at least equal to his analytically modern stress on scientific analysis of the complexities of the Soviet Union's crisis and the need for a disciplined approach to overcoming it.

In short, Gorbachev's time orientation, as displayed in the address to the Twenty-seventh Party Congress, was charismatically impersonal in the classic Marxist-Leninist sense. The new general secretary, in focusing on Soviet domestic politics as the proper arena for revolutionary endeavor, in breaking with the neotraditional stress on orthodoxy characteristic of Brezhnev, and in outlining an alternative vision of *uskorenie* as the key to unlocking the inherent dynamism of the socialist economy, sounded themes that had real meaning for cadres steeped in Leninist norms of discourse and practical activity. Indeed, Gorbachev's success in convincing a significant percentage of the party establishment to back reform policies that from the beginning threatened their basic material interests can only be explained by understanding how Gorbachev's program resonated on the level of Leninist *ideals.* After years of unrealizable utopianism followed by decades of unrevolutionary defense of the status quo, Gorbachev's call for the "radical reform" of Soviet institutions at last promised the party a chance to do something simultaneously heroic and realistic.

But just how this promise would be translated into an actual program for institutional change was not clear in 1986. At first, Gorbachev's economic

STEPHEN E. HANSON

program remained very similar to Andropov's in its stress on ~~increased labor~~ ~~discipline, sobriety, and crackdowns on corruption~~. As during Andropov's reign, this set of policies produced short-term payoffs as the most egregious violations of norms of work and party activity were attacked. But by the beginning of 1987, there were already signs that these methods of stimulating economic production had begun to bog down. Sugar began to disappear from store shelves as the production of *samogon* (moonshine) skyrocketed in the absence of state-supplied vodka. The arrest on charges of corruption of Brezhnev's son-in-law, Yuri Churbanov, rather than presenting the image of a newly cleansed party apparatus, had the effect of demonstrating that the CPSU as an institution had become rotten to the core. At the same time, efforts to enforce labor discipline and efficiency in time use in the Soviet economy began to run up against inherent limits. Early attempts to introduce a three-shift system in Leningrad factories, in order to keep machinery in operation twenty-four hours a day, and thus in principle overcome problems of idleness in industrial production, were abandoned as complaints poured in from workers about the impossibility of living normally on the night shift in the absence of twenty-four-hour grocery stores and nighttime child care.[30] The Andropov strategy for enforcing cultural Leninism—mass disciplined enthusiasm for work *within* Leninist institutions—had failed.

The beginning of 1987 found Gorbachev at a crossroads. He could intensify the campaign for discipline, but with the most obvious violations of discipline already under attack, this would have necessitated a neo-Stalinist reliance on punitive sanctions, and potentially large-scale police violence against Soviet workers, that directly contradicted Gorbachev's professed anticentralism. At the same time, Gorbachev had decisively rejected both the Khrushchevian strategy for eliciting work enthusiasm from the Soviet population—charismatic promises of a quick end to economic scarcity—and the Brezhnevian attempt to enforce political, social, and economic orthodoxy despite increasing cultural anomie. There remained the "right-wing" option: explicitly to reject the possibility of achieving socialist cultural transformation except perhaps in the very long run, and to concentrate on introducing true marketization and on producing or importing more consumer goods to inspire Soviet workers to work harder. But when this strategy was articulated by the prominent economist Nikolai Shmelev in the summer of 1987,[31] is too proved to be unacceptable to Gorbachev. Like Bukharin's right-wing strategy for economic development in the 1920s, Shmelev's proposals relied ultimately on the specter of unemployment as a tool for enforcing work discipline where positive work incentives had failed, and this was incompatible with Gorbachev's platform. Gorbachev had promised socialist renewal; adopting the right-wing strategy would have meant accepting the necessity of yet another long-term period of retreat, which would no doubt have been ruinous for a party already substantially corrupted and in danger of losing its revolutionary ideals altogether.[32]

THE "HUMAN FACTOR"

Faced with these rather unpalatable choices, Gorbachev began to rely increasingly on a group of close advisers who had worked at the Novosibirsk institute of the Academy of Sciences in the late Brezhnev era, a group centered around the sociologist Tat'iana Zaslavskaia. Beginning in the late Brezhnev era, and then increasingly publicly since Gorbachev's rise to power, Zaslavskaia and her colleagues began to put forward an alternative analysis of the problems of declining work discipline and economic stagnation in the USSR—an analysis that came to be known as the "human factor" approach to economic reform. In a series of prominent articles in Soviet academic journals, Zaslavskaia argued that the overwhelming centralization of Soviet economic life that developed under Stalin and became ossified under Brezhnev had acted to prevent the expression of an otherwise natural enthusiasm of labor under socialist conditions. As she put it: "A great deal depends on the worker's recognition of his involvement in the common cause, on the degree of his subjective 'involvement' in the production process, on the level of his identification with the collective and with the contents of his job."[33] The more the worker identified with his work, Zaslavskaia argued, the greater "the fulfillment of plans and norms and the effectiveness of utilization of labor time."[34] Under Brezhnev's rule, however, because of the lack of any correspondence between the worker's effort and his material reward, "people with a high skill level and the ability to do excellent work did not want to work with maximum intensity and preferred the 'quiet life'."[35]

But Zaslavskaia's analysis did not lead her to accept, as did Shmelev, the idea of unemployment as a solution to problems of worker idleness. She argued that a cultural transformation in the USSR, bringing about widespread enthusiasm for labor, was the only answer: "There is but one truly promising solution: the inculcation of all categories of workers with the capacity of self-monitoring based on a high degree of professionalism, personal dignity, pride in the excellent quality of job performance, and an aversion to careless work."[36]

Zaslavskaia remained somewhat vague on the issue of how this "inculcation" would take place; her assumption seemed to be that the mere experience of taking part in a "radically reformed" socialism in the USSR would provide enough impetus for workers to change their cultural attitudes toward labor: "The crucial conditions for accelerating social development are activation of the human factor, fuller and more effective use of the individual's labor and intellectual potential, and reawakening the creative energy of the masses and channeling it into the mainstream of social interest."[37]

To create the preconditions for such a "reawakening" might, Zaslavskaia admitted, require a short-term concentration on narrow economic goals— weeding out truly lazy or incompetent workers, changing the system of incentives to reward hard work more effectively, and so on. But this "subordination of social goals to economic goals" could be justified "only for short periods of time, limited to one or two five-year periods. Over the longer term, the principal goal of the development of socialism becomes the creation of a more progressive system of social relations that will ensure the all-round development of the individual, the realization of personal aptitudes, and the remuneration of representatives of all social groups in accordance with work performed."[38] Thus, in rejecting Stalinist centralism without advocating any new centralism to take its place, Zaslavskaia implicitly held out the possibility that in a reformed USSR, for the first time in history, a truly self-actualized and self-disciplined working class would emerge. The Soviet Union would then have achieved a "qualitatively new level of development of social relations, and consequently, of man himself."[39]

In sum, Zaslavskaia's articles painted a heroically optimistic picture of the state of the Soviet economy and the potential efficiency of the Soviet work force under the auspices of reformed Leninism. Under Brezhnev, the lazy had been rewarded more than those who took the initiative; reversing this equation would unleash a surge of enthusiastic, high-quality work which, combined with the high technology now available in the USSR, would begin to transform the Soviet Union into a qualitatively new type of social order. Upon closer examination, there was little in Zaslavskaia's work to indicate concretely what institutional changes the party should implement to change the Brezhnevian incentive structure. She called for increased penalties for violations of labor discipline but stopped short of advocating the ultimate penalty of unemployment; she called for greater pay differentials to reward skilled and high-quality labor but stopped short of recommending a free labor market, insisting on the need to "channel" individual interests to serve social needs. The one consistent policy implication of her analysis was a negative one: the overcentralized system of economic planning inherited from Stalin must be destroyed before the "human factor" could be activated and socialism's unique potential to "fully reveal man's abilities and develop his creative activity as an actor in social life" could be realized.[40]

PERESTROIKA AND CHARISMATICALLY IMPERSONAL TIME

The implications of the "human factor" approach to the reform of Leninism were concretized in the new slogan and strategy Gorbachev introduced in a decisive way in January 1987—*perestroika,* or restructuring.[41] The general secretary's call for the *perestroika* of existing Soviet institutions marked Gorbachev's final break with Andropovism and his emergence as a full-fledged innovator in the tradition of Marx, Lenin, and Stalin. Having realized the ultimate unworkability of right, left, or center strategies in the post-Stalin era for realizing the potential of a fully socialist cultural transformation in the USSR, Gorbachev drew the logical conclusion: Stalin's socioeconomic institutionalization of Leninism was itself to blame for the dead end in which the movement found itself. The natural tendency of socialism, after all, was to be dynamic, to outstrip time. Something in the existing institutional structure of the Soviet economy and society must therefore be acting as a "braking mechanism" on this process.[42] Before an acceleration of Soviet socioeconomic progress could be achieved, therefore, it would be necessary in effect to begin all over again from 1928 and "restructure" the Soviet economy along new lines. This would be possible, moreover, without merely substituting a new set of mechanisms of central control for the old centralized planning system, because, as Zaslavskaia's analysis had insisted, Soviet society had "matured" to the extent that a more dynamic socialist culture would emerge naturally as Stalinism itself was destroyed.

Perestroika, then, was to be the cultural equivalent of Lenin's "professionally revolutionary" seizure of state power in Russia or Stalin's combination of "American efficiency and Russian revolutionary sweep" in Soviet socioeconomic institutions.[43] It represented a practical and disciplined, yet revolutionary, movement to introduce a fourth and final period of development in Marxism-Leninism, one based on a continual dynamic internalization of norms of "revolutionary discipline" on a mass basis; in this sense it was "in its Bolshevik daring and in its humane social thrust ... a direct sequel to the great accomplishments started by the Leninist Party in the October days of 1917."[44] As Gorbachev rhapsodized:

> The success of perestroika will be the final argument in the historical dispute as to which system is more consistent with the interests of the people. Rid of the features that appeared in extreme conditions, the image of the Soviet Union will gain a new attractiveness and will become the living embodiment of the advantages that are inherent in the socialist system. The ideals of socialism will gain fresh impetus.[45]

The stakes were clear: a successful implementing of *perestroika* would not only reinfuse socialism with "fresh impetus," but would provide the "final argument in the historical dispute" between socialism and capitalism. As Gorbachev never tired of insisting, then, *perestroika* in its conception did not involve any rejection whatsoever of socialist values. It was meant to bring "more socialism" into the Soviet way of life and to cleanse the deformations of socialism that took place during the "era of stagnation."[46]

However, formal intentions are not the same as practical outcomes. Operating on the theory articulated by Zaslavskaia and others, that a "mature" Soviet culture awaited only the destruction of overcentralized control by the party-state over socioeconomic life to blossom into a disciplined and dynamic force for economic development, Gorbachev defined *perestroika* in almost purely negative terms. *Perestroika* in practice meant the disciplined revolutionary destruction of Stalinism, not the construction of any particular institutions to take Stalinism's place. The constructive side of *perestroika*, the creation of new forms of socialist life, was to be left to the popular initiative of the masses; any departure from this principle was held to be a reversion to

Brezhnevian or Stalinist ways of thinking. If the theory of Soviet society under which Gorbachev was operating had been correct, a new culture of disciplined revolutionary activity in everyday life should have begun to emerge
in the USSR—not all at once, as Khrushchev had imagined, but gradually,
and then more and more dynamically. New "plans" for revitalizing society
from the center, in this view, would only slow down this process.[47]

Accordingly, the three major campaigns associated with *perestroika*—for
glasnost', for *demokratizatsiia*, and for "new thinking" in Soviet foreign
policy—were each directed mainly *against* the existing order rather than toward the creation of a new order. *Glasnost'*, which encouraged the open
exposure in the Soviet press of the horrors of Stalinism, of current party corruption, of Soviet social problems, and, most consequentially, of Soviet nationality disputes, was designed to discredit for all time the centralized form
of Leninism that had taken shape under Stalin and fossilized under
Brezhnev—a task it performed with unparalleled effectiveness. *Demokratizatsiia*, in its original implementation, was designed to elicit mass pressure against the continuing tenure of die-hard Brezhnevites in party and
state positions, and to provide a political opening for grass-roots innovation.
Even the dramatic creation of the legal foundations for a more independent
Supreme Soviet in the fall of 1988 was designed above all to provide an alternative power base for Gorbachev in his struggle to destroy the existing party
and state apparatus, rather than as an attempt to establish Western norms of
liberal parliamentarianism in the USSR.[48] And the "new thinking" in Soviet
foreign policy amounted to an absolute rejection of the fundamentals of
Brezhnevian norms of "socialist internationalism," most importantly in relations with the regimes of Eastern Europe, without any clear articulation of
new principles according to which the Soviet use of its military and economic
power abroad might be justified.

Glasnost', *demokratizatsiia*, and "new thinking" thus did not add up to a
concrete vision of a "restructured" Soviet Union. Nor were they supposed
to. They were designed to unleash popular initiative for the destruction of
the corrupt, bureaucratized USSR which had emerged under Brezhnev, and
to make the process of *perestroika* within Leninist institutions "irreversible."
In this task the three campaigns succeeded perhaps beyond Gorbachev's expectations. Within two years after the full-scale implementation of
perestroika in 1987, every existing Leninist institution at home was under attack, and abroad the former Soviet bloc had crumbled into nothingness.

But this was not success in the form Gorbachev had originally imagined it.
The Soviet economic situation, rather than undergoing steady improvement
with the unleashing of mass initiative from below, simply continued to dete-
riorate as the Stalinist planning system lost whatever coherence it had still
possessed in the Brezhnev era. New political openness had not merely
relativized the role of the party apparatus but had led to the formation of
powerful groups actively hostile to every aspect of party rule in the USSR,
including far-right fascist groups such as *Pamiat'*, liberal capitalist groups

such as the Democratic Union, and national separatist movements in practically every Soviet republic. The rejection of the Brezhnev Doctrine in Eastern Europe had not created a new multipolarity in international relations. It had resulted in the outright defection of the most strategically important Soviet allies—Poland, East Germany, Hungary, and Czechoslovakia—to the capitalist camp.

Worse yet for Gorbachev, *perestroika* itself, having already accomplished much of its destructive mission, had by 1989 begun to run out of steam. Already, as in earlier periods of revolutionary fragmentation in the history of the Marxist-Leninist movement, right, left, and center interpretations of *perestroika* itself had begun to emerge. The "left" interpretation, true to its charismatic essence, argued for a rapid destruction of the remnants of Leninism in the USSR, which would bring about a quick, miraculous return to "normal" life under the auspices of the market; such an antiparty interpretation of *perestroika* was at the core of the political platform of Boris Yeltsin. The analytically modern, "right" interpretation of *perestroika* saw reform as a gradual, long-term process of the institutionalization of norms of liberal democracy in the USSR, with no possibility of any miraculous resolution of Soviet economic or political problems; this interpretation was argued most forcefully by Andrei Sakharov until his death (December 4, 1989). Finally, a "center," analytically neotraditional interpretation of *perestroika* itself began to emerge, emphasizing the preservation of Leninist party rule in any "reformed" Soviet Union and calling for crackdowns on the left and right alike, which were seen (perhaps correctly) as objectively anti-Leninist. This theme was most consistently expounded by Yegor Ligachev.[49]

Gorbachev responded to the new splits in the *perestroika* movement in typical fashion. Rejecting, like Ligachev, both Sakharov's democratic "right" and Yeltsin's populist-charismatic "left," but at the same time painting Ligachev himself as symbolizing nothing more than a return to the discredited neotraditional policies of Brezhnevian orthodoxy (which would in fact have been the likely outcome of a Ligachev victory), Gorbachev in early 1990 called for the continuation of *perestroika*. But *perestroika* was now to be directed not only against Stalinist socioeconomic centralism but against Leninist *party* centralism as well. In pushing for the repeal of Article 6 of the Soviet Constitution, which guaranteed the party's "leading role" in Soviet society, Gorbachev did not reject the notion of the vanguard party per se. But in Gorbachev's claim that the party would henceforth have to "earn" its leading role through concrete deeds, and in competition with other political forces, an implicit departure from Lenin's political thought began to manifest itself. For the implication of this argument was that the party itself could, in practice, become a "brake" on socialist progress, rather than being, as in Lenin's ideology, the ultimate *guarantor* of the socialist nature of socioeconomic and cultural development. Gorbachev's logic had led him to the conclusion that revolutionary Leninism might in principle require the destruction of the Leninist party itself.

Thus, although Gorbachev formally remained within the Marxist tradition even as late as 1990, substantively he had moved to a theoretical position that precluded any practical institutionalization of the Marxist ideal in political life. In his effort to put into practice a vision of cultural communism similar to Khrushchev's without becoming an unrealistic, Khrushchevian sort of "leftist," Gorbachev had called for the disciplined dismantling of Stalinism. But this had resulted in his becoming like an earlier leftist, Leon Trotsky—railing against the Stalinist bureaucracy without any concrete economic alternative besides a vague faith in the enthusiasm of the masses. Aware that he had once again reached an impasse, Gorbachev in 1990 began to associate himself with the disciplined dismantling of Leninism itself, acquiescing in, and even seeming at times to encourage, the emergence of a fundamentally anti-Leninist political coalition centered around Boris Yeltsin in Russia and the de facto breakup of the rest of the Soviet Union along the lines of its constituent republics. And the continuation of this political line—if indeed Gorbachev continued to pursue it—would very quickly leave him in much the same position as the original Marxist "leftist," Rosa Luxemburg: a pure revolutionary romantic, believing absolutely in the creative power of the masses, unable to countenance in principle any concrete institutionalization of revolutionary politics that might stifle this creativity, and therefore doomed to be defeated by others who had no such scruples.

By the summer of 1990, *perestroika* had led to an incipient loss of control by the CPSU leadership over the Soviet Union's political future. Essentially, under Gorbachev, Leninism had self-destructed.[50] Yet this was, in one sense, a fitting conclusion to the 150-year historical progression linking Marx to Gorbachev. Marx had begun that progression by calling for the political establishment of communism as "the *real* movement which abolishes the existing state of things," a movement disciplined by its scientific analysis of time-bound history but uncompromising in its ultimate rejection of time. Lenin had made communism a political reality for the "professional revolutionaries" of the Bolshevik party in 1917; Stalin had made communism a socioeconomic reality for the Stakhanovites and revolutionary managers who had heroically overfulfilled their norms and plan targets in the early years of Soviet industrialization. But Marx's vision of communism as a permanent *cultural* ideal—as a principle of day-to-day life for the masses—was inherently unachievable, at least in a world still governed inexorably by time constraints. With the failure of Khrushchev's charismatic promises and Brezhnev's defense of orthodoxy as strategies for the creation of socialist culture, Soviet socialism after Stalin's death had inevitably itself become part of the "existing state of things." Gorbachev's *perestroika* abolished this state of things, and did so in a remarkably disciplined and revolutionary manner. In working to destroy Stalin's and Lenin's historical legacy, he was thus a faithful Marxist.

NOTES

1. See, for example, the classic works of Hannah Arendt, *The Origins of Totalitarianism* (New York: Harcourt Brace, 1951), and Carl Friedrich and Zbigniew Brzezinski, *Totalitarian Dictatorship and Autocracy* (Cambridge: Harvard University Press, 1956).

2. This is the memorable expression used to describe Gorbachev by Vice President Dan Quayle in the early days of the Bush administration.

3. For an insightful analysis of the assumptions underlying the modernization paradigm within American political science in general and Soviet studies in particular, see Andrew C. Janos, *Politics and Paradigms: Changing Theories of Change in Social Science* (Stanford: Stanford University Press, 1986).

4. For a pre-Gorbachev analysis of Soviet politics in this vein, see Stephen F. Cohen, "The Friends and Foes of Change: Soviet Reformism and Conservatism," in *Rethinking the Soviet Experience: Politics and History Since 1917* (Oxford: Oxford University Press, 1985).

5. The assumption of an "end of ideology" in post-Stalin party politics is quite widespread in Soviet studies; for an early argument of this sort, see Robert C. Tucker, "The Deradicalization of Marxist Movements," in *The Marxian Revolutionary Idea* (New York: Norton, 1969).

6. The most interesting theoretical account of Gorbachev and his policies from this perspective is provided by Jerry Hough, *Russia and the West: Gorbachev and the Politics of Reform*, 2d ed. (New York: Simon and Schuster, 1990).

7. For an exceptionally clear statement of this thesis, see Moshe Lewin, *The Gorbachev Phenomenon* (Berkeley: University of California Press, 1987).

8. There are, of course, other important theoretical paradigms within the discipline of political science and social science in general. But most remained undeveloped in the field of Soviet studies, for various reasons. Marxist approaches to the analysis of the USSR were closely associated with Trotskyism and never became a major trend within the Western academic mainstream. Attempts to apply world-systems analysis and structuralism to the Soviet scene were, as of 1990, still few and far between. Rational choice theory had yet to be employed in a major study of Soviet politics, owing to the lack until quite recently of sufficient statistical resources on which to base quantitative analysis. This left the totalitarian model and the modernization paradigm as the two major contenders for theoretical predominance in the field of Soviet studies.

9. Max Weber, *Economy and Society*, Vols. 1, 2, ed. Guenther Roth and Claus Wittich (Berkeley: University of California Press, 1978).

10. Max Weber, *The Protestant Ethic and the Spirit of Capitalism* (New York: Scribner, 1958), pp. 181–82.

11. Kenneth Jowitt, *The Leninist Response to National Dependency* (Berkeley: Institute of International Studies, University of California, 1978), pp. 34–44.

12. Stephen E. Hanson, "Time and Industrialization in the USSR," Ph.D. dissertation, Department of Political Science, University of California, Berkeley, 1991.

13. David Landes, *Revolution in Time: Clocks and the Making of the Modern World* (Cambridge: Harvard University Press, 1983).

14. The conception of "cycles of development" I am using here owes a great debt to Jowitt's three "stages of development" in Leninist (and other) regimes: transformation, consolidation, and inclusion. See Jowitt, "Inclusion and Mobilization in Euro-

pean Leninist Regimes," *World Politics* 28:1 (1975), pp. 69–97. I have also been influenced by the periodization given in Mark Beissinger, *Scientific Management, Socialist Discipline, and Soviet Power* (Cambridge: Harvard University Press, 1988).

15. The term "communist neo-traditionalism" was first formulated by Ken Jowitt in "Soviet Neo-Traditionalism: The Political Corruption of a Leninist Regime," *Soviet Studies* 35:3 (1983), pp. 275–97. It was later applied very persuasively by Andrew Walder in his *Communist Neo-Traditionalism: Work and Authority in Chinese Industry* (Berkeley and Los Angeles: University of California Press, 1986). In my dissertation I argue that the phrase can be applied to the policies of two analogous figures in the earlier theoretical and political cycles of the development of the charismatically impersonal conception of time: Karl Kautsky and Grigorii Zinoviev.

16. Karl Marx, excerpt from *A Contribution to the Critique of Political Economy*, in *Basic Writing on Politics and History: Karl Marx and Friedrich Engels*, ed. Lewis S. Feuer (Garden City: Anchor/Doubleday, 1959), p. 44.

17. Karl Marx, *The German Ideology*, in Robert C. Tucker, ed., *The Marx-Engels Reader* (New York: Norton, 1978), p. 162, emphasis in original.

18. V. I. Lenin, *What Is To Be Done?* (New York: International Publishers, 1972), pp. 108–24.

19. For a detailed historical study of the idea of "rationalization" in the Soviet Union in 1920 and beyond, see Beissinger, *Scientific Management*.

20. The crucial role of generational turnover in understanding Gorbachev has been stressed by Hough, *Russia and the West*, pp. 17–43. However, Hough and I read the experience of the Gorbachev generation very differently. He argues that Gorbachev and his cohort developed an unambiguously pro-Western orientation even during their early years rising through the educational establishment of high Stalinism. While a detailed critique of Hough's position is beyond the scope of this essay, it seems to me at least doubtful that such influences as Soviet pro-American propaganda during the period of wartime alliance between the United States and USSR, the reading of prerevolutionary Russian literature in Stalinist secondary schools, and some exposure to classical philosophy in law school were decisive in shaping Gorbachev's cultural outlook, as Hough implies.

21. In *Perestroika: New Thinking for Our Country and the World* (New York: Harper and Row, 1987), Gorbachev recounts his impressions of the period of postwar reconstruction in revealing terms (pp. 41–42):

> In the West they said at that time that Russia would not be able to rise even in a hundred years, that it was out of international politics for a long time ahead because it would focus on healing its wounds somehow. And today they say, some with admiration and others with open hostility, that we are a superpower! We revived and lifted the country on our own, through our own efforts, putting to use the immense potentialities of the socialist system.
>
> And we cannot but mention one more aspect of the matter which is frequently ignored or hushed up in the West, but without which it is simply impossible to understand us, the Soviet people; along with the economic and social achievements, there was also a new life, there was the enthusiasm of the builders of a new world, an inspiration from things new and unusual, a keen feeling of pride that we alone, unassisted and not for the first time, were raising the country on our shoulders.

Later, Gorbachev explicitly compares the period of postwar reconstruction with the present era (p. 68):

We are living through no ordinary period. People of the older generation are comparing the present revolutionary atmosphere with that of the first few years after the October Revolution or with the times of the Great Patriotic War. But my generation can draw a parallel with the period of the postwar recovery. We are now far more sober and realistic. So the enthusiasm and revolutionary self-sacrifice that increasingly distinguish the political mood of the Soviet people are all the more valuable and fruitful.

22. That Gorbachev took the cultural ideal of disciplined time transcendence seriously on a personal level is evidenced by his being awarded, at the age of eighteen, the Order of the Red Banner of Labor for his work as an assistant to a combine harvest operator. See Dusko Doder and Louise Branson, *Gorbachev: Heretic in the Kremlin* (New York: Viking Penguin, 1990), p. 6.

23. It is crucial to note that the *corruption* of one's faith and the *rejection* of one's faith are two quite different things. Scholarly analysis of the Brezhnev era has too often equated the massive corruption of the party elite with its loss of faith in Marxist-Leninist values. In fact, a corrupt Marxist-Leninist will behave quite differently from a straightforward political opportunist, for the former and not the latter can still feel *shame*. Despite the stagnation of the movement under Brezhnev, the elder members of the Politburo preserved the capacity to feel *ashamed* at the extent of the corruption of Marxist-Leninist revolutionary ideals in the USSR that had taken place under their watch. The selection of Andropov and Gorbachev as general secretaries of the party by the former high priests of Brezhnevism would be inexplicable without taking this into account.

24. "Leninist Romantic" is aptly used to describe Gorbachev in Jowitt, "Gorbachev: Bolshevik or Menshevik?" in Stephen White, Alex Pravda, and Zvi Gitelman, eds., *Developments in Soviet Politics* (Durham: Duke University Press, 1990), pp. 270–92.

25. Jerry Hough, "The Politics of Successful Economic Reform," *Soviet Economy* 5 (January–March 1989), p. 6.

26. Mikhail Gorbachev, *Political Report to the 27th Party Congress of the CPSU*, translated in *FBIS*, February 26, 1986.

27. Ibid., p. 32.

28. Ibid., p. 1. At the same time, Gorbachev implicitly rejected both "left" and "right" responses to the Soviet crisis, arguing instead that charismatic "grandeur" and modern "realism" must be combined in party policy. As he put it, "It is our task to conceptualize broadly, in Lenin's style, the times we are living in, and to work out a realistic, thoroughly weighed program of action that will organically blend the grandeur of our aims with the realism of our capabilities."

29. Ibid., p. 9.

30. V. Urchukin, "Intensivnye metody ispol'zovaniia rabochevo vremeni," *Voprosy Ekonomiki*, March 1988, pp. 95–96.

31. Nikolai Shmelev, "Avansy i dolgi," *Novy Mir*, June 1987.

32. Shmelev himself, after his article was severely criticized within the CPSU, later retracted his views on unemployment, saying he "got carried away" on this question. See the interview with Shmelev in *Sovetskaia Kultura*, October 17, 1987.

33. Tat'iana I. Zaslavskaia, "Economic Behavior and Economic Development" (1981), p. 5; quotations from Zaslavskaia's work are from the English translation of her recent articles provided by Murray Yanowitch, ed., *A Voice for Reform: Essays by Tat'iana I. Zaslavskaia* (Armonk, N.Y.: M. E. Sharpe, 1989).

34. Zaslavskaia, "The Social Mechanism of the Economy" (1985), *Essays*, p. 59.

35. Zaslavskaia, "Economic Behavior and Economic Development," *Essays*, p. 13.

36. Zaslavskaia, "Social Justice and the Human Factor in Economic Development" (1986), *Essays*, p. 86.

37. Zaslavskaia, "Urgent Problems in the Theory of Economic Sociology" (1987), *Essays*, p. 123.

38. Ibid., p. 129.

39. Zaslavskaia, "Creative Activity of the Masses: Social Reserves of Growth" (1986), *Essays*, p. 74.

40. Ibid., p. 75.

41. Indeed, the phrase "human factor" is repeated numerous times in Gorbachev's book, *Perestroika*. The slogan *perestroika* had been used by Gorbachev from the start, but it only started to become prominent in late 1986.

42. Ibid., p. 19.

43. Joseph Stalin, *The Foundations of Leninism*, in *Selected Works* (Tirana: "8 Nentori" Publishing House, 1979), p. 100.

44. Gorbachev, *Perestroika*, p. 50.

45. Ibid., p. 131.

46. Ibid., p. 36.

47. Indeed, Gorbachev in *Perestroika* notes with apparent pride that *perestroika* involves "no ready-made formulas" for a reformed USSR. This ideological inhibition against creating new "formulas" for imposing reform from above also accounts for the oft-noted vagueness and ineffectiveness of the Gorbachev program for Soviet economic revitalization, which merely worked to destroy the old Stalinist planning system without building any concrete alternative. See Marshall I. Goldman, "Gorbachev the Economist," *Foreign Affairs* 69:2 (Spring 1990), pp. 28–44.

48. As Jerry Hough points out, the formal procedure for the selection of the new Congress of People's Deputies, which guaranteed a substantial percentage of seats to members of so-called public organizations—such as the Communist Party itself!—was in principle far less democratic than the old direct elections to the Supreme Soviet had been on paper. Had Gorbachev wanted to introduce true parliamentarianism in 1988, he could have simply allowed for multiple-candidate elections to the existing Supreme Soviet. See Hough, *Russia and the West*, p. 205.

49. Although according to the theoretical framework adopted here, Sakharov's evolutionary model of convergence between capitalism and socialism can be seen as a "right-wing" position, Yeltsin's call for the immediate dismantling of centralism as a "left-wing" position, and Ligachev's neo-orthodoxy as a "center" position, the utility of this terminology by 1989 was beginning to break down. Thus Sakharov and Yeltsin became allies—though still disagreeing on fundamental issues—within the Interregional Group of Deputies in the Supreme Soviet, which began to refer to itself as the "left" and to the Ligachev faction as the "right." Rather than invalidating the analysis given above, such terminological shifts merely illustrate the process of collapse of Marxist-Leninist ideological categories in the late Gorbachev era. Indeed, it could be argued that the formal alliance of Gorbachev's opponents on both the "right" and the "left" as a unified bloc against the old party center marked the end of the distinctive Marxist-Leninist tradition of political discourse extending from Marx to Gorbachev.

50. In arguing that Leninism essentially self-destructed under Gorbachev's leadership, I am *not* claiming that the Communist Party as of 1990 had ceased to be an

important player on the political scene in what for the time being remains the Soviet Union. The reverse will be true as long as the party continues to control the military and the secret police and as long as the opposition lacks any comparable mechanisms for enforcing its political will. In fact, one possible outcome of the current crisis in the USSR would be the restoration of order by a coalition of hard-liners in the party, army, and KGB hierarchies; such a coalition might even claim to rule in the name of "Leninism." But such a regime of militarized quasi-Leninism would resemble the old Leninist system about as much as Louis Napoleon's rule in nineteenth-century France resembled that of the original Napoleon—aping the formal symbolism (perhaps, like Louis Napoleon, even mixing in monarchical symbolism where appropriate) but maintaining none of the substance of Marxism-Leninism, that is, the ethos of charismatic impersonalism. Furthermore, the "internationalist" veneer of the Soviet empire would almost certainly be stripped away under these circumstances, forcing such a leadership to declare itself Russian rather than Soviet.

Of course, such attempts at social science "prediction" in an environment of political and social turmoil are probably best avoided. The crucial point is that by having forced the Leninist elite to confront the fundamental unworkability of its claim to legitimacy by demonstrating the impossibility of *cultural* charismatic impersonalism, Gorbachev "irreversibly" broke the historical chain linking the revolutionary founders Marx and Lenin to the current party leadership. This being the case, it is possible to state unequivocally that no matter what form of rule (or lack of rule) emerges in the coming years, Leninism in the form in which it has existed since 1917 has now reached the end of the line in the territory currently known as the USSR.

3

Eastern Europe and the Soviet Union:

A Technological Time Warp

W. W. ROSTOW

ALTHOUGH, on and off, I have been involved with Eastern Europe and the Soviet Union as an academic and public servant for forty-five years, it took me some time on the ground to develop a clear picture of their problems and possible remedies. In part, of course, this is because seen close up the countries of Eastern Europe differ greatly among themselves. This was true even at the peak of Soviet dominance. And evidently the Soviet Union differs in many important respects from Eastern Europe. These societies face an unprecedented array of political, diplomatic, and economic problems all at once. It is quite enough to give the governments vertigo, let alone peripatetic observers from abroad.

Politically, there is the problem of creating the constitutional base for democratic politics and setting in motion its substance; making or rediscovering viable rules of the political game; reshaping bureaucracies so that they will respond positively to their policies rather than impede or sabotage them; coping with an ample share of the regional problems that have surged in intensity all over the world as the cold war subsides—problems with distinctive roots, but all marked by an acute sense of old grievances demanding urgent redress.

Diplomatically, East European leaders confront inescapable issues of the first order of magnitude: they must make or participate in urgent decisions with respect to the Soviet Union, Western Europe, and the security structure of Europe as a whole, which will cast long shadows in history, while reorienting almost every day-to-day bilateral diplomatic relation in the light of new realities.

Economically, the agenda for the leadership consists of problems unprecedented in scale if not in kind: privatizing the bulk of the means of production now publicly or socially owned, but also substantially obsolete; introducing competitive price setting in private markets geared to those of the world economy; setting rules for the purchase by foreigners of means of production; maintaining a short-run balance between control over inflation and offloading excess labor from inefficient plants, and at the same time coming to terms with socially and politically acceptable levels of unemployment; rebuilding a good deal of the physical infrastructure and beginning the enormous task of rolling back the pollution of the environment, carried to extraordinary lengths by their predecessors. Above all, in almost all the East European countries the new leadership is weighed down by heavy debt commitments incurred by their predecessors, loans generally spent for nonproductive purposes.

It is the widespread sense of these converging problems that accounts for a tone of pessimism in the region, more acute in the USSR than in Eastern Europe, but in both cases not unlike the tone of pessimism in postwar Western Europe before the emergence in June 1947 of the possibility of the Marshall Plan. It was, in fact, the analogy with postwar Western Europe that provided the first clue to a coherent view of the central problem of the region and of the route to its remedy. In both cases—1945–46 in the West, 1989–90 in the East—great things had happened: victory over Hitler and peace in the one case; the return to national independence and political freedom in the other. But in both, blessed release was accompanied by continued deterioration of economic circumstances. Teaching at Oxford in 1946–47, having spent 1942–45 in London, I can attest that postwar rationing was tougher than during the war years. But the economic regression in 1945–47 was general.

So far as development economics is concerned, the key common characteristic of the contemporary Eastern region is not unrelated. One cannot look about in Warsaw or Moscow, Budapest or Zagreb, Krakow or Sarajevo without knowing that this part of the world is caught up in a technological time warp. Conditions vary, of course, and these areas are not physically damaged like postwar continental Europe. But things have the look of West European technology of the early to middle 1950s. As Jean Monnet said of France in 1945, "What is really wrong . . . is that our capital equipment and production methods are out of date."[1] The central development task in Eastern Europe and the USSR is, then, to create circumstances by which the region can rapidly absorb the enormous backlog of highly relevant technology that has accumulated in the past two generations.

I shall consider later the policy implications of that task; but first it is important to explain why the region as a whole tumbled off its growth curve into stagnation or worse.

FALLING OFF THE GROWTH CURVE

The overall growth rate of a reasonably healthy economy is sustained by the successive introduction of major innovations. Fresh innovations are required because the normal path of a given sector incorporating a once-new technology is one of progressive deceleration.[2]

Responding to the widespread view of the late 1950s that the Soviet Union was on its way to overtaking total U.S. production levels, in 1960 I wrote as follows in *The Stages of Economic Growth*: "First, it is necessary to beware of linear projections. A variety of forces at work in Russia, already evident in her projected figures for expansion, are making for deceleration. The E.C.E. [Economic Commission for Europe] Survey in 1957 (published in 1958) presented, for example, the official projected rates of growth in key sectors of Russian industry. . . . "[3] The table giving those projected growth rates is reproduced as Table 3.1 below.

TABLE 3.1

[Projected] Rates of Growth in Soviet Industry (%)

Annual Average Rate of Increase	Coal	Oil	Pig Iron	Steel	Electric Power	Cement
1955–60	8.6	13.6	10.0	8.5	13.5	19.5
1957–72	2.8	9.4	5.3	5.3	9.7	8.6

I went on to say: ". . . the composition of Russian output must certainly change. The present higher Soviet rate of increase in GNP is the product substantially of a peculiar concentration of investment in certain sectors. If steel is not to be used for military purposes, what will it be used for? An enormous heavy industry, growing at high rates, is not a goal in itself; nor is it an intrinsic international advantage."

I then suggested that to sustain its growth rate the USSR would have to introduce strongly the sectors associated with high mass consumption: those linked with the automobiles, durable consumers goods, and the life of suburbia. These include strip steel, machine tools, oil refining, rubber production, synthetic fibers, and plastics.

As we now know, Soviet growth rates in the classic heavy industry sectors did decelerate, as foreshadowed by Moscow's central planners of the 1950s; but the leading sectors of high mass consumption never took hold sufficiently to counter the drag of the decelerating older sectors. The overall rate of industrial growth, therefore, progressively declined (Table 3.2).[4]

TABLE 3.2

Average Annual Growth
of Soviet Industrial Output
1961–85 (%)

1961–65	6.5
1966–70	6.4
1971–75	5.5
1976–80	2.7
1981–85	1.9

Meanwhile, other forces helped bring the Soviet Union to the Brezhnev stagnation of the 1980s: the need to allocate increased investment resources to a perverse, inherently low productivity agricultural system; the need to rely increasingly on distant and expensive sources of raw materials and energy; and the continued allocation of the society's best scientific, engineering, and entrepreneurial talent to military production, including space.[5] These depressing forces were compounded by extraordinary neglect of the physical environment and demographic trends. The latter yielded an absolute decline in the able-bodied population of European Russia, where most of Soviet industry is located. This circumstance rendered further Soviet growth increasingly dependent on accelerated improvement in productivity rather than on population increase or the transfer of the work force from rural to urban areas. In fact, the rate of productivity increase declined.

This grinding to a virtual halt of a massive economy—investing more than 30 percent of GNP to achieve an increase in output that barely matched its decelerating rate of population increase—was climaxed by the palpable inability of Soviet society, endowed with ample cadres of well-trained scientists and engineers, to absorb and diffuse efficiently the array of new technologies that moved from invention to innovation during the mid-1970s: microelectronics, genetic engineering, lasers, and a batch of new industrial materials. The Soviet system, with its bureaucratic compulsion to meet quantitative targets irrespective of quality, set up powerful perverse incentives that discouraged innovation except in the one field where Russia inescapably confronted international competition—the military. I have the impression from discussions with Soviet officials in the Gorbachev period that the image of a Soviet Union falling rapidly behind the United States, Japan, and Western Europe in the new technologies may have significantly helped to crystallize a consensus in an important part of the elite that a radical restructuring of Soviet society was imperative.

At some risk of caricature, the Soviet system emerges, in terms of stages of growth, as one that could manage and even expand output using incrementally improved pre-1917 heavy industry technologies: steel, electric power, cement, general purpose machine tools, basic chemicals. But it was a system that could not bring itself to make the political, social, and economic transition to the attitudes and technologies of the age of high mass consumption, or to make the profound institutional and policy changes required to absorb efficiently the post-1975 technologies. With respect to the latter, the Soviet system simply could not cope with the extraordinary rate of obsolescence of these technologies, stemming from their close linkage to areas of science that were themselves moving at a revolutionary pace and from their highly diversified character far beyond what central planners can handle. Thus a system at technological maturity after 1945 found it impossible either to move into high mass consumption or to maintain itself at the always outward-moving technological frontier after 1975. Therefore, it tumbled off its growth curve and ceased to be technologically mature. Ironically, we have witnessed an extreme version of a Marxist clash between technological change and an out-moded economic, social, and political superstructure. And one cannot walk the streets of Moscow or look out over the farmland without echoing Mon-net's terse diagnosis of 1945 France: "What is really wrong . . . is that our capital equipment and production methods are out of date."

In different degrees the countries of Eastern Europe shared this descent to societal as well as economic bankruptcy, their dissidence heightened by two ultimately irrepressible forces: nationalism and a desire for the dignity of human freedom. But their present difficulties are not as starkly bleak as those of the USSR, for certain identifiable reasons. First, they have not lived with communism as long as the Soviet peoples. The problem of changing at-titudes is real, but not quite as difficult. Moreover, there have been reforms that loosened the bonds of central management in agriculture and the ser-vices. Difficulties with former communists clinging to power and privilege exist in certain East European countries, but they are not as formidable as in the Soviet Union, where Gorbachev often seems like a nineteenth-century reforming tsar trying to move forward against the undertow of a still active if corrosive feudal nobility. Except in Yugoslavia, the forces of fragmentation in Eastern Europe are less powerful. And there is an intangible asset: in Eastern Europe, most of those now in power took real risks to help bring about liberation; and this is a source of national pride in a region where the people themselves could rarely shape their own destiny. There is an aura of defeat in the USSR, as well as shame and cynicism at having been cowed or taken in by the communists for so long.

With all these (and other) differences taken into account, both Eastern Europe and the Soviet Union face the same basic problem: how can these so-cieties be transformed to move out of their stagnant technological backwater to the fast-paced technological frontier now available? Another broad conclu-sion flows from this perspective. If the Soviet society can succeed in trans-forming itself into a system with strong incentives for regular innovation, an enormous backlog of technology awaits. Like Japan from, say, the mid-1950s, Russia may one day enjoy an extraordinary phase of economic growth as it moves from its present laggard position to the technological frontier now occupied by Western Europe, Japan, and the United States. The same can be said of Eastern Europe, which may well demonstrate this potentiality sooner than the USSR, because it is likely to be easier there to break defini-tively the grip of single-party rule and central bureaucratic control over economies.

WHAT IS TECHNOLOGICAL ABSORPTIVE CAPACITY?

The possibility of a great boom in the region evidently depends, then, on a large increase in what development economists sometimes call technological absorptive capacity. That concept sounds neat, antiseptic, even measurable.

In fact, it consists of three large elements that go to the heart of a society, its organization, and its morale.

1. *An adequate pool of scientists, engineers, managers, and workers of appropriate training and skills.* By and large, the countries of Eastern Europe and the Soviet Union contain such pools of educated personnel, although a good deal of updating will be required. To give this notion some rough quantitative substance, it is worth noting that since 1960 the proportion of those students in higher education who are between the ages of twenty and twenty-four in Eastern Europe may have doubled, to a present level of about 15 percent. This is something like the West European level in 1960 and about half the current level. With purposeful public policy and some help from abroad, the East European proportion could be lifted to the current Western level in a decade or so.

2. *Institutions built around incentives for technological innovation as well as a physical infrastructure capable of supporting a technologically up-to-date economic system.* Here there are multiple critical problems inhibiting rapid absorption of new technologies in the region. The institutions inherited from communism are geared to centrally imposed quantitative targets. They therefore actively discourage quality control and technological innovation, and thereby reduce output in the short term. They even inhibit adequate production of spare parts, since output is measured by complete units. Moreover, major innovation generally requires not merely change in one plant—or even in one industry. Coordinated changes are difficult to come by in a system where different ministries administer the major sectors.

In addition, physical infrastructure—except in the military—is grossly inadequate in telecommunications, computers, transport facilities, and so forth.

3. *Finally, a critical factor impossible to measure: the national will to catch up.* In the case of France after 1945, there was not only a widespread will to make up for the humiliation of defeat and occupation but an extraordinary generational coalition. Leadership in modernization was assumed by a small group of men who knew the world before 1914 (e.g., Monnet and Schuman) and carried in their memories an image of what Europe could be. They associated themselves with intelligent young men who had fought in the war from British bases or in the underground and were determined to look forward and build a France and Europe of which they could be proud. There were equivalent coalitions throughout Western Europe led, for example, in Italy by De Gasperi, in Germany by Adenauer.

This is so fundamental a point it is worth elaboration. Perhaps the situation most similar to Eastern Europe's is that of Spain before its remarkable recovery after 1958. In the 1930s Spain was hit severely by the world depression and then by a brutal civil war, which was followed politically by a one-party dictatorship and economically by a system of autarkic corporate fascism that cut Spain off from Western Europe more effectively than the Pyrenees ever did. For more than twenty years Spain was trapped in a time warp.

In the course of the 1950s, as West European dynamism asserted itself, Franco began to rejoin Spain to the West. Leadership in technological modernization and economic growth was taken by a small group led by Lopez Rodo. Their objective was ultimately political. They aimed to prove that, contrary to Franco's endless assertions, Spain could manage a stable democracy. To ensure that outcome they sought a high rate of growth that would put Spain foreseeably in the European Common Market, where membership would, as it were, lock Spain into democracy. Their indicative planning, combined with widespread educational and clandestine political activities, helped to yield the sustained 7 percent average growth rate that brought Spain into a position to join the Common Market.

In Asia, the single-minded drive of Japan for a maximum economic and technological role in the world is clearly linked to a determination to make up for military defeat. The even more remarkable performances in Taiwan and South Korea are clearly, in the minds of the leadership and many of the people, also routes to places of security, consequence, and dignity in a threatening world.

This should not surprise Americans. It was, after all, Alexander Hamilton who wrote in 1791: "Not only the wealth but the independence and security of a country appear to be materially connected with the prosperity of manufactures." And Thomas Jefferson, Hamilton's initial ideological opponent, came—out of the vulnerability of an agricultural former colony—to agree.

I shall consider below what the ideological basis for a drive to catch up might be in Eastern Europe and the Soviet Union; but first I will discuss the elements of policy and action required to overcome the sense of stagnation— or worse—that pervades the region and to set Eastern Europe and the Soviet Union on the fast track to the technological frontier.

WHAT IS TO BE DONE

In the light of the analysis presented thus far, I propose the following eight-point program for the Eastern region in collaboration with Western Europe, Japan, and the United States. As will become apparent, the internal and external elements in the program are closely interrelated. The vital interests of Western Europe, Japan, and the United States which justify such assistance are set out at the end of the chapter.

Point 1: *A double jump start.* As this program as a whole makes clear, the gathering of momentum in Eastern Europe and the Soviet Union—like any other development task—can be accomplished only by the men and women who live there, deploying intelligently their own resources. But external assistance can be a critical margin—a catalyst—as it was in post-1945 Western Europe, Japan, and a good many other countries where, as it were, the batteries were low but not dead and could respond to a jump start.

In the summer of 1990 there was a certain technical legitimacy to the wry question put by a young Soviet reporter to a group of American scholars at a press conference in Moscow: "All right, you've won the cold war. Where's our Marshall Plan?"

In fact, of course, there's a great deal more to be corrected in the Eastern region than a dollar shortage, although additional foreign exchange is part of this package. The first requirement is the efficient introduction of, say, fifty large Western and Japanese firms into the Soviet Union, and twenty-five into Eastern Europe. (Incidentally, Canada, South Korea, Taiwan, and others might join in the barn raising.) These firms would be guaranteed by their governments perhaps via World Bank and IFC procedures; but the real guarantee would be the scale of the collective effort. This is an occasion where, quite literally, there is safety in numbers.

The Eastern countries could choose the sectors in which the plants would operate. Food processing, modern machine tools, computers, telecommunication equipment, energy-efficient motor vehicles, and firms with foreign exchange earning potential might well be candidates. They might be joint ventures, if appropriate partners exist; but total foreign ownership would be permitted. On the other hand, a certain amount of ownership shares would be made available for local purchase, by mutual agreement, with the passage of time.

This proposal is designed to serve multiple purposes: to supply quickly state-of-the-art technology; to demonstrate the collective support of the advanced industrial world; to serve as training schools for local managers and the work force; and, above all, to force the pace of adoption of other essential structural measures, some of which are set out below.

But there is a second essential jump-start element especially for Eastern Europe: a radical reduction in the debt burden that the present political leadership inherited in all the countries except Czechoslovakia and Romania. These debts have risen to levels several times the annual level of exports in convertible currencies. Neither lenders nor borrowers expect the debts to be fully repaid; both now settle for interest payments, but these are so high that the East Europeans are forced to increase their total debt to meet the interest payments. It is not a viable situation to have to borrow further to pay interest.

Conventional official borrowing by the Soviet Union and the countries of Eastern Europe might be focused on infrastructure investment where very large programs will be required (see point 6, below).

Point 2: *Conversion of an important part of the Soviet military complex to civil production.* Soviet society proved it could produce competitive manufactured goods in the one area where intense international competition could not be entirely avoided: military (including space). I cannot assess the relative real cost and efficiency of this Soviet performance or the level of quality control. We do know that something like 25 percent of Soviet GNP has been devoted to the task, including an extraordinary proportion of the ablest scientists, engineers, managers, and workers. And we also know from the testimony of Soviet leaders of the Gorbachev era that the effort grossly distorted the Soviet economy as a whole.

Nevertheless, it is evident from the gap in quality between Soviet military and civil production that the military-industrial complex is a substantial potential asset in moving the society to the contemporary technological frontier. There is reason to believe that this is fully appreciated by the Soviet leadership; but there has been a good deal of difficulty in generating an important civil contribution from the military-industrial complex. Such a contribution should be easier to induce as part of the massive concerted effort envisaged here to jump start the Soviet economy.

Point 3: *Price and fiscal reform.* It is evident that the long-discussed, long-delayed introduction of a competitive price system, along with drastic reduction in the monetary overhang, will have to be faced if the foreign plants being introduced (and rehabilitated Soviet plants) are to operate rationally. The experience of Poland and Yugoslavia—as well as a great deal of development experience—is that what might be called the "IMF formula" works only if strong forces are simultaneously generated on the supply side, as was true of the post-1945 German and Japanese currency reforms. Without such supply stimulus the outcome is likely to be a hard currency trap, with low growth and heavy unemployment, broken finally by political and social unrest leading to another bout of inflation.

Point 4: *Western food and consumer goods loans.* Western Europe and Japan can, however, play an important ancillary role in price and fiscal reform, aside from the double jump start set out above. The removal of subsidies from essential foods and other basic consumer goods will and should raise their prices, which now bear no relation to costs of production in much of the Eastern region. But in some cases this kind of necessary adjustment has been accompanied by hoarding and panic buying, which pushed prices much higher than justified merely by the removal of subsidies. Outside assistance in the form of well-publicized loans (or grants) of food and basic consumer goods might avoid such panic and ease the necessary transition to market prices.

Point 5: *Fundamental agricultural reform.* Marginal external food assistance in the context of price reform would be an illusory contribution to the revival of the Soviet economy unless accompanied by long-term agricultural reform. This is not the occasion to analyze and prescribe for all the ills that have created the extraordinary—almost unbelievable—perverse and pathological state of Soviet agriculture. But two policy steps appear fundamental: provision for unambiguous, definitive landownership by farmers; and, against a background of ownership and price incentives (point 3, above), prompt provision of transport and storage infrastructure radically to reduce the substantial wastage of Soviet harvests.

Point 6: *Infrastructure and unemployment.* For the fifty new foreign firms to operate efficiently in the USSR will require not only a stable currency and a competitive price system but also an efficient infrastructure, notably an updated telecommunications system. One is sometimes told in the USSR that the military have a separate and quite efficient telecommunications system. Given the role of nuclear weapons, missiles, and space in the Soviet military establishment, as well as the enormous geographical spread of Soviet forces, including submarines, this is likely to be so. In that case, the extension of existing technologies to the civil economy may be the heart of a solution. In any case, heavy investments in telecommunications will be required.

But the most casual observation of life in the Soviet Union underlines the enormous backlog of the most mundane forms of infrastructure that must be made good, such as roads, bridges, housing, water supply, and sewerage. All of this is quite aside from the investment required to bring under control and roll back the physical deterioration wrought by gross neglect of the environment.

Like many crises, as the Chinese characters for the word dramatize, the Soviet and East European infrastructure crisis is an opportunity as well as a danger. The shakeout of the Soviet economy as it moves to a competitive price system will require initially a radical reduction in overmanned, inefficient industrial and government employment. As the economy subsequently expands rapidly, these workers will be productively employed. In the meanwhile it would be wholly irrational for them to be paid a subsistence income on the unemployment rolls. The Soviet Union and the countries of Eastern Europe should mount large-scale public works programs to make good the infrastructure backlog. The workers might be paid slightly more than those on unemployment insurance. As in some New Deal programs in the United States, Soviet military officers (or ex-officers) might be used to organize this effort. The Soviet Union might even consider drawing on another American example, by engaging some engineering units on active duty in sophisticated infrastructure projects.

Point 7: *Exports.* The international stability of the hard competitive currencies yielded by the financial and fiscal reforms discussed under point 3 will depend on the generation by the countries of the Eastern region of a greatly increased flow of exports. Private and official capital imports as well as a rise in tourism can help in the short run, as can the international debt reduction commended in point 1. Moreover, a reasonably efficient agriculture could shift the region from a scandalously heavy net import position in agricultural products to a net export position—a status already achieved by Hungary. But in the end, their stage of growth and potential technological absorptive capacity suggest that the Soviet Union and most of the countries of Eastern Europe should be competitive net exporters of manufactured goods before long. The relatively low labor costs of the region should help achieve this result as should the whole complex of measures outlined here to elevate the region's technological level. But the European community could help, as Margaret Thatcher suggested it should, by granting preferential status to East European exports, dramatizing a mutual intent that these countries one day join the Common Market and the other European institutions.

In the short run, such assistance to the countries of Eastern Europe is further justified by their sudden loss of the USSR as both a source of soft-currency oil and gas and as a rather uncritical market for inferior manufactured goods.

Point 8: *Institutional Change.* As Eastern Europe and the Soviet Union move toward a competitive price system and the quality control disciplines of competing in hard-currency world markets, the policy changes outlined in points 1–7 will evidently have to be accompanied by institutional changes and, in some cases, changes of attitude reaching deep into their societies.

The criteria for good management under regimes of central planning are so perverse that a good deal of training and retraining for management in competitive markets will be required. (One of the most effective instruments of the Spanish economic reformers was to set up in Barcelona the Instituto de Estudios Superiores de la Empresa [IESE], a high level business school.) Given the critical role of the efficient absorption of new technologies, it would be wise for the countries of the region to build on their strong engineering traditions and focus their curricula more sharply on manufacturing and innovation than is typically the case in American business schools. The business schools of the East will also have to devote a good deal of attention to workers' morale and productivity.

Evidently workers will have to make the transition from "They pretend to pay us, we pretend to work" to "Pay by productivity." In addition, efforts to recapture pride in workmanship and a sense of identification of hard work with large public purposes will be required. The experience of East Germany as it joins the West may permit some assessment of the seriousness of this problem. I am inclined to believe that if workers are paid fairly according to performance and can buy goods of high quality with their income and save with reasonable confidence in the stability of the currency, much of this problem will dissipate. But that remains to be seen.

In the reaction against centralized planning and government ownership of the means of production, rather simplistic views of modern capitalism have been current in Eastern Europe and the Soviet Union. A proper emphasis on the critical importance of private property and competitive markets has led to a neglect of the role of government in modern capitalist countries. Among the major OECD countries, for example, government expenditures as a percentage of GDP ranged from Japan at 27 percent to Sweden at 58 percent. The American figure, 35 percent, is near the bottom of the list despite relatively high military expenditures. Outlays for social security by employees and employers in the United States amount to more than 8 percent of GDP, close to the OECD average. Governments finance the bulk of expenditures on education, and in many cases also on health; a high proportion of R&D; and virtually all infrastructure investment. Clearly, such social functions will continue to be managed by governments in Eastern Europe and the USSR.

A PHASE OF INDICATIVE PLANNING?

For a Western economist, one of the most heartening contemporary sights is the extremely large, empty building along the Danube in Budapest that used to be the Central Planning Ministry. On the other hand, the inescapable role of Eastern governments in making the transition to modern competitive free enterprise economies makes it, in my view, unwise for them to abandon all planning. Indeed, the importance of assistance from abroad, and the likelihood of a persistent foreign exchange shortage during the transition, will make some planning inevitable. The rationing of scarce foreign exchange has been a much more powerful force than ideology in generating planning in noncommunist countries. The model here should be Jean Monnet's: he chose for his Planning Commissariat a modest town house on the East Bank of the Seine; and he never permitted a senior staff of more than thirty officials. In fact, Monnet made all the critical decisions himself with a closely knit team of five or six. As he was well aware, an institution of that size can never aspire to run the economy in detail. Indeed, it was forced to work closely with the relevant ministries, the private sector, and the trade unions. And that was the point. Monnet's dictum belongs on the wall of every planning unit in a democracy: "Since the implementation of the Plan will require everyone's collaboration, all the vital elements in the nation must help to draw it up."

If such planning emerges in the Eastern region, it should be a transient phenomenon. It should fade as foreign exchange constraints are overcome and the economies absorb increasingly sophisticated technologies yielding highly diversified products. Such economies are likely to maintain extremely important economic functions for government but are unlikely to persist even with selective indicative planning.

INTERESTS: EAST AND WEST

This final section bluntly addresses three questions. Why should Western Europe, Japan, and the United States care about the economic fate of Eastern Europe and the Soviet Union? Aside from their own economic and social welfare, what larger objectives should underpin and inspire the rather heroic efforts of transition required of the Eastern peoples to convert their societies into their own versions of democratic market economies? Are the interests of Western Europe and Japan consonant with the larger hopes and ambitions of the Eastern peoples?

Separating Eastern Europe and the Soviet Union for a moment, why should Eastern Europe not go on being the contentious, fragmented relative backwater it has been since the Industrial Revolution or, at least, since 1914—moving forward in modernization for a time, then set back by tragic events beyond the region's control, always lagging the West?

A first answer might be that World War I was triggered by an assassination on a short, narrow street in Sarajevo; World War II was triggered nominally over the fate of Danzig; and the cold war became irreversible for more than forty years when Stalin judged correctly that he could safely violate his Yalta commitment to support free elections in Poland.

At the moment, there is no reason to expect another great war—hot or cold. And there is clearly hope that the next century will not see repeated the fratricidal European tragedies of the century now ending. Nevertheless, there is the possibility of all manner of dangerous and unpleasant trouble in the region if the hopes of democratic leaders in Eastern Europe are not fulfilled. It would not be wholly irrational for the West to act on the proposition: "Never again." Thus a strong Eastern Europe, incorporated in the European Community, is key to a stable European balance of power.

But the fear of trouble is not the ultimate rationale. The ultimate rationale is the real possibility that a dream can, in fact, be brought to life. That dream is of a great federalized continent, each state within it cherishing proud, unique memories and traditions, but united by a marvelously complex common culture, common religions, and a common scientific heritage created by men and women from every quarter of the continent.

A West prepared to commit itself to that dream, to reach out now—at this critical juncture—to the peoples of the East as children of a common culture and partners in a great adventure, not only would set a pattern of creative federalism for other regions of the world to follow but would constitute a powerful force for global peace in the next century.

As for Japan, the stability of Europe and an enlarged market for its products are less intimate but still extremely important stakes. But is this what the East Europeans want? Is the vision of authentic dignified partnership in a Great Europe as compelling as it is in the West? On the face of it, the old parochial quarrels going back to the Ottoman and Austro-Hungarian empires—complicated by arbitrary boundary settlements after the First and Second World Wars—have revived, with potentially dangerous consequences. For what it is worth, I am convinced that only the reality of the coming to pass of a Great East–West Europe can push these old quarrels into the past and keep them in proportion.

As for the Soviet Union, fragmentation and violence in a great country replete with nuclear weapons represent an authentic global danger. With a potential pull toward Europe in the west, toward the Moslem world in the south, and a residual Chinese sense that a Soviet Eastern Siberia is a product of tsarist imperialism, the Soviet Union could become a lethal bear pit. But a Soviet Union—its tsarist imperial inheritance transformed into a new, authentically federal structure—finding and sustaining its position at the technological frontier, might be a critical key to a stable global balance of power. The question is: Would such a Soviet Union be content to seek its security in cooperation with other powers focused not on hegemony but on the maintenance of a secure global balance of power and the rule of law? No one can answer that question with absolute confidence. The hopeful evidence is two-fold: first, the Soviet Union found its extremely costly cold war pursuit of hegemony frustrated by the nationalism of others; second, the foreseeable rise of new massive nation-states to technological maturity (notably India and China) and the emergence of a whole range of substantial nation-states to that status (e.g., Indonesia, Brazil, Mexico) show the urgency of collective efforts to sustain the global balance of power. It is almost as if Saddam Hussein, with his poison gas and nuclear yearnings, had been sent among us to make this point.

I conclude, therefore, that if Western Europe, Japan, and the United States stay together in alliance (putting aside chimerical mercantilist temptations), a vital Soviet Union—recapturing its unity on a more civilized basis as well as economic momentum—is much more likely to join the club of advanced industrial powers seeking to bring to life the United Nations Charter than to make a second try for hegemony.

These are the more fundamental considerations which underlie this eight-point jump-start program.

NOTES

1. Jean Monnet, *Memoirs,* trans. Richard Mayne (Garden City: Doubleday, 1978), p. 107.

2. Historically, the classic sequence of such leading sectors was: cotton textiles; railroads and iron; steel, chemicals, and electricity; and the automobile industry. The normal path of such sectors is one of progressive deceleration, as the initial technological breakthrough is exploited, followed by lesser refinements, while other dampening forces operate on both supply and demand. In Britain, for example, a graph of historical production in these leading sectors shows just such a pattern, with rapid increases, followed by slowing growth, and, eventually, gradual decline. If a new leading sector with new technologies is not developed, the decline of previously leading sectors risks turning into a general economic decline. W. W. Rostow, *The World Economy: History and Prospect* (Austin: University of Texas Press, 1978), pp. 105–7.

3. W. W. Rostow, *The Stages of Economic Growth: A Non-Communist Manifesto* (Cambridge: Cambridge University Press, 1960), pp. 102–3.

4. Laurie Kurtzweg, "Trends in Soviet Gross National Product," in *Gorbachev's Economic Plans*, Volume 1: *Studies Submitted to the Joint Economic Committee of the Congress of the United States* (Washington, D.C.: U.S. Government Printing Office, 1987), p. 140. Recent analyses suggest these growth rates may be even higher than the reality, but they capture adequately the extraordinary deceleration of the past two decades.

5. For a discussion of the process of deceleration in the 1970s, see Rostow, *The World Economy*, pp. 436–37.

4

The Leninist Extinction

KEN JOWITT

MASS EXTINCTION

THE SECOND WORLD WAR was the twentieth century's Big Bang. Its end marked the defeat of the gravest threat in two hundred years to liberal Protestant capitalist democracy, and, more fundamentally, to modernity as a way of life based on the individual, impersonalism, association, and tolerance. Nazism was a unique assertion within Western Europe of an antimodern way of life based on a corporate ("racial") group, hierarchy of SS "heroes,"[1] their genocidal intolerance, and the Führer's charismatic leadership of a movement employing and subordinating traditional (German) nationalism and modern (German) science.

The outcomes of the Second World War have defined our political universe, as well as its features, issues, and boundaries. The most immediate outcome was the elimination of nazism and fascism in their German and Italian forms; the second was the appearance of nuclear weapons. The third was the social mobilization of African Americans and American women, along with the development of the American West (California). Decolonization and its replacement by the so-called Third World was yet another major outcome of the war.

The emergence of the United States of America as the most powerful and prestigious reviver and guarantor of world liberal capitalist democracy was the most momentous outcome. But the emergence of the Soviet Union as a European continental power (soon to be allied with a Leninist regime in China) and, in short order, a nuclear, thermonuclear, and global power, must rank a close second.

The "promise" identified by many in the October Revolution of 1917, the view of the Soviet Union as a socialist hierophany, the nucleus of a superior successor to the world capitalist order—and a view tarnished for many by the purges, Nazi-Soviet Pact, and initial Nazi victories—was reclaimed in 1945. A heroic Soviet Union emerged, soon to be multiplied by a set of geographically contiguous replica regimes, from Czechoslovakia to Vietnam. Physically devastated by war, still a largely peasant and "backward" country, the powerful Soviet Union was filled with self-confidence in its institutional performance and promise. This promise was shared by some in the West, who, like Le Carré's fictional Bill Haydon, saw in the Soviet Union a crude but Rousseauian reality superior to the vulgarity of American material euphoria and nuclear power.[2]

With Stalin's death in 1953, the Soviet Union began to change substantially, if not essentially.[3] Coercion replaced terror. The party once again ruled over the secret police, not the other way around. Khrushchev lowered the Soviet foreign policy drawbridge (or raised the "iron curtain") by recognizing the existence of an unaligned ex-colonial world and diplomatically engaging the West.[4] He also drained the moat of terror between Soviet society and the party by repudiating the Stalinist notion "enemy of the people" and Lenin's internal class war tenet.[5]

In fact, Khrushchev's repudiation of class war in his 1956 de-Stalinization speech was an ideologically mortal blow to the integrity and vitality of Leninism as a Soviet and international phenomenon. With this action, Khrushchev removed the ideological and political rationale for juxtaposing the party as the locus of a superior, more "real" way of life against an "unreconstructed, culturally contaminating" Soviet society. With his ideas of the "state of the whole people" and the "party of the whole people," Khrushchev diluted the ideological and political tension between the party and its host, Soviet society. He weakened the party's conviction that it had a still unfulfilled mission requiring internal discipline. Khrushchev's revisions left a party increasingly unable to distinguish between the party City of God and the Soviet City of Man: between the cadres' particular interests and the party's general interest.

Stalin was a perverse giant, a malevolently mysterious Leninist Wizard of Oz. Under his rule, the party, the Soviet Union, and his personage were objects of fearful adoration and awe. Khrushchev demystified the party, the Soviet Union, and Leninism. Who could imagine Stalin thumping his shoe at the United Nations or wanting to visit Disneyland? This is not the place to analyze Khrushchev's decision to de-Stalinize, but to emphasize Khrushchev's belief that the Soviet regime should do more to engage and less to estrange the Soviet population, to be more Aquinian and less Augustinian. However, his party companions supported only those revisions that enhanced their collective and personal security, perquisites, and status. The party elite favored Khrushchev's party Magna Carta—that is, strictures against a sultanlike Stalin, and his possible use of a patrimonial secret police against the leadership itself. The party elite also supported Khrushchev's repudiation of the ideological underpinnings of Stalinism, such as the terms "enemy of the people," "dictatorship of the proletariat," and "class war." But it was predictably unwilling to lose its monopoly of political power, economic perquisites, and elite status. Khrushchev's notion of "state and party of the whole people" implicitly undermined the categorical and exclusive position of the party's relation to society, while his attempt to create a plebiscitary relationship with the party "laity," its mass membership, directly threatened the politically superior role of the party bishops (i.e., the members of the central and regional party and ministerial apparatus). Khrushchev's political revisions of Stalinism threatened both the corporate status of the party leadership *and* his own ability to withstand a threat to his power.

With Brezhnev came an end to the Leninist "promise," an end to the confidence that a compelling, viable, superior way of life would appear in the Soviet Union. What emerged instead was a Leninist polity with a parasitic party, booty economy, and scavenger society. Plekhanov's sarcastic comments about Lenin's Inca-like socialism found morbid resonance in the persons of Brezhnev, Andropov, and Chernenko. In the 1980s, the Soviet leadership closely resembled the mummified Incan rulers of Cuzco.[6] During the thirty years between Stalin's death and Brezhnev's, a civil society had indeed been created, *within* a Soviet Communist Party bearing exactly the features Marx had identified—unrestrained ego, selfishness, and greed.[7]

As for the Soviet economy, the term itself was misleading. Soviet economic organization and culture resembled a traditional *oikos* as much, perhaps more, than a modern economy.[8] But of even greater importance was the relation that developed during the Brezhnev era between the party and Soviet society. More a protection racket than a social contract, Soviet (and Polish, Romanian, Chinese, Hungarian, Cuban) subjects were forced to act as supplicants and scavengers or be treated by the regime as psychotics.

The Soviet Union's international position and condition resembled the Soviet domestic situation. True, in the 1970s one could regularly hear Brzezinski, Kissinger, Reagan, and others talking about the Soviet Union as the most aggressive, successfully expansive empire in history. Yet as one of the only two global thermonuclear powers in world history, Soviet imperial expansion in the post-Stalin era was limited to Cuba, Laos, Kampuchea, Ethiopia, Angola, Mozambique, Benin, Congo-Brazzaville, part of Yemen, and Afghanistan; all of which it would very likely have traded for the half of Austria it gave up in the mid-1950s. To a Soviet leader looking at Soviet "internationalism" in the early 1980s, it must have come as a depressing shock to realize that the expansion begun in the early 1920s with "third world" Outer Mongolia was repeating itself—less successfully—in "third world" Afghanistan. As I pointed out over ten years ago, the Soviet Union was converging domestically and internationally but with the wrong world—the "third," not the "first."

What explains the failed promise of Leninism? There are four "big" reasons and three "little" ones.

The first "big" reason was Khrushchev's ideological disarming of Lenin's "party of a new type"—a combat party, as Selznick correctly noted,[9] whose organizational integrity rests on its regular ability to prevent the ritualization of its combat ethos and the transformation of deployable party agents into nondeployable party principals. Khrushchev's ideological reconciliation with Soviet society, his definition of it as "benign" (as opposed to politically equal) decisively undercut the party's ability to identify and act on a social combat task.

The second was the Brezhnev leadership's adamant refusal to substantiate formal ideological reconciliation with the political integration of Soviet society. The Brezhnev regime rejected a political framework in which the Soviet subject could become a Soviet citizen—a framework in which the party cadre would no longer be the sole political actor nor the party the polity. The result: a situation in which a "lazy party monopoly"[10] ruled an increasingly articulate and alienated Soviet society. The Brezhnev pattern was paralleled by a comparable but singular development in Gierek's Poland, where Solidarity heralded the "end of Leninism."

Solidarity is the most powerful and consequential liberal democratic revolution since the French Revolution. A striking illustration of the ironical—not dialectical—nature of historical development, Solidarity was a liberal democratic revolution[11] carried out by a working—not middle—class: a working class created by an antiliberal Leninist party and nurtured by an antiliberal Roman Catholic Church.

If part of a Leninist party's uniqueness rests in its political conflation of the state and public realms, in its effort to have the cadre fuse the roles of state official and citizen, then Solidarity's challenge is immediately apparent. Solidarity was more than a threat to party power. It offered an opposing definition of political leadership and membership. It confronted the party cadre with the national citizen. As a politically "self-limiting"[12] movement, Solidarity was an organized public whose membership consisted of voluntarily associated individual citizens opposed to a hierarchical corporate party polity. Solidarity and the party were mutually exclusive ways of life.

If to Solidarity's political "constitution" one adds the persistent inability, after 1980, of the Polish United Workers Party to find a variant of inclusion[13] capable of restoring party discipline and confidence and undermining Solidarity's national citizen appeal, then one can see why Polish developments in the 1980s were both traumatic and prophetic for some Soviet leaders. Part of the Soviet elite drew a profound conclusion from the inability of the Polish party—and military—to successfully fragment and co-opt Solidarity: inclusion of social forces was no longer an adequate strategy to maintain the party's monopoly. The ongoing Polish drama in the 1980s heightened and crystallized the impatience and frustration at what some Soviet leaders must have come to consider a curse—namely, their regime's apparent inability to develop a political format that could sustain social support, economic growth, and the party's political integrity. They concluded that the party's political leadership and organizational rectitude required them to risk "losing its life to save it." In good measure, Solidarity is responsible for Gorbachev and *perestroika*.

In essence, *perestroika* has been an effort to relativize the position of the apparatchiki within the Soviet Communist Party, the party within Soviet society, and the Soviet Union in the world. Previous Soviet leaders had adaptively reconfigured the party's features to new internal and external task environments,[14] but each preserved the party-regime's absolutist constitution. Stalin absolutized the party in the person of its leader, himself; Brezhnev absolutized the party cadres; Khrushchev attempted to absolutize the party as a mass organization. Gorbachev's novelty and tragedy as a Leninist

lies in his effort to relativize the absolutist quality of the party-regime by upgrading the Soviets and relativizing the party committees, by upgrading the
presidency and relativizing the office of general secretary, by upgrading the
Supreme Soviet and relativizing the Central Committee, and by upgrading
the individual party members and relativizing the power and status of the
apparat. But a politically relativized Bolshevism is Menshevism.[15]

Organizations can be compared in terms of their "strength." Deutsch has
argued that greater strength is to be found in "the social group . . ., which
can undergo the widest range of changes without losing its cohesion in a few
essentials, so as to be able to include other patterns and structures within itself without losing its identity or its continued capacity for growth."[16] A
Leninist party regime's strength depends on its ability to adapt without sac-
rificing its combat competence *or* its status as a self-contained (absolute) polity. Brezhnev's ritualization of the party's role in society weakened the
party's "strength"; Gorbachev's relativization of the party as *the* Soviet polis
has destroyed it.

The "four big reasons," then, for the end of Leninism are Khrushchev's
disavowal of class war, Brezhnev's neotraditionalization of the Soviet polity,
the appearance of a revolutionary national citizen class (Solidarity) in Poland,
and Gorbachev's relativization of Lenin's absolute party.

What are the "three little reasons"?

I have in mind, first, the Soviet Union's reconciliation with China. If the
twenty-year conflict with China helped sustain the inertial political quality of
the Brezhnev regime, the end of that conflict allowed some members of the
Soviet leadership to focus more intently on their own regime's internal de-
bilitation.

The Strategic Defense Initiative (SDI) should be included among the
"little reasons." Its fantastic quality, and the enormity of its policy implications for the Soviet order, undoubtedly interrupted the inertial quality of Soviet politics. So did the increasingly undeniable reality of scientific, technological, and industrial developments in the West, and among the newly
industrialized countries (NICS)—dramatic reminders that, after seventy
years of murderous effort, the Soviet Union had created a German industry
of the 1880s in the 1980s. (See Chirot, this volume, chapter 1.)

This combination of "four big" and "three little" developments created a
particular and peculiar environment for the Soviets and other Leninist regimes. Some leaders and regimes approached the situation with caution; all
viewed it with apprehension; a few saw it in terms of promise; many viewed
it with urgency; and, in the summer of 1989, one leader, Gorbachev, viewed
the situation as an emergency. At that point, Gorbachev acted preemptively,
striking out against the emerging coalition of *perestroika*'s East European
opponents (Jakes, Zhivkov, Honecker, and Ceausescu) and those in his own
party. The significance of Gorbachev's actions in 1989 is that he was willing
to accept the possible collapse of Leninist rule in Eastern Europe in order to

maintain it in the Soviet Union—not that he intended or foresaw the political collapse of Leninism in Eastern Europe.

If in 1918 Lenin "offered" Imperial Germany the Ukraine to save Bolshevik Russia, in 1989 Gorbachev offered East Germany to West Germany (and Eastern Europe to Western Europe) to save the Soviet Union. Lenin's Brest-Litovsk gamble succeeded, while Gorbachev's failed. In the Soviet (East European) environment I have described, Gorbachev's nonresponse to the flight of East German tourists was the catalyst that produced one of the most remarkable political events of the twentieth century, *the mass extinction of Leninist regimes.*

Intellectual perplexity and personal amazement are natural responses to the events of 1989 in Eastern Europe and the Soviet Union. There are, after all, two rare types of historical development.

As a rule, history is Protestant, not Catholic. The primary feature of world history tends to be cultural, institutional, and ideological diversity. However, episodically, a "universal" ideological "word" becomes institutional "flesh," and an authoritatively standardized and centered institutional format dominates a highly diverse set of cultures. Christianity with its standardized Mass, universal use of Latin, international stratum of bishops, all centered for hundreds of years in Rome, is one instance. Liberalism with the gold *standard,* parliamentary democracy, and free trade, all centered for a century in "the City," is a second. Leninism between 1947 and 1989—with a vanguard party, "correct line," collectivization, and combat industrialization centered in Moscow—is a third. To witness the emergence in the twentieth century of what Toynbee called a "civilization" is extraordinary. To also witness its mass extinction is unique, for mass extinctions are even rarer than the appearance of "universal" states.[17]

Paleontologists devised the concept *mass extinction* to describe the abrupt and accelerated termination of species that are distributed globally, or nearly globally. Their speed and comprehensiveness, as well as the absence of species "origination," distinguish mass extinctions from background extinctions. In light of the fantastic quality of events in the Leninist world during 1989, this concept is pertinent and valuable.[18]

In relation to the natural world, there are two contending explanations for mass extinctions (e.g., of dinosaurs at the end of the Cretaceous period). One is physical, the other biological. The physical explanation is that an asteroid struck the earth, drastically changing the climatic environment; and that, in short (geological) time, destroyed the dinosaurs. In contrast, and sometimes in opposition, to this perspective is a more gradualist biological one that emphasizes general deterioration over a long period, ending again with a unique pattern of mass extinction. Gould combines the two by arguing that the extinction of the dinosaur was a "complex combination of dramatic end superimposed upon general deterioration."[19]

I have argued here that "biological" reasons best explain the extinction of the Leninist regime in the Soviet Union. All "big four" reasons are internal to the Soviet polity or to developments within its regime world (e.g., Poland), while each of the "little three" are "physical" (external to the Soviet order). In examining the "extinction" of Leninism in Eastern Europe, one might opt for a "physical" explanation. Gorbachev's relativization of the Communist Party of the Soviet Union (CPSU), with all its attendant ideological and policy correlates, was the equivalent of a political asteroid for the Czechoslovak, Bulgarian, East German, and Romanian regimes. More than anything, these regimes, like their Brezhnev prototype, were politically and ideologically corrupt and inertial, lacking purpose and confidence, and relying for power on their Soviet patron. Their "extinction" perfectly fits Gould's notion of a "dramatic end superimposed upon general deterioration."

It's worth staying with paleontology a while longer. Paleontologists distinguish between mass mortality and mass extinction: "Mortality is the death of a single individual or individuals; extinction implies the elimination of the last member of a species, and is, of course, forever."[20] In light of this distinction, my claim that Leninism—as an international political order with distinct boundaries and international membership—is extinct might be considered premature. Literally, yes; essentially, no. A Leninist regime has three character-defining features: the primacy of social combat, of class war, in relation to its social host; a monopoly of historical-political insight whose incarnation at any given time is the "correct line"; and the exclusivity of the party as the sole locus of political leadership and membership. Khrushchev attenuated the party's identity by marginalizing the first of these characteristics, and Gorbachev has rejected the remaining two. Given the "founding" stature of the Soviet regime, and its historical role as origin, authoritative author, and model (to varying but always substantial degrees) for all other members of the Leninist regime world, its "death" signals extinction, not simply widespread mortality, for the entire family. One can point to Vendée Leninism in Albania, Cuba, China, Southeast Asia, and North Korea. But without (even an ambivalent) point of (Soviet) reference, it will wither. The only question left is: which will be the last Leninist dinosaur?

Several former Leninist regimes, including some in Eastern Europe and among the Soviet republics, will experience pseudoextinction. Regimes of this type, such as those of Romania and Bulgaria, will maintain features directly related to their Leninist predecessor, but will be recognizably distinct.[21] Point: even regimes whose new political profiles will contain elements recognizably derived from their Leninist predecessors will no longer be Leninist or part of an international regime world. In 1989 the world became more "Protestant."

A final feature of mass extinctions crucial to my thesis is that they typically affect more than one species. In this respect, the collapse of European Leninism may be seen more as a political volcano than as an asteroid. A volcano's eruption initially affects a circumscribed area (in this case limited to Leninist regimes), but, depending on its force, the effects gradually but dramatically become global. The Leninist volcano of 1989 will have a comparable effect on liberal and "Third World" biota around the globe.

The obvious and immediate consequence of Leninism's mass extinction is the dramatic clearing-away process in the area previously known as the Soviet bloc, empire, or Leninist regime world. Extinctions make room for new regime types. Poland, Hungary, and Czechoslovakia are examples (whether they become liberal or authoritarian capitalist). So are Romania and Bulgaria, despite the continued powerful, even predominant presence of leaders groomed by their Leninist parents. Leninist progeny may exercise power, but they do (and know it) in a decisively different national and international environment. Priests without *the* Church aren't Catholic; cadres without *the* party aren't Leninists. Pseudoextinction does not mean a "faked regime death."

The clearing-away effect of a mass regime extinction has an international as opposed to a national impact—ask East Germans! But rather than fixating on the German boundary change, one should appreciate the possibility that it may signal a number of boundary changes of extraordinary import. Yugoslavia and the Soviet Union have already begun attempts at federal-confederal reconfiguration that may readily turn into national disintegration.

Nor can we expect the clearing-away effect of the Leninist Extinction to be self-contained—a political storm that considerably loses its force as it approaches "coasts" of the West and the Third World. Nothing could be further from the truth.

For practically half a century—no time at all geologically, but a substantial and consequential period politically—international and national boundaries and identities have been shaped by a Leninist regime world led in different ways and to different degrees by the Soviet Union. For half a century we have thought in terms of East and West, and now there is no East as such. The primary axis of international politics has "disappeared." Thermonuclear Russia hasn't, but the Soviet Union/Empire most certainly has. Its "extinction" radically revises the framework within which the West, the United States itself, the Third World, and the countries of Eastern Europe, the former Russian Empire, and many nations in Asia have bounded and defined themselves.

The Leninist Extinction will force the United States to reexamine the meaning of its national identity. The persistent hysterical strain in American political culture has expressed itself for some seventy years now as an acute anxiety over communism, its latest expression being an SDI "condom" capable of keeping out the Evil Empire's nuclear and ideological "AIDS."

One could read the Brzezinski and Huntington book on political power in the USA and USSR and never get an inkling of this quite unpragmatic dimension of American political culture.[22] Fortunately, the movies *Dr. Strangelove* and the *Invasion of the Body Snatchers* brilliantly capture the hysteria Brzezinski and Huntington miss. But, with the remarkable exception of the South African Communist Party, one is hard put to find a genuine

Leninist party anywhere in the world on anything more than inertial glide toward political extinction. That leaves the three-hundred-year-old hysterical dimension (from "witches," to "reds," to "evil empire") of American political culture in search of an expression. In short, internationally and nationally, the Leninist Extinction will have a direct impact on America's political self-definition.

The Third World has also bounded and defined itself from its Bandung beginning by distinguishing itself from the West *and* the Leninist world. Whatever shared political identity the "unaligned" world of African, Asian, and Middle Eastern states had, it has for the most part been a negative one—neither liberal nor Leninist. The Third World's ideological identity, its geographical borders, and its capacity to secure developmental aid have all depended on the conflict between two universal states, the American liberal and the Soviet Leninist. The field within which the Third World of genuine and fictive national-states bounded and defined itself has disappeared. A telling example can be found in Latin America, where the state security ideology of the Brazilian, Peruvian, and Argentinian armies are oriented to and dependent on the international communist threat and Soviet-American hostility. Stepan has argued that a key theme in the Brazilian military's ideology was that the "underdeveloped" (or Third World) countries were "under great internal pressure . . . because of global ideological conflict, which had deep ramifications for the internal security of the country."[23] The Leninist Extinction removes a powerful rationale for one of the most persistent phenomena in Latin America, military coups.

The Leninist Extinction will directly affect political life, national identities, and international boundaries throughout the world. The world has entered a period of "tectonic" and traumatic, complicated and confusing changes, a period that would test even the skills of old "Halitherses, keenest among the old at reading birdflight into accurate speech."[24] As Sorensen has recently pointed out, the Leninist Extinction presents us with a conceptual vacuum.[25] How we characterize the features of the emerging world will directly affect its future boundaries and identities.

GENESIS

According to the Bible, "In the beginning . . . the earth was without form and void."[26] To say that this describes the political condition of the world today would exaggerate reality and frighten those academics and political figures for whom a known and controlled world is a psychological and political necessity. However, the global impact on boundaries and identities begun by the Leninist Extinction is more likely to resemble the world outlined in Genesis than the stingy and static view of development Fukuyama presents in "The End of History?"

In Fukuyama's view, "the triumph of the West, of the Western *idea*, is evident first of all in the total exhaustion of viable systematic alternatives to

Western liberalism."[27] Fukuyama's allowance for the "sudden appearance of new ideologies or previously unrecognized contradictions in liberal societies" is a throwaway. For him Hitler, the Nazi revolution, and World War II were a "diseased bypath in the general course of European development."[28] Similarly, his allowance that the "fascist alternative may not have been played out yet in the Soviet Union" is a liberal Goliath's view of a possible fascist David. (I leave it to the reader to develop the analogy.)

Fukuyama's homogenization thesis finds its complement in Hough's version of Soviet history in which "Khomeini Leninism" is replaced by a "Western" Gorbachev generation reared in an urban milieu, with wives dressed in Yves Saint Laurent clothes (and at least one, Raisa Gorbachev herself, holding a degree in sociology), all ready to undo the Bolshevik Revolution's "unnatural break with Russian history."[29] But historical "exceptions" of this order (the Nazi and Bolshevik revolutions) don't prove the "liberal rule." One almost destroyed it, and the other had the nuclear power to do it.

I have no quarrel with Fukuyama's observation that liberal capitalism is now the only politically global "civilization" or his suggestion that "the present world seems to confirm that the fundamental principles of socio-political organization have not advanced terribly far since 1806." But I do reject his idealist, ahistorical assertion that liberal capitalist "civilization" is the "end of history," the last "civilization." And in the next section I will show why liberal capitalist democracy will always generate opposing challengers. In the immediate future, the Leninist Extinction is likely to dramatically, and in some instances traumatically, challenge and undermine the national boundaries and political identities of Third World nations, Western nations, and the character of the Western world itself, as well as create obvious and serious obstacles to stable and viable elite and regime replacements in the Soviet Union, Eastern Europe, and Asia.

Jehovah's response to a world void and without form was twofold: *he created boundaries between and named the new entities.* His task was greater, but our task is comparable: to respond to a world that will be increasingly unfamiliar, perplexing, and threatening, in which existing boundaries are attacked and changed and in which the task will be to establish new national and international boundaries; as well as to "name" or to identify the new entities. Fukuyama's "End of History" and my "Genesis" images are exaggerations; but if a theorist's only choice is what type of error to make, I offer mine as more accurate and helpful in assigning meaning and attempting to influence the type of world we are entering.

In one respect, we are currently on the type of "full sea" Shakespeare had in mind when he had Brutus observe, "There is a tide in the affairs of men, Which, taken at the flood, leads on to fortune; Omitted, all the voyage of their life Is bound in shallows and in miseries." (*Julius Caesar*, act 4, scene 3). In more mundane terms, we may have reached what Gerschenkron liked to call a "nodal point," a situation of opportunity and the related risk of missed opportunity.[30] However, even Shakespeare's and Gerschenkron's more contingent sense of developmental possibilities in risky environments may be too optimistic. Both Shakespeare and Gerschenkron formulate a discernible point where action brings about successful and (pace Fukuyama) *novel* developments. But the current environment in the Soviet Union increasingly resembles the earth "without form and void." In September 1990, Premier Ryzhkov felt compelled to say: "I don't want to dramatize things. I don't want to frighten anyone. I have no right to do that. But laws are not obeyed, resolutions are not obeyed. There are massive violations, to say nothing of criminal violations."[31] We must temper our Enlightenment optimism with the recognition that a crisis is not automatically a developmental opportunity. Today and for the near future, crises—not developmental opportunities—may be the rule. Nodal points may or may not appear in the Soviet Union. Similarly in Eastern Europe, the facile and pacific notion of "transiting to democracy" (where, having entered at the "Lenin station," one gets off at the "liberal station") is challenged by the not-so-latent ethnic-economic maelstrom extending from Bulgaria to Czechoslovakia.

If not Fukuyama, if not Gerschenkron, then are we not left with spreading chaos? Possibly! Certainly, in coming to grips with the Leninist Extinction's global impact, we must be prepared to witness and respond simultaneously to chaos in some areas, nodal points in others, and the unlikely but persistent possibility of new "civilizations" emerging inside and outside the liberal West.

The first imperative is to anticipate an international environment whose primary characteristic will be turbulence instead of the stereotypical, fundamentally apolitical quality of international life during the cold war,[32] and national environments characterized by conflict along both civic-ethnic and regional fault lines. Turbulent environments produce more than their share of simultaneous emergencies (e.g., reconceiving or abolishing NATO, the disintegration of the Soviet Union, and Iraq's invasion of Kuwait) for a significant number of national and subnational elites. An emergency environment calls for different political skills and leaders than does the stereotyped bipolar environment of the largely contained, and occasionally ritualized, emergencies characteristic of the cold war.[33]

On balance, leaders will count for more than institutions, and charisma for more than political economy, in a turbulent world environment. It is in epochs when existing boundaries and identities—international and national, institutional and psychological—are challenged and assaulted that "great men," or leaders who want to be considered great, offer themselves as points of certainty and promise. We can expect their appearance. William James said, "Societies . . . at any given moment offer ambiguous potentialities of development. . . . Leaders give the form."[34] That is particularly true of Genesis environments.[35]

Charismatic leaders in the former Leninist world, in the now politically and ideologically adrift Third World, and in the liberal West itself who are constrained to act in the context of existing state institutions will be of real but limited consequence: they can affect the distribution of power in a larger or smaller area but are unable to act as the catalyst for a new way of life. The truly remarkable feature of turbulent, dislocating, traumatic Genesis environments is the dissolution of existing boundaries and related identities and the corresponding potential to generate novel ways of life.

A new *way of life* consists of a new ideology radically rejecting and demanding avoidance of existing institutions—social, economic, religious, military, administrative, political, cultural—and calling for the creation of alternative, mutually exclusive institutions with "superior" features (this invidious element is essential); a new political idiom, language, and vocabulary that, in Genesis-like manner, "names" and establishes the boundaries of the new way of life; a new powerful and prestigious institution (be it religious, economic, military, or political); the emergence of a social base from which members and leaders can be drawn to complement and substantiate the new ideology; the assignment and acceptance of a heroic historical task and related strategy, explicitly calling for risk and sacrifice; and, finally, a core area—geographical or institutional—which, for whatever set of accidental and social reasons, generates a surplus of resources consistent with the task of creating a new way of life.

Some historical examples should help make the argument more evocative. Liberal ideology asserted a new social ontology in which the individual, not the corporate group, was the basis of social identity and responsibility. In the first instance, liberal capitalism (as Polanyi so brilliantly grasped) was the call for a new way of life, not for the mere redistribution of power.[36] Nazism and Leninism made ideological demands of the same order, not of the same content.

All new ways of life depend on a new political vocabulary. Absolutism is unimaginable without Jean Bodin's radical reformulation of authority and sovereignty. Anderson may exaggerate a little, but there is much in his contention that "the practice of Absolutism corresponded to Bodin's theory of it."[37] Leninism is unimaginable without its language of "dictatorship of the proletariat," "vanguard party," "correct line," and "democratic centralism."

Similarly, every new way of life, whether social, economic, political, or cultural, has a novel institution, a partisan pattern of authoritative behavior, associated with it. Absolutism had the court (as Versailles), liberalism the market and parliament, Leninism *the* party and plan.

For each new way of life a social base must be uprooted from its previous identity,[38] available for a new one, attracted to and validated by the features of the new ideology—a social base from which a new elite stratum emerges (courtiers in absolutist states, ascetic entrepreneurs in liberal capitalist states, Bolshevik cadres in Leninist regimes, and the SS in Nazi Germany).

For a new way of life to assert itself, a social minority must completely identify with and accept an imperative task, such as establishing the superiority (not simply the power) of the king, or of free trade and the market, or the "race" and the Führer, or the party and the *kollektiv*—for a critical period during which new elites, practices, organizations, and beliefs institutionally coagulate.

Finally, the emergence of a new way of life requires the existence of a core area generating, concentrating, and then "exporting" a surplus of leadership talent and resources to the "unreconstructed" society it intends to transform. Versailles, Cluny, *the* party, London, Rome, Mecca-Medina, and Gdansk all played this creative role.

I am not prophesying the inevitable appearance of a new way of life in response to the Leninist Extinction. I am saying the clearing-away and traumatizing effect of this event will act as a stimulus and create potentials for such a development within the former Leninist world and its Western and Third World ecumene. In the next decade and beyond an unusual number of leaders and movements will appear, making claims about a new way of life or the restoration of a former period of glory. Saddam Hussein's call to the Arab-Muslim nation is only the first effort of this kind. Most aspirants will fail; perhaps all of them. But their appearance and actions will reflect and contribute to a world marked by increasing national and international disorder. We can expect conflict over geographical boundaries (in the Soviet Union, Yugoslavia, Canada, and the Middle East, where Pakistani visions have as great a threat potential as the Iraqi). We can expect civic-ethnic violence in any number of countries around the world. The United States will have to deal with a growing number of "intermestic"[39] issues—issues like those in Israel, South Africa, Mexico, and Canada that are simultaneously national and international. All this does mean the "end of history," a history of the last forty-five years and very possibly that of the last two hundred years. It does not mean the inexorable assimilation of the world to the current liberal Western way of life, nor even the continued adaptive "strength" of the liberal West.

THE WEST AND THE "REST"

The introduction of disorder and turbulence, appearance of charismatic leaders and movements, and possible evolution of new ways of life will occur in a political universe that may now be inertial, but is, for the moment, still well delineated nationally and internationally. History is more often Protestant in its cultural and institutional diversity than Catholic, and uniform over cultural space. However, that diversity is finite. As Miss Marple once observed: "You'd be surprised if you knew how very few distinct types there are in all."[40] Indeed, in the last hundred years, liberal capitalist democracy, fascism-nazism, Leninism, and some variant of military rule exhaust the range of regime types. To predict, as I do in this article, the emergence and proliferation of Genesis environments does not require that developments be either apocalyptic or unintelligible. Precisely because Genesis environments develop in, out of, and in opposition to more delineated and "named" environments, the theorist is positioned to grasp the connections and meanings of some developments. I completely agree with the fictional William of

Baskerville's commentary: "at a time when as philosopher I doubt the world has an order, I am consoled to discover, if not an order, at least a series of connections in small areas of the world's affairs."[41] With the (initial) extinction of fascism-nazism, and now the extinction of Leninism, the question is: what types of political response developments are likely in a world dominated by an uncontested liberal capitalist democratic "civilization," or way of life? I confidently predict one general response.

Liberal capitalist democracy has generated a heterogeneous set of opponents: romantic poets, Persian ayatollahs, aristocrats, the Roman Catholic Church, and fascists. However, for all the genuine and substantial differences separating these diverse oppositions, one can detect a shared critique. Liberal capitalist democracy is seen as one-sided in its emphasis on individualism, materialism, achievement, and rationality. While the Roman Catholic preference for the family over the individual and the Nazi preference for "race" in place of the individual are radically different critiques, the general critique is the same: liberal capitalism fails to adequately provide for the essential group needs and dimension of human existence.

Similarly, liberal capitalism has regularly evoked passionate criticism and hostility in connection with its materialist bias and emphasis on achievement, its tendency to ignore or marginalize the human need for security, and its repression of expressive human action. But nothing has been more central to liberal capitalism, and more capable of sustaining and eliciting opposition over the last two hundred years, than its rational impersonalism. Liberal capitalist democracy's rejection of the heroic ethic of awe and mystery, which throughout most of history was seen as separating man from the world of animals and necessity, has generated countermovements as diverse as the English romantic poets and Roman Catholicism, and as perverse as nazism and Stalinism.

My point is that liberal capitalist democracy's victories over the Catholic Church, then fascism-nazism, and now Leninism are particularly momentous, but, most of all, particular victories. Precisely because liberal capitalist democracy has a bounded, distinctive, partisan identity, it cannot be all or do all things in equal measure. As long as the West retains its partisan liberal capitalist democratic identity, it will regularly generate movements—internally and externally—opposing or attacking, attempting to reform or destroy it; movements that in one form or another will emphasize the values of group membership, expressive behavior, solidarist security, and heroic action. One locus for such is the so-called Third World.

Beginning with India's independence in 1947, the Third World has been regarded by many as a source of promise. For some in the West, it was the promise of actually extending and revitalizing liberal capitalist democracy. Panchayats in India, colonially sponsored "gentry" in Nigeria, and the tradition of "consensual" decision making in East Africa were to enrich and extend the promise of the West. With Khrushchev, the Soviet Union added its political and ideological enthusiasm for (and thereby created a rivalry with the United States over) the Third World. It was to be the Soviet Union's international "virgin lands." West African and Egyptian leaders became heroes of Lenin, Cuba a Leninist apostle.

But some Third World political leaders, intellectuals, and Western supporters went further and saw it as the source of revolutionary promise; the locus of a novel, compelling, and better way of life, neither liberal nor Leninist. For Fanon, it was a question "of the Third World starting a new history of man, a history which will have regard to the sometimes prodigious theses which Europe has put forward, but which will also not forget Europe's crimes, of which the most horrible was committed in the heart of man, and consisted of the pathological tearing apart of his functions and the crumbling away of his unity." Third World countries were "to do their utmost to find their own particular values and methods and a style which shall be peculiar to them."[42]

But the "promise" has not (yet) been realized. No new way of life has emerged anywhere in the Third World. No new ideology has been embraced by leaders who go on to create a new political vocabulary for, and recruit a new leadership stratum from, a mobilized social base that "populates" innovative institutions, pursues historically extraordinary tasks, and draws from as well as relies on a powerful, prestigious core area. No London, Moscow, Mecca, or Rome has appeared in the Third World. In stark contrast to a new international way of life, for the most part one finds depressingly familiar examples of tyranny, corruption, famine, and rage in prenational settings. Still, it is premature to write off the Third World as a potential source for a new way of life. After all, the ex-colonial world has been independent for less than half a century.

The core sites around which novel clusters of institutions comprising a new way of life develop are often marginal areas: the development of monotheism in Israel is one example; the emergence of liberal capitalism in a fragment of the Eurasian continent that for most of its existence was quite underdeveloped, one might even risk saying backward, is another. Do such areas exist in the Third World? South Africa may be one.[43] It offers the analyst a striking tableau: intraracial violence between Inkhata and the ANC, interracial violence between Afrikaaner *verkramptes* and the nonwhite population; the sole militant communist party in the world (the SACP); and an African leader, Nelson Mandela, who skillfully linked the African black struggle to American politics and ideology with his suggestion to the American Congress that "one of the benefits that should accrue to both our peoples and to the rest of the world should surely be that this complex South African society, which has known nothing but racism for three centuries, should be transformed into an oasis of good race relations where the black shall to the white be sister and brother . . . an equal human being, both citizens of the world."[44] South Africa's industrial, racially conflictual, tribalurban, Christian, and revolutionary society is a potential recipe for destructive brutality and/or constructive realities affecting a good part of the world.

However, even if there is some reason to consider South Africa a long-shot core area for a new way of life, there are other developments in the Third World (including South Africa) with more immediate developmental implications in light of, and in response to, the Leninist Extinction and the victory of the West.

I want to examine four such developments: wars between Third World countries; the status of the NICs and the related issue of democracy; immigration; and, above all, Movements of Rage.

The Leninist Extinction favors an increase in the number of wars fought between Third World nations. The geographical boundaries of many Third World countries are arbitrary and their national identities fictive. The Soviet-American rivalry supported existing boundaries insofar as any change would indicate a possible shift of influence toward one and away from the other superpower. Minus that rivalry, latent Third World irredenta will express themselves more readily and aggressively. Their significance will vary from the regionally contained Liberian variant, with its civil war and consequent invasion by several divided West African nations, to the Iraqi invasion of Kuwait and its consequent international repercussions. The Iraqi invasion is an example of a Third World leader attempting to create favorable new boundaries and political identities in what he sees as a disrupted, promising, and threatening environment.[45]

The emergence of NICS in the Third World predates the mass extinction of Leninist regimes. I am not primarily concerned with the institutional strategies, or the cultural and international settings, that underlie their economic development. My focus is their political identity. Not one is a stable liberal capitalist democracy. Nor do I see any reason to think democracy will fare well in any part of the Third World. Like individualism, democracy is a historically rare and deviant phenomenon, requiring not only a certain level of economic and social development, talented leadership, and a dash of *fortuna,* but also intense cultural trauma. As the liberal Ralf Dahrendorf has noted, it took a far from predictable sequence of Nazi revolution and American victory and democratization to create liberal capitalist democracy in West Germany.[46] It took war, American victory, occupation, constitution writing, and military protection to help create Japan's incomplete liberal democratization. The democratic movement in Poland, Solidarity, is unimaginable without the traumatic dislocation and migration of five million Poles to the Western Territories in the context and aftermath of World War II. Nor did Spain and Greece simply "transit" to democracy; they both experienced a wrenching civil war in the twentieth century that has had a direct sociocultural bearing on their ability to sustain a liberal capitalist democratic constitution.

In a world environment in which basic political identities are at stake, and where the political rules of the game are unclear, countries like South Korea or any number of Latin American countries with democracy on their political agenda are likely to remain undemocratic even as they talk about democratization. I am amazed by the facility with which Latin Americanists, who quite recently were gloomily talking, conferencing, and writing about the "break-down of democracy," are now enthusing about the "transition to democracy," not only in Latin America but by acontextual extrapolation to Eastern Europe and the Soviet Union. Economic and social development places democracy on a nation's political agenda; but *irreversible* breakthrough to democracy depends on quite different sociocultural and institutional factors. Argentina's history bears perpetual witness to this. More economically distressed regimes, such as the Philippines, whose democratic institutional facade finds little correspondence or support in the country's social and cultural "constitution," or the military's political culture (seven coups have been attempted in the four and a half years of Aquino's governance), are even more likely to find the breakthrough to democracy beyond their current reach. Even India's circumscribed and faulted, but substantial, democracy is threatened by a growing potential for national disintegration along regional, linguistic, and religious lines as it loses its Congress-based, pan-Indian generation of bureaucrats, officers, and politicians.

For years, perhaps decades, to come, one is more likely to see the emigration of people out of, rather than the immigration of democracy into, the Third World. And emigration out of the Third World means immigration into the West. The most immediate and significant consequence of liberalism's "historic victory" is not the exporting of liberal capitalist democracy to the Third World and Eastern Europe; it is the importing of Third World *and* East European populations into the West. This immigration directly challenges the balance of civic-ethnic identities within the West itself.

In the near future, the most extraordinary development within the Third World may be the emergence and victory of Movements of Rage. These also predate the Leninist Extinction, but it creates environments within which Nazi-like revolutionary substitutes for Leninism will appear.

I am thinking of movements that to date have not been theoretically connected: the Mulele uprising in Kwilu Province in what is now Zaire, the Tupamaros in Uruguay, the Khalq in Afghanistan, the Khmer Rouge in Kampuchea, and the Sendero Luminoso in Peru. I am referring to revolutionary movements with a Leninist-Maoist vocabulary but a Fanonist ethos and character—movements whose motive force is nihilistic rage against the legacy of Western colonialism. These movements typically originate among provincial elites: men and women filled with hate for the culture of the capital city, and at the same time angered by their exclusion from it. Their murderous rage is directed against those "contaminated" by contact with Western culture: those wearing ties, speaking French, or educated in a Western university.

Movements of Rage are nihilistic political responses to failure—the failure of the Third World to create productive economies, equitable societies, ethical elites, and sovereign nations. They are desperate responses to the fact that nothing seems to work. The anticipated magical effect of adopting the label "one-party democracy," or "Leninist," or, as is becoming fashionable, "market capitalist democracy" has turned out and will turn out to be weak developmental magic for most Third World countries. Movements of Rage are violent nativist responses to failure, frustration, and perplexity. It is ironic that the man who called on the Third World to generate a superior way of life is the same man who claims: "violence is like a royal pardon. The colonised man finds his freedom in and through violence"; and "violence alone, violence committed by the people, violence organised and educated by its leaders, makes it possible for the masses to understand social truths and gives the key to them."[47] True, Fanon was speaking to the colonized, but the Pol Pots, Hafizullah Amins, and Guzmans are quite ready to apply Fanon to the culturally "colonized" people of Kampuchea, Afghanistan, and Peru.

To my knowledge, only one person has identified this phenomenon, V. S. Naipaul. While academia has had all of its attention monopolized by studies of state building and the political economy of commodity regimes, in *The Return of Eva Peron* and *Among the Believers* Naipaul has insightfully described the potential in the Third World for nativist state-destroying movements that treat the economy as booty.[48]

One can question whether I have established a sufficient case for the existence of a new type of revolutionary movement, a variant of fascism-nazism in the Third World. In addition, one should critically observe that few of these movements have come to power, and when, as in Afghanistan and Kampuchea, they have, they self-destruct. So did the Nazi regime—at the cost of fifty million lives. Furthermore, had the Nazis possessed nuclear weapons, the Waltz thesis that proliferation of nuclear weapons reduces the chances of war when the opponent has a protected second-strike capability, would have been put to the test—and come up short![49] Waltz fails to understand that there are different types of cultural-ideological rationality.[50] For him, persons who consider the destruction of their own regime are mad, psychotic. But the issue isn't psychological; it is primarily cultural and ideological. Pol Pot wasn't mad: he operated within a cultural and ideological framework that rejected the cultural premises underpinning the global balance of power epitomized by MAD (Mutual Assured Destruction).

I mentioned another potential criticism of my Movements of Rage thesis: very few have ever come to power. True, but that tells us little about the potential for these movements in a post-Leninist world, unless one believes that the Leninist Extinction is a self-contained event. The burden of my entire argument has been to challenge that assumption. In the new, more turbulent Genesis environments emerging in the aftermath of the Leninist Extinction, species that didn't fare well earlier may do much better. After all, mammals didn't appear after the dinosaurs. Rather, as long as dinosaurs existed, mammals were rather puny things with a restricted range of adaptive radiation. They didn't grow in strength or "come to power" until the "clearing away" of the dinosaurs. In sort, one cannot gauge the potential for future Movements of Rage by generalizing from their failure prior to the Leninist Extinction.

Instead, one must imagine a Third World increasingly neglected by the United States and Soviet Union (as each attends to domestic crises) except when a very clear and present emergency occurs in a strategic location; a Third World where aggression occurs more and more frequently; a world where the technology of nuclear weapons becomes more widely dispersed; a world where the few democracies that have any standing (such as the Indian one) fail; and where checks on emigration to the West remove a vital escape valve. In that far-from-fantastic world the "movements of rage" might indeed become a very disruptive international force, especially in a country like Mexico. This may be too speculative for many in academia, with its narrow perspective, one "with plenty of brain, but with a brain which, while seeing clearly and in detail all that is on the horizon, is incapable of conceiving that the horizon may change."[51] But that is what has already happened.

The Leninist Extinction is not a surgical historical strike that will leave the liberal and Third World "friendlies" unaffected. Everyone's horizons, including the West's, will be dramatically affected. But doesn't the worldwide rush toward liberal capitalist democratic idioms, policies, and institutional facades refute this claim? And what of the shift by socialist parties to positions that differ insignificantly from their historic capitalist antagonists (see Lipset, this volume, chapter 9); the tentative moves toward a multiparty system in African "socialist" regimes;[52] the belief of many East Europeans in the market's miraculous quality? These are not illusory phenomena; they are real. But how substantial, consistent, or persistent? If one interprets these phenomena in developmental—not static—terms, their significance also rests in the expected surge of anger that will follow the failure (in most cases) of the market and electoral democracy to produce sovereign, productive, equitable nations in the greater part of Eastern Europe, the former Soviet Union, and the Third World.

Those who currently presume a permanent identity and universal triumph for the liberal capitalist democratic way of life should remember Hobsbawm's observation that "the progress of democratic politics between 1880 and 1914 foreshadowed neither its permanence nor its universal triumph,"[53] and read Weber's passage about the liberal capitalist "iron cage."

Weber said, "No one knows who will live in this cage in the future, or whether at the end of this tremendous development entirely new prophets will arise, or there will be a great rebirth of old ideas and ideals, or, if neither, mechanized petrification, embellished with a sort of convulsive self-importance. For of the last stage of this cultural development, it might well be truly said: 'Specialists without spirit, sensualists without heart; this nullity imagines that it has attained a level of civilization never before achieved.' "[54] Note that Weber balances his pessimistic and damning comments about liberal capitalist nullities with his open appreciation of the possibility of "entirely new prophets," and perhaps the "rebirth of old ideas and ideals" (in the Western world). Like Daniel Bell (though with some of Weber's pessimism), I believe that "we stand with a clearing ahead of us. The exhaustion of Modernism, the aridity of Communist life, the tedium of the unrestrained self, and the meaninglessness of the monolithic political chants all indicate that a long era is coming to a close."[55] It was an era whose general origin is the Enlightenment and the French Revolution, and whose particular origin is the Big Bang of the Second World War.

How the West responds to this "clearing" and what new boundaries and political identities emerge depend more than anything else on how America interprets and reacts to the Leninist Extinction. To date, the reaction and interpretation have been *inertial*. In American foreign policy, the Bush administration's fetishlike emphasis on maintaining NATO is a major example. Another is the belief that an American cavalry charge to Iraq will prevent international chaos and shape a new consensual international order. With his Iraqi policy, Bush is trying to force the world to stay within its postwar boundaries and identities. This effort is consistent with what Louis Hartz insightfully called American liberal absolutism. According to Hartz, what distinguishes America, particularly since the Civil War, is the near absolute quality of liberal capitalist (Protestant) democracy as the (ideological) American way of life. The consequence has been the inability and unwillingness of American political elites to grasp or accept our cultural, ideological, and national relativity. As Hartz put it, the issue for the United States is whether "a nation can compensate for the uniformity of its domestic life by contact with alien cultures outside it. It asks whether American liberalism can acquire through external experience *that sense of relativity*... which European liberalism acquired through an internal experience of social diversity and social conflict."[56]

Throughout the twentieth century, the United States has oscillated between national messianism and isolationism, two sides of the same absolutist coin. How the political universe evolves depends in good measure on whether the United States stays within the stingy confines of absolutism: the belief that unless we are omnipotent we must be impotent, currently expressed in the dead-end debate over decline (Kennedy: We are! Nye: We're not!).[57]

I see two competing political futures: one *dogmatic*, the other *tolerant*. If the current American administration remains nationally and internationally inertial, we face serious to severe crises and dogmatically intolerant isolationist and nativist responses.

Should the United States continue to cast itself primarily as military leader of the West, the domestic results will be increasing economic disorder, and consequent racial violence that will make the 1960s look benign. Internationally, conflict will increase with a Japan that is more culturally absolutist than we are ideologically absolutist. Western Europe will explicitly reject the reactionary American conception of Western leadership. The American response to these developments is likely to be a bitterly isolationist mentality coupled domestically to a nativist backlash against the hostile ethnic and racial fragmentation (described by some as multicultural diversity) manifesting itself in the United States.

In the setting of a West at odds with and in itself, and the former Leninist world, far from having "transited" to liberal capitalist democracy, forced to cope with a growing civic versus ethnic maelstrom (exacerbated by latent boundary conflicts);[58] and a Third World reacting to economic, cultural, and political failure with increasing rage—in that world environment, one should not ignore the potential political role of the Roman Catholic Church. Like fascism, the Church may find new life in a post-Leninist world. Antiliberal, anticapitalist, antimodern, the Church retains and espouses an identity, a way of life, that is corporate, solidarist, charismatic, and international. Under this pope, a Roman Catholic Church could serve as a focal point for an antiliberal capitalist democracy movement embracing religio-ethnic movements in Eastern Europe, right-wing anti-immigration movements in the West, and some Movements of Rage in the Third World. (The Church did, after all, manage its relations with the Nazis quite well.) A development of this order would surprise many, and shock others, but Genesis environments are full of surprises and shocks.

In shaping those environments, in delineating new boundaries and "naming" new political entities, at least one thing works in John Paul II's and even Gorbachev's favor; unlike the American president, they know Fukuyama (and Hegel) are wrong. They know we stand on the threshold of a decisive reordering of world boundaries and identities, and as the Pontifical Biblical Institute's "Father Jorge," Malachi Martin, says, they are actively attempting to shape the outcome of what he calls the millennium endgame.[59] Both John Paul II and Gorbachev proceed from a dogmatically intolerant ideological base. Cardinal Siri "spoke" for Lenin when he asserted that "tolerance . . . is not a virtue. It's a mere expedient, when you cannot do otherwise."[60] Roman Catholic dogma faces challenges within the Church, and Leninist dogma has been eroded to the point of extinction in Moscow. But dogma remains actively dominant in the Church and inertially and latently dominant in what is left of the CPSU. It would be historically perverse if the West, specifically the United States, denied its greatest historical achievement—religious and political toleration—by dogmatically adhering to a liberal absolutist vision of its place in the West and the world.

A tolerant future world depends on America's recasting—not rejecting—its self-conception, its place in the West, and its relation to the former Leninist and "third" worlds. The key to a more tolerant future is a relative sense of American identity domestically and internationally.

Domestically, it means rejecting the absolute emphasis many now place on ethnic, racial, and gender identities, with its "tower of Babel" implications; *and* the backlash "white castle" alternative. A nation that invented the inclusive political party must now invent an ideological and institutional framework for integrating privately diverse and publicly shared identities.

Internationally, the Iraqi crisis highlighted the American predilection for an absolute political identity. Thus 1990 could have been 1950. The United States acted and organized world support in an absolutist manner. Just observe the Bush administration's rejection of the Soviet effort to place primary responsibility for opposing Iraq with the United Nations' dormant military committee. Bush refused to relativize America's role and power in a superordinate international framework. The American inability or refusal to envisage a role for the United States that is central, even primary, but not absolute is deeply embedded in both American experience after the Second World War and an absolutist political culture. And this bears directly on the future of the West.

The West has survived and thrived because of its relatively supple identity. Based on three revolutions that created the grounds for liberal capitalist democracy (the British, American, and French), the Western way of life has a "trinitarian" base, unlike the monotheistic Leninist world with its unique October Revolution. This helps explain the remarkable shift from nineteenth-century British to twentieth-century American leadership of the liberal world. The shift was not automatic, or free of conflict and risk. In fact, it occurred in response to the near mortal assault on the West by the Nazis. The immediate question is whether the United States will facilitate or obstruct a twenty-first-century shift in Western leadership. Will it take a trauma comparable to that of the Nazi assault to recast the West's self-conception and leadership in response to the changes occasioned by World War II, and those that will follow the Leninist Extinction?

Japan is a most unlikely contender for the Western leadership. So is a unified Germany. A new united Western Europe is a more likely candidate, but the most desirable outcome would be a more complementary relationship between all three parts of the Western "trinity," with the United States more interested in joining the Common Market and less obsessed with maintaining an American NATO. An American initiative to deliberately and prudently integrate America's, Japan's, and Western Europe's economies, cultures, and in certain respects military and governmental operations would be difficult, but not as costly as a failure to imagine that "future." A more humble, less smug, appreciation of how valuable the discovery of political ethics and individual dignity in Eastern Europe is to the revitalization of the West's way of life is called for. A more deliberate, even organized, approach to some Third World issues and countries, one that relativizes the political autonomy of all involved—Western and non-Western—should be considered. Otherwise, the "last shall stay last." But to inhibit the appearance of Movements of Rage, these new relations should at one and the same time be more intrusive and less callous than those now in place.

A world without Leninism must decide whether fundamental social change always proceeds from traumatic, uncontrollably violent "big bangs," or whether reason and courage can limit violence, while respecting surprise and novelty and "naming" it in a tolerant spirit.

NOTES

1. On the SS, see Gerald Reitlinger, *The SS: Alibi of a Nation, 1922–1945* (New York: Da Capo Press, 1989), and Charles W. Sydnor, Jr., *Soldiers of Destruction: The SS Death's Head Division, 1933–1945* (Princeton: Princeton University Press, 1977).

2. In John Le Carré, *Tinker, Tailor, Soldier, Spy* (New York: Knopf, 1974).

3. Ken Jowitt, "Moscow 'Centre,' " *Eastern European Politics and Societies* 1:3 (Fall 1987), pp. 296–348.

4. The Cuban Missile Crisis was a nearly fatal error on Khrushchev's part. However, the placement of missiles was intended as an act of military diplomacy, not as aggression.

5. See Jowitt, "Moscow 'Centre.' "

6. See Burr Cartwright Brundage, *Lords of Cuzco: A History and Description of the Inca People in Their Final Days* (Norman: University of Oklahoma Press, 1967), a good introduction to the Incas and their "mummy bundles."

7. See Karl Marx, "On The Jewish Question," in Robert C. Tucker, ed., *The Marx-Engels Reader* (New York: Norton, 1972), pp. 24–52.

8. I elaborate on the *oikos* quality of the Soviet economy in "Soviet Neo-Traditionalism: The Political Corruption of a Leninist Regime," *Soviet Studies* 35:3 (July 1983), pp. 275–97.

9. Philip Selznick, *The Organizational Weapon* (New York: McGraw-Hill, 1952).

10. I am adapting Albert Hirschman's notion of a "lazy (economic) monopoly." See his *Exit, Voice, and Loyalty: Responses to Decline in Firms, Organizations, and States* (Cambridge: Harvard University Press, 1970), p. 59.

11. I do not mean to ignore socialist, anarchist, and Catholic components of Solidarity, but only to identify its defining thrust.

12. See Jadwiga Staniszkis's stimulating work, *Poland's Self-Limiting Revolution* (Princeton: Princeton University Press, 1984).

13. See Ken Jowitt, "Inclusion and Mobilization in European Leninist Regimes," *World Politics* 28:1 (October 1975), pp. 69–97.

14. See Jowitt, "Moscow 'Centre,' " for an analysis of Leninism's developmental history.

15. Bertram D. Wolfe, *Three Who Made a Revolution: A Biographical History* (New York: Stein and Day, 1984). See chapters 13–15.

16. Karl W. Deutsch, *Nationalism and Social Communication: An Inquiry into the Foundations of Nationality* (Cambridge: Technology Press of the Massachusetts Institute of Technology; New York: Wiley, 1953), p. 49.

17. See Arnold Toynbee, *A Study of History* (abridgement of vols. 1–6 by D. C. Somerville) (New York: Oxford University Press, 1974), pp. 1–48.

18. On mass extinction, see Stephen Jay Gould, *The Flamingo's Smile: Reflections in Natural History* (New York: Norton, 1985), pp. 415–51; by the same author, *Hen's Teeth and Horse's Toes* (New York: Norton, 1983), pp. 320–52; Kevin Padian et al., "The Possible Influences of Sudden Events on Biological Radiations and Extinctions," in H. D. Holland and A. F. Trendall, eds., *Patterns of Change in Earth Evolution* (New York: Springer-Verlag, 1984), pp. 77–102; David M. Raup, "Approaches to the Extinction Problem," *Journal of Paleontology* 52:3 (May 1978) pp. 228–34. I thank my colleague, Kevin Padian, for trying his best to educate me.

19. Gould, *Hen's Teeth*, p. 324.

20. Padian et al., "The Possible Influences," p. 86.

21. Ibid.

22. Zbigniew Brzezinski and Samuel P. Huntington, *Political Power USA/USSR* (New York: Viking Press, 1971), pp. 7–71.

23. Alfred Stepan, *The Military in Politics: Changing Patterns in Brazil* (Princeton: Princeton University Press, 1971), p. 179. I thank Matt Marostica for suggesting this change in the Latin American military's new environment.

24. Homer, *The Odyssey*, trans. Robert Fitzgerald (New York: Vintage Classics, 1990), p. 23.

25. Theodore C. Sorensen, "Rethinking National Security," *Foreign Affairs* 69:3 (Summer 1990), pp. 1–19.

26. *The New Oxford Annotated Bible With the Apocrypha*, revised standard version (New York: Oxford University Press, 1977), p. 1.

27. Francis Fukuyama, "The End of History?" *The National Interest* 16 (Summer 1989), p. 3.

28. Ibid., p. 16.

29. Jerry Hough, *Russia and the West: Gorbachev and the Politics of Reform* (New York: Simon and Schuster, 1988), pp. 7–44.

30. Alexander Gerschenkron, *Economic Backwardness in Historical Perspective: A Book of Essays* (Cambridge: Belknap Press of Harvard University Press, 1962).

31. Nikolai Ryzhkov quoted in the *Oakland Tribune*, September 30, 1990.

32. See Kenneth Jowitt, *Images of Detente and the Soviet Political Order* (Berkeley: Institute of International Studies, University of California, 1977).

33. The regular "discovery" of gaps between overstated Soviet and understated American military capacity in presidential election years is one example of ritualized emergency.

34. William James, *The Will to Believe and Other Essays in Popular Philosophy, and Human Immortality* (New York: Dover, 1956), pp. 227–28.

35. In *The Eighteenth Brumaire of Louis Bonaparte, With Explanatory Notes* (New York: International Publishers, 1963), Marx (following Engels) makes his famous statement: "Men make their own history, but they do not make it just as they please; they . . . make it under circumstances directly encountered, given and transmitted from the past. The tradition of all the dead generations weighs like a nightmare on the brain of the living." While this is always true, what distinguishes Genesis environments is the relative leeway charismatic leaders enjoy in defining boundaries and identities.

36. Karl Polanyi, *The Great Transformation: The Political and Economic Origins of Our Time* (Boston: Beacon, 1965), in particular chapters 3–10.

37. Perry Anderson, *Lineages of the Absolutist State* (London: Humanities Press, NLB, 1974), p. 51.

38. The classic statement about "social mobilization" is found in Karl Deutsch, "Social Mobilization and Political Development," *American Political Science Review* 55:3 (December 1961), pp. 493–514.

39. See Bayless Manning, "The Congress, the Executive, and Intermestic Affairs: Three Proposals," *Foreign Affairs*, January 1977, pp. 306–24.

40. Agatha Christie, *The Murder at the Vicarage* (New York: Dell, 1958), p. 193.

41. Umberto Eco, *The Name of the Rose* (New York: Harcourt Brace Jovanovich, 1980), p. 394.

42. Frantz Fanon, *The Wretched of the Earth* (New York: Grove, 1966), pp. 255 and 78.

43. To my mind, the best analysis of the current South African situation appears in Robert Price, *South Africa: The Process of Political Transformation* (New York: Oxford University Press, 1991).

44. The quote is from "Nelson Mandela's Address to the U.S. Congress, June 26, 1990" (a special reprint by the Washington Office on Africa, 1990).

45. The "promise": Hussein might have seen the end of the cold war creating a larger zone of indifference for regional actors. The "threat": at the same time, he may have concluded that the cold war's end put a premium on staking one's claim in the Middle East before the full brunt of the American-Israeli military monopoly (with the Soviet withdrawal) was felt.

46. Ralf Dahrendorf, *Society and Democracy in Germany* (Garden City: Doubleday, 1967), chapter 25.

47. Fanon, *The Wretched*, pp. 67, 117.

48. V. S. Naipaul, *The Return of Eva Peron* (New York: Vintage Books, 1981); and *Among the Believers: An Islamic Journey* (New York: Vintage Books, 1982). It would be interesting to see how many academics dealing with Latin America, the Middle East, South Asia, and comparative politics assign any portion of these books for their students to read.

49. As do the "enthusiasts" who belong to the school of rational choice theory (what one of my colleagues at Columbia University calls "rat" choice theory).

50. Kenneth N. Waltz, "Nuclear Myths and Political Realities," *American Political Science Review* 84:3 (September 1990), pp. 731–47.

51. *The Recollections of Alexis de Tocqueville*, trans. Alexander Teixeira de Mattos (New York: Meridian, 1966), p. 18.

52. On the rationale of African "socialism," see my "Scientific Socialist Regimes in Africa: Political Differentiation, Avoidance, and Unawareness," in Carl G. Rosberg and Thomas M. Callaghy, eds., *Socialism in Sub-Saharan Africa: A New Assessment* (Berkeley: Institute of International Studies, University of California, 1979), pp. 133–73.

53. Eric Hobsbawm, *The Age of Empire, 1875–1914* (New York: Pantheon, 1987), p. 111.

54. Max Weber, *The Protestant Ethic and the Spirit of Capitalism* (New York: Scribner, 1958), p. 182. Fortunately for him, Weber was spared reading Fukuyama and Hough, as well as members of the Bush administration.

55. Daniel Bell, *The Cultural Contradictions of Capitalism* (New York: Basic Books, 1978), p. xxix.

56. Louis Hartz, *The Liberal Tradition in America* (New York: Harcourt, Brace, 1955), p. 14, emphasis added. The last chapter, "America and the World," remains as insightful a piece as has ever been written about American foreign policy.

57. See Paul Kennedy's rich work, *The Rise and Fall of the Great Powers* (New York: Random House, 1987). For an example of Nye's position, see his *New York Times* editorial, "No, the U.S. Isn't in Decline," October 3, 1990. (Actually, Professor Nye is literally correct; for the time being, it is merely in denial.)

58. I discuss this in my contribution to "A Survey of Opinion on the East European Revolution," *Eastern European Politics and Societies* 4:2 (Spring 1990) pp. 193–97. Adam Michnik has recently made the same point to a much wider audience

in a typically compelling manner; see his "The Two Faces of Europe," *New York Review of Books*, July 19, 1990.

59. See Malachi Martin, *The Keys of This Blood: The Struggle for World Dominion Between Pope John Paul II, Mikhail Gorbachev and the Capitalist West* (New York: Simon and Schuster, 1990), passim.

60. Ibid.

5

Illusion, Critique, and Responsibility:
The "Revolution of '89" in West and East

BRUCE CUMINGS

The bourgeoisie, by the rapid improvement of all instruments of production, by the immensely facilitated means of communication, draws all nations, even the most barbarian, into civilization. The cheap prices of its commodities are the heavy artillery with which it batters down all Chinese walls. . . .

The Communist Manifesto

Capitalism always runs ahead of the critique.

Jean Baudrillard

History does not flow from socialism to capitalism but vice versa.

Kim Il Sung

WHAT ARE WE to make of the "Revolution of '89"? What sort of revolution was it? How has it been interpreted in the West? As a revolution against Stalinism, why was it limited to Eastern Europe? Why are the East Asian communist systems still standing? What are our responsibilities as intellectuals and teachers in the post-1989 world?

These are some of the questions I hope to answer, by looking at the stunning events of recent history through four optics: the elusive quality of the events, understood less as fact than as filtered through various illusions; the putative "end of Marxism," where I ask if there is anything useful left in that doctrine, and argue that Marx's critique of capitalism still has value; the vantage point of "the East," where I hazard some generalizations as to why the East is "still Red," and dwell a bit on the "last communists," still running North Korea; finally I consider the optic of the American intellectual, and the irresponsibility of much commentary on the collapse of socialism and the dawning epoch of a world under capitalism. East European socialism's greatest failure may well be, as Daniel Chirot argues, in the moral realm. Can liberalism substitute for that moral vacuum?

TIME OF ILLUSION

The "Revolution of '89" did not end in 1989, but unfolds before our eyes today. We live in a time whose essential characteristic, beyond all the others one might mention, is flux and indeterminacy. We do not know the character of this revolution. Furthermore (most pundits to the contrary), we *cannot* know it. The reason is that we participate in a lived history, an active, open-ended experiment in which people throw over "history" as a dead weight and rediscover it as an active phenomenon—human beings giving a direction to the future. In the recent upheavals the peoples of Eastern Europe recaptured themselves as masters of their own destiny, and in so doing demolished one argument after another about the permanence of the socialist regimes under which they lived, and about the presumed extinction of their own individuality, their own capacity to act historically.

The revolt was, in part, against a past that seemed immutable: as it was for forty years, so would it be for eternity, the experience of Stalinism suggested. Instead, courageous acts of will, predicated on rejecting an illusory reality, liberated people to act in the present. Daring acts of protest and witness, with a little help from a friend in the Kremlin named Gorbachev, and the Stalinist regime and its illusory power collapsed.

This collapse detonated yet more illusions, however, especially in the United States. One purpose of history, as some historians write it, is to tell us what we cannot do. If our system is totalitarian, we cannot be free: we are condemned for eternity to be totalitarian. The right-wing theory was that totalitarian systems cannot evolve (Jeanne Kirkpatrick's "doctrine"). They have almost all *evolved*. One of the most unexpected things in the whole process was that, for the most part, people acted in evolutionary ways: a simple rejection of official lying, peaceful petition and protest, dogged persistence in the face of official repression and violence.

The American illusion is that all is for the best in the best of all possible worlds in a liberal polity that is also the model for mankind: truths held self-evident here are, or ought to be, self-evident everywhere else. A major study of "Revolutionary 1989," participated in by about sixty prominent scholars, government officials, and East European émigrés, concluded that as soon as East European peoples were done with communism, they "turned immediately to liberal democracy and the free market as the way of their future."[1]

My position—my own illusion—is also Louis Hartz's, that the American polity is a fragment of the European liberal tradition, knowing something but not all of what it means to maintain that tradition over time.[2] In the fragment is also a strong propensity toward a total politics: if our truths are self-evident, what reason would any human being have for believing differently? From that standpoint, in 1989 the worst happened: the American people were vindicated precisely in their instinctive liberalism, the tip of an iceberg of unexamined eighteenth-century assumptions that have little relevance to the United States as it prepares to enter the twenty-first century.

I have now given three illusions. Indeed, the title of this section might well be "What's My Illusion?" after the 1950s television show "What's My Line?" The "Revolution of '89" has elicited a hailstorm of commentary, in which people see their own illusions confirmed. Each illusion carries its own diagnosis and prognosis, its own set of I-told-you-sos, and its own time-bound subjectivity: we will not know who is right until years from now, or maybe we will never know.[3]

Jeane Kirkpatrick can conveniently forget her doctrine and find in the collapse of the East European system a vindication for cold war anticommunism going back to the Truman Doctrine. Christopher Hitchens can find in the same events an end to neoconservatism in American politics, with his own well-put collection of I-told-you-sos.[4] Francis Fukuyama can misread Hegel and declare the end of history, just as a forgotten history awakens from long slumber in the Balkans, or as Saddam Hussein dusts off a tried-and-true ploy of "history": aggressive war. So are we at the end of history, or back to 1914? And just as this happens, Richard Gardner can resuscitate Wilsonian internationalism as if we are back to 1919.[5] So are we back to 1919 or 1914—or perhaps 1848, or is it 1815?

A. M. Rosenthal of the *New York Times* would have you believe we are back to a different time, the 1930s. Unified Germany, he has intoned in numerous op-ed columns, may well be a horror like the old unified Germany. Meanwhile, amid the end of the cold war, the *New York Times* discovered that there were not just two systems in the world (communist and free), but three: the first two plus the East Asian system of state-dominated industrial economies. This is what Robert Reich calls "national capitalism," as opposed to "cosmopolitan capitalism" (that's us), and what political economist Jude Wanniski calls "state corporate capitalism," as opposed to "entrepreneurial capitalism" (that's us). Or, as Wanniski politely explains, these economies—Japan, of course, but also South Korea—are "what we used to call fascism."[6]

Here is what we might call a discourse of eternal mistrust, in which the German and Japanese future must always be measured against the 1930s. I agree that the uniqueness of the Holocaust makes Germany deserving of mistrust, if not perhaps for eternity. I cannot see that Japan deserves the same (let alone South Korea), especially when the *New York Times* editorial cites as its expert testimony (see note 6, above) Karel von Wolferen's *Enigma of Japanese Power*, a well-wrought version of age-old stereotypes about "the East" (enigmatic, inscrutable).

What is true about Germany and Japan, perhaps, is that they won the cold war and the USSR lost it. The United States may also have lost it, "if we remember the fate of over-extended empires of the past." If Germany and Japan won, does this mean a twenty-first century under dual hegemony—a new axis? Has it all been a horrible mistake, this past forty years, showing that "those who forget history are condemned to repeat it"?

Now we have two allusions to two illusions: Gibbon on Rome and Santayana on history. Whether Gibbon was right or wrong about the decline and fall of the Roman Empire need not detain us; it is, however, decidedly unclear whether the United States is in decline or rather in a new, mature phase of hegemony. (For "declinists," see Paul Kennedy; for "still hege-

monic" see Joseph Nye, Jr.)[7] It would seem today, however, it is a bit premature to place America in a period "after hegemony." Instead the United
States is now the only "superpower," and likely to remain so for some time.
It also seems that Paul Kennedy rushed to judgment on the causes of American decline. And that was just as Saddam Hussein was about to stimulate a
new wave of military Keynesianism—the reigning (if surreptitious) doctrine
of American political economy since 1950.

As for Santayana, I wonder if such a fine philosopher could really have said
such a silly thing about history. Henry Ford was closer to the truth when he
said that "history is bunk." Remembering history is not a protection against
repeating it, and forgetting it does not obligate repetition. As for the United
States, it would be closer to the truth to say that Americans think that history
can be erased every generation.

Whatever Santayana may or may not have said, "history" is the last refuge
of every platitude. Consider William Pfaff, whose essays are often enjoyable,
but who begins his recent book this way, as preface to a discussion of American ahistoricity: "The accounts that history presents have to be paid. Past has
to be reconciled with present in the life of a nation. History is an insistent
force: the past is what put us where we are. The past cannot be put behind
until it is settled with."[8] Not a single sentence has meaning. If historical accounts have to be paid, why was Germany unified in 1990 and not Korea? If
past must be reconciled with present in the life of a nation, why is Pol Pot
again contesting for power in Cambodia? The past obviously put us where
we are, but where are we? The American people *are* ahistorical, Pfaff is right
about that; but what does this really mean?

I think Murray Sayle's prognosis for "the Pacific Rim in the 21st century"
(another favorite theme for pundits), however facetious, provokes more
thought than Pfaff's platitudes:

> Britain and Ireland could respectively be Japan's Hong Kong and Macao, well
> placed for the European entrepot trade, the U.S. will be Japan's fabulously
> wealthy India, *terre des merveilles*, while Australia can be Japan's Australia,
> land of rugged adventure and heavy drinking, the appropriate place of exile for
> Japanese dissidents and remittance men. This would leave only table scraps for
> the others: Holland, perhaps, for the Indonesians, France for the Vietnamese.[9]

So we live in a time of illusion. The cascading daily events call forth a discourse about the past, each event offers evidence for the truth of one or another version of history, and we can all parade our diagnosis, prognosis, and
I-told-you-sos. It is almost as if Jeane Kirkpatrick or Christopher Hitchens or
Richard Gardner or William Pfaff speaks, and after the first sentence you can
write the rest.

If we adopt Gardner's internationalist assumptions, for example, we can
"see" the dawning of a new Versailles without its three "errors": the error of
the hard peace for Germany, the error of American unwillingness to join the

League of Nations, and the error of Bolshevism. Now Germany has a soft peace, America is able and willing to be hegemonic, and the Bolsheviks have declared themselves to be a seventy years' error. This optic enables us to "see" the entire crisis from 1919 to 1989 as the outcome of the real Versailles: no end to the European civil war, the rise of Bolshevism and fascism, the depression and the breakdown of the world economy, World War II, and its "settlement"—which only came unstuck in 1989.

If we adopt another version of internationalist theory, Immanuel Wallerstein's world-system assumptions, we can "see" that the Bolshevik error was to begin the revolution in the semiperiphery, not the core, and then to run the semiperiphery (of Russia and Eastern Europe) into the ground by trying to fashion an alternative "socialist" world-system to compete with the capitalist world-system, one century too early and in the wrong place. (It was the wrong system at the wrong time in the wrong place.) And thus, Eastern Europe finally realizes its telos and slides back into the semiperiphery of the world capitalist system, as the inevitable result of the revolution of 1989. Both Gardner and Wallerstein appear "right" all along, if for different reasons, as long as they interpret the recent past according to their old views.

Francis Fukuyama's "The End of History?" became the intellectual *cause célèbre* of 1989, announcing "the triumph of the West, of the Western *idea.*" "Fukuyama's bold and brilliant article," according to Allan Bloom, who sponsored Fukuyama and published the article in *The National Interest,*[10] "is the first word in a discussion imperative for us, we faithful defenders of the Western Alliance. . . . [For Fukuyama] it is the ideas of freedom and equality that have animated the West and have won [*sic*] by convincing almost all nations that they are true. . . . " (Fukuyama says that unbelievers exist only in "Managua, Pyongyang, or Cambridge, Massachusetts.")[11]

Even before Fukuyama had become famous, Charles Krauthammer wrote that the burning question going back to Plato—"What is the best form of governance?"—has been answered: "After a few millennia of trying every form of political system, we close this millennium with the sure knowledge that in liberal, pluralist, capitalist democracy we have found what we have been looking for."[12] Well, that settles it.

The discourse of the "Left" on the meaning of '89 calls forth more illusions. We have the argument that the East European systems were never really socialist, that the Soviet Union under Stalin was not either, that working-class power has never really been tried, that new forms of community and solidarity—socialist and not capitalist—undermined the Stalinist regimes of the East, and so on.[13] Samir Amin is content merely to refute several "liberal axioms" and spin out his own "socialist" axioms ("the values of socialism have scientific justification," socialists ought to "encourage embryos of world government," etc.), as if nothing of moment happened in the 1980s to disturb socialist verities.[14]

It seems to me that anyone on the left who did not know the character of the Soviet-imposed East European systems in 1956 (Hungary) should have learned it in 1968 (Czechoslovakia); anyone who did not learn it in 1968 should have by 1980 (Solidarity); and anyone who did not know it by 1980 was beyond help. It was precisely the meaning of the New Left, from the Port Huron statement forward, to separate itself from the nightmare of Stalinism. Having been a part of that history, I can remember nearly breaking my television when a bulletin came through in August 1968 about Soviet tanks having crushed Dubček's attempt at democratic socialism. As we have learned recently, a generation of young people in Czechoslovakia felt a certain solidarity with the youth rebellion of the 1960s in the West; it was not for nothing that Václav Havel invited the Rolling Stones to the first "official" Czech rock concert. The demise of Dubček, thus, was in many ways the event that ensured that whenever Eastern Europe became democratic, it would assuredly *not* be socialist.

Our dilemma, running the length of the political spectrum, is that we can remember history, or forget it; we can repeat it, or not. It all depends on *what* history we remember, and what moral valence we attach to it. Our historical method ought to be more than grinding an ax, of course, but our assumptions inevitably grind the glass through which we peer. And no glass, no matter how well ground, can enable us to see our future, or even subject our dynamic present to a scrutiny that is free of "world view." In other words, Hegel was right to say that the owl of Minerva flies at dusk, and Marx was right to find in human history an unpredictable dialectic.

MARXISM: WHAT IS LEFT?

Being a Marxist today in America is like being an isolationist on December 8, 1941, or perhaps a spoilsport at an orgy. Being designated a Marxist or a leftist in America means you are responsible for everyone from Stalin to Pol Pot, from Eldridge Cleaver (whose son was delivered in Pyongyang, and who is now a Moonie) to Shirley MacLaine (who penned a Maoist text titled *You Can Get There From Here*). Perhaps America pioneered "market Marxism," in which any form of inanity has purchase, provided it is carried on in full public view.

I am sometimes called a Marxist by people who do not like my work. That is, the label functions semiotically to connote moral valence: this is bad work. This is the way "Marxism" has always functioned in America. A non-European people use a European political argot to talk about their politics, thus engaging in endless cases of mistaken identity. Most Americans labeled "Marxists" are progressives like Eugene Debs, or Studs Terkel, or the late and much-missed historian William Appleman Williams.

The labels are misapplied because few Americans understand Marxism. It starts at the top. In July 1989, George Bush spoke at Karl Marx University of Economics in Hungary (the Karl Marx was replaced by "Budapest" shortly

after the fall of the communist regime); his address was described by the
New York Times as "the most eloquent" of his European visit.[15] Here is what
he said about Marxism:

> Some historians argue that Marxism arose out of a humane impulse. But Karl
> Marx traced only one thread of human existence and missed the rest of the tap-
> estry of humanity. He regarded man as hapless, unable to shape his own envi-
> ronment or destiny.
>
> But man is not driven by impersonal economic forces. He's not simply an ob-
> ject, acted upon by mechanical laws of history. Rather, man is imaginative and
> inventive. He is artistic, with an innate need to create and enjoy beauty. He is a
> loving member of a family and a loyal patriot to his people. Man is dynamic, de-
> termined to shape his own future.

Here is what Shlomo Avineri, author of books on Hegel, Marx, and Moses
Hess, and holder of various posts in the Israeli government, wrote about
Marx:

> To Marx reality is always human reality not in the sense that man exists within
> nature, but in the sense that man shapes nature. The act also shapes man and
> his relations to other human beings; it is a total process, implying a constant
> interaction between subject and object. . . . Marx's way to socialism is not a col-
> lectivism which subsumes the individual under an abstract whole; it is rather an
> attempt to break down barriers between the individual and society and to try to
> find the key to the reunion of these two aspects of existence. . . . Marx discovers
> the paradigm of the future in the family . . . as a general model of the structure
> of human relations in socialist society.[16]

And here is what Marx said:

> The materialistic doctrine that men are products of circumstances . . . forgets
> that it is men that change circumstances and that the educator himself needs ed-
> ucation.[17]

The deeper problem with Marxism is that there was only one Marxist, and
he is buried in Highgate Cemetery. In his utterly subversive text *The Anti-
Christ*, Nietzsche wrote that "there has been only one Christian and he died
on the cross."[18] This is part of an involved passage in which Nietzsche casti-
gates Christians for misunderstanding Christ's teaching, for institutionalizing it politically in a church, for imposing it on frail humans incapable of
living by its precepts, and for failing to live Christ's teaching themselves,
thus perpetuating and deepening a rank hypocrisy. Above all, he says,
Christianity begets not more Christs, but the moral fanatic, whose "'glad ti-
dings' are precisely that there are no more opposites." In other words "dia-
lectics are . . . lacking," the doctrine "simply does not know how to imagine
an opinion contrary to its own."[19]

The East European communist had the same characteristics, if with less fanaticism or zeal in the recent period: misunderstanding Marx, institutionalizing this failed understanding in the ubiquitous party, imposing the doctrine in circumstances where it could not possibly succeed, proceeding to live a life of relative privilege, and thus perpetuating a system whose main characteristic was its hypocrisy. Above all, from Stalin forward, official Marxism denied the flux and human qualities of a lived history, a dialectic of opposites, in favor of a metaphysical, formulaic doctrine that "does not know how to imagine an opinion contrary to its own."

Nietzsche reserved his greatest contempt for those "Christians" who no longer believed a word of Christ's teaching but professed religion anyway and trotted off to church—so many of them in his time, indeed, that "it is indecent to be a Christian today." It is precisely this that characterized the party hack, and that has created a situation where, in most of Eastern Europe, it is indecent to be a communist today. The indecency was in the corrosive rot spread throughout the system precisely by the nonbelievers holding power, at the point of the knout. The result today is predictable: just as Nietzsche thought he would see the last Christian in his own lifetime, many people now think they will soon see the last Marxist. I expect them to be as wrong today as Nietzsche was a century ago.

Marx was the founder of a way of thought, and in that sense was an original, a genius. By and large the followers do not measure up, almost by definition because they *are* followers, concerned with not straying from some procrustean straight-and-narrow, or with announcing a partial interpretation of his thought as immutable truth.

Is there anything left of "Marxism"? There is still Marx's lifework, the critique of capitalism. We and most of the world now live under, or soon will, a single regime of capitalism. Is the critique still useful?

A couple of examples of a Marxian insight later rendered into fine scholarship will serve us in good stead in figuring out why, in fact, the American system is limited in what it can offer democratic revolutions abroad: it can offer the market, but not its form of liberal politics.

In an essay entitled "Bastiat and Carey," Marx argued that the North Americans belonged to:

> a country where bourgeois society did not develop on the foundation of the feudal system, but developed rather from itself; where this society appears not as the surviving result of a centuries-old movement, but rather as the starting-point of a new movement; where the state, in contrast to all earlier national formations, was from the beginning subordinate to bourgeois society, to its production, and never could make the pretence of being an end-in-itself; where, finally, bourgeois society itself, linking up the productive forces of an old world with the enormous natural terrain of a new one, has developed to hitherto unheard-of dimensions . . . , and where, finally, even the antitheses of bourgeois society itself appear only as vanishing moments.[20]

This is the kernel idea behind the best comparative politics account of the American system, Louis Hartz's *Liberal Tradition in America,* and behind Hartz's neglected text on the developing world, *The Founding of New Societies.*[21]

When Marx thought about European democracy, he thought about the French Revolution, and about the German failure or inability to host a similar revolution, and especially about Hegel. Hegel's writings anticipated the essence of pluralist arguments as they were later developed by political scientists, and thus Marx's critique extended from Hegel to the general conception of representative democracy.

It is little remembered that Marx located the Hegelian conception not just in Hegel's tacit presumption of capitalist property relations, untouched by the flux of politics, but in a specific German configuration of "late" development. "The struggle against the German present is the struggle against the past of modern nations," Marx said. "We Germans have lived our future history in thought, in *philosophy.* What for advanced nations is a *practical* quarrel with modern political conditions is for Germany, where such conditions do not yet exist, a *critical* quarrel with their reflection in philosophy." What is his point? That Germany "did not pass through the intermediate stages of political emancipation at the same time as modern nations. . . . How is Germany, in one *salto mortale,* to override its own limitations but also those of modern nations. . . ?" The German state was the result of only *"partial* victories over the Middle Ages." Hegel's state was an amalgam of the feudal, the organic, and the democratic. Whereas in England and France "it is a question of the solution," in Germany, Marx said, "it is only a question of the collision."[22]

Hegel implicitly recognized this amalgam, and the impending collision, but hoped to overcome both through extolling the historic role of the middle class: and if it did not exist, or existed imperfectly, then, in Hegel's words, it was "a prime concern of the state that a middle class should be developed." If Hegel dwelt on romantic notions mingling an old organic conception of the state with the modern parliamentary form, while fostering a middle class that would prepare a new bourgeois synthesis, for Marx this merely indicated "late development," something that was bound to pass because it had passed in England and America.

It is obvious that this is the starting point for one of the finest texts in comparative history, Barrington Moore's analysis of three paths to modernity, each hinged dramatically on the relative weight of the middle class, with a mostly implicit assumption that the three paths correlated with early, late, and Stalinist industrialization (the respective paths taken by the English, the Germans and Japanese, and the Soviets or Chinese). As Moore says in his preface, there is something called the bourgeois revolution,[23] which produced parliamentary democracy, and it happened in England, France, and the United States. This emphasis on timing and on amalgams of lord, peasant, and bourgeois deeply influenced the Hartzian notion that the Latin

American amalgam brings together, but never fully realizes, a North European, an Iberian, and an indigenous politics (liberal, corporate, and nativist models in a mix, to put it simply).[24]

Born free in an unfree world, the North American cannot grasp the *Sturm und Drang* that marked the birth of liberal politics—nor grasp the revolutionary project itself. Not knowing feudalism, the North American cannot know socialism, but instead takes liberalism to be the natural form—God-given—and seeks to impose it elsewhere, only to be frustrated.

This somewhat involved argument is, in my view, the best place to start in a responsible assessment of the prospects for democracy in "postcommunist" Eastern Europe. As Fredric Jameson and Zygmunt Bauman have argued (from different premises),[25] the communist party was the instrument of radical intellectuals determined to transform their societies in the model of Western Europe, but without the "necessities" in the form of developed working and middle classes and the "regime of high productivity and advanced technology" envisaged by Marx as the precondition for revolution (and which "wishful thinking cannot conjure into being").[26] Thus they used party and state to substitute for and to build these necessities, only to find their project a failure four decades later.

Today, quite predictably, their place has been taken by yet more intellectuals determined to use newly found power to introduce liberal democracy and market mechanisms. A kind judgment based on the above analysis would suggest that their way will not be easy; here is Jameson's unkind prognosis (p. 250):

> In effect, what follows the abdication by the Party . . . is a vacuum in the state which is at once, but only provisionally, filled by the spectacle of intellectuals, or the intelligentsia itself, in power; some future Marx may outdo the analogous pages of *The Eighteenth Brumaire* in satirizing the euphoria with which this caste celebrates and seals the acquisition of its own professional guild-values ("freedom" of speech and "free" elections) and then aimlessly confronts its production crisis. . . .

If by this account the prospects for liberalism are slim, what about the prospects for "the market"?

ONE CHEER FOR THE MARKET

Like Hartz and Moore, Karl Polanyi's work similarly stood on Marx's shoulders; like them he was not "a Marxist." He has much to tell us about where our world-in-flux is going.

In *The Great Transformation*, Polanyi sought to understand the coming of the Second World War: the breakdown of world order, the end of the "hundred years' peace," and the collapse of nineteenth-century civilization, manifest in the First World War but especially in the Great Depression of the

1930s. He found the cause of this crisis precisely in today's panacea for "postcommunism," in the reigning doctrine of American and British political economy: the Smithean thesis on the unregulated market, which was "fount and matrix" of the old system. The idea of a self-adjusting market, Polanyi wrote, "implied a stark utopia": it could not exist for long "without annihilating the human and natural substance of society"; in its industrial form it would have "destroyed man and transformed his surroundings into a wilderness," unless society "took measures to protect itself."[27]

The "Hundred Years' Peace," he thought, was due to a strong "peace interest" on the part of *haute finance* and the concert of powers in Europe. Wars between and upon small countries—which went on throughout the nineteenth century—could be isolated and contained. War between the big powers was, however, a dire threat, because it threatened the system of world trade. Thus "trade had become linked with peace."[28] Polanyi treated World War I as an unfortunate nineteenth-century war, the results of which further undermined the old system. But only with the end of the gold standard and the proliferation of autarkies in the 1930s did the nineteenth-century system collapse.

The Great Transformation was written at the end of what E. H. Carr called the twenty-years' crisis. It was meant as a caution to the postwar world *not to forget*, and thus not to constitute the world again on the basis of the unregulated market. A sense of crisis permeates the book, all the more so since when he published it in 1944, Polanyi's own people (Hungarian Jewry) were facing extermination.[29]

By "market" Polanyi always meant a system that was capitalist (production for profit rather than use) and that had an inherent tendency toward expansion (who says market says world market). Thus his understanding of the motive force of capitalism was a "circulationist" one: production for profit in a world market. The invention of industry, however, gave to the ups and downs of this market a great new velocity, speeding it around the planet and encompassing more and more of the "backward areas."

This expansion is of the market, not political imperialism. Unlike Lenin, Polanyi saw no necessity in imperialism. Empires carve up the world market into currency blocs and impose irrational barriers; "fast communications turned colonies into an expensive luxury." The avatar of the world system, for Polanyi, was really the anti-imperialist and card-carrying charter internationalist, Woodrow Wilson.[30] By "society" Polanyi meant the actions people take to subordinate and control the market, ranging from poor laws to the minimum wage, Corn Laws to "nontariff barriers," bread laws to industrial unions, utopian to "actually existing" socialism, from the Keynesian mechanisms of the New Deal to the autarky of fascist political economy.

What would Polanyi have to tell us today, when the events of the 1980s seem to trumpet the virtues of the market and to announce the death of socialism, in the precise sense Nietzsche meant when he said a century ago that God is dead (i.e., Christianity isn't dead historically; it has died as a way to grip men's minds). We live in the most bourgeois period in world history, when neither the reaction of the landed aristocracy nor the progressivism of socialists places a significant brake on capitalism. It is not just that East European Stalin-style socialism died a deserving death; in the citadels of capitalism the market reigns, and everything else seems silenced. Democratic socialism mimics Reaganism and Thatcherism, the idea of industrial unions is dead, the New Deal is dead, the Democratic Party has no program, the British Labour Party has none either, and hardly anyone believes that anything good can be achieved through the architecture of politics. The most political people of our time, those in Eastern Europe, are the best example: audacious and creative in ways to bring down the *ancien régime*, their best thought of what to do next is to copy Western parliamentary and market systems. Be that as it may, at this juncture it would seem that Polanyi is the last place one would turn for a prognosis on our future.

But Polanyi's optic gives us a different way of thinking about the demise of Stalinism. His position is that only one world system exists, the world market. When it collapsed in the 1930s, "society" reacted on the international level in the form of nations withdrawing from the system, always in idiosyncratic ways: National Socialism, the Greater East Asia Co-Prosperity Sphere, the Stalinist autarky. The Bolshevik Revolution was perhaps an accidental outcome of World War I; in any case, the real Soviet revolution came with Stalin and his "socialism in one country," and above all with the forced-pace industrialization of the 1930s, accomplished mostly on a self-reliant basis.

This was also a form of "late" industrial development, expressing the Soviet version of the hell-bent-for-leather race toward industrial might that has occupied the world since the middle of the last century. The Stalinist program was the most furious example of "late" industrialization, in which the state occupies almost the whole market, private property disappears, and "society" in the form of central planners, bureaucracies, and the *nomenklatura* supplants the market's function in delivering goods and services.

This 1930s revolution was the most violent in history, and yet paradoxically brought the Soviet Union to its most influential position in the world: it "emerged as the representative of a new system which could replace market economy," its industrialization appearing to less modern nations as an "amazing success."[31]

When combined with the Soviet defeat of Hitler's legions, in the early postwar period this system seemed to have some talismanlike power to transform backwardness overnight and confer national power. The system was imposed with brute force in Eastern Europe (although not without significant domestic support, depending on the country), but its power is more evident in Stalinism becoming a model for the industrialization of countries where the revolutions were indigenous: China, Vietnam, North Korea, Cuba, and several more. Stalinism had nothing to do with the humane ideals of Marxism and socialism; it had much to do with finding an alternative to the ravages of the market and dependency on the advanced capitalist economies (as perceived in Havana, Beijing, Hanoi); above all, it was a way to "catch up."

When the People's Republic of China was founded, the leadership decided to catch up by following the Stalinist heavy-industry-first model. When Mao became disenchanted with the Soviet model, he inaugurated the Great Leap Forward: a program designed to "catch up" with Britain in fifteen years. At the same time, North Korea launched the *Ch'ŏllima* movement, named for a horse that could leap one thousand *li* at a jump. When Mao died, his successors began the program of the Four Modernizations, designed to make China into a modern nation by the year 2000. In Eastern Europe, too, Stalinism meant simultaneous development of heavy industrial bases in every country, rather than a transnational division of labor. (On reflection, it was an odd way to run an empire.) All were to become industrialized in the Valhalla of Stalinism, from Poland to Cuba to Guinea-Bissau, and swiftly, swiftly.

The result a generation later is a ruthless destruction of the environment and a tawdry, depressing urban modernism that would have scandalized Polanyi or Marx. And none of these countries have "caught up." Instead, Stalinist development was a kind of *wall*, not just to keep out the West, like the real Berlin Wall, but to hide underdevelopment and husband resources. If it was a wall erected against the backwash of the Depression in the 1930s, it became a barrier against the reality of postwar wealth in the capitalist world, a way to keep out the technologies and commodities that "batter down all Chinese walls."

But what is evident today was not evident in the 1940s, nor was it incipient until perhaps the mid-1960s. In a country like Czechoslovakia, which had its own industrial development before World War II and a background of democracy, Stalinism fit like a rough peasant's glove on the hand of a ballerina. Elsewhere in the Soviet bloc, however, modernization came under the rude auspices of Stalinism, and until 1970 or so it still seemed to "work." (North Korea, for example, had a higher per capita income and much greater industrial development than South Korea in 1970.)

Furthermore, and this is crucial, there was enough industrial development in most socialist states to change peasants into workers, rural dwellers into urbanites, and their children into middle class consumers, or would-be consumers. Those "children" appeared first, and predictably, in Hungary and Czechoslovakia (see, for example, the film *Time Stands Still*, about James Dean style rock-and-rollers in a 1950s Hungarian high school). They are appearing last, perhaps, in Mongolia, where a rock band was part of the vanguard of that 1989 revolution. When I turn on MTV in 1990, I can see the aspirations of East European youths: Walkman jammed in the ears, blue jeans, Reebok shoes, Michael Jackson. They are like our youth; they just have fewer creature comforts.

The wall of Stalinism was always more permeable than people in the West imagined, but what brought it down was the latest industrial revolution: high technology communications, information systems, computers, and the application of the new techniques to industry. And, of course, what is carried on the circuits: consumer pop culture. A recent traveler reported that even in Nepal, street urchins tag at the sleeves of Westerners, shouting "Michael Jackson, Michael Jackson." This revolution made closed-system, self-reliant industrial development obsolete. If a country like North Korea shows that it is still possible in the 1990s to "jam" the new technologies assaulting Stalin's walls, it also shows that a failure to adapt those new technologies to production, or to the development of human capital (home computers, etc.), condemns one to stagnation.

Timothy Garton Ash called the recent upheavals "tele-revolutions," which they were, and they were vetted through global networks like CNN and the typical commentary of the American liberal anchorperson. Witness the demonstrators: whether they were disciplined East Germans marching in Leipzig every Monday night, courageous communists in the Romanian Army tracking down evil communists in the "Securitate," or Lithuanians giving Gorbachev hell—they all wanted freedom, they all wanted to be just like us.

One had to read the fine print in our paper of record to discover such an alternative interpretation: "As [Hans] Modrow explained to Mr. Baker, the push for unification from East Germans is being driven . . . not by visions of a grand Germany, but visions of videocassette recorders."[32] Or this interpretation, at the tag end of a long article: "In [businessman] Mr. Summers's view an independent Lithuania (or Estonia, or Latvia for that matter) would be able to attract capital—and modern factories—from nearby Scandinavia. "Where else," he asks, "can you hire high-quality labor for one-eighth the wage of South Koreans?"[33] This is how the market expands, now to encompass a whole new mass of consumers, and by no means against their will.

What is left after the end of Stalinism and cold war bipolarity is, of course, the possibility of intercapitalist conflict. Yet through the optic of the world market we can see a "peace interest" today like that of the nineteenth century: it is not just that the "antisystem" now wants to join up; we also find several great powers of roughly equivalent weight, with a stronger interest in creating wealth than in accumulating power. This constitutes our "one cheer for the market."

It is remarkable that in 1986 Britain, France, and Italy were all economies of about $800 billion GDP; allegedly gargantuan West Germany was at $950 billion.[34] The addition of East Germany, it now seems, will not do much for the German economy except in the long run; in the short run it may be a drain. In other words, it is unlikely that one nation will have its way in Europe, given that the other industrial economies, whether alone or in concert, are also formidable. This augers well for a genuinely cooperative European Community.

The United States and Japan do tower over other industrial economies in their respective regions. (Japan has a GDP of nearly $2 trillion, compared with South Korea's nearly $200 billion, one-half the size of Spain's. No economy comes close to the United States in the Americas.) But Japan and the United States are so interdependent, the American market is still so essential to Japan, that "trilateral" cooperation is much more likely than conflict and the emergence of regional blocs (about which there is much punditry).

The existence of nuclear weapons carries its own inherent "peace interest." These weapons have never been used against nations possessing them, owing to the principle sometimes called "Mutual Assured Destruction." All the industrial countries either have nuclear weapons or can acquire them in short order. A small quiver of such weapons and reasonably up-to-date means of delivery are all that is needed for effective deterrence, quite unlike the nineteenth century.

Finally, the very idiosyncracies through which the 1930s "withdrawals" were defined, and that produced fascism, no longer exist.[35] European regimes before World War II were not completed democracies, but embodied more or less liberal political form simultaneously with the intersection or "triangulation" of continued agrarian or aristocratic dominance, the incipient emergence of an industrial revolution with novel technologies (telephones, automobiles—consumer durables produced for mass consumption), and "the imaginative proximity of social revolution."[36]

If Western Europe's ultimate trajectory was liberal, that was not certain until 1945. Until that time liberal progressivism had to contend with romantic reaction on the right and social revolution on the left, both of them antimarket: the conjuncture embodied "a still usable classical past, a still indeterminate technical present, and a still unpredictable political future." The Second World War finished off this conjuncture, according to Perry Anderson, leaving universal bourgeois democracy in Western Europe. The revolutionary prospect faded away—bequeathing a "closure of horizons: without an appropriable past, or imaginable future, in an interminably recurrent present." This, at least for Anderson, is the contemporary terminus of the bourgeois revolution: what is celebrated now in Eastern Europe is for him "an oppressively stable, monolithically industrial, capitalist civilization."[37]

The moral valence Anderson attaches to contemporary liberalism is perhaps not widely shared. I cite his analysis to show why the "discourse of eternal distrust" is likely to fade in regard to Japan and Germany: they had their democratic revolutions, even if it took World War II to get them.

But then what is there of value in Polanyi's critique, now that fascism and Stalinism have vanished in Europe, and in the wealthiest industrial countries in general? What he still has to offer, I would argue, is a rich appreciation of the limits of the market in promoting equitable economic growth, a daunting analysis of the destructive effects of industry on the environment (whether industry is socialist or capitalist in form), and a cogent understanding of how liberal politics has come about—an understanding that refutes American universalism. In short, Polanyi's analysis brings into question the assumption that the fall of socialism will result in a universal move toward liberalism. What took place through more than two centuries of violent conflict in the West, and which culminated in the catastrophe of the middle of the twentieth century, may mean a traumatic passage in the rest of the world before it can happen, if it ever does.

Perhaps the best example of the latter point is East Asia, where we find many competitive industrial societies but only one liberal democracy— Japan's—and that country's democratic revolution was achieved the hard way.

THE EAST IS STILL RED

Perhaps it took a Deng Xiaoping or a Saddam Hussein to remind us that Eurocentrism is provincialism. The years 1989 and 1990 were euphoric with news of the end of the cold war, the demise of Stalinism, and the unification not just of Germany, not just of Europe, but of the world. With peace and good will breaking out everywhere, perhaps even the glimmering light of a "peace dividend" might be found at the end of the tunnel of American military Keynesianism. The invasion of Kuwait burst that last illusion in the summer of 1990, just as the bullets ricocheting on Changan Boulevard in June 1989 had announced earlier that the rumored death of Stalinism was, at the least, premature.

Outside of Europe "actually existing socialism" persists, above all in "the East." There is no break yet in Asian communism, with the predictable exception of Mongolia. China thus announced that "the center of socialism has moved East."

The East is forever being viewed through lenses forged and polished in the West. A deep, pervasive, and often unconscious "Orientalism" brings the familiar into focus just as it obscures indigenous authenticity. It is no curiosity that the original political model used by Western experts to interpret the "People's Republics" in China, Korea, and Vietnam was the East European one of "people's democracies." That is, the PRC, the DPRK, and the DRV were impositions of a Soviet-derived system lacking legitimate revolutionary credentials. Wlodzimierz Brus saw the people's democracy form as "a *model* [sic] of socialist structure," a transplantation and "concentrated form" of Stalinism; he also refers to the people's democracies as "brutal instruments of foreign domination," opposed ipso facto to nationalist ideologies of legitimation.[38] This was the dominant paradigm of interpretation, the accepted wisdom, about China and Vietnam throughout the 1950s and early 1960s. It was unlearned very slowly, and only through the clear emergence of the Sino-Soviet conflict, the many labors of Asian scholars, and the long debate on Vietnam. It remains today the dominant interpretation of the Democratic People's Republic of Korea.

In nearly all the Western literature, North Korea is depicted as a classic Soviet satellite and puppet in the 1940s and 1950s; only in the late 1950s did the DPRK flirt with emulating another foreign model, the Chinese, and only in the 1960s did it seek an independent path to building socialism. Few grant that North Korea even in the recent period has developed much independence, and until Gorbachev began rapping Kim Il Sung's knuckles, it was routinely called a Soviet satellite.

North Korea is also thought to fit the East European pattern, especially the East German one, better than any other Asian example. Both "belong to the imposed variety," according to Robert C. Tucker. Contrasted to this would be Russia, China, Vietnam, Yugoslavia, Albania, and Cuba, where the revolutions took place "fundamentally as an indigenous process involving a substantial level of mass participation." Tucker hypothesized that the imposed regimes would have problems of legitimacy, would be dependent on Soviet succor, and would not reflect native national-cultural "domestication."[39]

DPRK internal politics is thought to be as Soviet-influenced as any European socialist regime, a pure form of "Stalinism in the East."[40] This is given an added fillip with the assumption, most often tacit, that Stalinism itself is "Oriental," and that Maoism and above all "Kimilsungism" were wretched excesses of the Stalinist-Orientalist tendency. One can hear this from Soviet as well as American specialists, and from British leftists. Trotsky, Bukharin, Isaac Deutscher, and Karl Wittfogel all likened Stalin to Eastern potentates, especially Genghis Khan and Tamerlane, and thought his system a species of Oriental despotism, the worst features of the Asiatic mode of production coming to the fore. It is stunning to see Trotsky open his biography of Stalin with a first sentence remarking that the old revolutionist, Leonid Krassin, "was the first, if I am not mistaken, to call Stalin an 'Asiatic'"; and he goes on to talk about "Asiatic" leaders as cunning and brutal, presiding over static societies with a huge peasant base.[41] Perry Anderson once wrote of the theory of the "Asiatic mode of production" that in the night of our ignorance, all forms take on the same hue; in this case, the portrait contains the "people's democracy" model, Stalinism, Genghis Khan, Tamerlane, Mao Zedong, and Kim Il Sung.

With the demise of the "people's democracies" in Europe, the *Wall Street Journal*, predictably, ran an article by Nick Eberstadt under the title "The Coming Collapse of North Korea."[42] Strange, therefore, that the most recalcitrant outpost of communism today is in North Korea, which seems almost a museum of 1950s–60s revolutionary socialism. Today it is the most interesting communist nation, because it is the last unadulterated redoubt of what all the others used to be: the last communist, like Nietzsche's last Christian. So, we will direct more attention to it than to the other candidate for imminent collapse, which is not all that close to collapse either, as Nicholas Lardy suggests in his essay in this volume.

The simplest answer for the seeming anomaly of persisting Asian communism is the Chinese claim that "the center of socialism has moved East." It may in fact have moved there after World War II, or perhaps even in the

1930s. Only three Marxist-Leninist revolutions won power in any part of Europe: the Bolshevik, as an outcome of World War I, and the Yugoslav and Albanian, as an outcome of World War II. The Russian Revolution belongs to the history of "the West," the hoped-for "spark" of more such revolutions in Europe. But the European revolution died in Germany shortly thereafter, and there has not been a serious threat of indigenous Marxist-Leninist revolution since.

Yugoslavia and Albania belong to the "Eastern" or, more properly, the "Third World" pattern of Marxism-Leninism mingled with guerrilla warfare and revolutionary nationalism; and power was conquered indigenously against opponents far weaker than the middle-class parties of Western Europe. But the example par excellence is the Chinese revolution, of which the Vietnamese and Korean revolutions were in many ways extensions. The core revolutionaries found success in organizing not the small proletariat of the cities but the vast masses of the countryside; their appeals centered on the land question, and on resistance to foreign imperialism. Thus Western observers could not decide if they were communists, "agrarian reformers," or nationalists. They were all three, but in any case no one thought to ask such a question about East Germany or Czechoslovakia.

Once in power the Asian Marxist revolutionaries became Weberian: they all adopted the "Soviet model" of high bureaucratized power, central planning, and minimal role for the market. In the East, too, this model proved adept at "late" development of the third industrial revolution but a failure in going beyond it. Nonetheless, all those of the Third World pattern are still standing as communist systems, even Yugoslavia (or at least Serbia), in spite of economic crisis and near ethnic bifurcation; and also Cuba, despite its being a little island off the coast of Florida, a once-and-future dependency of Miami.

This is not to say that these systems do not feel deeply threatened by the events of 1989. The response of Asian communisms to the collapse of the East European system was publicly muted; privately they were terrified and panicked. (Only the Laotian communists acknowledged this publicly, however, saying that 1989 was a terrible year for socialism.)

The most reformist of these systems is probably Vietnam. It has taken dramatic steps both internally and externally in recent months: pulling its army out of Cambodia, turning away from the Soviet model of industrialization, handing nearly 80 percent of the land over to private ownership, courting ties with Japan and the Asian NICs. Visitors note a surprising degree of openness as part of the *doi moi* (renovation) by which the reforms are known. The leadership has some of China's problems in trying to balance economic and political reforms, but none of its political instability. Its weak economy necessitated remarkable dependency on the Soviet Union recently, and now Soviet aid is ending; but it is unlikely that central power will be threatened. Perhaps the euphoria and legitimacy won by defeating the world's greatest power fifteen years ago still have not worn off; perhaps also the capitalist fleshpot we knew as Saigon can return to life as a Southeast Asian entrepôt, if with an inapposite name: Ho Chi Minh City.

The most predictable reforms came in Mongolia, where Moscow's influence was greatest, but not without surrealism and postmodern flourishes. Here we have the Bulgaria of Asia, getting Soviet domination for decades and liking it because the alternative was Chinese rule. Ulan Bator saw big political demonstrations last year, punctuated not by bullets but by a rock-and-roll group called The Honk, and Golden Horde cries of "Mongols to your horses." Meanwhile they still love Lenin, who kept China at bay.

China is the subject of other papers in this volume, and so I will limit myself to a few comments. The PRC is, of course, distinguished by having followed Erich Honecker's "Chinese solution" in June 1989, before Honecker thought of it. (It was probably the disastrous result of Deng's solution that encouraged Egon Krenz and others to oust Honecker rather than clean up a bloodbath.)[43] Somehow Deng, Li Peng, Yang Shangkun, and the other hard-liners (an understatement) contrived to achieve something that even Mao's Cultural Revolution could not: to demolish the legitimacy of the Chinese Revolution. Never before, I think, has the Chinese Communist Party been so widely hated as in China today; not since the Cultural Revolution has it been so isolated in the world (although China-expert George Bush's assiduous courting, the renewed Japanese investment, and some recent World Bank loans may be ending that).

China is truly between a rock and a hard place. First, until the collapse of 1989 it had gone further than any European socialist regime in economic reform and opening to the outside world; even Hungary had nothing resembling the bustling capitalism of the many coastal special economic zones (SEZs), mushrooming joint ventures, PRC–World Bank transnational planning, and the like. Second, over the past fifteen years the leadership has so eviscerated their presumed ideology ("Marxism–Leninism–Mao Zedong Thought") that their programmatic statements seem ever more foolish, especially when in the wake of the Tiananmen violence they revived many old slogans, tired programs, and even Cultural Revolution golden oldies like the "emulate Lei Feng" campaign. These blasts from the past are coincident with Li Peng trying to resuscitate foreign business interest in China's "good investment climate."

The leadership has no theory of what it is doing. Thus it is mired in a peculiar and mostly unprecedented immobilism, barely masking a schizophrenia at the level of theory and practice, and a bifurcated elite (e.g., the hero of the Tiananmen students, Zhao Ziyang, is still not purged). Marxism-Leninism–Mao Zedong Thought remains today merely a justification for one-party rule. The economic reforms hang in a balance, or along a spectrum, from a young urban and coastal crowd which is following the capitalist road blazed by the Four Tigers (Singapore, Hong Kong, Taiwan, and South Korea), an old crowd whose preferred Marxism is the Stalinist variety (central planning, heavy-industry-first), and the still-vast peasantry for whom nobody but Mao had a policy—other than that they should disappear as a class, by becoming workers, urbanites, or the latest slogan, by "getting rich." (In forty years of communism perhaps half a billion of them have done none of the above.)

All these contradictions are hardly being "correctly handled," as Mao urged, but rear their heads in the daily press. Liu Guoguang of the Academy of Sciences pledges to keep to the road of "opening to the outside world," while again regurgitating the dialectic of centralization versus decentralization (first one, then the other, then a new mix of both) through which the leaders have sought to make Stalinism work in China for forty years.[44] Liu wants markets and he wants planning. He wants "macrocontrol mechanisms" and micromarkets. He is likely to get macroproblems and microprofits.

Wu Shuqing, president of Beijing University, does not like bourgeois liberalization![45] But the past decade has shown that Chinese leaders will tolerate much more of it than the other communist states of Asia will, as long as it doesn't threaten their power, and as long as their young people do what ours now do: consume rather than protest. How else explain the prostitution in the SEZs, the circulation of X-rated videotapes, the rock-and-roll music played by teenagers, the green hair in aerosol cans available from the local black market?

Wu also remarked that "the capitalist road of primitive accumulation" was "ridden with disasters for the broad masses" (i.e., the peasants); yet this is another (Maoist) concern that Deng placed on the back burner for a decade, leading to enormous dislocations in which tens of thousands of peasants a day would arrive in Guangzhou and other big cities looking for work.

The communist system still stands in China, I would argue, because the leadership has combined the political and international gains of its revolutionary nationalism (national unity, internal discipline, China's position as a big and respected world power) with fairly adept economic reforms that undid many of the irrationalities of Stalinist centralism. But its current problems are political ones, and enough to daunt anyone; they express themselves in the muted but obvious immobilism of the statements I have just cited. One would wish them on the architects of the rape of Beijing.

For monochromal communism without schizophrenia or qualms, North Korea takes the Lenin prize. It, too, has been blanketing the party newspaper with blasts from the past, especially after the fall of Ceausescu, which seemed to unnerve the North Koreans remarkably (and for good reason, since Gorbachev did not pull the plug there, and Ceausescu had emulated Kim Il Sung). Most of Kim's texts from the 1950s have been reprinted in the past several months, along with new calls to "strengthen the mass line," new "speed campaigns to reach the heights of the Ten Great Tasks," and more moves toward installing Kim's son in power when the founder passes. The difference is that in the antiquarian, bucolic atmosphere of Pyongyang the texts have a contemporary ring. They have never been revised, the program then is the program now, and so cognitive dissonance is not a Korean problem. When Li Peng, in his statement calling a halt to martial law in China in January 1990, pledged to "unswervingly follow the socialist road," it was understood that it was, in fact, a road with innumerable potholes, hairpin turns, and cloverleaf reversals over the past several decades of Chinese "communism." In North Korea the claim to consistency is justified.

Mincing words is not a problem in Pyongyang, either. As North Korea's close European friends, the East Germany of Honecker and the Romania of Ceausescu, crumbled to the ground in late 1989, Kim Il Sung's scribes let loose one of their vintage programmatic documents, entitled "Let Us Vigorously Advance Along the Road of Socialism, Repulsing the Challenge of the Imperialists."[46] Taking off after the Fukuyamas who proclaim "the victory of the free world," the authors instead project "the inevitable doom" of capitalism and imperialism. "History does not flow from socialism to capitalism but vice versa," they quote their leader as saying, reversing the East European dictum that capitalism is the highest stage of socialism. "A person with money enjoys the freedom of buying everything, unlimited freedom of buying not only things, but also human conscience and dignity." The imperialists, they write, are "shameless" enough to ask us to open our market, but "a door flung open [will] allow the infiltration of corrupt imperialist ideology and culture."

To the Koreans the East European crisis resulted not from communism but from not enough communism: it was "a crisis resulting from the poverty of communist ideology," which should be robust and should be inculcated on a daily basis. Freedom of the press is deemed "a prelude to a counterrevolutionary riot to overthrow socialism." Instead of pluralism, they like organic politics, organic society: the whole society should be "united in one sociopolitical organism." And so North Korea will hew to its well-trod path, in a society where: "There is nobody who is exceptionally better off, nobody who goes ill-clad and hungry..., no jobless people, no people who go bankrupt and wander around begging, no drug addicts, alcoholics and fin-de-siecle faggots [sic] who seek abnormal desires."[47]

Nothing can be understood in a vacuum, "in itself," without comparison. If North Korea is not East Germany, South Korea is not West Germany—a stable, liberal polity with a strong safety net of welfare measures. Quite the contrary. Many have forgotten that South Korea had its own "Tiananmen" in Kwangju in May 1980, when somewhere between two hundred (regime figure) and two thousand (opposition figure) young people and workers were massacred by security forces. It had its own East European–style popular mobilization in June 1987, when hundreds of thousands massed in the streets and forced through direct elections for the president. There is, in fact, much more similarity than most analysts realize between the events of 1987 in Korea and those of 1989 in Eastern Europe, and between the nature of student protest in Korea and the abortive student protests in China. The similarity derives, ultimately, from similarities in the regimes that do not follow our communist-versus-capitalist distinction.

For forty years, a deadly anticommunism using prewar Japanese methods (forced confessions and political recantations, reeducation camps for political dissidents) has ruled the roost in the South. If it is a crime to be a libertine or a capitalist in North Korea, it is a crime punishable by death or lifelong imprisonment to be a communist in South Korea. The definition of communist is stretched, furthermore, to encompass everyone from opposition leader Kim Dae Jung to Catholic fathers to Buddhist priests to liberal professors. The ROK maintains huge security bureaucracies that penetrate the lives of everyone; they are more restrained today than before 1987, but they have not been dismantled. Indeed, in late 1990 it was revealed that the Army Security Command still kept files on the political activities and beliefs of some thirteen hundred political leaders. No significant political party has yet made a coalition with labor (with the exception of the South Korean Labor Party of the 1940s, which was attacked with every means available); no regime has been inclusionary of labor.

No need for all this in the North, of course; there is no opposition, at least none that scholars know about. Yet there may be as many as a hundred thousand political prisoners in work and reeducation camps.

North Korea might be vulnerable to collapse on the Romanian model, if not the German. It was Ceausescu and his Lady Macbeth of a wife who patterned their personality cult after North Korea's. But Ceausescu ruthlessly drove living standards down for a decade, something few leaders of any stripe could survive, whereas Kim has incrementally improved them in recent years. Nor do we know of significant differences between the security apparatus and the army, although they may well exist. There has been no breakaway dissent from former officials, no major new repressions that we know about, as there had been in Romania. Finally, Kim is the founder, like Castro, and will probably hold things together until he dies. It is perhaps the son, Kim Jong Il, a good facsimile of Ceausescu's profligate offspring Nicu, who will find his tenure insecure.

North Korea's main vulnerability is external, where its two biggest allies assiduously court the South, and where its diplomacy was made a shambles by the events of 1989. Nearly all the East European nations have opened relations with Seoul, as has Moscow. North Korea's political economy was in some ways the East Germany of Asia, with a comparable population (22 million in the DPRK, 18 million in the GDR) and the highest industrial proportion of GNP among the Asian communist nations. Like East Germany, North Korea had an active African and Middle Eastern diplomacy, selling weapons and sending military and intelligence advisers, economic missions, and so forth. Kim Jong Il reportedly attended school in East Germany.

There was a much closer affinity to Romania, however, especially in the common ideology of self-reliance, opposition to dependency, and nation rather than class as the unit of struggle with capitalism; in the leadership system; and in the preference for great monuments on an inhuman scale in the capital (Pyongyang has erected the tallest hotel in the world, and the tallest building in Asia, at 105 stories; shaped like the Transamerica building in San Francisco, it is empty most of the time).[48] Now North Korea has no friends in Eastern Europe save Albania, to which it was never very close, and Albania itself has begun sliding down the steep slope toward heresy. The only thing left is to heighten ties with Cuba! So Castro visited Pyongyang in 1989, and Kim and Castro now correctly see themselves as the last of a breed.

It is unlikely however, that a "Romania" will occur in North Korea, because of the security structure in which the Korean peninsula has been imbedded since the Korean War.

STILL THE COLD WAR IN KOREA

In 1949, the eminent Asianist Owen Lattimore uttered a prophetic mouthful: "Korea appears to be of such minor importance that it tends to get overlooked, but Korea may turn out to be a country that has more effect upon the situation than its apparent weight would indicate."[49] If you wish to see and remember the heyday of the cold war, today you can go to Korea: like North Korean communism, here too is a living museum. Panmunjom is best, where the American "Manchu" unit holds the line; it got its name from the Boxer intervention at the turn of the century. And just as at the dawn of the cold war, Korea is again being overlooked. Or it is viewed through lenses ground in Eastern Europe: North Korea is going to collapse.

Consider that Kim Il Sung and his top aides have shared revolutionary experiences going back to the resistance against Japan and to the Korean War, that their independently controlled army is the size of Saddam Hussein's with comparable equipment (but probably much better disciplined), that they have their own chemical weapons and budding nuclear facilities, and that the Silkworm missiles shipped to the Middle East, which some experts said were Chinese, may have been of Korean manufacture. Consider, also, that South Korea, which has a stunning record of political instability, also has a gigantic, well-armed military of its own, that it jails anyone who visits North Korea without state permission, that it retains a draconian National Security Law forbidding even praise of North Korea, and that its younger generation is so sick to death of the regime's lying that it looks longingly to that other set of liars in North Korea. Add to this the presence of 43,000 American troops and at least 150 U.S.-controlled nuclear weapons on the ground in the South. When I think of all that, I think we ought to write not about the "coming collapse" but the "coming cataclysm."

Is it really likely that North Korea will go quietly, like East Germany? It is much more likely that they will deepen their already remarkable fortress mentality, and bolster their position by any and all means. Read what the North said recently about its intentions:

> If the Soviet Union establishes "diplomatic relations" with South Korea, it will mean the formation of a tripartite alliance, with the Soviet Union joining the

U.S. and South Korea in a conspiracy to topple the socialist system in the DPRK. . . . The Korean-Soviet Treaty of Alliance will automatically be reduced to a mere name. This will leave us no other choice but to make measures to provide for ourselves some weapons for which we have so far relied upon the alliance.[50]

Whereupon the Soviets announced that they would establish diplomatic relations with South Korea.

North Korea had a nonnuclear ace up its sleeve, however, which was to play a Japan card by inviting Kanemaru Shin, kingmaker in Japan's Liberal Democratic Party, to visit Pyongyang.[51] This illustrates a subterranean current in Japanese-Korean relations. Kim Il Sung fought against Japanese imperialism while many South Korean leaders fought for it (including the current Prime Minister Kang Young Hoon and the late Park Chung Hee), whence comes an element of respect for Kim and for his always anti-Japanese republic.[52] Something else is felt about the leaders of the South. Americans can understand this if they reflect that many Vietnam veterans enjoy visiting with Viet Cong veterans, but few seek out Nguyen Van Thieu or Nguyen Cao Ky.

If Japan were to bring North Korea out of isolation, like West Germany it would reestablish ties with its former economic hinterland, where Japan built industries and extracted raw materials in the 1930s. Recently, Japanese experts have been asked to come back and work big gold mines in North Korea formerly owned by Japanese firms. Japan has dramatically deepened its investment and trade with the Asia region since 1985. Perhaps Kim Il Sung will end his career by helping to reestablish the Greater East Asia Co-Prosperity Sphere. With the USSR moving closer to the South, and to the Americans, why not?

As usual, the United States is the anachronism, persisting in a policy of isolating the North and hoping for it to collapse. Unbeknownst to most Americans, the United States still exercises operational control of the ROK Army, conducts the largest military exercises in the world in the spring of every year in South Korea, bellies up to the Korean People's Army along a portion of the DMZ, and gives every manner of support and special pleading to the South. Thus the South is rarely pressured to do anything significant in the way of reducing tension and opening relations with the North. While Gorbachev and Kanemaru wheel and deal, the State Department moves at a snail's pace, dropping its objection to North Korean scholars visiting the United States, and engaging in desultory talks with the North at a low diplomatic level in Beijing.

To the extent that Americans notice North Korea at all, it is the country they love to hate. On the "MacNeil-Lehrer News Hour," in August 1990, Edward Luttwak was well into a rendition of why Saudi Arabia was the most disgusting place on earth, when he paused to remember North Korea: sorry, that's the worst place on earth. That place, however, was the site of three years of genocidal bombing by the U.S. Air Force which killed perhaps two million civilians, dropped oceans of napalm, left barely a modern building standing, opened large dams to flood nearby rice valleys and kill thousands of peasants by denying them food, terrorized the population with simulated atomic bombing runs, and went far beyond anything done in Vietnam in a conscious program of using air power to destroy a society—a society "of a new type," as it was called in the 1950s.

This well-documented episode (by the Air Force itself)[53] is remembered in the North as if it ended yesterday, and perhaps explains some of the extremism of North Korean politics. It makes a unification like the German one, on American and South Korean terms, exceedingly unlikely. This experience, however, merits not the slightest attention or moral qualm in the United States. This is an unknown aspect of the unknown war we fought in Korea; if it is known, it is usually dismissed as unimportant to our contemporary involvement in Korea. In fact it is *our* responsibility as Americans, as teachers, as intellectuals, to reflect back on this terrible episode and to seek reconciliation with our Korean enemy.

CONCLUSION: ILLUSION AND RESPONSIBILITY

The vocation of the intellectual is to be a critic. Above all in America, if the critics are not the intellectuals, who will perform this necessary task? Instead, once the Vietnam War ended in the mid-1970s, many intellectuals merged again with the broad middle, the liberal mainstream. After a decade that raised important and continuous challenges to the powers-that-be in all walks of American life, intellectuals did what was easy (the critique of communism) instead of what was hard (the critique of one's own society). A period of critical quietism ensued when criticism should have been at its loudest, during the Indian summer of the cold war and the unregulated market in the Reagan years. The American left, itself, illustrated the trend, with its increasing interest in postmodernism, another form of quietism.[54]

Many intellectuals indulged in an ideological discourse in which they dispensed with the homegrown critique that emerged in the 1960s, measured American society against the standard of the imposed regimes of Eastern Europe, breathed a sigh of relief at our freedoms, and identified with the opponents of Stalinist rule. This identification would have been all to the good, if it had been combined with an equally critical eye cast on our own society, or that of our clients around the world such as South Korea. But it was not, at least in the writings of many of our leading lights who have championed the East European dissidents. This includes all the neoconservatives, of course, but also fine thinkers such as Susan Sontag and Philip Roth, many of those who write for the *New York Review of Books*, and all of those who write for *Commentary*.[55]

Through their writings we learned of the moral collapse of East European society, the stultifying and stupefying behavior of the party-hack politicians, the cowardice of the academics, the degradation of civic life, the crumbling infrastructure, the polluted waters, the industrial rust belts, the decaying cities: good thing we don't have any of that here in America.

As Eastern Europe came unstuck, this one-eyed bias leaped forth as a celebration of liberalism and the market. But the episode also highlights the absence of any visible political alternatives to Reaganism and Thatcherism, the twin apotheoses of liberalism and the unregulated market. In that limited sense, Fukuyama is right: not that the whole world is becoming liberal, but that we have had just two kinds of modernism, both devouring the planet. In 1989 one of them showed itself incapable of sustaining political power.

It is tribute to Barrington Moore's insight that two decades ago he hinted at the "historical obsolescence" of both Western liberalism and Soviet socialism. "Industrialism, as it continues to spread," he wrote, "may in some distant future still these voices forever and make revolutionary radicalism as anachronistic as cuneiform writing."[56] Moore reminds us that market-driven liberalism also carried a radical antipathy to all previous ways of life, and that its radical presuppositions about politics could easily give way to technocratic justifications for system maintenance and the exercise of power. In this respect he was extending Karl Polanyi's argument against unregulated liberalism.

Perhaps both Moore and Polanyi were wrong about Western liberalism. But the "Revolution of '89" has done us a big favor in clearing the Erich Honeckers from our vision, thus recentering the debate on our own society, so that these questions can again be raised.

NOTES

1. Study Group on Central and Eastern Europe, United States Institute of Peace, "Prospects for Conflict or Peace" (Washington, D.C.: Institute of Peace, May 1990), p. 1.

2. Louis Hartz, *The Liberal Tradition in America* (New York: Houghton Mifflin, 1955).

3. Shortly before he died, Mao Zedong was asked to comment on the real meaning of the French Revolution. He responded that not enough time had yet passed to know.

4. Christopher Hitchens, "How Neoconservatives Perish: Good-bye to 'Totalitarianism' and All That," *Harper's*, July 1990, pp. 65–70.

5. Richard Gardner, "The Comeback of Liberal Internationalism," *Washington Quarterly* 13:3 (Summer 1990), pp. 23–39.

6. *New York Times*, "Some Lines on the Rest of the Millennium," December 24, 1989. These opinions were expressed in a symposium on predictions for the 1990s in the *Times*.

7. Joseph Nye, Jr., *New York Times*, October 3, 1990; Paul Kennedy, *The Rise and Fall of the Great Powers* (New York: Random House, 1987).

8. William Pfaff, *Barbarian Sentiments: How the American Century Ends* (New York: Hill and Wang, 1989), p. 3.

9. Murray Sayle, "Bowing to the Inevitable," *Times Literary Supplement*, April 28, 1989.

10. I first heard of Francis Fukuyama when Allan Bloom invited him to lecture at the University of Chicago in the spring of 1989; shortly thereafter, the lecture appeared as "The End of History?" *The National Interest* 16 (Summer 1989).

11. Fukuyama, "The End of History."

12. Charles Krauthammer "Democracy Has Won," *Washington Post*, March 24, 1989, p. 23.

13. The literature here is immense, but for an example of the blinders and disarray of the American left, see the account of a conference on "Socialist Upheaval and the U.S. Left," by Elizabeth Martinez, in *Z Magazine*, September 1990, pp. 60–63; and for a cogent, but I think romantic, view of grassroots politics of the "left" in Eastern Europe, see Mary Kaldor, "After the Cold War," *New Left Review*, March–April 1990, p. 33. Ms. Kaldor has been one of the most clear-sighted analysts of the cold war system.

14. Samir Amin, "The Future of Socialism," *Monthly Review*, July–August 1990, pp. 10–29. Of thirteen footnotes, twelve refer to Amin's own published work.

15. *New York Times*, July 13, 1989, comment by R. W. Apple, Jr.

16. Shlomo Avineri, *Social and Political Thought of Karl Marx* (London: Cambridge University Press, 1968).

17. Karl Marx, *The German Ideology*, 3d rev. ed. (Moscow: Progress Publishers, 1976).

18. *The Anti-Christ*, trans. R. J. Hollingdale (New York: Penguin, 1968), p. 151. Friedrich Nietzsche published *Der Antichrist* in 1895.

19. Nietzsche, *The Anti-Christ*, pp. 144–45.

20. Karl Marx, "Bastiat and Carey," in *Grundrisse: Foundations of the Critique of Political Economy*, trans. Martin Nicolaus (New York: Vintage, 1973), pp. 883–88.

21. For further elaboration of my ideas in this section, see my essay "The Abortive *Abertura*: Korean Democratization in the Light of the Latin American Experience," presented at the annual meeting of the Latin American Studies Association, March 1988, and published in *New Left Review*, March–April 1989, pp. 5–32.

22. Marx, "Critique of Hegel's Doctrine of the State," p. 116; "Critique of Hegel's Philosophy of Right," pp. 247–49, 253, both in Lucio Colletti, ed., *Karl Marx: Early Writings* (New York, 1975).

23. Barrington Moore, Jr., *Social Origins of Dictatorship and Democracy* (New York: Beacon, 1966).

24. Louis Hartz, *The Founding of New Societies: Studies in the History of the United States, Latin America, South Africa, Canada, and Australia*, 1st ed. (New York: Harcourt, Brace and World, 1964), pp. 13–33.

25. Fredric Jameson, *Late Marxism: Adorno, or, the Persistence of the Dialectic* (London and New York: Verso, 1990); Zygmunt Bauman, "Intellectuals in East-Central Europe: Continuity and Change," *Eastern European Politics and Societies* 1:2 (1987), pp. 162–86.

26. Jameson, *Late Marxism*, p. 250.

27. Karl Polanyi, *The Great Transformation* (Boston: Beacon, 1944), p. 3.

28. Ibid., pp. 14–15.

29. See in particular Polanyi's last chapter in *The Great Transformation*, "Freedom in a Complex Society," which ends with moving passages on "the three constitutive facts in the consciousness of Western man: knowledge of death, knowledge of

freedom, knowledge of society," followed by the unexpectedly Nietzschean conclusion that "life springs from ultimate resignation."

30. Ibid., pp. 22, 212.

31. Ibid., p. 247.

32. *New York Times*, December 14, 1989.

33. *New York Times*, April 19, 1990.

34. Central Intelligence Agency, *Fact Book, 1990*.

35. Polanyi, *The Great Transformation*, p. 133.

36. Perry Anderson, "Modernity and Revolution," *New Left Review*, March–April 1984, pp. 96–113.

37. Anderson, "Modernity and Revolution," p. 106.

38. Wlodzimierz Brus, "Stalinism and the 'People's Democracies,'" in Robert C. Tucker, ed., *Stalinism: Essays in Historical Interpretation* (New York: Norton, 1977), pp. 239–41, 252–53.

39. Robert C. Tucker, "Communist Revolutions, National Cultures, and Divided Nations," *Studies in Comparative Communism* 7:3 (Autumn 1974), pp. 235–45.

40. See, for example, Chong-sik Lee, "Stalinism in the East: Communism in North Korea," in Robert Scalapino, ed., *The Communist Revolution in Asia* (Englewood Cliffs, N.J.: Prentice-Hall, 1969).

41. Leon Trotsky, *Stalin*, 2d ed. (New York: Stein and Day, 1967), pp. 1–2, 358. See also Stephen Cohen, *Bukharin and the Bolshevik Revolution* (New York: Vintage, 1979), p. 291, for Bukharin's depiction of Stalin as a "Genghis Khan"; also Isaac Deutscher, *Stalin: A Political Biography* (London: Oxford University Press, 1949), p. 472: Stalin was "primitive, oriental, but unfailingly shrewd."

42. *Wall Street Journal*, June 26, 1990.

43. It was widely reported that Honecker ordered security forces to fire on demonstrators, and even readied hospitals for the expected casualties. See Timothy Garton Ash, "The German Revolution," *New York Review of Books*, December 21, 1989.

44. "Retrenchment: A Boon to Reform," *Beijing Review*, January 15–21, 1990.

45. "The Course for China's Reform and Opening," *Beijing Review*, January 1–7, 1990.

46. *Nodong Sinmun* [Worker's Daily], December 22, 1989.

47. Ibid.

48. On the affinity between Romanian and North Korean communism, see Ken Jowitt, "Moscow 'Centre,'" *Eastern European Politics and Societies* 1:3 (Fall 1987), p. 320.

49. "Transcript of Round Table Discussion on American Policy toward China," State Department, October 6–8, 1949, Carrollton Press Retrospective Collection 1977, item 316B.

50. *Minju Chosôn* [Democratic Korea], September 18, 1990.

51. *Chosôn Ilbo* (Seoul), October 1 and 2, 1990.

52. Citizens are still constantly urged to live like and follow the tradition of the anti-Japanese guerrillas. Kang and Park were both officers in the Manchurian Kwantung Army, who were then vetted through the Korean military academy in 1945–46 during the American occupation. Kang was a vice-commander of the 38th parallel region, which saw much fighting in the summer of 1949, a year before the Korean War.

53. The attacks came just after the laborious, backbreaking work of rice transplant-

ing had been done. The Air Force was proud of the destruction created: "The subsequent flash flood scooped clean 27 miles of valley below, and the plunging flood waters wiped out [supply routes, etc.]. . . . The Westerner can little conceive the awesome meaning which the loss of [rice] has for the Asian—starvation and slow death." Many villages were inundated, "washed downstream," and even Pyongyang, some 27 miles south of one dam, was badly flooded. Untold numbers of peasants died, but they were assumed to be "loyal" to the enemy, providing "direct support to the Communist armed forces." (That is, they were feeding the northern population.) The "lessons" adduced from this experience "gave the enemy a sample of the totality of war . . . embracing the whole of a nation's economy and people." This was Korea, "the limited war." See "The Attack on the Irrigation Dams in North Korea," *Air University Quarterly* 6:4 (Winter 1953–54), pp. 40–51. For an excellent account of the air war and the breaking of the dams, see Callum A. MacDonald, *War Before Vietnam* (New York: Free Press, 1987), pp. 241–42; for more documentation, see Cumings, *Origins of the Korean War*, vol. 2 (Princeton: Princeton University Press, 1990), chapter 21.

54. See the critique of postmodernism on the left in Norman Geras, *Discourses of Extremity* (New York: Verso, 1990), pp. 61–168.

55. For a good account of what I am suggesting, see Russell Jacoby, *The Last Intellectuals: American Culture in the Age of Academe* (New York: Basic Books, 1987). The exceptions to my generalization come mostly from intellectuals of the Catholic left, like Roberto Mangabiera Unger, and especially Alasdair MacIntyre, who are trying to find an alternative to what MacIntyre calls modern society's oscillation "between a freedom which is nothing but a lack of regulation of individual behavior and forms of collectivist control designed only to limit the anarchy of self-interest." See his books *After Virtue: A Study in Moral Theory* (Notre Dame: University of Notre Dame Press, 1981), p. 33, and *Whose Justice? Which Rationality?* (Notre Dame: University of Notre Dame Press, 1988).

56. Barrington Moore, Jr., *Social Origins of Dictatorship and Democracy*, pp. 505–8.

6

Intellectuals and Tiananmen:
Historical Perspective on an Aborted Revolution

ELIZABETH J. PERRY

OF ALL THE momentous political upheavals in 1989, few captured wider attention and sympathy than the Chinese democracy protests that spring. Taking full advantage of the international media (then focused on Beijing to cover first the Asian Development Bank meetings and then the Gorbachev summit), the protesters engaged in a style of political showmanship that seemed tailor-made for their new global television audience: festive marches complete with colorful banners and contemporary music, somber hunger strikes punctuated by the wail of ambulance sirens, even a twenty-seven-foot "goddess of democracy" guaranteed to strike a resonant chord with foreign viewers.

Undoubtedly this adept handling of symbolic politics contributed to the widespread publicity and enthusiasm that the Chinese democracy movement elicited around the world. The revolutions in Eastern Europe later in the year were surely stimulated in part by the Chinese example. But although the Berlin Wall came tumbling down, the walls surrounding Tiananmen Square stand more heavily fortified than ever. International opinion was obviously not sufficient to break a Chinese regime whose leadership operated according to its own political logic. Moreover, despite the apparent sophistication of the young Chinese protesters in dealing with the international media, their movement also remained for the most part within a distinctly Chinese political tradition. The shared assumptions of rulers and rebels served to reinforce preexisting authority relations, ensuring that China's democracy movement did not become its revolution of 1989.

WHY NO REVOLUTION IN 1989? THE STANDARD EXPLANATIONS

Compared with the head-spinning transformations in Eastern Europe, the Chinese outcome has been tragically anticlimactic. To account for this difference, two sorts of explanations are commonly given. The first, ironically enough, points to China's revolutionary heritage. In contrast to most of Eastern Europe, China became communist after a hard-fought civil war. Won from within, rather than imposed by alien tanks, the Chinese system was said to enjoy a much higher level of popular legitimacy than its East European counterparts.

In the early 1960s, Chalmers Johnson highlighted China's (and Yugoslavia's) indigenous revolutionary experience—which he termed "peasant nationalism"—as an explanation for the emergence of the Sino-Soviet rift.[1] At that time it seemed that nationalist revolutions had engendered independent and dynamic variants of socialism: Maoism in China, Titoism in Yugoslavia. Today, however, that same revolutionary heritage (lingering in Cuba, Vietnam, and to some extent North Korea as well) reputedly acts as a brake on further political transformation; moribund regimes cling to their revolutionary memories like a dying man to his life-support system.

If legitimacy was once the product of a revolutionary past, however, it is surely being eroded by a repressive present. Presumably, then, this explanation for contemporary political stagnation is a short-lived one; as the reservoir of popular support is drained by the heavy-handed tactics of obsolescent polities, the rulers' claim to revolutionary legitimacy is rendered less and less convincing.

A second type of explanation would seem to have more staying power. This is the view that stresses the *peasant* nature of China. Mired in poverty and ignorance, the 800 million rural dwellers are held responsible for China's political impasse. The tendency to lay the blame for tyranny at the feet of the peasantry is familiar in social science analysis on both the left and the right. Marx's attribution of the rise of Louis Napoleon to those French "potatoes in a sack" dovetails with the explanation for Third World dictatorships proffered by many a modernization theorist. Among Chinese intellectuals, this line of reasoning has been especially pronounced. Mao's cult of personality—and the resultant tragedies of the Cultural Revolution and its aftermath—are said to have sprung from the benighted peasantry's undemocratic messianic yearnings. It was these peasants, we are told, who were so attached to the anthem of the Cultural Revolution: "The East is red, The sun is rising, China has given birth to a Mao Zedong; He works for the people's happiness; He is our great savior." The same adulation that had propped up imperial despots for thousands of years was now being transferred to communist tyrants—first Mao and then Deng Xiaoping. Little wonder that democracy advocates like Fang Lizhi allude to the need to limit peasant political participation; democracy demands an enlightened citizenry—something that in China only the intellectuals claim to be.[2]

The use of peasants as convenient scapegoats is an old practice among Chinese thinkers. Whenever political change failed to occur in the desired manner, the fault could always be said to lie with the backward inhabitants of the countryside. In fact, however, most of China's twentieth-century political follies have been centered in the cities where intellectuals themselves have played a central role. Certainly this was true of the Cultural Revolution; not ignorant peasants, but educated students proved the most zealous disciples of Chairman Mao. In the post-Mao period as well, intellectuals were a bastion of support for Deng Xiaoping through much of the 1980s. History might well have taught them better. In 1957, Deng had taken charge of implementing the notorious antirightist campaign that ruined the careers of hundreds of thousands of the nation's finest intellectuals.[3] In 1979–80, Deng's harsh crackdown on the Democracy Wall movement again indicated his intolerance for intellectual criticism. Yet despite this record of repression, Chinese intellectuals continued to express great enthusiasm for Deng Xiaoping. More than peasants (most of whom have, after all, benefited materially from Deng's agrarian reforms), it is the intellectuals whose complicity in despotism seems based less on realistic interests than on traditional patterns of authority.

INTELLECTUAL TRADITIONALISM

To explain the weaknesses of China's democracy movement, one must not stop with her revolutionary heritage or peasant population. The very people who launched the Tiananmen protest—urban intellectuals—were perhaps the greatest fetter on its further development. The seemingly cosmopolitan and contemporary style of the demonstrations masked a deeper reality that was essentially Chinese.

Educated Chinese have tended to identify closely with the regime in power. For much of imperial history, this identification was of course institutionalized in the examination system; the highest honor for a Confucian scholar was to win an official position by an outstanding examination performance. While a vigorous tradition of remonstrance did develop among Chinese intellectuals, it remained for the most part within officially prescribed channels. In contrast to early modern Europe, an alienated academy did not emerge in China until the twentieth century under foreign tutelage. The May Fourth Movement of 1919 revealed the explosive potential of this new critical stance, but it was a short-lived Enlightenment indeed. The tendency for subsequent generations of Chinese intellectuals to invoke the May Fourth model—most recently on the seventieth anniversary of that historic occasion—reflects nostalgia for a truncated event rather than the completion of its critical mission.[4] Contemporary intellectuals have fallen into the trap that the literary critic Lo Changpei so presciently warned against on the eve of liberation in 1949: "The old tune of May Fourth cannot be replayed. . . . Without May Fourth, we would not have the present. If we continue to grasp forever at the spirit of May Fourth, we will have no future."[5] In trying to imitate the May Fourth exemplar, recent generations of intellectuals have been guilty of the same "emperor-worship mentality"—characterized by submission to a familiar pattern of ceremonial politics—against which the May Fourth Movement was directed.

A dramatic example of this recycling of tradition was seen on April 22, 1989, the day of government-scheduled memorial services for former Party General Secretary Hu Yaobang. As they had on many previous occasions (e.g., the Qingming remembrance for the late Premier Zhou Enlai thirteen years earlier, which sparked the momentous Tiananmen Incident of April 5, 1976), students managed to convert an official ceremony into a counter-hegemonic performance.[6] The inversion of state rituals has been used to considerable effect by protesters in other parts of the world as well, of course.[7] In taking charge of the occasion (in the Chinese case by claiming control of the official site for such events, Tiananmen Square), the demonstrators are aable to challenge the legitimacy of the regime and gain a forum for conveying their own political messages. Yet a striking feature of the April 22 counter-ceremony was its adherence to traditionally sanctioned modes of behavior. Three student representatives attempted—in the age-old manner of Chinese scholarly remonstrance—to present a petition demanding an explanation for the ouster of the late general secretary, Hu Yaobang, and a meeting with the current premier, Li Peng. Denied entrance to the Great Hall of the People, the young emissaries suddenly fell to their knees and began to kowtow. Embarrassed officials eventually opened the doors, allowing the students to present their petition to a low-ranking functionary, who summarily rejected the demands.[8] The obsequious demeanor of the petitioners was a stark reminder of the degree to which contemporary intellectuals remain bound to traditional styles of protest.

Perry Link, a specialist in Chinese literature who was an eyewitness to the memorial demonstration, offers an insightful account:

> ... the students knelt on the steps of the People's Hall and asked the Premier, "Will you just come out and see us, just give us your acknowledgement of our trying to be patriotic and trying to help?" From our point of view the demand for dialogue with somebody might not really have punch. But for them it was really important, and in fact I can view that whole square through those thrilling days of April and May as a Beijing Opera Stage... in that morally charged Beijing Opera sense... when one after another unit would come out, and say, "Here we are with our banner." This to me meant two things. It meant literally, "We have shown up," but it also meant, "We have presented ourselves in this drama."[9]

The presentation of banners representing one's unit was both a theatrical convention and a standard form of protest.[10] It was, moreover, a tradition not confined to Beijing. When a delegation of graduate students from the Shanghai Academy of Social Sciences attempted on May 25 to present their banner to the Shanghai Garrison Command,[11] the scene was reminiscent of the presentation by the Shanghai workers' militia of their banner to Chiang Kaishek following a major labor uprising in the spring of 1927.[12] In all these instances, the protesters were in effect seeking recognition from the ruling authorities of their unit's place on the political stage.

THE LIMITS OF TRADITION

To be sure, the protesting units had changed somewhat since the Republican period. Although schools remained central, gone now were the native-place associations, guilds, and professional societies that had served as the building blocks of urban unrest during the first half of this century. Thanks to the reordering that took place under communism, in 1989 many of the participating groups were the *danwei* (units) created by the state itself. In fact, at one point members of more than ten organs directly under the Central Committee of the Chinese Communist Party—including the Propaganda Department—could be counted among the marchers.[13]

The incestuous relationship between state and society that had developed as a consequence of communism rendered familiar forms of protest ineffective. Although *danwei* could serve as a vehicle to mobilize millions of people for a Tiananmen demonstration, the fact that these units (whether schools, factories, or party organs) were ultimately dependent on the state for their very survival meant that they could easily be *de*mobilized once the state leadership was united in its determination to take action. The frailty of "civil society" in contemporary Chinese cities, even when compared with the late imperial and Republican scene,[14] has made much of the old protest repertoire anachronistic. Lacking autonomy from state domination, urbanites restage the pageant of May Fourth without the *social* power that invigorated the initial performance.

The actors in the most recent rendition of this continuing drama were certainly capable of putting on an exciting show. Joseph Esherick and Jeffrey Wasserstrom, who have characterized the 1989 protest as "street theater: untitled, improvisational" but following a "historically established 'repertoire' of collective action,"[15] offer the following judgment:

> Once one recognizes the movement as an instance of political theater, it becomes tempting to rate the performances. One of the best acts was put on by Wuer Kaixi in the May 18th dialogue with Li Peng. The costuming was important: he appeared in his hospital pajamas. So, too, was the timing: he upstaged the Premier by interrupting him at the very start. And props: later in the session, he dramatically pulled out a tube inserted into his nose (for oxygen?) in order to make a point. Especially for young people in the nationwide television audience, it was an extraordinarily powerful performance.[16]

But if the theatrics were first rate, the politics were less impressive. A particularly disappointing feature of this self-styled "democracy" movement was its fickle search for patrons. Hu Yaobang, posthumous hero to the students of 1989, had been vilified in the huge demonstrations that broke out during his tenure as general secretary just a few years earlier. In the winter of 1986–87, a popular protest slogan had called for the overthrow of Hu Yaobang, comparing him unfavorably to the Gang of Four of Cultural Revolution notoriety.[17] Yet once Hu was ousted in January 1987, and particularly after his death from a heart attack April 15, 1989, he became a martyr to the movement. Hu's successor as general secretary, Zhao Ziyang, now suffered the wrath of the students. Whereas Hu had been criticized for his buffoonery, Zhao was attacked for the corruption of his children.[18] Even so, when Zhao deigned to visit the hunger strikers in Tiananmen Square on May 19, he became an instant hero, with students clamoring for his autograph. And just as soon as Zhao was deposed, he too attained martyrdom status.

While it would be grossly unfair to accuse the 1989 activists of anything close to the degree of adulation that surrounded Mao's cult of personality during the Cultural Revolution, nevertheless the longing for heroes remained disturbingly evident. Among many young intellectuals, this tendency found expression in support for the doctrine of New Authoritarianism (*xin quanweizhuyi*), which looked to a political strongman—in the tradition of Chiang Kaishek in Taiwan or Park Chung Hee in South Korea—to push forward the economic reform. While there were important differences among advocates of this doctrine,[19] a number of its adherents played a leading role in the early stages of the 1989 demonstrations.[20] To them, state strengthening was the sine qua non of democracy—an argument which, as Andrew Nathan has shown, has been common among Chinese "democrats" since the late nineteenth century.[21] But whereas earlier generations lived under imperial and republican regimes that were indeed too weak to effect the economic and political transformation of which young activists dreamed, the current dilemma is of an entirely different sort. Genuine change will almost certainly require breaking, not buttressing, the state's tentacles of control.

The students' deference to state authority was seen in their demand for dialogue—for a place on the political stage, as it were. Xinhua News Agency reported on April 30, "Dialogue has become a household word here as millions of Beijing residents watched last night and tonight the television program of the dialogue between Yuan Mu, the spokesman for the State Council, and the college students."[22] Dramatic as it was, the demand for dialogue was also an admission of the hold the state continued to exert; protesters wanted a role in the official political pageant, which for them remained the only real show in town. In sharp contrast to Eastern Europeans, Chinese urbanites certainly were not "simply beginning to turn away from the state, by refusing to take it seriously" (see Chirot, this volume, chapter 1).

Perhaps the most distressing aspect of the demand for dialogue was the limited cast of characters included in the request. Perpetuating a Confucian mentality which assigned to intellectuals the role of spokesmen for the masses, students assumed that they were the only segment of society whose voice deserved to be heard. The disregard for peasants and workers was a prejudice that intellectuals shared with state leaders. Deng Xiaoping, like Chiang Kaishek and Yuan Shikai before him, was a reformer who viewed the Chinese peasantry as an obstacle to the fulfillment of national objectives. When each of these reformers turned repressor, he pointed to the "backward" peasants as the reason why China's march toward representative government would have to be postponed.[23] Similarly, in the 1989 "democracy" movement, students were reportedly "horrified at the suggestion that truly popular elections would have to include peasants, who would certainly out-vote educated people like themselves."[24]

From the perspective of the students, the peasants and workers appear motivated by crass materialism whereas their own politics are selflessly pure. The link to Confucian morality is evident here. When hunger strikers wrote out their last testaments—vowing to sacrifice their very lives for their beliefs—they joined an ancient tradition of scholar martyrs dating back to the third century B.C.[25]

The intense moralism of the Tiananmen protesters has been noted by many analysts. Lee Feigon writes of the hunger strikers: "By fasting they hoped to contrast the *moral* righteousness of their behavior with that of the corrupt and despotic government against which they protested."[26] Dorothy Solinger highlights the "proclivity to *moralize* and demand high behavioral standards from rulers."[27] And Esherick and Wasserstrom point out: "The slogans, big-character posters, pamphlets, open letters, and speeches of the protesters were replete with emotive statements of commitment and dissent. They were proclamations of personal positions, *moral* statements of resolve."[28]

In this respect, the Chinese case would seem to fit comfortably into Daniel Chirot's interpretation of the revolutions of 1989; the cause was essentially moral (this volume, chapter 1). Chirot links "the endless corruption, the lies, the collapse of elementary social trust, the petty tyranny at every level" to a moral backlash. Similarly, at the height of the Chinese protests, Fang Lizhi offered the following analysis: "The corruption is so obvious now. People see it every day in their factories and offices. Everybody understands what is going on. The blatant profiteering of state officials is now the focal point of the movement because it is this profiteering that has directly led to the failure of the economic reform."[29] An attitude survey conducted in Beijing at about the same time provided support for Fang's assertions; the overwhelming majority of respondents saw anticorruption as the most important goal of the movement and predicted that corruption was the most likely precipitant of future unrest in China.[30] A startling indication of this moralism was the nostalgia for Chairman Mao that surfaced during the spring protests.[31] One popular ditty expressed the general sentiment: "Mao Zedong's son went to the front lines (and was killed as a soldier in the Korean War); Zhao Ziyang's son smuggles color television sets."

The 1989 demonstration was, in David Strand's words, "a morality play done in Beijing opera style."[32] As a morality play, it shared many features of the East European scenario. But its Beijing opera style limited the stars of the show to the Confucian elite: scholars and officials. Indeed, the criticisms that Mao's wife Jiang Qing had leveled against the Beijing opera during the

Cultural Revolution could be applied with equal force to the Tiananmen drama. The plot followed a standard format that denied heroic roles to workers and peasants.

RANK AND FILE PARTICIPATION

That the ordinary populace is in fact fully capable of dramatic action is revealed not only by its revolutionary history but by its recent behavior. In the post-Mao era, despite major gains for agriculture under the reforms, unrest in the Chinese countryside has been remarkably prevalent.[33] Significantly, this rural protest is accompanied by a strong resurgence of folk religion; many of the incidents have involved shamans, ancestral temples, "jade emperors descended to earth," and the like. Undoubtedly the popular religion of the contemporary countryside differs significantly from its pre-1949 forerunners; the socialist experience has left a visible imprint on the mentality of today's peasantry.[34] But regardless of how old or new these practices may be, they suggest the fuzzy outlines of a "civil society"—in the sense of a domain of public interaction not fully controlled by the state. The drive to institutionalize this domain (as seen in the privately financed rebuilding of local earth god temples or rewriting of lineage genealogies, for example) further attests to the efforts of the rural populace to carve out a niche of independence from state authority. Admittedly, we are not seeing here a Chinese Solidarity or Neues Forum. Yet we are witnessing the consolidation of organizational forms that have for centuries provided a foundation for popular protest.[35] When they join state officials in dismissing these practices as "feudal superstition" *(fengjian mixin)*, contemporary intellectuals mirror the prejudice of their Confucian forefathers as well as of the ruling regime. In failing to take seriously the peasantry's capacity for collective action, would-be democrats deny themselves a powerful and essential ally.

Equally damaging to the democratic project has been the exclusion of other key social groups: entrepreneurs and workers in particular. With the liberalization of marketing under the post-Mao reforms, an explosion in entrepreneurship occurred. Enticed by the profits to be made in commercial activity, hundreds of thousands of peasants and town dwellers rushed to join the burgeoning ranks of the *getihu*, or independent entrepreneurs. Their transactions gave new life to that realm of nongovernment economic activities which Hegel, Marx, and Gramsci all viewed as central to the emergence of civil society. The importance of the growth of this commercial class for the advent of democratic politics is succinctly posited in Barrington Moore's memorable formulation "No bourgeoisie, no democracy." The defense of property and profits encourages ordinary citizens to fight for the freedoms associated with liberal democracy.[36]

The support provided by Chinese entrepreneurs for the student protests in 1989 was in fact substantial. In Shanghai, on May 21 "hundreds of people with 'entrepreneur' banners staged a sit-in" in sympathy with the students.[37]

Unlike most Chinese, the independent *getihu* could engage in political action without fear of sanctions from their work units. Many of them were, moreover, financially well off. It was their monetary contributions that made possible the purchase of battery-operated megaphones for the student leaders.[38] One of the largest of the new private enterprises, the Stone Corporation, is estimated to have donated tens of thousands of dollars worth of sophisticated equipment—including facsimile machines—to the protesters.[39] As military intervention grew imminent, members of the Flying Tiger Brigade of *getihu* on motorbikes delivered news of troop movements to the students. After the crackdown, it was the pedicabs of the *getihu* that carried off the casualties.

Despite this crucial help, the entrepreneurs received from the students the same disparaging appellation that the regime used to discredit them. Intellectuals and officials alike referred publicly to the *getihu* as "*xiansan ren*"—or idle drifters.[40] In Communist China as in Confucian China, commercial elements are scorned as rootless, amoral figures who cannot be trusted. (Significantly, the Chinese societies in which merchants *have* flourished—Taiwan, Singapore, and Hong Kong—are also societies where the link between state and scholar was broken by colonialism.)[41] The recent experience of Taiwan in particular establishes the catalytic role that the commercial middle class can play in the democratization process. Similarly, Chirot points to the centrality of the East European middle class in the upheavals of 1989 (this volume, chapter 1). In denigrating this key social element, Chinese students undervalued the contributions of one of the most enthusiastic supporters of their cause.

Another group relegated to a role in the Tiananmen drama well beneath its actual performance ability was the urban working class. A review of Chinese popular movements of this past century reveals the extraordinary power of a worker-student alliance. The May Fourth Movement of 1919, which began as a demonstration by three thousand students in Beijing, became a historical watershed only after it had been joined by tens of thousands of Shanghai workers in a general strike the following month. It was this participation by labor that persuaded the government to disavow the terms of the Versailles Treaty which threatened to turn China's Shandong Province into a virtual colony of Japan. And it was this same worker activism that persuaded young student organizers to establish in 1921 a communist party dedicated to the proletarian cause. Four years later the influence of this new party was seen in the momentous May Thirtieth Movement of 1925—again precipitated by a worker-student protest against imperialism—which marked a high point of communist strength in the cities. Although subdued by Chiang Kaishek's white terror in the spring of 1927, the urban coalition regained force after the Japanese invasion of 1937. Fueled first by anti-Japanese sentiment and then, after 1945, by anti-Americanism, worker-student nationalism was a key ingredient in the communist victory of 1949.[42]

The founding of the People's Republic, although ushering in a self-proclaimed "dictatorship of the proletariat," certainly did not spell the end of labor unrest. In fact, every decade has brought a new round of widespread strikes. In 1956–57, the Hundred Flowers Movement saw a major outburst to protest the inequities of the First Five-Year Plan.[43] In 1966–67, the Cultural Revolution prompted another explosion of labor protest.[44] In 1974–76, resentment against the austere policies of the Gang of Four resulted in a further display of working-class dissatisfaction.[45] And in 1986–88, strikes erupted at factories across the country to protest the inflationary consequences of the post-Mao reforms.[46] In contrast to the pre-1949 situation, however, the contemporary upheavals elicited little enthusiasm from students. To be sure, much of the explanation for the separation of worker and student politics in the socialist era can be attributed to the effectiveness of state controls.[47] But a certain amount of the responsibility must also be assigned to the intellectuals' disdain for a working class whose aspirations are dismissed as crass "economism."

That workers are actually attracted to larger social causes than many intellectuals give them credit for is shown in their reaction to recent student demonstrations. When tens of thousands of students marched in Shanghai during the winter of 1986–87 to demand freedom of expression and an end to police brutality, an even larger group of workers gathered in support. Although a tight police cordon was formed to prevent anyone without a valid student identification from entering the center of the demonstration, sympathetic workers stood just outside the police lines yelling "younger brothers, your elder brothers support you!" and tossing in bread and cigarettes as a gesture of solidarity. The immediate precipitant of this massive demonstration was the police beating of a college student during a concert by an American rock group in Shanghai. When fellow students erupted in fury, the then mayor of Shanghai (and now secretary general of the CCP), Jiang Zemin, went to the campus of the injured student to offer an explanation. The police, he assured his audience, had mistaken the young concertgoer for a worker; had they realized he was an intellectual, such heavy-handed treatment would never have been applied. Most members of the campus community reportedly found nothing improper in the mayor's line of reasoning.[48]

Many workers, increasingly disadvantaged by the post-Mao industrial reforms, had ample cause for concern about government policy. For one thing, double-digit inflation was threatening their standard of living. For another, the reforms promised to put more money into industrial reinvestment at the expense of workers' housing and bonuses. "Economistic" as such issues may be, they could form the backbone of a lively protest. Moreover, workers were no less aware or intolerant of corruption and petty tyranny than other Chinese. In short, the basis for a potent worker-student alliance seemed to exist. As in the pre-1949 era, such an urban coalition might have been constructed on the foundations of both *consumer* and *citizen* identity. As consumers, urbanites could unite against the debilitating effects of runaway inflation (also a central issue during the general strikes of May Fourth and the Civil War years). As citizens, they could condemn government corruption (again an issue, along with imperialism, in all the major pre-1949 urban movements). Orthodox historiography notwithstanding, it was not *class* identity (or protest against on-the-job exploitation) that had fueled the massive worker strikes of early twentieth-century China. Labor was accustomed to performing on a larger stage than the narrow confines of the workplace.[49]

In the spring of 1989, workers again sought to play a major role in the drama unfolding in Tiananmen Square. On April 20, laborers from a number of Beijing factories made speeches at the square, proclaiming that "workers and students should work together for the introduction of a more democratic and less corrupt system."[50] Fearing the dangers of growing working-class participation, especially as the May Fourth anniversary drew near, the Beijing city government issued an order forbidding any worker to take leave of absence between April 25 and May 5.[51] At this same time, Deng Xiaoping— explaining that "the movement might soon spread to workers and peasants, as in Poland, Yugoslavia, Hungary, and the Soviet Union"[52]—arranged for two divisions of the 38th Army to be called into the city. But the leadership's fears of a worker-student coalition were in fact ungrounded. As Anita Chan and Jonathan Unger have observed, until the very end of the movement, "the students had disdainfully tried to keep the workers at arm's length."[53] This was literally the case, with students linking arms to prevent workers from joining directly in their ranks.[54] Only during the last week of May, beleaguered by the growing threat of military suppression, were student delegations sent to the major factories to seek support.[55]

Considering the lack of student initiative, the extent of worker participation was rather remarkable. In late April an unofficial workers' group calling itself the Beijing Workers' Autonomous Association issued a statement condemning inflation and the gap between wealthy government leaders and the ordinary people. The group called for wage raises, price stabilization, and publication of the personal incomes of party and government officials.[56] A month later, claiming a membership of more than six thousand workers, the group's goal was "to set up a nationwide non-Communist union along the lines of Poland's Solidarity trade union."[57]

Pressured by this competition from an autonomous labor group, the official All-China Federation of Trade Unions began to assume a more active role in responding to working-class concerns. On May 1 (Labor Day), the president of the ACFTU conceded that government-sponsored unions "should fully support workers in their fight against corruption."[58] Thanks to this encouragement, workers became more involved in the demonstrations. On May 17, as the hunger strike entered its fifth day:

> Millions of workers, peasants, and clerks from government organs, personnel from cultural and publishing circles and from the press took to the streets to show they supported and cared for the students. . . . Particularly noticeable were the massive marching columns of workers. They came from scores of en-

terprises such as the Capital Steel Corporation, the main factory of the Beijing Internal Combustion Engines, Beijing Lifting Machinery Factory and the state-run Number 798 Factory. The demonstrating workers were holding banners and placards carrying slogans stating: "Students and workers are bound by a common cause" and "Workers are grieved seeing students on hunger strike."[59]

The next day the ACFTU took the bold step of donating 100,000 yuan (about U.S. $27,000) for medical aid to students in the sixth day of their hunger strike. Explained a spokesperson for the Federation, "We workers are deeply concerned about the health and lives of the students."[60] The same day, the Shanghai Federation of Trade Unions added its voice in support of the movement: "Workers in the city have expressed universal concern and sympathy for the patriotism of students who are demanding democracy, rule of law, an end to corruption, checking inflation, and promoting reform. The municipal council of trade unions fully affirms this."[61]

But there were limits beyond which the official unions could not go. On May 20, a mass of workers gathered in front of the ACFTU offices to demand that the unions order a national strike.[62] Three days later, after the declaration of martial law, Beijing television announced:

> In the last few days, there have been rumors in some localities saying that the All-China Federation of Trade Unions has called for a nationwide general strike. A spokesman for the Federation said that this is merely a rumor with ulterior motives. The spokesman emphatically pointed out that the ACFTU has recently stressed that the vast number of staff members and workers should firmly stay at their posts and properly carry out production work.[63]

By the end of the month, Ruan Chongwu, a former minister of public security, had been appointed to the post of labor minister. His brief was "to ensure that workers remain loyal to the party and government—and that they not take part in activities that challenge the regime."[64] Reported the Hong Kong press, "A top priority with Mr. Ruan and the restructured leadership of the trade unions federation will be to prevent nonofficial unions from being organized."[65]

In the drive to recapture control of labor, three leaders of the Beijing Workers' Autonomous Association were detained by the police on May 30. Also rounded up were eleven members of the Flying Tiger Brigade—the contingent of three hundred motorbikers, at least two hundred of whom were independent entrepreneurs—which was providing information on troop deployment to the students.[66] Once again workers and other nonstudents were being made to pay the price for a movement in which they had played only supporting roles.[67] Even so, many continued to defy the authorities. On June 9 at a huge demonstration and memorial service in Shanghai for victims of the June 4 massacre, among the marchers were about a thousand workers holding high a banner which read "Shanghai Autonomous Federation of Labor Unions."[68]

CONCLUSION

The tragic ending to China's uprising of 1989 is explained neither by the salience of its revolutionary ideology nor by the silence of its rural inhabitants. If the persistence of "tradition" served as a brake on political transformation, the relevant tradition was not that of the committed revolutionary or the conservative peasantry. Ironically, it was the very instigators of the Tiananmen protest—the urban intellectuals—who appeared most wedded to a limiting legacy. In their *style of remonstrance* (presenting petitions and banners and demanding dialogue with the authorities), their *search for political patrons* (emphasizing the need for state strengthening and switching quickly from one "hero" to the next), and above all their *stress on moralism* (contrasting their own selfless martyrdom to the crass materialism of the masses), the students evinced a brand of political behavior and belief replete with the stigmata of the past.

The traditionalism of student protesters was not due to some immutable Confucian culture, forever lurking like a sea monster beneath the surface of China's political waters—waiting to seize and sink any unsuspecting would-be democrat who happened to swim by.[69] Rather, the intellectuals' political proclivities were shaped by the close links between state and scholar that persist in contemporary China.

Although the Confucian examination system was abolished in 1905, the communists instituted a *fenpei* (allocation) system whereby the state assigns college graduates to jobs commensurate with their scholastic records, political loyalties, and of course personal connections. Even more than under the imperial regime, the socialist state exercises a virtual monopoly over meaningful job opportunities for intellectuals. Little wonder, then, that these intellectuals—even in the act of protest—should evidence such state-centric tendencies. It was only during the Republican interregnum, when the state's hold over the scholar was effectively severed, that a different sort of student protest emerged. That "May Fourth Tradition," which held sway from 1919 until the founding of the PRC in 1949, was a brilliant but brief chapter in the history of Chinese popular protest. Occurring during an unusual period of state retrenchment (at least with respect to control over intellectuals), the protests of that generation demonstrated an unprecedented independence and enthusiasm for active alliance with workers, peasants, and merchants. It was these qualities of autonomy and mass involvement that imbued the collective action of the Republican era with such social fire. By contrast, contemporary intellectuals who attempt to resuscitate the spirit of May Fourth are hampered by the inability to liberate themselves from the hegemonic claims of the state and thereby embrace the interests of other social elements. As a consequence, their rendition of the May Fourth drama is much less powerful—politically, if not necessarily theatrically—than pre-1949 performances.

The omnipresence of the Chinese communist state, even more than its

Confucian forerunner or its East European counterparts, has inhibited the florescence of "civil society" and rendered the formation of cross-class coalitions correspondingly difficult and dangerous. Accordingly, Andrew Walder cautions against interpreting the Tiananmen upheaval "as a direct expression of the growth of an independent society. Such independence was greatly restricted in China relative to Poland, Hungary, and the Soviet Union."[70] But if the answer lies not in a developed "civil society," how *do* we explain China's recent turmoil? For Walder, "the key to the 1989 upheaval appears to be the splintering of the central leadership and the Party-state apparatus after the initial student protests of April." There is considerable merit in Walder's emphasis on elites and political institutions. As we have seen in the case of the All-China Federation of Trade Unions, elements of the state did indeed play a significant role in facilitating the protest movement of 1989. At the same time, however, we must not underestimate the potential for self-generated political action by nonstate entities. The traditions of Chinese civil society are admittedly weaker and different from those of Eastern Europe. Absent in China are the Catholic Church of Poland, the old democratic parties of Hungary, or the dissident intellectual circles of the Soviet Union and Czechoslovakia. Yet there is evidence that recent reforms have encouraged the resurgence of meaningful traditions of extrastate economic and associational behavior in China, just as in Eastern Europe. Today's independent entrepreneurs, practitioners of folk religion, and members of autonomous labor unions are all building on patterns of collective identity and action with proven records of resisting state domination in the Chinese context. These practices may well lack the democratic character of the institutions of civil society in Eastern Europe.[71] But as David Strand has noted, "When Chinese seek to revive a democratic tradition, it is a tradition of movements, not institutions, they are drawing upon."[72] And China's merchants, peasants, and workers—as well as students—can rightfully lay claim to a vital part of that inheritance.

In accounting for the timing of the 1989 protest movement, it is clear that the efforts of the Chinese state to undertake reform have played a major hand in encouraging dissent on the part of both political elites and ordinary citizens. Although the relationship between reform and revolution is poorly understood, it is obviously significant. As the history of modern China shows, reform is often the harbinger of revolution. The Revolution of 1911 which toppled the imperial system followed upon the Hundred Days Reform and New Policies of the ailing Qing dynasty. The reformist New Life Movement of Chiang Kaishek's Guomindang (Kuomintang) heralded the imminent demise of the Nationalist regime. Serious reforms exact substantial costs on at least some sectors of both state and society. Furthermore, they raise expectations to levels that can seldom be attained. Most important, reforms are admissions by the regime of its own inadequacies. As a result, they encourage widespread disbelief. This is especially unsettling in communist systems, where claims to ideological truth have been so central. When the leadership publicly repudiates many of its past practices, it invites ordinary citizens to engage in open criticism as well.

The Tiananmen uprising was a dramatic expression of the Chinese people's appetite and aptitude for political criticism. Influenced by forty years of socialism as well as by international cultural currents, the demonstrators staged an innovative performance. Dunce caps from the Cultural Revolution, rock music from Taiwan, headbands from South Korea, and a hunger strike from Gandhi's India all contributed a seemingly contemporary and cosmopolitan flavor. Yet in its core values the student movement was in fact remarkably traditional. Thanks to the special bond between state and scholar that had persisted for so long under the imperial system and was reconstituted (on different terms, to be sure) under the socialist system, Chinese students engaged in an exclusionist style of protest that served to reinforce preexisting authority relations. At the same time, however, other social groups showed themselves ready to reclaim the true spirit of the May Fourth Movement—in which a fledgling civil society had challenged a troubled Chinese state on both moral and material grounds.

NOTES

1. Chalmers Johnson, *Peasant Nationalism and Communist Power* (Stanford: Stanford University Press, 1962).

2. Richard C. Kraus, "The Lament of Astrophysicist Fang Lizhi," in Arif Dirlik and Maurice Meisner, eds., *Marxism and the Chinese Experience* (Armonk, N.Y.: M. E. Sharpe, 1989), pp. 294–315.

3. On Deng's role in the antirightist campaign, see David Bachman, *To Leap Forward: Bureaucracy, Economy and Leadership in China, 1956–57* (New York: Cambridge University Press, 1991), chapter 8.

4. Vera Schwarcz, *The Chinese Enlightenment: Intellectuals and the Legacy of the May Fourth Movement of 1919* (Berkeley: University of California Press, 1986), pp. 283–91. Schwarcz argues convincingly that the incompleteness of the May Fourth enlightenment is linked to the tension in twentieth-century China between commitment to cultural criticism and commitment to national salvation. Those who raised the most serious criticisms have been open to the charge of being unpatriotic.

5. Quoted in Vera Schwarcz, "Memory, Commemoration, and the Plight of China's Intellectuals," *Washington Quarterly*, Autumn 1989, p. 124.

6. Examples of this technique during the Republican period can be found in Jeffrey Wasserstrom, *Student Protest in Twentieth Century China: The View from Shanghai* (Stanford: Stanford University Press, 1991).

7. See Charles Tilly, *The Contentious French* (Cambridge: Harvard University Press, 1986), for a discussion of comparable protest behavior in France.

8. Lee Feigon, *China Rising: The Meaning of Tiananmen* (Chicago: Ivan R. Dee, 1990), p. 146; *Foreign Broadcast Information Service (FBIS)*, April 27, 1989, pp. 11–12.

9. Quoted in David Strand, "Civil Society and Public Sphere in Modern China: A

Perspective on Popular Movements in Beijing, 1919–1989," *Working Papers in Asian/Pacific Studies* (Durham: Duke University Asian/Pacific Studies Institute, 1990), pp. 30–31.

10. On the continuity with earlier student movements, see Jeffrey Wasserstrom, "Student Protests in the Chinese Tradition, 1919–1989," in Tony Saich, ed., *Perspectives on the Chinese People's Movement: Spring 1989* (Armonk, N.Y.: M. E. Sharpe, 1991). At least since the May Fourth Movement, groups of students had paraded with banners naming their alma mater as they marched from school to school, calling on those at other institutions to join in the task of saving the nation.

11. *Bajiu Zhongguo minyun jishi* [Annals of the '89 Chinese Democracy Movement] (Cambridge: Harvard University Press 1989), p. 446.

12. Jean Chesneaux, *The Chinese Labor Movement, 1919–1927* (Stanford: Stanford University Press, 1968).

13. *FBIS*, May 18, 1989, pp. 49–50.

14. On the earlier situation, see William Rowe, *Hankow: Conflict and Community in a Chinese City, 1796–1895* (Stanford: Stanford University Press, 1989); Susan Mann, *Local Merchants and the Chinese Bureaucracy, 1750–1950* (Stanford: Stanford University Press, 1987); and Mary Rankin, *Elite Activism and Political Transformation in China* (Stanford: Stanford University Press, 1986).

15. Joseph W. Esherick and Jeffrey Wasserstrom, "Acting Out Democracy: Political Theater in Modern China," *Journal of Asian Studies* 49:4 (November 1990), p. 839.

16. Ibid., p. 841.

17. Personal observation, Shanghai, December 1986. The slogan was "Dadao Hu Yaobang; Ningyuan Sirenbang!" (Down with Hu Yaobang; Better the Gang of Four!).

18. A son who had allegedly used his family connections to make huge profits from an illicit trading company in Hainan was the cause of much of the public hostility.

19. The Beijing variant, formulated by Rong Jian and others close to Zhao Ziyang, argued for a coercive government to carry out radical liberalization of the economy. The Southern variant, as formulated by Xiao Gongqin at Shanghai Normal University, favored a more gradual reform program. See Xiao Gongqin, "Lun guodu quanweizhuyi" [On Transitional Authoritarianism], *Qingnian xuezhe* 2 (1989).

20. Feigon, *China Rising*, chapter 6.

21. Andrew J. Nathan, *Chinese Democracy* (Berkeley: University of California Press, 1985).

22. *FBIS*, May 1 1989, p. 50.

23. Ernest P. Young, "The Reformer as Repressor," paper presented at the annual meeting of the American Historical Association (1989).

24. Mary S. Erbaugh and Richard C. Kraus, "The 1989 Democracy Movement in Fujian and Its Consequences," *Australian Journal of Chinese Affairs* 23 (1990), p. 153.

25. Esherick and Wasserstrom, "Acting Out Democracy," pp. 856–57.

26. Feigon, *China Rising*, p. 196, emphasis added.

27. Dorothy Solinger, "Democracy with Chinese Characteristics," *World Policy Journal*, Fall 1989, p. 625, emphasis added.

28. Esherick and Wasserstrom, "Acting Out Democracy," p. 846, emphasis added.

29. *South China Morning Post*, May 22, 1989, p. 23.

30. *China Information* 4:1 (1989).

31. Feigon, *China Rising*, p. 206. The carrying of Mao posters was one expression of this phenomenon.

32. Strand, "Civil Society and Public Sphere," p. 16.

33. Elizabeth J. Perry, "Rural Collective Violence: The Fruits of Recent Reform," in Elizabeth J. Perry and Christine Wong, eds., *The Political Economy of Reform in Post-Mao China* (Cambridge: Harvard University Press, 1985).

34. For this argument, see Helen Siu, *Agents and Victims in South China* (New Haven: Yale University Press, 1989). See also Elizabeth J. Perry, "Rural Violence in Socialist China," *China Quarterly*, September 1985, pp. 414–40.

35. On rural religion as a basis for antistate rebellion, see Susan Naquin, *Millenarian Rebellion in China: The Eight Trigrams Uprising of 1813* (New Haven: Yale University Press, 1976). On kinship and village as organizational bases of rural protest, see Elizabeth J. Perry, *Rebels and Revolutionaries in North China, 1845–1945* (Stanford: Stanford University Press, 1980).

36. For a dissenting view, see Nina P. Halpern, "Economic Reform and Democratization in Communist Systems: The Case of China," *Studies in Comparative Communism* 22:2/3 (1989).

37. *Bajiu Zhongguo minyun jishi*, p. 355.

38. Feigon, *China Rising*, p. 183.

39. Ibid., p. 184.

40. Interviews with participants, Seattle, April–May 1990. An exception was the dissident writer Wang Ruoshui, who argued for an affinity of interests between intellectuals and entrepreneurs. See the interview with Wang in *Jiushi niandai* [The Nineties], April 1989, p. 37.

41. In Taiwan, the role of intellectuals was further weakened after the KMT takeover via a land reform that undermined their traditional economic base and (by compensating dispossessed landlords with stock in nascent industries) converted the intellectuals themselves into members of the bourgeoisie.

42. Suzanne Pepper, *Civil War in China* (Berkeley: University of California Press, 1980).

43. François Gipouloux, *Les cents fleurs dans les usines* (Paris: École des Hautes Études en Sciences Sociales, 1986).

44. Hong Yung Lee, *The Politics of the Chinese Cultural Revolution* (Berkeley: University of California Press, 1978).

45. Lowell Dittmer, *China's Continuous Revolution* (Berkeley: University of California Press, 1987).

46. Interviews at the Shanghai Federation of Trade Unions, May 1987 and September 1988.

47. See Andrew Walder, *Communist Neo-Traditionalism: Work and Authority in Chinese Industry* (Berkeley: University of California Press, 1986). Walder provides an insightful discussion of the operation of state controls in state-owned factories. In my view, however, he underestimates the possibility of autonomous worker protests.

48. Personal observations and interviews, Shanghai, December 1986–January 1987.

49. Elizabeth J. Perry, *Shanghai on Strike: The Politics of Chinese Labor* (Stanford: Stanford University Press, forthcoming).

50. *FBIS*, April 20, 1989, p. 18.

51. *FBIS*, April 26, 1989, p. 17.

52. Feigon, *China Rising*, p. 153.

53. Anita Chan and Jonathan Unger, "China After Tiananmen," *The Nation*, January 22, 1990, pp. 79–81.

54. Feigon, *China Rising*, p. 203.

55. *FBIS*, May 26, 1989, p. 52.

56. *FBIS*, April 28, 1989, p. 11.

57. *FBIS*, May 30, 1989, p. 9; May 31, 1989, p. 44.

58. *China Daily*, May 1, 1989.

59. *FBIS*, May 18, 1989, p. 49.

60. Ibid., p. 76.

61. *FBIS*, May 22, 1989, p. 91.

62. Ibid., p. 45.

63. *FBIS*, May 23, 1989, p. 58. Whatever the ACFTU leadership may really have felt about a general strike, theirs was one of the last government/party units to express support for martial law. See *FBIS*, May 30, 1989, p. 9.

64. *FBIS*, May 30, 1989, p. 9.

65. Ibid.

66. *FBIS*, May 31, 1989, p. 44.

67. On the detention of additional workers and entrepreneurs in early June, see *FBIS*, June 2, 1989, p. 11.

68. *Bajiu Zhongguo minyun jishi*, p. 787.

69. The "unchanging China" argument can be found in Lucian Pye, *The Spirit of Chinese Politics* (Cambridge: MIT Press, 1968); Richard Solomon, *Mao's Revolution and Chinese Political Culture* (Berkeley: University of California Press, 1971); and Lucian Pye, "Tiananmen and Chinese Political Culture: The Escalation of Confrontation from Morality to Revenge," *Asian Survey* 30:4 (April 1990), pp. 331–47. Pye and Solomon argue for a unitary Chinese culture (across time and social class) instilled during childhood socialization experiences.

70. Andrew G. Walder, "Political Upheavals in the Communist Party-States," *States and Social Structures Newsletter* 12 (Winter 1990), p. 8. See also Walder, "The Political Sociology of the Beijing Upheaval of 1989," *Problems of Communism*, September–October 1989, pp. 39–40.

71. This is the conclusion of Esherick and Wasserstrom, "Acting Out Democracy."

72. Strand, "Civil Society and Public Sphere," p. 3.

7

Is China Different?

The Fate of Its Economic Reform

NICHOLAS R. LARDY

IN THE AFTERMATH of the events of Tiananmen, the demise of economic reform in China has been widely proclaimed.[1] The contrast between the dismantling of communist regimes in most of Eastern Europe and the crushing of the movement of Chinese students and, to a lesser extent, workers is stark. Although more difficult to portray, there is also a growing sense of the contrast between the regimes in Eastern Europe, rushing headlong to jettison the heritage of central planning and state control, and their counterpart in China, where an initially successful turn away from a similar heritage has given way to an image of retreat and recentralization of economic decision making. The turn away from economic reform, which some observers feel was evident even in the months prior to June 1989,[2] was accelerated by dramatic developments in Eastern Europe in the latter part of 1989, leaving the Chinese leaders with an acute sense of political vulnerability and exposure, reinforcing their tendency to pursue repressive domestic political policies.[3]

While there is an element of truth in the observations summarized above, my view is that many writers have been too quick to declare the expiration of economic reform in China. A more tentative judgment is that we tend to link economic and political reform too closely.[4] No doubt over the long run a competitive market economy must be paired with a pluralistic political system. But authoritarian governments in East Asia pursued market driven economic growth for decades without relaxing their hold on political power. Only after sustained economic growth had created per capita incomes several times those of present-day China did pressures for political reform become compelling. Moreover, unlike several countries in Eastern Europe or the Shatalin plan in the Soviet Union, the Chinese Communist Party has never embraced the goal of a market economy. Western observers, encouraged by a vocal minority of reformers in China who sought to privatize state industry, too frequently argued that China was going capitalist. Even President Reagan on a trip to China referred publicly to the Chinese leadership as being composed of "so-called" communists.

But these writers as well as the president overlooked the heart of the most authoritative reform document ever endorsed by the Chinese Communist Party Central Committee.[5] That document, dated October 1984, called for the establishment of "planned commodity economy, not a market economy that is entirely subject to market regulation." Yet it allowed for market forces to determine the allocation of resources and the distribution of output in a wide sphere of the economy. And it forecast a significant change in the planned sector of the economy in which compulsory plans would be reduced in scope and more reliance would be placed on economic levers to achieve plan aims. This was a deliberately vague formulation, reflecting the lack of consensus on the ultimate objectives of economic reform in China. But it certainly fell far short of endorsing the creation of a market economy.

DIFFERENCES IN CHINESE AND SOVIET ECONOMIC REFORM

Indeed, one of the difficulties in comparing economic reforms in China with those in the Soviet Union is a fundamental difference in style. Chinese reforms have been under way for more than a decade without a comprehensive reform plan. Beginning with the rural reforms of the late 1970s, reform has proceeded by incremental stages, with each successive policy initiative leading to seemingly unanticipated adverse consequences.[6] These consequences are then addressed by yet more far-reaching reform policies. By contrast, at least to this observer, economic reform in the Soviet Union has been paralyzed by the attempt to map out a comprehensive reform in advance. This process brings out conflicts of interest among contending bureaucratic, regional, and social interest groups and has left the Soviet economy in a state of near collapse. Thus while the plans for economic reform in the Soviet Union far surpass the modest Chinese documents, the reality is that Chinese economic reforms are light-years ahead of the Soviet ones. The perception in many quarters, based on comparison of the most recent detailed Soviet blueprint for reform with much vaguer Chinese statements, is that China is retreating to old-fashioned, centralized planning while the Soviets are embracing market capitalism, disagreeing among themselves only on whether the transition can be accomplished in five hundred days or somewhat longer.

Two examples may clarify this fundamental difference. Perhaps the most significant is the question of ownership. The Soviets seem mired in a debate about whether and, if so, how to convert state assets into private property. The most recent manifestation of this is Gorbachev's proposal to conduct a national referendum on the issue of landownership prior to implementing the Shatalin plan. While debate has raged on the ownership question for many years, virtually nothing has changed. No significant amount of rural land has been transferred to the peasantry, and manufacturing remains essentially a state monopoly. Even in Poland, where reform is said to be following the "big bang" model, over 90 percent of industry remains in state hands.

The contrast with China is stark. It is, of course, widely appreciated that collective farming has been dismantled throughout China. In most places this occurred almost a decade ago. Peasants have been provided land on increasingly favorable terms. Lease contracts, initially as short as one to three years, were lengthened to three to five years prior to the mid-1980s, and now terms of thirty years are common. Moreover, the state has introduced other changes that enhance the property rights associated with these leases. Leases are inheritable and, with few restrictions, transferable to nonfamily members. Land held under a lease may also be rented out on a short-term basis without transferring the underlying contract. The state has also encouraged the development of rural labor markets, so leaseholders have the option of hiring laborers to farm their land as well as the option of renting out the land. In short, while rural lands still nominally belong to the state, peasant-use rights to the land seem well established. This, in turn, has contributed substantially to increased farm output and productivity.[7]

What is less widely understood is that what I call the entrepreneurial portion of the manufacturing sector of the Chinese economy has also grown significantly over the past decade. This sector includes urban collective firms, township and village enterprises, equity joint ventures, private firms, and so forth—any manufacturing firm that is not subject to the economically suffocating direct bureaucratic management of the state.

While Chinese reform documents continually uphold the principle of "public ownership of the means of production," the reality is quite different. Even in the industrial sector, where the legacy of borrowing from Soviet economic practices is most apparent, the share of output produced by nonstate firms rose continuously throughout the 1980s. From an initial share of less than 20 percent when reform began, the output of nonstate firms rose to 45 percent by 1989.[8]

In short, in the period during which the Soviets have been debating whether and how to privatize land and other state assets, the share of state-managed industrial output in China has plunged. The rising share of output produced by entrepreneurial firms is all the more extraordinary because it occurred in the decade in which the average annual rate of industrial growth exceeded 12 percent.[9]

The significance of the sharply declining share of manufactured goods produced by state-owned firms is that almost half of manufactured goods are now produced in a marketlike setting.[10] Entrepreneurial firms generally pay something close to the real value for their capital, both fixed and working, rather than relying on budgetary allocations from the state; they purchase the bulk of their inputs on relatively free markets, rather than receiving materials allocated by the government supply bureaucracy at fixed prices; they pay their workers wages based on their productivity, rather than following the pattern of fixed wage scales used by state firms; and they sell most of their output at market prices, rather than delivering it to the state at a fixed price.[11]

The same transformation is under way in retailing and even construction. Less than a decade ago, 80 percent of all retail sales were made by state firms. By 1988 their share had fallen to less than 40 percent.[12] This change largely reflects the rise of private retailing, which barely existed a decade ago but now accounts for a fifth of all retailing, and the surge of direct selling by individual farmers to urban residents. As reform got under way in rural areas in the late 1970s, these private farm sales to urban residents were just 2 billion yuan. By 1989 these sales amounted to 70 billion yuan.[13]

In the construction sector, the share of state employment has fallen from more than half to under a third, with the difference made up by sharply rising employment in township and village firms that are collectively owned and managed and in rural construction teams.

Only in transport does the state still dominate, largely because of the continued predominant reliance on railroads for medium and long distance transport.

A second example—currency convertibility—provides a similar contrast in Soviet and Chinese approaches to fundamental economic reform. The Soviets for years have embraced convertibility as a goal of economic reform. The specific timetable has been delayed more than once, but the objective has not been in doubt. By contrast, one can look high and low and still not find any public statement by a Chinese official that convertibility is even an ultimate goal. Even the official document supplied by the Chinese to the General Agreement on Tariffs and Trade, as part of China's proposed accession to the GATT, contained not a word about convertibility of the domestic currency.[14] The apparently astonished members of the working party appointed by the GATT Secretariat to examine the merits of China's effort to become a contracting party wasted no time in offering the Chinese side an opportunity to correct what they apparently felt must have been an oversight. In the first round of interrogatories designed to clarify ambiguities in China's initial memorandum, the GATT Working Party asked, "Is China planning to move over time towards the convertibility of the Renminbi?" The answer could not have been clearer: "The free convertibility of RMB is not under consideration at present."[15]

But in practice the Chinese have moved quite far toward allowing supply and demand on an open market to determine the value of their currency. This process began by moving the official exchange rate toward a more realistic level throughout the 1980s. The Bank of China has devalued the yuan repeatedly, so that the official exchange rate in the fall of 1990 stood at 4.7 yuan to the dollar compared with 1.5 yuan to the dollar at the beginning of the 1980s. The process of using the market to allocate scarce foreign exchange was also under way as early as 1980–81, when the Bank of China and its local branches began to facilitate foreign exchange transactions among state units at prices diverging from both the official exchange rate and the internal settlement rate used by the Bank of China to settle merchandise trade transactions in the period 1981–83. More formal foreign exchange markets were established in major urban centers and several special economic zones in the mid-1980s to allow joint venture firms to buy and sell foreign exchange among themselves. In 1987–88 these markets were opened up to domestic firms, and the state authorities abandoned their most blatant efforts to control prices of these transactions.

The volume of transactions expanded from $4 billion in 1987 to $6.3 billion in 1988.[16] In 1989, when some argue reform was in full retreat, the volume of transactions rose almost 40 percent to reach $8.6 billion.[17] The upward trend continued in the first half of 1990, with transaction volume up 30 percent over the first half of 1989 in Shanghai, site of the largest foreign exchange market.[18]

The economic significance of this development is that for a large and growing share of Chinese trade transactions, importers are paying the opportunity cost of earning foreign exchange rather than continuing to be subsidized by the still somewhat overvalued official exchange rate.[19] In 1988, when the official exchange rate was 3.7 yuan per U.S. dollar, the average swap market price of foreign exchange was 6 yuan, a premium of almost two-thirds over the official rate. Moreover, the black market rate for foreign exchange was only about one-fourth higher than the swap rate in 1988, and by mid-December 1989 the premium was under 5 percent. After a further devaluation of the official rate in late December 1989, the spread widened, but only moderately.

In the early months of 1990 the situation was as follows: the official exchange rate was 4.7, the swap rate was 5.7, and the black market rate was 6.5.[20] What this suggests is that the swap market rate may be close to representing an equilibrium exchange rate and that the official exchange rate only moderately overvalues the domestic currency.

Contrast this situation with that in the Soviet Union. The official exchange rate for trade transactions in the fall of 1990 was .625 rubles per dollar, and, in contrast to China, this rate had not changed in recent years. The rate on the black market in 1989 varied by city but was rarely less than 10 and was as high as 20 in Leningrad and the Baltic Republics. In the very limited official bimonthly auction market initiated by Vneshekonom Bank in late 1989 in Moscow the rate—around 15 rubles per dollar—was a premium of 2,400 percent over the official rate.[21] The value of the ruble subsequently fell, with buyers of foreign exchange paying as much as 20 rubles per dollar at some auctions. The wide differential between the official and the auction market rates led officials to postpone until 1991 a previously announced regularization and expansion of these foreign currency exchanges. In short, the ruble is grossly overvalued, and users of imported goods are highly subsidized, as they have been for decades.

Although the view that the Chinese were ahead of the Soviets in economic reform was commonplace during much of the 1980s, the consensus shifted sharply in 1989. But much of the commentary on China mistakenly views austerity policy endorsed by the third plenum of the CCP's Thirteenth Central Committee in September 1988 as evidence of a major retreat from economic reform.

However, the main objective of the austerity program was to reduce excess demand and inflationary pressure, not to roll back economic reform. It is important to recognize that credit offered to enterprises, which had grown only moderately more rapidly than the economy in the early 1980s, grew excessively after the mid-1980s. These expanded credits were used to add to industrial capacity and to raise the wage bill. Money supply growth was soon virtually out of control, with currency in circulation expanding by almost 50 percent in 1988 alone.[22] A major reason for this sharp increase is that local branches of the state bank were beholden almost entirely to local government authority. These governments urged banks to extend more credit to stimulate local economic growth, in the process usurping the authority of the newly established central bank.

In the second half of 1988, China was heading for a major economic crisis. Excess demand from an inappropriately high rate of investment and huge increases in money in circulation quickly became apparent. Panic buying in the summer and fall of 1988 stripped many commodities from store inventories, and prices began to rise rapidly. The officially compiled cost of living index, for example, in December 1988 was 28 percent higher than in December 1987.[23] Without the austerity program initiated in the fourth quarter of 1988, China would soon have been consumed by hyperinflation.

The effectiveness of the austerity program can be judged in part on the basis of the performance of the economy in 1989, the first full year of the new program. Most significant, the rate of expansion of national income was brought down from an unsustainably high 11.4 percent in 1988 to 3.7 percent in 1989.[24] There were also significant achievements on the monetary and inflation front in 1989. Currency in circulation rose only 9.8 percent, compared with 46.8 percent in 1988. Retail prices increased by 17.8 percent for the year as a whole, a high rate by historic standards. But the monthly trend, which is more revealing of the direction of change, was far better. In the last quarter of 1989, retail prices were falling in absolute terms.

Even more surprising, given the predicted effects of the Tiananmen debacle of June 1989, China's external sector came through the year with reasonably good results. Exports grew by more than 10 percent, while the growth of imports was held to 7 percent. Again, contrary to predictions of collapse, the inflow of foreign direct investment rose for the tenth consecutive year to reach $3.3 billion.[25] Two-thirds of the investment came in the second half of the year, after the Tiananmen debacle. While earnings from tourism and overseas labor services fell, the declines were less than predicted. Despite the moratorium on new lending to China imposed by the World Bank and the Asian Development Bank, credits dispersed by international organizations from previously approved loans ran in excess of $1.2 billion in 1989, up almost 50 percent over 1988. Official bilateral credits to China, however, fell sharply. Moreover, Chinese foreign commercial borrowing also declined dramatically in 1989. But the drop dates from the beginning of 1989, prior to the imposition of foreign economic sanctions in

June. In short, it reflects mostly reduced Chinese demand for commercial loans rather than the reduced supply of loans by foreign banks. In part because net commercial borrowing was a negative $2 billion (i.e., repayments were $3.2 billion while new borrowing was only $1.1 billion), China's foreign exchange reserves dipped by about $500 million in 1989. However, at just over $17 billion, year-end reserves still provided a relatively comfortable coverage of three months' imports.

These basically positive developments continued in 1990. The rate of price inflation has been in the very low single digits; and the external sector has been recording its best performance ever, at least as measured by the merchandise trade balance. Exports have continued to grow at double-digit rates, while imports have fallen in response to sluggish domestic growth. Industrial growth, which had slowed considerably during the course of 1989 and early 1990, apparently began to turn upward around midyear. Thus, at least by some measures, the macroeconomic picture improved significantly between 1988, when austerity began, and 1990.

PROSPECTS FOR A RESUMPTION OF REFORM

As I have suggested above, in my judgment much commentary over the past year or so has both overstated the degree of retreat from economic reform and underestimated the probability that economic reform might resume its former pace.[26] As I have already argued, there were some areas, such as monetary policy, where a recentralization of control was imperative. And there were certain actions, such as a supposed centrally directed squeeze on private and collective activity in manufacturing and services, that were resisted locally and in any case were motivated largely by fiscal rather than ideological concerns. In manufacturing the nonstate sector flourished in 1989, growing more rapidly than state-owned industry for at least the twelfth consecutive year. Although the number of nonstate enterprises fell in 1989, by other measures the entrepreneurial sector has been doing quite well in China's current economic climate.[27]

Moreover, in many spheres of the economy, reforms have continued to move forward over the past year or so. In late 1989 the Bank of China announced a 20 percent devaluation of the yuan, the first such change in the official exchange rate since July 1986. And, as already discussed above, the State Administration of Exchange Control allowed a significant further expansion of the market for foreign exchange.

Another example of continuing reform on the external side is the increasing influence of foreign market prices on domestic prices. At the outset of the reform process the government sought to expand foreign trade while continuing to insulate domestic prices from both the level of foreign prices and fluctuations in those prices. By the end of the 1980s this insulation was significantly eroded. Nine-tenths of all imports were priced on the basis of world market prices and the exchange rate. Very few products were still eligible for subsidies from the central government—subsidies that once allowed the sale of imports on the domestic market with little or no regard for the world price of the commodity. Much of this progress occurred in 1989, and it continued in 1990. Similarly, producers of export goods in China increasingly receive prices tied to the international price rather than the domestic price of their goods. Again, this trend continued in 1990.

The increased influence of foreign prices in the domestic market is a significant development because it makes it possible for Chinese traders to make economically more rational choices. It also substantially increases the utility of the exchange rate as an instrument of government policy. In the early 1980s exchange rate changes had little or no effect either on the domestic prices of a broad range of imported goods or on the profitability of exporting a broad range of manufactured goods. That has now changed, paving the way for more active and effective exchange rate policy.

Reform and innovation have also continued in domestic financial markets. For example, the state has made active use of interest rate policy to influence private consumption and savings behavior. To dampen excess demand in late 1988 they introduced medium- and longer-term savings deposits in which the interest rate was linked to the consumer price index. Similarly indexed government bonds were introduced in late 1989. This gave consumers an incentive to increase their savings. Thus inflationary pressure was reduced by paring the incentive to shift from financial to real assets as rapidly as possible in order to avoid the erosion of the purchasing power of money. More recently, in the early months of 1990, the state lowered the interest rate on most savings deposits in order to stimulate sluggish consumer demand.

It would be premature to evaluate the success of these policies. But it is worth noting that the active use of interest-rate policy to influence consumption and savings is unusual in centrally planned economies. In the Soviet Union, individual savings accounts earn interest rates of only 2 to 3 percent. These rates have not been adjusted in recent years.

Although still limited in scope, price reform has been continued by the state. Significant price reform for transportation has been instituted over the past year, and discussion is under way for similar far-reaching price adjustments for energy. Huge price increases for passenger transport and increases for freight transport are particularly significant because basic transport prices were last changed in the mid-1950s. As the prices of energy, labor, and materials increased significantly over the ensuing decades, the transport sector was pushed into the red. Unable to reinvest to expand capacity, the sector became a bottleneck, dragging down the overall performance of the economy. Increases in passenger fares alone, which on average more than doubled, are expected to add almost 6 billion yuan annually to revenues of the railroads, civil aviation, and water transport systems. Combined with the additional revenues generated by higher freight rates, the sector will be able to finance more of its own expansion and upgrading, thus over time alleviating the bottleneck this sector has posed in recent years. Although less significant in purely economic terms, the prices of domestic postal services were more than doubled in 1990. As in the case of transport, this was the first change in prices in almost four decades and was designed to reduce the budgetary subsidies to this sector.

Crude oil and coal have also been significantly underpriced in recent years, leading to wasteful use of these scarce resources. A modest increase in the price of crude oil was instituted recently, and there is the prospect of as much as a doubling of the price of coal. However, as has been true for at least a decade, adjustments in the price of coal are fiercely contended. Competing bureaucratic interests may fight each other to a standoff with no more than a token price rise finally approved. But the debate on this topic appears as vigorous as ever.

Some economists, including some in China, argue that these examples of bureaucratically engineered price changes demonstrate how little reform has occurred in 1989 and 1990. In principle, of course, freeing up all prices, to let them be determined by supply and demand, would be desirable. In practice, many Chinese prices are so far from market clearing levels that preliminary bureaucratic price resetting is necessary. There are many examples over the past decade where this has ultimately led to a complete freeing up of prices.

In short, although the pace of reform has lagged compared with the early 1980s, selective but important reform measures have gone forward in 1989 and 1990. Moreover, I believe that the prospect is for an eventual resumption of more rapid reform. That judgment is based on several considerations.

First, in marked contrast with the Soviet Union, there is a substantial constituency in China for further reform. And it is not limited to a small urban intellectual class that supports economic reform because of the expectation it will lead to political reform. The vast majority of China's population benefited enormously from the first decade of reform, and their appetite for further reform appears to be substantial. This constituency includes not only the roughly 100 million workers in state-run units where nominal and real wages have tripled and doubled, respectively, over the past decade but even more particularly hundreds of millions of rural farm households; tens of millions of households that have benefited from the rapid growth of village and township enterprises; several tens of millions of urban Chinese who live in the various special economic zones, open cities, and technical and economic development zones that have benefited from China's opening to the world economy; and the families of 20 million entrepreneurs throughout China engaged in private service and manufacturing ventures. These latter groups in particular are likely to be strong supporters of further reform.

Substantial acceleration of both economic growth and personal income in China in the 1980s has created this constituency for further reform. True, it has been undermined by increased inequality that is the result of corruption. But rapid economic growth has provided the lubricant to reduce the frictions

of the transition to a more market oriented economy. The average rate of real
growth of the Chinese economy in the 1980s was approximately 10 percent,
about 9 percent in per capita terms. Thus average real consumption more
than doubled. The contrast with the Soviet Union (and perhaps, in the not
too distant future, even Poland) is marked. Official Soviet data show a
growth rate of around 3 percent in the 1980s, while Western estimates place
the rate at about 2 percent. The lagging growth rate and the increasing shortages in Moscow, and perhaps other urban centers, of the most basic goods,
such as bread, meat, salt, and soap, have enormously negative effects on
popular attitudes toward reform.[28] The population may be less likely to welcome reforms, with their attendant transitional costs of restructuring and increased inequality, when real living standards are perceived to be under
acute pressure. By contrast, a double-digit rate of real growth provides substantial benefits to virtually all members of society, cushioning the dissatisfaction caused by rising inequality and intersectoral and regional conflicts.

In addition, the sluggish Soviet economy, in the view of some, has created
or at least compounded a technical constraint on economic reform. Both
Western specialists and Soviet planners are preoccupied with the problem of
ruble overhang—the huge quantities of rubles held by the population, in the
form of either currency or savings deposits.[29] These rubles are held, it is argued, only because of a shortage of goods on the market.[30] Since these funds
are relatively liquid and would be used to bid up prices for scarce goods if
prices were freed, forced savings are perceived to represent a permanent
threat to price stability. Thus it is argued that the regime must somehow absorb the ruble overhang before introducing greater reliance on markets.

Two methods are discussed most often. The first is the sale of state assets.
However, it is countered that in the absence of a well-established market for
shares in state enterprises these sales would be manipulated and result in
huge transfers of wealth to a few individuals. Thus unless markets are well
established, the ruble overhang cannot be addressed. But the overhang itself
is an obstacle to allowing markets to develop. The most commonly proposed
solution, to simply distribute shares to the work force and allow a secondary
market to develop subsequently, would not contribute to a reduction of the
ruble overhang.

A second proposal is to either borrow internationally or sell a portion of
the state's gold holdings and use the proceeds to import large quantities of
high-quality consumer goods from the West that could be resold at high
ruble prices. The obvious drawback of this approach is that it would not directly contribute to the development of an increased capacity to export to
earn foreign exchange to repay the initial borrowing or restore the initial
level of state foreign exchange and gold reserves.

Superficially, it might appear that China suffers a similar problem. Individual savings soared in China during the first decade of reform—from 31
billion yuan in 1978 to 445 billion yuan at the end of 1989.[31] Individual sav-

ings accounts in 1989 were the equivalent of 35 percent of national income, roughly the same proportion as in the Soviet Union.

However, the favorable interest rates on longer-term deposits in China have resulted in a significant reduction in the liquidity of these savings. Moreover, the extremely rapid growth of the economy over the past decade has placed China in a fundamentally different position from the Soviet Union's. The Chinese economy actually suffers from a surplus of consumer goods, even durables. The regime, as alluded to above, is trying to stimulate consumer demand. As inventories of durables have piled up, the regime has been forced to curtail production of cameras, bicycles, household refrigerators and washing machines, and even color televisions. Chinese citizens are sitting on what for them are mountains of savings not because there is nothing to buy but largely because they expect prices to fall in the future. And Chinese reformers are not preoccupied with the threat of renminbi overhang.

A second factor underlying my somewhat optimistic judgment on the prospects for reform is that changing leadership at the top could again bring forth a leader, like Zhao Ziyang, strongly committed to economic reform. Indeed, one cannot rule out Zhao's comeback. Moreover, the party has not repudiated the instrumentalist approach it has embraced over the past decade or more.

In the wake of the collapse of communist regimes in 1989, the more conservative members of China's leadership orchestrated the drafting of an ideological document intended to buttress the legitimacy of the Chinese Communist Party. The resulting document repudiated developments in Eastern Europe and even much of Gorbachev's reform program and upheld China as the last remaining bastion of communism. Deng Xiaoping himself reportedly quashed this effort and admonished the supporters of the document that they should focus their energies not on ideological matters but on solving China's problems, particularly its economic difficulties. Thus Deng continues to see the legitimacy of the party as deriving not from its ideological leadership but from its ability to ensure rising living standards as reflected in increased consumption of food, clothing, housing, and so forth.

But the policies that have been most successful in raising living standards are those of the reformers. Even Li Peng, who is less than enthusiastic about reform, may feel compelled to support further reform measures as a means of increasing the underlying productivity of the economic system and thus improving its capacity for raising living standards. Indeed the sharp drop in economic growth in 1989 and the continued softness of the economy through much of 1990 has weakened Li's position, so that he may become increasingly receptive to reform proposals designed to raise the underlying productivity of the economic system.

Finally, most of the institutes and informal advisory groups that were the fount of ideas for reform over the past decade are in place and still functioning. Indeed, the vigor of the debate on economic reform in these organizations in 1990 was remarkable. This debate was reflected in a broad range of publications as well as in informal discussions, meetings, and so forth. Of course, these reformers do not necessarily enjoy the access and influence they once had with the highest levels of China's political leadership. But the debates continue, and for reasons described above I think it is highly likely that the influence of the proponents of reform will rise once again.

The main obstacle to the resumption of more rapid economic reform in China, in my judgment, is not the demand of students and intellectuals for a more pluralistic political system. China's leadership has not stepped back from its commitment to reform because they fear economic reform will lead to escalating demands for political reform. In the wake of the Tiananmen tragedy, many Western observers speculated that the conservatives would have to mollify an alienated urban population by abandoning the policy of austerity that had begun to impose real economic costs on the population. In a word, reflation would be used to defuse the threat to political stability posed by the urban working class. Instead, the regime initially did the opposite: it pushed through unpopular retail price increases, held down investment spending (thus leading to the layoff of millions of additional workers in construction), and held down the rate of wage increases, particularly bonus payments. None of these actions suggests a regime that perceived incipient popular unrest.

The challenge the regime faces is to deal more successfully with the problems of a semireformed economy. Roughly two-thirds of China's national income is produced by units over which the state exercises indirect control. Only a third is produced in state-owned units that to some degree are subject to the traditional planning system. That means the regime must rely increasingly on the policy instruments of a market-oriented economy, notably monetary and fiscal policy, to influence the pace of economic growth. Yet development of the institutions that would make this possible has just begun.[32]

The second key problem is to deal with the endemic corruption. It is a direct result also of the semireformed character of the economy. Many inputs and final goods are sold at widely varying prices depending on whether they fall under the purview of the shrinking state plan or the rapidly expanding more decentralized portion of the economy where the influence of state price control is limited. The profits that accrue to arbitrage between these two sectors can be huge. Because even state-owned plants are allowed and encouraged to produce for the uncontrolled sector, it is virtually impossible to separate legitimate profit seeking activity from the illegal diversion of planned materials and output to the decentralized market.

The regime has sought to deal with this problem in two ways, one short term and the other longer term. The former is evident in a seemingly more vigorous campaign against economic corruption. As in the war on drugs in the United States, it is difficult to judge whether the heightened anticorruption campaign is reducing the level of illegal activities.

The second policy is the decision, in principle, to do away with what is referred to as the dual track pricing system, which is the ultimate source of the economic incentive for illegal transactions. So far this is a decision only in principle. It does not mean, as some have suggested, that price controls will be reimposed on the large share of output that is now distributed through the market. The state-fixed prices for some goods will be abolished and all of the output will be distributed through the markets. For other goods the state-fixed price will be raised significantly, reducing the gap between the state and market prices. And for some goods, state price controls will be reimposed on the share of output now distributed via the market. Obviously, this process will take time, and it will not soon be possible to judge the relative importance of these three alternative means of reducing the price disparities of the dual-track system.

NOTES

1. Adi Ignatius, who has articulated this view consistently, wrote in the fall of 1989, "four months after the Beijing massacre, it's apparent that the hard-line stance that brought in tanks and troops to clear Tiananmen Square also has swept away plans to let market forces play a greater role in the economy." "China's Economic Reform Program Enters Hibernation," *Wall Street Journal*, September 26, 1989, p. A18.

2. Editorial, "China Steps Back from Reform," *New York Times*, April 11, 1989.

3. Developments in Eastern Europe at the end of 1989 went virtually unreported in the Chinese media, largely because of the fear of reviving domestic political opposition. Steven Erlanger, "China's Lonely Press Tries to Look the Other Way," *New York Times*, December 24, 1989.

4. One notable exception to this perspective is Zbigniew Brzezinski, who, at least prior to 1989, thought that China could substantially reform its economy without a radical political reform. *The Grand Failure: The Birth and Death of Communism in the Twentieth Century* (New York: Scribner, 1989).

5. Chinese Communist Party Central Committee, *China's Economic Structure Reform* (Beijing: Foreign Languages Press, 1984).

6. For analyses of this phenomenon see the essays in David M. Lampton, ed., *Polity Implementation in Post-Mao China* (Berkeley: University of California Press, 1987).

7. One estimate places the share of increased farm output between 1978 and 1984, due to improved incentives, at more than three-quarters. The balance of the growth, just over a fifth, is attributed to higher prices paid to farm producers during the same period. John McMillan, Jon Whalley, and Lijing Zhu, "The Impact of China's Economic Reforms on Agricultural Productivity Growth," *Journal of Political Economy* 97:4 (August 1989), pp. 781–807.

8. State Statistical Bureau, *Chinese Statistical Yearbook 1985* (Beijing: Statistical Publishing House, 1985), p. 306; *Chinese Statistical Abstract 1990* (Beijing: Statisti-

cal Publishing House, 1990), p. 68. These shares are calculated based on the gross value of industrial output measured in current prices.

9. *Chinese Statistical Abstract 1990*, p. 3.

10. For an illuminating analysis of the evolution of the private sector and its significance for reform of socialist systems, see János Kornai, "The Affinity Between Ownership Forms and Coordination Mechanisms: The Common Experience in Socialist Countries," *Journal of Economic Perspectives* 4:3 (Summer 1990), pp. 131–47.

11. For the most comprehensive analysis of the economic environment in which the township and village industries operate, see William Byrd and Lin Qingsong, eds., *China's Rural Industry: Structure, Development and Reform* (New York: Oxford University Press, 1990).

12. State Statistical Bureau, *Chinese Statistical Yearbook 1983* (Beijing: Statistical Publishing House, 1983), p. 372; *Chinese Statistical Yearbook 1989* (Beijing: Statistical Publishing House, 1989), p. 601.

13. *Chinese Statistical Yearbook 1989*, p. 601; *Chinese Statistical Abstract 1990*, p. 90.

14. Ministry of Foreign Economic Relations and Trade, "Memorandum on China's Foreign Trade Regime." Submitted to the General Agreement on Tariffs and Trade, February 1987.

15. Working Party on China's Status as a Contracting Party, "Questions and Replies Concerning the Memorandum on China's Foreign Trade Regime" (Geneva: GATT, 1987), pp. 149–50.

16. Reporter, "Initial Steps in the Establishment of China's Foreign Exchange Market," *Jinrong Ribao* [Banking Daily], February 15, 1989, p. 1.

17. Wang Guanghua and Wang Xiangwei, "Swap Centers Will Be Updated," *China Daily*, May 6, 1990.

18. Staff Reporters, "New Steps for Money Exchange," *China Daily*, August 17, 1990, p. 2.

19. Importers paying the opportunity cost of earning foreign exchange include not only those purchasing foreign exchange in the swap market but those exporting firms that use some of their retained foreign exchange to import goods rather than selling it on the market. The magnitude of these purchases is not known but could have been as high as $12 billion in 1988, since total foreign exchange retained by exporters was $18.51 billion. The latter volume is equal to almost half the volume of China's imports in 1988, as reported by the Minister of Foreign Economic Relations and Trade.

20. Chen Weihua, "Dollar Up Only Slightly in Shanghai Money Market," *China Daily*, December 19, 1989, p. 2.

21. Compared with the Chinese foreign exchange market, the Soviet auction is limited both in size and in the kinds of enterprises permitted to participate. The volume of foreign exchange sold at one auction in the fall of 1989 was reportedly $13.7 million. At this rate, the yearly Soviet volume of exchange would be one-tenth of China's in 1989. The Soviet auction market is open only to state-owned firms, whereas in China not only state firms but also joint ventures, collective firms, and to a limited extent even individuals are allowed to buy and sell foreign exchange. "Ruble Shrinks Again," *Wall Street Journal*, November 13, 1989. Peter Passell, "The Ruble's Next Move," *New York Times*, October 26, 1989, p. C2. Bill Keller, "Soviets to Open Exchanges for Free Trading in Rubles," *New York Times*, August 8, 1990, pp. C1–C2.

22. Currency in circulation rose from 145.4 billion yuan at year-end 1987 to 213.4

billion yuan at year-end 1988. State Statistical Bureau, *Chinese Statistical Abstract 1989* (Beijing: Statistical Publishing House, 1989), p. 74.

23. *China Statistics Monthly* 1:12 (March 1989), p. 57.

24. State Statistical Bureau, "Statistical Communique on China's 1989 Economic and Social Development," *People's Daily* (overseas edition), February 21, 1990, p. 2.

25. This is actual investment. The annual volume of contracted investment also rose, to $6.3 billion.

26. For example, the fundamental premise of Christopher Wren's treatment of China is that no reform is possible until the Chinese Communist Party is dumped into the wastebin of history. *The End of the Line: The Failure of Communism in the Soviet Union and China* (New York: Simon and Schuster, 1990), p. 315.

27. Western commentators, in my view, have missed the point in citing the failure of large numbers of private, collective, and village and township enterprises as evidence of the state's effort to reconcentrate industrial capacity in firms under its direct control. It is true that in 1989 the number of collective industrial enterprises fell from 18.5 to 17.5 million, and there were 24,000 fewer private industries than in 1988. Township and village enterprises also fell, from 18.9 to 18.7 million. However, it is not consistent to decry the state's propping up its own enterprises through loans and other financial subsidies and to expect nonstate firms to avoid the influence of market forces. Moreover, much of the turnover of these nonstate enterprises is encouraged by laws that exempt them from paying most taxes for the first three years of their operation. Many of these enterprises go out of business at the end of the third year and then, reflecting the creativity of the entrepreneurs that control them, are reestablished under a different name in a slightly different product line the following year. I prefer to look at the shares of employment and output in this sector. These indicators reflect the buoyancy of the nonstate sector.

28. A dissenting view is presented in Robert J. Shiller, Maxim Boycko, and Vladimir Korobov, "Popular Attitudes toward Free Markets: The Soviet Union and the United States Compared," Yale University, Cowles Foundation Discussion Paper 952, August 1990. In a random survey in the Soviet Union and the United States in May 1990, they found that Soviet attitudes toward price changes, profits, income inequality, work incentives, entrepreneurial activities, free markets, and savings did not differ significantly from the attitudes held by Americans who were surveyed at random in the same period. However, the survey was telephonic and limited to Moscow, so one might be skeptical about the validity of the findings for the Soviet Union. The authors conclude that the transition to a market system in the Soviet Union is not inhibited by popular attitudes but by entrenched bureaucratic interests that resist change.

29. For an interesting discussion of the conceptual problems in measuring the overhang and a brief review of some Soviet writings on this subject, see Gregory Grossman, "Monetary and Financial Aspects of Gorbachev's Reform," in Christine Kissides et al., eds., *Financial Reform in Socialist Economies* (Washington, D.C.: World Bank, 1989), chapter 1.

30. An exception to this perspective is Shiller et al., "Popular Attitudes" (p. 35), who found in their survey that there is virtually no difference between the savings motivations of Soviets and Americans. Both save overwhelmingly for retirement or to accumulate financial resources to make major purchases such as cars and vacation homes. Only 6 percent of the Soviet respondents in the survey indicated that they save because goods are not available on the market.

31. *Chinese Statistical Abstract 1990*, p. 35.

32. Barry Naughton, "Macroeconomic Obstacles to Reform in China: The Role of Fiscal and Monetary Policy," forthcoming in a conference volume edited by Hung-dah Chiu. For an insightful analysis of the problems of economic stabilization during the transition to a more market-oriented economy in the Soviet Union, see William D. Nordhaus, "Soviet Economic Reform: The Longest Road," *Brookings Papers on Economic Activity*, no. 1, 1990, pp. 287–318.

8

American National Interest and the New Europe:

The Millennium Has Not Yet Arrived

DAVID CALLEO

A NEW WORLD ORDER

FUTURE RELATIONS between America and Europe will depend heavily on how the overall global situation evolves, and what general geopolitical roles and strategies the United States and the Europeans choose to pursue. The global situation has remained essentially static for so long, and national strategies have remained so constant, that this truism about the interdependence of regional and global policy is perhaps harder to grasp than it ought to be. Throughout the long postwar period, with its bipolar global dispensation, America's commitment to European defense was never seriously in question, nor was Europe's desire for it. And both were firmly committed to the liberal world political economy of the Pax Americana. It was this harmony of transatlantic interest that made the postwar global system possible. Thanks to the transatlantic alliance, a Eurasian balance contained the Soviets on their own home ground and left the United States the predominant power throughout the rest of the globe. Today, at the beginning of the last decade of the twentieth century, the Soviets have rapidly abandoned the cold war, retreated from Central Europe, and embarked upon profound if uncertain reforms to democratize their politics, liberalize their economy, and federalize the remainder of their empire. In effect, the bipolar global dispensation has collapsed.

So complete a Western victory threatens to destabilize many habitual relationships, the transatlantic alliance among them. The destabilization has been, first of all, intellectual. The cold war provided a simplistic but highly serviceable way to view the problem of order in the world. It focused American efforts on building the military forces to deter Soviet aggression and the military, political, and economic coalitions needed to contain Russian ambitions.

For our West European allies, America's anti-Soviet preoccupation was preferable, in many respects, to the diffuse and relatively unlimited American aims of the wartime period. President Roosevelt and Secretary of State Hull had dreamed of a global system of free trade, where Europe's old colonies would become liberal democracies, Germany and Japan would be severely punished, and the United States, together with its Western allies and the Russians and Chinese, would use the United Nations Security Council to enforce collective security against "aggression." This early vision of the "American Century" elicited grave reservations in Western Europe. The British and French, as well as the Soviet government, felt threatened by the overwhelming military and economic power of a United States beginning to enjoy its hegemonic destiny.

Stalin asserted dreams of his own, and brutally imposed Russian predominance in Eastern Europe. By allying with a newly communist China, he appeared to have cemented a vast Eurasian bloc, an "evil empire" that was, potentially at least, a global challenger to the Pax Americana. It was certainly a real enough threat to Western Europe. But the resulting cold war had advantages from a West European perspective. It restrained America's universalistic pretensions within the more manageable goal of containing the Soviet challenge. Building a grand anti-Soviet alliance inclined the United States into a series of compromises with European and Japanese aspirations. Out of this came the Marshall Plan and Germany's rearmament, as well as America's support for Japan's resurrection and the European Economic Community. As the United States contested Soviet influence, in the Third World anticommunism modified anticolonialism and aid supplemented free trade.

In some respects, the cold war probably limited interstate conflict. A Europe clearly divided into two blocs, both heavily armed with nuclear and conventional forces, made a new European war extremely improbable. And dividing the Third World into U.S. and Soviet clients gave a much-needed definition to relations among the bewildering crowd of uncertain states emerging from the old European empires. The two superpowers, mesmerized by their nuclear balance of terror, drew back from direct confrontations with each other and tried to restrain their respective clients from challenging what were perceived as the vital interests of the other. After Korea at least, wars in the Third World were mostly instigated by local clients for their own purposes, as in Arab-Israeli clashes, or resulted when a superpower miscalculated the strength and determination of indigenous, nationalist forces—as in Vietnam or Afghanistan. While it seems perverse to wax enthusiastic over the benefits of an order that brought so much oppression, and wasted such huge resources on armaments, nevertheless the cold war's restraints were certainly preferable to the violent military conflicts and economic convulsions of the twentieth century's first half.

The sudden end of the Soviet "threat" now requires a redefinition of the fears, ambitions, and policies of both the Americans and the Europeans. The nature of the future world order will very much depend on the degree to which those redefinitions are harmonious with each other. For the United States, one immediate tendency is to turn back the intellectual clock to the more universalistic aspirations of the wartime era. Without the Soviet threat to provide focus and discipline, America's global mission can once more be defined as stopping "aggression" in general. The ever-serviceable Munich analogy can become a sort of intellectual hair trigger, ready to invoke retribution at any use of force to settle grievances against the status quo.

This tendency is encouraged by America's present exceptionally high degree of military readiness.[1] The Soviet retreat, following the great Reagan military buildup, leaves the United States with a relatively high capacity to impose its will through superior military force. Gorbachev's retreat, leaving the United States the lone superpower, entices us into the role of world policeman, perhaps even more than Stalin's relentless probing.[2]

In a world full of thwarted national aspirations, unsettled grievances, artificial boundaries, and reckless dictators, the risks of such a policeman's role are considerable. Becoming a sort of global Metternich seems a formula destined to alienate a good part of the world, Europe included, and exhaust ourselves in the process. Avoiding such risks will presumably require a world vision more receptive of change, more discriminating about defining and protecting American interests, and more alert to the possibilities for using the initiatives of others.

If the sudden Soviet retreat has greatly confused America's geopolitical strategy, it has revolutionized the perspectives of the Europeans. For a start, America's geopolitical weight in Europe is now considerably depreciated. So long as the formidable Soviet army was deployed in the middle of Germany, a Western Europe that wished to preserve its independence and prosperity urgently needed the Atlantic Alliance. Today's Russia may possibly remain a military colossus, but it has a very different posture in relation to its West European neighbors. These neighbors now begin to look upon the Soviet Union, with its vast undeveloped resources and hunger for consumer goods, more as a target of economic and political opportunity than as a military threat. America's military and political role in Europe is thus devalued from being the almost indispensable protector against an urgent danger to being a prudent insurance policy against a remote contingency.

While Russia's sudden retreat has brought the need for new American and European roles and strategies to a head, the need has, in fact, been long anticipated. The trend away from a bipolar world has been a long-standing one. Signs of a more plural distribution of economic prowess and political vitality have been abundant in recent years. Japan's spectacular industrial and financial development has been followed by the rise of highly competitive manufacturing in other Asian countries, not too long ago classified as underdeveloped. This has had profound implications for American and European economies. Revolutions in every postwar decade—from Algeria in the 1950s to Iran in the 1970s—have also made manifest the dynamic energy and the unstable structures of postwar Moslem civilization. Iraq's assault on Kuwait challenged not only the regimes and economic relationships but the state system itself left over from the era of Western domination.

Over the past decade, Europe has produced perhaps the most beneficent signs of pluralist vitality. Progress toward a more integrated West European Community has taken several significant steps, among them the European Monetary System and the Single European Act. Russia's retreat now has brought Germany's peaceful reunification and Central Europe's return to its traditional Western orientation. Even the less developed Balkan states are being drawn into Europe. At the same time, the halting Soviet progress toward a liberal economy and democratic federation presents Europe with huge long-term economic prospects. The political dangers are obvious, but so is the enormous promise.

Any trend toward a more plural world implies a concomitant relative "decline" of the superpowers. For the United States at least, this relative decline is not in itself undesirable. That Europe is richer and stronger in relation to the United States than in 1950 or 1960 is hardly surprising, and can be attributed in good part to the success of deliberate American policies. The same might be said of the rise of Japan or other rapidly developing Asian states. But relative decline can also become absolute and pathological—a weakening of the springs of national strength. For the superpowers, the principal cause for this absolute kind of decline is not the rise of others but their own inappropriate policies. In a world growing more plural, superpowers trying to continue their traditional roles without adapting to the new circumstances risk overstretching their resources to the point where they do real harm to their own long-term national prospects.

It seems self-evident that the Soviet Union has been its own worst enemy. Many analysts suspect that the United States is on a similar course.[3] The most obvious evidence of America's overstretching lies in its twin deficits—fiscal and external—that must be largely financed either by capital borrowed from abroad or by inflation.[4] These chronic deficits have now endured well over a decade, going back to the unbalanced fiscal policies and unsound financial practices of the 1970s and before. Behind these accumulated problems lies an erratic contest for priority between military and civilian aims, resolved too frequently by a resort to easy money that the dollar's international position has made too possible.

These practices have increasingly damaged the American economy's long-term prospects. The litany of weaknesses has grown familiar. The federal government now struggles with an exceptionally high level of debt service that progressively constrains its resources.[5] Neglect of the country's physical infrastructure, education, and health needs over several years continues to weaken the economy's productive base. So does crime, drug addiction, and a swelling underclass. Excessive credit creation, often to offset fiscal shortfalls, has discouraged saving and encouraged a dangerous level of debt among firms and too much speculative investment in general.[6] Thanks to the consequences of macroeconomic malpractice, the American economy now has a high propensity for inflation that needs to be repressed by periodic bouts of savagely tight monetary policy. This stop-go policy, coupled with the sharply oscillating exchange rates that are one of its consequences, discourages long-term investment. Low and misdirected investment saps the growth of productivity needed to keep American industry competitive at home or abroad.[7] High debt, low savings, and the regular urgent need to borrow from abroad all greatly constrain the flexibility of macroeconomic policy in the face of future recessions, at the same time as the high level of public and private debt makes any deep recession dangerous for financial stability. Conditions of this kind have made the United States increasingly unattractive for foreign investors, at the same time as it has grown highly dependent on a regular inflow of foreign capital to finance its swelling debt. Under these circumstances, the United States is not only unable to participate actively in recapitalizing Central and Eastern Europe but must fear the diversion of European capital away from financing American debt.

In short, the retreat and apparent collapse of Soviet power is not the unequivocal American victory that might have been expected. The United States itself manifests too many characteristics of national decline for comfort. Soviet decline has to be counted, then, as less a sign of American triumph than of a more plural world in general. The problem for the United States is how to foster a new order out of those plural elements, while avoiding a fate for itself similar to that of the Soviets.

KEEPING THE PEACE

America's economic improvement and geopolitical redesign are, of course, closely interdependent. The Soviet retreat seemed to offer the United States some fiscal relief through cuts in military spending. But the Gulf crisis that erupted in the summer of 1990 made clear that any such relief will prove ephemeral without basic changes in American geopolitical strategy.

The Gulf crisis demonstrated rather clearly what seem to be the basic characteristics of the new post–cold war order. At the outset, the United States was able to deploy a vast force without fear of Soviet reaction. On the contrary, the Soviet Union voted in the Security Council to legitimize the presence of the American forces and impose severe economic sanctions on Iraq. The Soviets even hinted that they might supply forces to a collective peacekeeping effort under United Nations command. The old dream of cooperation among the superpowers to impose world order suddenly revived. But while the Soviets undoubtedly had large military forces, their political and economic disarray made it unlikely that they would or could deploy them, let alone risk a lengthy campaign. Their large and restless Muslim population and recent disaster in Afghanistan make them leery of any superpower combination smacking of traditional great power imperialism against the Muslim world. All these constraints suggest that even with Russian good will, superpower condominium is an improbable organizing principle in the more plural system that is emerging.

As it happens, the bulk of non-American forces to counter Iraq had to come from Britain and France or from certain states of the region— principally Egypt, Saudi Arabia, and Syria. The entire, slow unfolding of the crisis demonstrated the difficulties of combining pluralistic peacekeeping with traditional American hegemony.

Caught unprepared for this particular crisis, the American military proceeded to deploy its huge forces according to an operation plan originally drawn up to counter a massive Soviet or Iranian invasion of the entire Gulf area. Military decisions also seemed to reflect putative lessons from the Vietnam War. Since gradual escalation did not work there, it was said, overwhelming force had to be applied in the Gulf from the very outset.

At the same time, the limits to American means were made vivid by the spectacle of the American secretary of state and the secretary of the treasury traveling around the world raising funds to defray the military costs. Except from the Saudis and the Kuwaitis, however, funds remained scarce for the American military effort, but relatively abundant for relieving the frontline states—Egypt, Jordan, and Turkey—of their considerable economic costs from enforcing the sanctions. Again, broad support around the world for a more plural conception of peacekeeping was combined with diffidence toward a unilateral American military role.

The military outcome of the 1991 Gulf War notwithstanding, the whole crisis illustrated rather well the possibilities and dangers for American policy in the present state of the global system. Political conditions seem unusually propitious for developing a concert of powers to maintain order against the more flagrant and brutal forms of aggression, at least in places critical to the collective national interests of Americans, Europeans, Japanese, and Soviets. The United States, however, is inhibited from genuinely pursuing a coalition strategy because it believes that timely and decisive military action requires preemptive American leadership and initiative. At the same time, whatever the practical difficulties of collective peacekeeping, the costs and dangers make it unlikely that the United States will sustain a unilateral policy for very long. Moreover, the United States acting unilaterally risks putting itself in the position of the world's principal reactionary power, the great enemy of all the forces around the globe urgently pressing for change. It remains to be seen whether the lesson can be grasped in advance or has to be learned through painful and costly experience.

However the lesson is learned, and whatever the final outcome of the Gulf crisis, America is in no position to return to its hegemonic dreams of 1945. Financially, the United States has grown dependent on the inflow of foreign capital and can reduce its dependency only by reducing its fiscal deficit—a difficult course quite incompatible with sustaining its present military establishment, let alone transforming it into a world police force. In fact, the United States is unlikely to follow such an ambitious geopolitical course, if for no other reason than that the American public is unlikely to support it through any prolonged test of strength, and properly so. America's global problem, then, is how to build an effective concert. While the United States undoubtedly still has the leading role in building the new machinery, Europe, as during the cold war, remains the partner needed for success. Western Europe is still the principal region in the world, and in some respects the only one, that combines economic, financial, and military power on anything like the American scale. Whether the transatlantic partnership endures obviously depends on how Europeans, as well as Americans, assess its value in the more plural world now emerging. That assessment depends at least partly on how well the partnership adapts its inner arrangements to fit the new world.

NEW EUROPEAN PERSPECTIVES

Throughout the cold war, the Atlantic Alliance ensured Europe's independence as well as America's global predominance. On balance, Europeans had good reason to find the terms favorable. With Russia's retreat, Europe is unlikely to feel the same urgent need for the American alliance; the transatlantic relationship is thus fated to change its character. But both the West European states and the United States will continue to have vital interests in each other. They share profound cultural ties and they remain the only parts of the world where liberal political and economic traditions are deeply implanted and reliably practiced. But the new European scene, transformed by the Soviet retreat, now has different threats and different opportunities for both European and American policy. The principal common threat is that the recent changes in Europe will prove too great for either the European or the international system to contain. The worst danger might come from the disintegration of the Soviet Union itself. While a genuinely federated Soviet Union, with its elements open and liberal, ought to prove a great boon for Europe, a Soviet Union that breaks up in domestic chaos and internecine conflict could easily bring Europe closer to war than it ever was during the cold war. No one can say how Gorbachev's grand experiment will evolve. But the extremely pessimistic expectations for his economic reforms, widespread among the experts, do not permit any facile optimism about the stability of the Soviet Union, the longevity of its nascent democracy, or even its current friendly posture toward its Western neighbors. In any event, whatever regime evolves will remain a military giant. Europe's political safety will require that Russian military power be balanced in some effective fashion. The Soviet Union is obviously not the only potential source of instability. Those Central and East European states now free of Soviet tutelage will have enormous difficulty transforming their economies rapidly enough to relieve the long frustrated expectations of their populations.

While Eastern and Central Europe have been struggling with their new freedom, the nascent West European confederacy has been riding a wave of optimism about its own prospects. But troubles in Central and Eastern Europe could easily cause dissension among the West European states and blight those prospects. The most critical issue for West European solidarity will be what happens within a reunited Germany. West Germany has been the great anchor of Western Europe's liberal prosperity and democratic stability. Together with France, the Federal Republic has led the European Community throughout its history. But absorbing the old German Demo-

cratic Republic now presents the Federal Republic with a challenge that can
be expected to absorb a good part of its energy and wealth for a generation.
Under the circumstances, Germany's traditional role in the European Community can hardly be taken for granted. Germany is more important for Europe than ever, but its policies will be less stable and predictable, and it will
have far fewer resources for resolving other people's problems.

German unification also poses a challenge to the rest of the Community,
France in particular. The threat of German hegemony dominated French
policy in the time of the Third and Fourth Republics. Under the Fifth Republic, a more robust and confident France shifted from a policy of hostile
containment to one of intimate partnership with Germany. This change was
possible partly because the French felt themselves stronger. Even if West
Germany was somewhat richer and more populous, France's economic performance was impressive. Whatever economic disparity existed seldom
seemed great enough to make the partnership seriously unbalanced and uncomfortable. France's superior status as an independent nuclear power with
considerable global outreach, bolstered by the exceptionally creative élan of
French diplomacy, seemed to more than compensate for any economic gap.
In recent years, moreover, the French economy has grown even stronger.
The French have restructured many of their leading industries and brought
their inflation rate slightly below Germany's.[8]

A reunited Germany undoubtedly affects this Franco-German balance,
but calculating the effect is not easy. In the near future, absorbing the East
will more likely weaken Germany's economic weight than strengthen it. For
the German government's finances, East Germany will be a heavy liability
well into the future.[9] For private firms, the economic possibilities in the East
are nearly all long term at best. French firms, of course, have not been inac-
tive in looking over the more lucrative possibilities. Insofar as German firms
are under greater constraint to invest in eastern enterprises generally, it may
not prove an advantage to them. In the long run, the real value of acquiring
several million well-educated and presumably hard-working and ambitious
countrymen should not be underestimated. But the short-term economic
costs may be very high.

Politically, the new Germany is even more elusive. Historically, the
Germans—east, west, south, and north—have not got on particularly well
with each other. Prussian domination was much resented in the old Reich,
and the return of even a radically truncated eastern region is not welcomed
as an unmixed blessing, even now. But the West German political system
has deep resources of tolerance and balance, and underneath its partisan
waves flows a stable current of common sense. Still, Germans and their
neighbors can hardly be blamed for some apprehension.

So far, the principal common reaction among the West Europeans has
been to press forward more frantically with plans for tightening integration
within the European Community. This merely reinforces a trend well under
way before the Soviet retreat reunited Germany and opened up the East.

The Single European Act of 1986 had already committed EC states to major new steps toward monetary union and general economic and political integration. Logically, however, Europe's new situation just as easily favors delaying as speeding up any "deepening" of the Community. A disparate crowd of Eastern states are now desperately eager to adhere to the West. Complicating matters further, Austria, Sweden, Switzerland, and Turkey would also like to join the Community. Faced with this situation, the EC is trying to deepen and widen simultaneously. But the declared priority has so far seemed to go to deepening. The prevailing theory has been that only by intensifying its Western core can the EC have enough inner strength to reach out and eventually incorporate the East. This has been preeminently the French view; and the Germans, eager to reassure their Western neighbors, and perhaps themselves, have been at pains to cater to it.

It is not clear how long this priority will prevail. From the start, the British, never enthusiastic about a Europe bound tightly together, have openly argued that the Community should forbear its internal tightening in order to incorporate the Central and East European states. The British position has a certain obvious logic and its appeal has been growing. On balance, it seems probable that the Community will strengthen its integrating structures somewhat, but not as much as many had hoped.

Institutional progress within the EC in recent years, combined with fear of the destabilizing effects of the Soviet retreat, has promoted a revival of the old dream of a federal Community whose structures will somehow replace the nation-states. That dream is likely to remain as great an illusion in the near future as it has been in the past. The Community is not a centralized state, nor does it seem about to become one. But by a more practical standard, the EC is an extraordinary success. Its success derives from the working balance it has achieved between national self-determination and collective needs. Its real progress has depended on Europe's national governments, elites, and publics developing an extended sense of self-interest in building a regional system. Building this system has not made Europe's nation-states disappear into a new super state. The old states remain the ultimate centers of political legitimacy and administrative authority. But they have developed among themselves remarkable openness and cooperation, kept functioning by a structure that provides for constant negotiating among the governments and bureaucracies. The success of the EC thus stems from its practical machinery for negotiating and harmonizing national interests. In the process, a considerable degree of common European feeling has most certainly grown up among both elites and the public at large. But this European feeling is not so much a diminishing of national loyalty as an extension of it.

In effect, Western Europe has not been creating a new superpower, on the American model, but a new political form, whose constitution embodies a balance between national and collective interests and identities. It has grown into a working constitution for much of the European continent. As a continental constitution, it is highly flexible, and for that reason more robust than it seems. It may prove ideal for absorbing the intense pressure in Europe to accommodate so many new forces. In the long run, it may prove better able to regulate the affairs of a whole continent than the more rigidly centralized national structures of the earlier continental systems, the United States and the Soviet Union. Certainly the troubles of the Soviet Union make evident its structural limitations. Unfortunately, the growing problems of governing the United States also suggest the limitations of a federal as opposed to a multinational continental system.

Whatever its advantages, a confederal system will not hold together unless its states have reached a certain acceptable equilibrium of power among themselves. Germany's unification will inevitably encourage tentative new alignments within the Community. The anti-German France of the Fourth Republic can be expected to revive sufficiently to look with new interest upon relations with its old allies—Britain, "Latin Europe," or Eastern Europe, including Russia itself. Heavy North African emigration will continue to remind the French not to ignore their Mediterranean neighbors. The Italians, too, have a Mediterranean preoccupation, but also historical ties to German Mitteleuropa; they have begun to promote a revived "Habsburg Europe"—to forge the states of the old empire into a cooperative block within the new enlarged Europe.

These sorts of constructions are no substitute for the European Community. But insofar as they develop, they will inevitably make for a different EC, with different alignments and centers of initiative. But whatever the new stresses and strains within the EC, it presents what is, by far, the most hopeful and attractive vision of how the new Europe should develop. West Europeans are not at all likely to throw away the immense political and economic capital they have invested and developed within it.

In the long run, the Central European countries like Czechoslovakia, Hungary, and Poland may well join the Community—along with the Austrians, Swedes, Swiss, and perhaps others. In the meantime, the Community can be expected to embrace its eastern neighbors with a proliferating network of "association" arrangements. The problem will be to regulate the pace. Full integration of the Central European countries has to be timed not to put intolerable strain on national resources and political systems in the West as well as in the East, or on the cooperative interstate relations that have already grown up within the Community. The more diverse the elements to be reconciled, the more important to have an informal directorate to play the role of political executive for the whole. Traditionally, the Franco-German partnership has filled that function. France has little choice but to continue, and hope that the new Germany is not too bemused or distracted. Meanwhile, the British and Italians will find themselves with greater incentive to assert themselves and more room to maneuver. Community politics will grow more complex and probably slower. Very likely, Community institutions will grow stronger to compensate in the process, but expecting to resolve the multinational tensions merely by strengthening the confederal structures is likely to prove a disappointing and potentially dangerous course.

For many obvious reasons, Europe will have a tendency to grow more inward-looking over the next few difficult years. But Europe's interdependence and vulnerability will not permit it to ignore the rapid changes and increasing troubles around it. The troubles of a more plural world should reinforce the impulse for European states to formulate compatible and concerted foreign and defense policies. This will require new institutional structures—logically in the EC framework but perhaps more probably in a format with more restricted formal membership and less cumbersome procedures. Depending on American policy, a troubled world should also prove a strong incentive for Europeans to maintain the transatlantic alliance.

AMERICA AND THE NEW EUROPE

As the European states struggle toward a broader unity and a new equilibrium among themselves, what should be the European role of the United States? Within the political-economic structures of the European Community, the United States remains a privileged outsider. Over the years, U.S. efforts to make a place for itself inside the structures of the European Community have been contentious but unsuccessful. So long as the EC is primarily an economic coalition, these efforts are not likely to succeed in any serious way. Inevitably, the United States is seen not only as a political ally but as a major economic rival. Given the great diversity and conflicting interests within the EC already, admitting the Americans inside the Community is bound to seem a formula to paralyze the already too cumbersome bargaining process. If the larger U.S. interest lies with a stable order for the new Europe, acquiring a stronger bargaining position over trade issues at the expense of weakening the Community's structures and solidarity makes for a bad exchange.

American trade interests, however, have an important political significance. The United States is inclined to blame its huge and chronic trade deficit on the mercantilistic protectionism of its allies. Disputes with the EC have been long and bitter. But American trade with Europe has, in fact, improved sharply in recent years.[10] The heavy growth in demand likely to follow from German unification and Central and Eastern Europe's liberalization should improve the American position still further. At the same time, traditional American goals, like an end to European agricultural or aircraft subsidies, are less likely than ever to be met. With all their other concerns, Europeans will not cut back their agricultural sector any more rapidly than they have been doing.[11] Nor are they going to abandon subsidies to high technology. Europeans, moreover, feel that the dollar's rapid fall in the late 1980s—over 50 percent against the DM since September 1985—already constitutes a major boost to American trade interests.[12] Since then, in fact, the American trade position has improved markedly. A trade war might well harm the American position much more than Europe's.

In any event, the real problem with U.S. trade lies in the accumulating imbalances and malformations of the domestic economy. The tendency to substitute advocacy of international trade reform for internal structural and macroeconomic reform is a dangerous evasion, likely to embitter our diplomatic relations without improving our trade. It seems particularly unjustified in U.S.-EC trade relations.

THE FUTURE OF NATO

If there are good reasons why the United States has never found a foothold in the European Community, the institution that makes Europe's collective economic policy, there have been equally good reasons why it has played the leading role in NATO, the institution that has managed Europe's collective security. Now, even though the cold war seems near its end, the United States has a natural tendency to try to preserve its NATO hegemony—both because the new Europe still needs some kind of security structure and because NATO remains the principal way that the United States has institutionalized its role as a European power.

Hanging on to the traditional NATO role is not, however, a good long-term strategy. NATO was formed to counter an urgent Soviet military threat. Negotiations have now institutionalized the Soviet military retreat. While there are still relatively few in Europe who would deny the legitimacy or usefulness of some American role in European defense, the traditional overweening hegemony of the United States in NATO begins to seem inappropriate and even oppressive. And to Americans, moreover, the huge cost of the NATO deployment—roughly half the defense budget in recent decades—also seems increasingly anomalous and insupportable. Even without arms control negotiations, America's fiscal problems will almost certainly lead to drastic cuts in U.S. forces in Europe. What then happens to America's hegemonic role in NATO?

Basically, there are two ways to resolve the issue: one is to scrap NATO and find some new way for the United States to participate in European security arrangements. The other is to reform NATO in some fashion that preserves its usefulness, along with an acceptable American role. Those who advocate ending NATO generally propose folding it into a pan-European security structure in which the United States participates. Thus some analysts want the apparatus of the Conference on Security and Cooperation in Europe (CSCE) to evolve into a "security community" that would include the United States, but dissolve the old alliance blocs completely.[13] Those who propose keeping NATO tend to want either to transform it into a more European organization with a lesser American role or expand its scope to global concerns that would freshly legitimize the old American role. Each solution has problems.

Scrapping NATO seems unwise so long as the Soviet Union remains a military superpower. While the major European NATO states bound together in alliance could make a reasonable military and political counterweight to Soviet power, a structure that dissolves NATO without creating at least a West European substitute would not be a very strong guardian for Europe's long-term security. This is not to deny the usefulness of some general pan-European security organization. A more structured form of CSCE could monitor Europe's security balance and negotiate the periodic adjustments needed. It might also conceivably give legitimacy and direction to some collective force to preserve order within Europe itself. With all the turbulence in the East, Europe may be happy to have some structure to legitimize and direct collective military interventions to restrain war or the slaughter of civilians.

A collective structure without a Western bloc could not, however, give stable resolution to Europe's major security problem—the military imbalance between the Russians and the individual states of Western Europe. Disturbing political-economic events in the East would probably provoke the major Western states to rearm. Serious German rearmament on a national rather than bloc basis would logically include nuclear forces. Preserving the Western military bloc as an integral part of the structure of European security from the very start seems a more prudent long-term strategy.

In any event, security and diplomatic interests cannot remain isolated from general political economic policies. European states cannot expect to sustain close economic cohesion within the EC if they are not in accord on fundamental security issues. To be sure, attempts to structure and intensify European military cooperation have never got very far, outside the NATO framework itself. The basic reason seems straightforward enough. So long as the Soviet Union was the principal and urgent threat to Europe's security, a secure American protectorate seemed the most satisfactory resolution. Some nation-states—notably Britain and France—used the leverage provided by the American protectorate to build up their own national strategic and global forces. But not even France ever wanted the American protectorate to end.

Russia's persisting military potential makes it unwise to scrap NATO entirely, but with the Soviet threat much more remote, how should the Atlantic Alliance be restructured—both to preserve an American military presence and a European consensus on security? Two solutions jostle for attention. The Gulf crisis has revived the old idea of changing NATO's focus from European to global security—a move that would presumably restore a range of threats great enough to justify America's traditional hegemonic role, even if the United States no longer maintains a huge European army.

The idea has been discussed since the beginning of the alliance but never got anywhere. European and American interests in other parts of the world, while often parallel, have not seemed sufficiently convergent to justify an alliance so closely structured and hegemonically organized as NATO. Some serious differences have surfaced over the years, principally in the Middle

East—where many European governments have found the United States too
tied to Israel—but also in Southeast Asia and even Central America.

Americans, too, have been diffident. A global NATO would tend to limit
U.S. global policies to suit the European allies. Such a commitment risks
paralyzing American global policy, and the United States seems far from
ready for it, as the Gulf crisis made quite clear.

Such complications suggest the danger of trying to refocus NATO on any
global agenda. The United States and Europe share a deep common interest
in maintaining a military balance within Europe itself. Straying beyond this
common purpose seems less likely to strengthen the alliance than break it
up. Countries like Germany, if pressured by NATO to join global policies
that have little public support, will soon generate powerful opposition to the
alliance itself. If the United States was unable to generate support for its
global policies in the era when U.S. support seemed essential to Europe's independence, it can hardly expect to do so now. European powers disposed
to join the United States in global peacekeeping, like Britain or France, can
do so outside NATO, and can tailor their collaboration to the degree of consensus between their aims and American ones.

If enlarging NATO's scope seems a dubious way to preserve it, what about
a Europeanized NATO? In its more extreme version, the Americans would
withdraw and some kind of European institution would replace NATO
entirely—a military dimension to the European Community or a drastically
rejuvenated West European Union. At present, such a course seems too radical for European governments—partly because they are not used to the
idea, but more fundamentally because a continuing American presence
seems good insurance against a Soviet or nationalist German military revival.

The basic outline of arrangements to shift primary responsibility to the
Europeans is not so difficult to imagine. Over time, the United States should
withdraw all but one or two divisions.[14] But more difficult questions follow.
With the U.S. contribution limited, and Europe's standing armies and reserves providing the bulk of NATO's forces, the United States cannot expect
the same leading role in the command structure. But can the American
forces remaining in Europe be expected to serve under foreign command-
ers?

In recent years, the American military has been notably opposed to serv-
ing under any direction but its own. This is an increasingly dysfunctional
view. To say that U.S. military forces can never serve under foreign com-
manders effectively limits U.S. military deployments to situations where
they will be the principal force. It deliberately renounces a good part of our
potential diplomatic influence and military strength in the plural world that
is fast coming upon us. It discourages genuine multinational military forces,
and handicaps any sharing of military labor among a concert of powers. It
will prove particularly discouraging for efforts at global peacekeeping. For
the American military to hold fast to such a position under all circumstances
suggests a deficient understanding of the relationship of military force to po-

litical power. It seems a serious intellectual and doctrinal deficiency at odds with the national interest.

Within NATO, however, the nuclear question greatly complicates the problem of a non-American commander. Traditionally, the United States has been unwilling to station ground forces in Europe unless accompanied by short- and intermediate-range nuclear weapons—first, because the conventional balance in the region always seemed to favor the Soviets; second, because the Soviets themselves deployed such weapons. For obvious reasons, the United States has insisted on controlling the use of American nuclear weapons, even when they were deployed among allied forces. With a Supreme Allied Commander in Europe, what happens to the chain of command between the American president and American nuclear weapons?

To raise these questions is not to assume that they can never be answered. Before the Soviet retreat, nuclear weapons were needed to compensate for an overweening Soviet conventional superiority that posed, in itself, an urgent threat. Europe's new arms-control regime will severely limit Soviet capacity for any westward attack before a long and obvious buildup of forces. Under these circumstances, the need for deploying short- and intermediate-range nuclear weapons has to be reconsidered. The Germans, upon whose soil the bulk of these weapons are deployed, will certainly do so.

Some longer range American "theater" systems, capable of striking the Soviet Union, will no doubt continue to be a welcome contribution to Europe's "strategic" nuclear deterrence. But these systems could remain under American command. It is no longer clear, in any case, why NATO's collective deterrent needs to be provided so exclusively by the Americans. Now that both the British and French are rapidly acquiring major strategic deterrents of their own, they can assume a more prominent role in Europe's general strategic defense.

Problems of nuclear control are obviously complex and cannot be resolved without prolonged reflection and negotiation. But with an entirely different European military balance in prospect, they do not form the same intractable impediment to a more European NATO as during the cold war. In short, both military and geopolitical factors favor a more European NATO. If the old alliance is to be saved, this is probably the only way to do it.

EUROPE WITHOUT AMERICA?

America has a primordial interest in keeping Europe from again becoming a major breeding ground for war. Confederal cooperation seems the best bulwark against European destabilization. But the United States also fears being excluded from the new Europe. And intensifying European cooperation sometimes enhances that fear. Europe is not only America's closest military and political ally, but also America's principal commercial rival. A "European space" that encompasses Scandinavia, the old Soviet sphere in Eastern Europe, and the southern Mediterranean countries poses economic threats as well as opportunities for the United States. Over the longer term, a newly opened Soviet Union is itself a prime candidate for incorporation into a Eurocentric bloc. With its vast natural resources and great appetite for capital and consumer goods, a transforming Soviet Union offers tremendous opportunities to its rich Western neighbors. The danger that a Soviet Union whose economy does not develop rapidly risks being destabilized politically, and returning to its old ways or worse, constitutes a further incentive for Europe to reach out to the Russians, politically as well as commercially.

Disquiet over this potential new alignment is already visible in fears that the Germans, ransoming their eastern half with economic blandishments, will be drawn too deeply into Eastern Europe, at the expense of their old links to the West. Other Western countries, like France, Britain, or Italy, might also feel compelled to compete with the Germans for Russian favors. The Japanese could hardly remain indifferent to such developments. In due course, a Russo-Japanese rapprochement would imply a further isolation of the United States. In the end, a vast Eurasian bloc might emerge. The end of the cold war, in effect, might usher in the end of the American Century.

Given the current economic disarray of Eastern Europe and the Russians particularly, such fears seem highly exaggerated. Over the longer term, however, they should not be ignored. The real issue is the appropriate strategy for addressing them. Trying to hang on to America's traditional military predominance over Western Europe is one familiar strategy: thus the impulse to make NATO into a globally oriented alliance. Another is to oppose vociferously the European Community's "inward looking tendencies" or its reaching out to incorporate its neighbors. Another is to cultivate our own special relationship with the Russians, perhaps around the old cold war dream of a global condominium. Yet another is to reinforce the cold war special relationship with Germany.

The United States can be expected to explore all of these impulses over the coming years. Each will have its appeal, but also its limits. Turning NATO into a global alliance, run by the United States, will not deflect Europeans from recognizing their own distinctive interests in the Third World. If the United States pushes too hard, it may well accelerate the process of transatlantic estrangement.

As for a Soviet-American condominium, while the Russians will certainly want to maintain good relations with the Americans, they are not likely to be drawn into a policy that estranges them from the Europeans. It is the Europeans who can offer most of what the Russians need. The brutal truth is that the United States no longer has the financial resources to play a dominant role in transforming the Soviet economy. And since the Russians are themselves in the process of renouncing an empire, their enthusiasm for a partnership designed to keep order around the globe will be more polite than fervent. They can be expected to remain firmly preoccupied with themselves for the foreseeable future.

For the United States to adopt a spoiler's role in Europe at this late date seems a strategy with limited appeal and dangerous risks. Trying to play off one European state against another would more likely embitter transatlantic relations than succeed in preserving American predominance. Europeans have innumerable rivalries and frictions but also a deep common stake in their collective prosperity and stability. They have been developing that stake for over three decades and are unlikely to be lured away from it by anything the United States has to offer.

Trying to take advantage of the uneasiness in Europe over German reunification seems a particularly unwise course. While continued close relations with Germany are obviously in America's interest, treating Germany as our particular ally in the European Community, and neglecting other links—particularly with the French—is not. Notions of Germany as the master of the new Europe are greatly exaggerated, and it is hardly in our interest to encourage delusions of this kind among the Germans. Nor should we try to manipulate the jealousies of Germany's neighbors to limit European cohesion.

We should not forget that Europe remains probably the one place in the world whose destabilization could still easily trigger a general nuclear war. Europe's postwar progress toward inner stability has been an incomparable advance toward world stability. Trying seriously to reverse that progress would be a crime against history, and a frivolous disregard of our own vital interests.

For these and other reasons, the United States will need to temper its assaults against the Common Market's "mercantilism." For the United States to attack the Community too severely risks a disintegration of European cooperation that would not be in anyone's interest. In any event, the United States does not have a compelling economic case. If the United States could get its own fiscal, financial, and industrial house in order, the trade problem would take care of itself. Indeed, the opening of the Soviet economy, and the huge rise in world demand that it implies, could provide a heaven-sent opportunity for the United States to reverse its chronic current-account deficit. But to eliminate the chronic imbalance between domestic production and absorption, we also need to resolve our fiscal crisis. Again, the problem abroad starts at home.

The same point may be made about the most effective strategy to prevent a Eurasian bloc from forming at the expense of transatlantic ties. So long as the world economy remains open and liberal, it is not in any nation's interest to be bound too exclusively into a relationship with another power or bloc of powers. The Europeans treasure their own union, but they are happier with each other if the Americans are nearby. Certainly Europeans would prefer to keep their relationship with the United States and limit their dependence on the Soviets. Nor will the Russians, or others in the East, wish to make themselves too exclusively dependent on anyone—the Germans, Europeans generally, or the Japanese. They will naturally welcome anyone with something to offer. A pluralistic approach to economic relations is not only the best way to guard political independence, it is manifestly the most efficient way to maximize economic benefits. So long as the world economy remains tolerably open, everyone's obvious enlightened interest is to keep it that way.

Should the liberal world economy collapse, however, blocs will grow difficult to avoid. If the world's market mechanisms break down generally, thanks to a depression or financial crisis, states can be expected to create limited zones of protected order within which they can hope to restart their stricken economies. Trade will become exclusive within these zones, and thus trade and investment will grow more and more intimately tied to competing political systems. This was the pattern for the imperial world of 1910 and, to a much greater extent, for the bloc world of the 1930s. Those were the kinds of world that the Pax Americana was meant to banish.

Ironically, today's greatest threat to the liberal Pax Americana is not from the Soviet Union but from the financial disorder of the United States. Belatedly, the Soviets have started adjusting to the inexorable realities of a more plural world. The Soviet Union's defeat as the rival superpower may thus mark Russia's rejuvenation as a nation. It is not clear, however, that the United States has seriously begun its own adaptation. On the contrary, the Soviet defeat seems to have revived the old postwar dreams of world hegemony. If those dreams prevail in American policy, America's triumph in the cold war may prove a very expensive victory. And one of the principal and earliest costs is likely to be the transatlantic relationship.

NOTES

1. During the 1980s, U.S. military spending was over $2,300 billion, the largest peacetime buildup ever, and involved significant qualitative as well as quantitative upgrading. Despite cuts in real military expenditure over the past two years, a 4 percent annual real reduction in U.S. defense spending over the five fiscal years 1990–94 would still leave the defense budget higher (after adjusting for inflation) than in any peacetime period in U.S. history before fiscal year 1983. Even an 8 percent annual reduction over the same period would leave the defense budget at the level inherited by the Reagan administration. *SIPRI Yearbook 1990: World Armaments and Disarmaments* (Oxford: Oxford University Press, 1990), pp. 147–48.

2. See, for example, Jim Hoagland, "The Counterforce to Saddam's Force Is Up to Bush," *International Herald Tribune*, August 8, 1990, p. 6; Hoagland, "So Far, Bush's Gulf Performance Looks Like a Winner," *International Herald Tribune*, August 18–19, 1990, p. 4; and William Safire, "Either Roll Saddam Back Now or Prepare to Roll Over Later," *International Herald Tribune*, August 8, 1990, p. 7.

3. The historic statement of this argument can be found in Paul Kennedy, *The Rise and Fall of the Great Powers* (New York: Random House, 1987). See also David P. Calleo, *Beyond American Hegemony: The Future of the Atlantic Alliance* (New York: Basic Books, 1987), and Walter Russell Mead, *Mortal Splendor: The American Empire in Transition* (Boston: Houghton Mifflin, 1987).

4. The U.S. federal government budget deficit for 1989 was $152.0 billion, raising gross federal debt to $2,866.2 billion. The current account deficit averaged $113.5

billion at an annual rate over the first three quarters of 1989. Foreign debt as a percentage of total expenditure and lending minus repayments totaled 29.40 percent in 1988, up from 17.87 percent in 1982. See *Economic Report of the President* (Washington, D.C.: U.S. Government Printing Office, 1990), pp. 45, 383; International Monetary Fund, *Government Finance Statistics Yearbook 1989* (Washington, D.C.: IMF, 1989), p. 50.

5. In 1990, estimated expenditure on net interest as a percentage of federal outlays was 14.80 percent. Office of Management and the Budget, "Table 3.2—Outlays by Superfunction in Percentage Terms," *Historical Tables: Budget of the United States Government, Fiscal Year 1990* (Washington, D.C.: U.S. Government Printing Office, 1989), pp. 47–51.

6. See John E. Silvia, "America's Debt: A President's Dilemma," *Challenge*, January–February 1989, pp. 27–33.

7. Increases in U.S. productivity have consistently lagged behind the averages of the Organization for Economic Cooperation and Development (OECD—the advanced industrialized capitalist countries of the world). OECD (not counting the U.S.) average increases in productivity (expressed in terms of real gross domestic product per person employed) were 5 percent per year from 1960 to 1968, 4.8 percent from 1968 to 1973, 2.3 percent from 1973 to 1979, and 1.9 percent from 1979 to 1987. In the United States the average yearly increases in productivity were 2.6 percent from 1960 to 1968, 1 percent from 1968 to 1973, 0 percent from 1973 to 1979, and 1 percent from 1979 to 1987. These data are from OECD, *Historical Statistics: 1960–1987* (Paris: OECD, 1989), p. 47.

8. The following tables demonstrate the point:

Gross Domestic Product

(billion U.S. dollars)

	1985	1986	1987	1988	1989
France	621.6	782.8	996.4	939.5	1054.8
Germany	743.7	995.2	1268.7	1185.6	N/A

Source: IMF, *International Financial Statistics*, September 1990, pp. 230–33, 240–43.

GNP/GDP Deflators

(percentage changes from previous period, seasonally adjusted at annual rates)

	Average			1989		1990 (est.)		1991 (est.)	
	1976–85	1987	1988	I	II	I	II	I	II
France	9.2	2.8	3.0	3.0	4.1	3.2	2.9	2.8	2.7
Germany	3.6	2.0	1.5	3.1	1.9	3.2	3.7	3.3	3.3

I = first half of the year; II = second half.

Source: OECD, *Economic Outlook 47* (June 1990), p. 127.

9. Using data supplied by Deutsche Bank and the West German Finance Ministry, *Business Week* estimates that the rebuilding of the East German economy will require $60 billion a year for the next ten years. A Barclays Bank study puts the figure at well over $100 billion per year and estimates that it will require DM1,000 billion just to raise East German capital investment per worker to West German levels. John Templeman, "Going for Broke: The Daring Plan to Rebuild the East," *Business Week*, April 2, 1990, pp. 50–54; Bruce Stokes, "Trans-Atlantic Shock," *National Journal*, April 21, 1990, pp. 952–57.

10. The following table shows both the growing importance of U.S. trade with the EC, and the narrowing gap between imports and exports.

U.S. Trade with the EC
(million U.S. dollars)

	1983	1984	1985	1986	1987	1988	1989
Exports	48430	50498	48994	53155	60169	75431	86570
Imports	47876	63413	71617	79520	84876	88844	88821

From 1983 to 1989, the volume of U.S. trade with the EC increased 82.1 percent, with an average annual increase of 10.6 percent, while the U.S. trade deficit with the EC has narrowed from $22.623 billion in 1985 to $2.251 billion in 1989. In 1989, U.S. trade with the EC constituted 20.47 percent of total U.S. trade. International Monetary Fund, *Direction of Trade Statistics Yearbook 1990* (Washington, D.C.: IMF, 1990), pp. 56–57, 402–4.

11. Indices for West European agricultural production per capita show a 4.3 percent decline from 1984 to 1988. (These are the most recent figures available.)

West European Per Capita Agricultural Production Indices
(1979–81 = 100)

1979	1980	1981	1982	1983	1984	1985	1986	1987	1988
99	102	100	104	102	108	105	105	105	103

Source: FAO Yearbook 1988: Production (Rome: FAO, 1989), p. 96.

12. From 1970 to 1975, the dollar depreciated 32.78 percent against the deutsche mark and from 1975 to 1980, a further 26.12 percent. From 1980 to 1985, the dollar appreciated 61.96 percent, only to fall again over 50 percent between 1985 and 1990. *OECD Economic Outlook: Historical Statistics, 1960–1985* (Paris: OECD, 1987), p. 19.

13. See, for example, Malcolm Chalmers, "Beyond the Alliance System," *World Policy Journal*, Spring 1990, pp. 215–50.

14. For a more detailed outline, see Sam Nunn, *Nunn 1990: A New Military Strategy* (Washington, D.C.: Center for Strategic and International Studies, 1990), esp. pp. 47–51.

9

No Third Way:

A Comparative Perspective on the Left

SEYMOUR MARTIN LIPSET

WHILE THE ATTENTION of the world has been focused on the startling transformation in the communist countries, equally important if less dramatic shifts have been occurring in the noncommunist parties of the left. Although less noteworthy, since they do not involve revolutionary economic and political changes, they are as significant ideologically, for they represent a withdrawal from the centralized redistributionist doctrines of the democratic left.[1] Their record confirms the conclusion of Pierre Mauroy, prime minister of France's first majority Socialist government, who noted in the spring of 1990: "We thought we could find a third way, but it turned out there isn't one."[2] In country after country, socialist and other left parties have taken the ideological road back to capitalism. This movement to the right, well advanced in many countries, stands in contrast to the behavior of our own traditionally moderate left party, the Democrats, in the last decade. Although opposed to socialism, and operating within the most antistatist society in the industrialized world, the Democrats have moved left, in direct contrast to left-of-center parties elsewhere.

This paper begins with a review of events around the social democratic world and ends by asking why the story of party principles and programmatic shifts is so different between the left in the United States and that in most of the other industrialized countries.[3] How can this conundrum be explained?

THE COMPARATIVE STORY: THE SOCIAL DEMOCRATS MOVE RIGHT

Beginning with the German Social Democrats in their Bad Godesberg platform in 1959, and gathering speed in the last decade, most of the overseas left parties have reversed their traditional advocacy of state ownership and domination of the economy in favor of market economy, tax reduction, monetarism, and deregulation. Many emphasize that increased productivity, rather than income redistribution policies, is the best way to improve the situation of the economically disadvantaged. Indian political scientist Radhakvishnan Nayar notes unhappily that "few among the Left, in the West at least," question free market beliefs: "The accent of the current debate inside the Western Left is how it can survive within a liberal capitalist system now assumed to be home and dry."[4] Marxist historian Eric Hobsbawm points out: "Today few socialist parties are happy to be reminded of their historic

183

commitment to a society based on public ownership and planning. . . . In the 1980s we find, probably for the first time in history, some nominally socialist parties whose leaders compete with Mrs. Thatcher in extolling the supremacy of the market and in increasing social inequality. . . . [I]n 1990 most socialists. . . competed with each other in the rhetoric of the supermarket."[5] The extent of these developments across almost every democratic country is worth exploring in more detail.[6]

Australia and New Zealand

The comparative story may start in Australia, a country whose Labor Party won majorities in a number of states as early as the 1890s. Labor parties have governed the Antipodes, including New Zealand, during the past decade. Coming to office in societies with a strong commitment to extensive welfare state programs and wage increases, these parties faced the dysfunctional effects on economic development of high taxes, government deficits, inflation, and steady growth in wages. Under Prime Minister Robert Hawke and Treasurer Paul Keating, the Labor government in Australia cut interest rates and income taxes, pursued "economic deregulation," and formed a successful accord with the trade unions to limit wage inflation, so that real wages have fallen by at least one percent each year since they took office.[7]

Hawke has gone around the world looking for investment capital, noting that his administration has maintained a policy of reducing the real income of Australian workers. He proclaims the new social democratic gospel that profits, savings, and dividends, rather than high wages and taxes, produce the capital for economic growth. Hawke contends that "if a social democratic government, such as mine, is going. . . to do as much for them [the poor outside the productive process] as we possibly can, then we have to have an economy which is growing as strongly as possible and I think in the early days [of the movement] some. . . didn't understand that. . . . [Y]ou have to be an idiot or just so blind with prejudice not to understand that you've got to have a healthy and growing private sector if you're going to look after the majority of the people."[8]

Complaining about an unjustifiably severe tax structure under his conservative predecessors, Hawke states that to give the private sector "the greatest incentive to invest and employ" it was necessary to get rid of the "appallingly high tax rate, 60 percent of the top bracket, which Labor brought down to 49, and plans to lower further. Beyond changes on the tax side. . . we've. . . [been] deregulating the economy."[9] On the subject of wage reduction, Hawke argues: "[T]he very reason why we are growing so strongly, why our employment growth rate is twice as fast as the rest of the industrialized world, is precisely because the Australian workers in this country have accepted lower wage levels. . . . [T]he move in the share of national income away from wages toward profits. . . has enabled us to grow. . . . "[10] In September 1990, Hawke and Keating announced a program of privatizing portions of the banking system, as well as airlines and telecommunications.[11] A subsequent party conference approved these policies and "officially abandoned its commitment to public ownership in favour of a policy reminiscent of early Thatcherism."[12]

The New Zealand story has been similar. Returning to power in 1984, the Labour Party, in office until October 1990, followed the most Thatcherite policy among Western governments, including the original in Britain. In its first year, the new administration "terminated all the exchange controls... , abolished all the price controls, wage controls, interest-rate controls, most of the industrial subsidies, agricultural subsidies, export subsidies and state-corporation subsidies introduced or intensified by the previous conservative government.... It... cut income tax across the board. This Labour government is also dismantling one of the oldest... welfare states in the world.... The stated objectives of the policy are to turn New Zealand from an over-controlled economy with high income tax, into a freer-market economy with low income tax; and to allow each enterprise... to be exposed to domestic and foreign competition."[13]

An article in a socialist magazine emphasizes that the Labour government continued to follow a free market economic policy. Prime Minister David Lange argued in 1986 that "social democrats must accept the existence of economic inequality because it is the engine which drives the economy."[14] The government removed rent controls and dropped regulations on banking, finance, and transportation. "Almost all supports for agriculture were removed.... Transport was deregulated... and mergers were regularly approved.... Universality was ended for all social programs; the needy were targeted.... Changes in the tax system ended the tradition of taxation according to ability to pay." Many state enterprises were privatized, including airlines, forestry, oil, coal, and electricity.[15]

Although a declining economy, reflecting world conditions, sharply reduced support for the Labour Party, the government responded by following the Australian model. In midyear 1990 it "struck a deal with the Council of Trade Unions under which it is to limit wage demands to just 2 percent for the coming year, less than half the current rate of inflation." This was reported by the president of the Council of Trade Unions as "an agreement on growth strategy." He said "the agreement safeguarded existing jobs."[16]

These economic changes do not mean the party has dropped its social concerns. *The Economist* comments that Lange "wants to make New Zealand richer so that he can afford to spend more money on what he regards as modern socialist causes": better education, a cleaner environment, and improvement in the situation of a "Maori underclass."[17] He also has "established a Guaranteed Minimum Family Income, set originally at $250 per week for a family with one child."[18] Labour has tried to retain support among the left intelligentsia by opposition to nuclear power and weaponry.

Southern Europe

Similar stories may be told of other regions. Summing up the situation of the socialists in four southern European countries (Greece, Italy, Portugal, and Spain), Tom Gallagher and Allan Williams note that "in each party by the late 1970s, the Marxist. . . statutes in the constitutions of the parties [were] being deleted or watered down or simply ignored. . . . [R]adical economic prescriptions and redistributive policies were absent or else were set out in an opportunistic fashion. However the phrase is defined, none of the governments attempted to implement a specifically socialist economic policy."[19] The four socialist parties, when in office, "all displayed a high degree of economic orthodoxy. . . , by implication, this means there has been little attempt to secure a substantial shift of resources to the working class, or to restrict the operations of private vs. socially owned capital." In the Portuguese case, when the conservative government replaced the socialists in 1988, the new right-wing prime minister "scolded the PS [Socialist Party] for having been too austere in its economic programme."[20] In Greece, the Panhellenic Socialist Movement (PASOK), which held office from 1981 to 1989, also followed "an austerity programme" from 1984 on, that depressed the income of wage earners while introducing tax "incentives for new investment."[21] A more detailed look at the patterns in Italy, which has had a socialist coalition government and large communist opposition, and Spain, with a socialist majority, is revealing.

In Italy, Bettino Craxi, the leader of a historically minor Socialist Party (PSI), much smaller than the Communist Party (PCI), became head of the coalition government with the Christian Democrats in 1983, and reversed the tradition of statism dating from Mussolini's rule. The public sector had been extended by the Christian Democrats, who emphasized corporatism and communitarianism, in the forty plus governments they headed since the end of the war. In the 1970s, Craxi, seeking a distinctive role for his party, and faced by the massive strength of the church-supported Christian Democrats and the working-class based communists, modified the party's socialist ideology. It "rapidly moved to the center of the spectrum," proclaiming to be "the only 'modern' party in the country and the only. . . [one] able to represent the rising group who were products of the country's increasingly advanced economic development." These include the "highly successful small businessmen, entrepreneurs and professionals."[22] Craxi's government lasted three years, a record among postwar regimes. It is noteworthy for starting a process of privatization of industry and pressing the unions for major concessions. It cut back on wage increases, regulated strikes, and reformed the welfare state, "gradually increasing the retirement age and adding tougher standards for disability pensions."[23] Rent control was gradually relaxed in order to open the housing market.[24]

The Italian Socialist Party has gained electorally to the point where it now threatens the PCI dominance of the left. For the first time since the war, the

PSI secured a higher percentage of the votes than the communists, in the May 1989 local government elections; 19.1 percent compared with 16.9.[25] During the 1970s, the PCI generally gained about one-third of the vote, while the PSI hovered near the 10 percent level.

As the Italian communists declined in votes and membership from their high point in 1976, they sought to modernize their appeal by emphasizing their independence from the Soviet Union, commitment to a multiparty pluralistic system, approval of Italian membership in NATO, and, increasingly, rejection of Marxism. The latter was marked by explicit recognition of the virtues of a market economy, even before Gorbachev came to office in the Soviet Union.[26] In early 1989, Daniel Singer noted that the party had given up "attacking capitalism. It has become a social democratic party in all but name, . . . [and] proposes to leave the Communist group in the European Parliament in Strasbourg in favor of the Socialist one."[27]

Achille Occhetto, the PCI secretary, proclaims, "We are not part of an international Communist movement. . . . There is absolutely nothing left to Communism as a unitary and organic system."[28] The ultimate change was to give up its name, as Secretary Occhetto proposed "to 'refound' the party under a new name" and "to join the Socialist International."[29] In October 1990 the PCI was renamed the Party of the Democratic Left. Occhetto insists: "We want democracy, no longer as a means to achieve socialism, but to achieve democracy as a universal end in itself. If our party were in America, we might call ourselves the Liberal Party." And in commenting favorably about the American political system, he describes it as "a system of alternatives, of weights balanced against counterweights, that allows moral questions to be solved better" than in Italy.[30]

In Spain, Socialist Premier Felipe Gonzalez, elected to a third term in 1989, converted his party, Marxist in its initial post-Franco phase, to support privatization, the free market, and NATO.[31] Some years ago, he noted in a near Churchillian formulation that a competitive free market economy is marked by greed and corruption, and results in exploitation of the weak, but *"capitalism is the least bad economic system in existence."*[32] More recently, in 1988, he commented, "My problem is not that there are rich people, but that there are poor people," in seeking to justify an emphasis on economic growth rather than redistribution.[33] Gonzalez's successful efforts to foster growth and reduce inflation have involved policies described as making his government "look somewhat to the right of Mrs. Thatcher's."[34] They include "low wage increases" and "tight money" policies that have led to conflicts with the unions.[35] Following his narrow electoral victory in October 1989, Gonzalez reemphasized the need to "pursue policies attractive to Spanish business executives and foreign investors," to continue the country's high economic growth rate. These hit the intended target. In reviewing the factors underlying the Socialist triumph of the polls, Alan Riding, a *New York Times* correspondent, quotes a leading industrialist: "The new right supports the Socialists. They . . . are completely committed to the market economy."[36]

France

The same wave of ideological and programmatic moderation is cresting north of the Alps and Pyrenees. In France, socialists have "come to realize that the creation of wealth must be given priority over the re-distribution of wealth to the less well-off."[37]

The French Socialists (PS), under François Mitterrand, sought in 1981 to implement their historic commitments to nationalization and income redistribution, but witnessed these changes producing economic reverses "and by the spring of 1983 they had effectively reversed almost every priority of their original plan." Minister Jacques Delors acknowledged: "The Socialists are in the process of making the adjustment that the Barre government [the conservative administration they had attacked and defeated in 1981] did not dare to do, politically or in terms of the social classes."[38] Nationalization turned out to be an economic disaster. Faced with the need to compete on the international market, "the government adopted a program of controlled austerity. Wages were deindexed, which meant that their real value fell and profits absorbed all of the positive gains from productivity."[39]

Mitterrand won reelection in 1988. His new prime minister, Michel Rocard, the leader of the social democratic forces in the party, resembles Craxi and Gonzalez in his approach to politics and economics. He, too, argues that the road to social and economic justice is paved with increased investment enhanced by tax cuts. He and his finance minister, Pierre Beregovoy, have emphasized the need for wage restraint, while putting off income redistribution.[40]

In the 1980s the Socialists moved away from their historic hostility to business as they came to acknowledge that entrepreneurship is the power behind increased productivity, behavior minimally present in state-owned industry: "Once the Socialists have understood that the goose of capitalism did not automatically lay the golden egg, they began to revise their ideas of the importance of enterprise, the entrepreneur and profit."[41] Jean-Pierre Chevènement, as minister of industry and research, noted the need to give "industry the respect it has always been begrudged in our country."[42]

During the 1988 election, Mitterrand and Rocard took the unusual step of arguing that it would be bad for the country if one party, their own, had a majority in Parliament as well as the presidency. The president said, "It is not healthy for just one party to govern." In effect, they argued that middle-of-the-road centrist government is preferable to control by an ideological tendency. Rocard in fact publicly promised an "opening to the centre."[43] Not surprising is the survey finding that as of the start of the 1990s, "61 percent of the French public see no difference between left and right."[44]

Germany and Austria

The Social Democrats of Germany and Austria rejected Marxism in favor of populist, rather than class, allegiance sooner than most of their continental brethren. As noted earlier, the German party set the path for the other affiliates of the International in its 1959 Bad Godesberg program. A recent history of Germany notes: "The program represented a fundamental shift in philosophical direction for the party, from primary emphasis on Marxism and Marxist solutions for problems of social and economic life, to primary emphasis on recognizing the achievements of liberal capitalism. . . . It therefore rejected the goal of state ownership of the means of production."[45] As political scientist Russell Dalton emphasizes, "Karl Marx would have been surprised to read this Godesberg program and learn that free economic competition was one of the essential conditions of a social democratic economic policy."[46] Speaking in 1976, Social Democratic Chancellor Helmut Schmidt noted his party's interests in extending profits: "The profits of enterprises today are the investments of tomorrow, and the investments of tomorrow are the employment of the day after."[47] The Social Democrats (SPD), when heading the government from 1969 to 1982, did not press for structural or other major changes. Proposed "reforms such as vacations from work for educational purposes, the building of investment funds in the workers' hands—as a contrasting program to nationalization—. . . were largely dropped from the [Schmidt] government's agenda." To control the national debt, the cabinet in the early 1980s publicly considered major cuts in social services for the lowest strata and in unemployment insurance, programs adopted by their Christian Democratic successors.[48]

After leaving office, the SPD sought to evaluate its basic commitments. In 1984, a party commission established to analyze the future of the welfare state noted that Social Democrats could "defend the welfare state successfully against its conservative and liberal critics only if they call publicly for its comprehensive reform." It concluded that "the economy simply will not support a social policy that aims solely at increasing the relative share of the social budget in the national income." Just to maintain existing social services will require a "substantial increase in taxes," which the commission doubted would be "either possible or desirable."[49]

During the 1980s, the SPD lost electoral support to the Greens. In reaction, at a national conference in December 1989, it adopted the Berlin Programme "described as Bad Godesberg plus feminism and environmentalism."[50] It notes that within "the democratically established setting, the market and competition are indispensable. The incalculable variety of economic decision-making is effectively coordinated through the market. . . . Competition benefits consumers and their free purchasing choice. The market is an instrument for attaining a balance between supply and demand."[51] Oskar Lafontaine, vice-president and the party's candidate for chancellor in the 1990 election, whose major following is among the "new middle class," seeks to deemphasize government intervention in the economic process. He states categorically: "Either you abolish the system, or you stick to the rules of the game."[52] These policies have won the SPD support among some "modern entrepreneurs," most notably Daimler-Benz (Mercedes) board president Edward Reuter, who is a dues-paying party member.

The Austrian party has held office either alone or in coalition with its major rival since World War II. The country has more public ownership than any other Western society as a result of the nationalization of all German-owned property at the end of the war. But the nationalized firms have operated like private companies with respect to investment decisions, collective bargaining, and dividends. The government has not attempted economic planning.[53] Regardless of electoral outcomes, business, unions, and government have adhered to a corporatist alliance policy designed to maintain economic stability, avoid strikes, and foster growth. The party-linked unions have "accepted lowish wage settlements and so helped keep costs down."[54] The party in government "pursues politics that focus on growth rather than redistribution."[55] From the mid-1980s on, as the country faced increasing economic difficulties and large budget deficits, the Socialist-led administration under Franz Vranitzky carried out a policy of gradual denationalization and deregulation.[56] State-owned banks and industries have either been sold to private companies, both domestic and foreign, or their shares have been floated on Austrian and foreign stock exchanges. These include energy, railway, mining, steel, plastics, and other businesses.[57] Socialist Finance Minister Ferdinand Lacina has reduced income taxes and is pressing to reform the pension system to allow private schemes.[58]

Both German-speaking parties continue to adhere to the Bad Godesberg orientation. They have accepted the monetarist tight money policies of the Bundesbank (which Austria follows since the schilling is tied to the mark). Given the existence of three parties, which makes it almost impossible to project majority governments, the Social Democrats do not differ much in domestic policy terms from their major Christian Democratic and People's Party rivals. Essentially the national politics of the two countries are characterized by competition between the center-left and the center-right. In Germany, the Socialists have been more critical of the close American connection and more supportive of environmental reforms than their major opponents.

Scandinavia

If we look north to the heartland of European socialist strength, Scandinavia, the story can be reiterated. The electorally most powerful socialist party, the Swedish Social Democrats, which has held office since the early 1930s with the exception of two terms between 1976 and 1982, has reversed its wage growth, high income tax, and heavy welfare spending orientations. Ironically, as Jonas Pontusson has noted, "the so-called 'bourgeois-parties'—Liberals, Centre, and Conservatives—nationalized more industry during their first three years in office [1976–79] than the Social Democrats had done in the previous forty-four years. And since they returned to office in 1982, the Social Democrats have undertaken several privatization measures."[59] Further, writes Michael Harrington "with the agreement of the unions, [Socialist Premier] Palme devalued the Swedish krona, made exports more competitive, increased employment *and* reduced the real income of those with a job, most of whom had voted for him. But Sweden (and Austria, which followed similar policies) has a labor movement that. . . is committed to 'solidaristic' values," that is, willing to "articulate a 'general interest' rather than the particular demands of a section of the work force."[60]

The Swedish Social Democrats decided in the mid-1970s to channel corporate taxes into a "worker-controlled" mutual fund to gradually buy up stock in large corporations. "In this form, the funds would have been a way of creating decentralized social ownership, which would eventually control the commanding heights of the Swedish corporate economy." The proposal was, however, drastically modified to set a limit of "8 percent of the stock in a given corporation." The public debate on the issue revealed that the population as a whole was not in favor of the proposal "and even Socialist voters were often negative about the reform," because they feared it would give the state too much power.[61]

Klas Eklund, a leading party economist, noted at the end of the 1980s: "The traditional Social Democratic strategy of the post-war period is no longer viable. That was to recognize a need, create a public service project to fulfill that need, and then raise taxes for it."[62] The party has been pursuing a vigorous tax cutting strategy as well as trying to curtail entitlements. The finance minister of most of the decade, Kjell-Olof Feldt, sought to reduce sharply the progressivity of his country's tax system, and emphasized the need for "accepting private ownership, the profit motive and differences of income and wealth." Writing in the Social Democratic Party's magazine, he stated: "The market economy's facility for change and development and therefore economic growth has done more to eliminate poverty and 'the exploitation of the working class' than any political intervention in the market's system of distribution."[63] Feldt argued that the party "must not. . . become the anti-capitalist party."[64] He therefore urged a "greater market orientation," and insisted that the growth of the welfare state must cease. Given increasing complaints about "the uneven state of health care, education and day care, the Government is seeking to inject more competition into providing services to increase quality and efficiency." Some Social Democrats have proposed to privatize some of the basic services, including hospitals.[65]

Swedish tax policy reflects these orientations. As Sven Steinmo points out: "In Sweden. . . taxes on corporate profits are inversely related to both profitability and size. In other words, the larger and more profitable a corporation, the lower its tax rate. . . . In 1980 among the OECD countries, Sweden had the. . . lowest yield from corporate taxes. The Swedish taxes that are exceptionally onerous in comparative perspective are the flat-rate local income tax (30 percent on average), the national VAT (24 percent), and the flat-rate social security tax (36 percent). . . . In addition, Social Democratic government policies have specifically encouraged the concentration of capital."[66] The revenues lost by the 1990–91 cut in the top rates for personal and corporate income tax will be replaced by extending the value-added tax "to a wider range of goods and services."[67]

The government's program for the 1990s calls for cutting the rate paid by most Swedes, including the wealthy and corporations, in an effort to encourage people to work longer and invest more.[68] Gunnar Lund, an assistant secretary of finance, noting "the low number of hours worked per capita... as a major cause of the [country's] economic woes," argued that "tax reform should stimulate people to work more and save more."[69] In October 1990, faced with severe economic problems and a declining currency, the cabinet proposed sharp cuts in social welfare programs, including the sickness insurance system, a reduction in "the proportion of national resources devoted to the public sector," and restrictions on wage increases.[70] Not surprisingly, a sympathetic British analyst notes: "Faced with contemporary economic problems, the social democratic government appears to have found certain Reaganite/Thatcherite principles uncharacteristically convenient."[71]

The Norwegian Social Democrats, who formed a minority government in October 1990, following a year out of office, have been trying to follow the policy lead of their Swedish neighbors. The earlier Labor government had prevented wage increases and devalued the currency, successfully reducing inflation, although the unemployment rate doubled.[72] During the 1980s, the party "pursued a programme of active 'self-criticism' in relation to its [traditional] ideological profile," writes William Lafferty, Norwegian political scientist. "This programme has... [been intended] to dissociate the party once and for all from the language and symbols of Marxism; and to make the party more flexible and competent as an all-round instrument for managing 'postindustrial' or 'late-capitalist' society." Lafferty anticipates that the ideological outcome of the process will be one in which "capitalism would no longer be perceived as the antithesis of socialist humanism; markets would no longer be understood as undesirable aberrations or rational planning... ; class conflict and class interests would no longer be understood as either irrevocable or determinative.... "[73]

Social democracy in Denmark has always been the most moderate, least anticapitalist in Scandinavia, in part because of the slower pace of early industrialization and greater continuity with preindustrial structures.[74] As Gøsta Esping-Andersen notes: "Probably no other socialist party has made its peace with parliamentary democracy and capitalism so subtly as the Danish party.... Danish social democratic economic policy has been imprisoned in the liberal [market] mold."[75]

Britain and Canada

The British Labour Party, the most important opposition left movement in Europe, suffered three successive electoral defeats to Margaret Thatcher's

Tories. Before Neil Kinnock led it into the ranks of the social democratic moderates in 1989, Labour had more statist and trade union–oriented economic policies than any other social democratic party, as well as the most dovish foreign policy. By moving his party toward the center, Kinnock hopes to reassemble the scattered votes of splinter groups on the edge of Labour's right.

In summing up the conclusions of a two-year policy review issued in May 1989, the party's leaders noted that it "has dropped its commitment to old-style nationalization and to unilateral disarmament, and has learned to love the market, consumers and capitalism."[76] *The Economist* comments that they "talk like a Michel Rocard or a Felipe Gonzalez."[77] The market is now seen as the "main motor of economic activity."[78] David Marquand, an intellectual leader of the Democratic Liberal Party, who quit the Labour Party as too far left, now notes "there can be no doubt that Labour. . . has become another European social-democratic party committed to. . . [a] mixed economy. . . . Labour has. . . taken a giant stride to the centre."[79]

Kinnock argues that his party's efforts should be addressed to making capitalism "work more efficiently, more fairly and more successfully in the world marketplace," that to continue to advocate nationalization of industry is "not socialism; that is dreaming."[80] Almost paraphrasing Oskar Lafontaine, he noted in 1989: "The economy that we are faced with is a market economy, and we have got to make it work better than the Tories make it work."[81] The party's most recent policy statement, *Looking to the Future*, has, however, given up the commitment to "full employment or even to a measureable reduction in unemployment," which is much higher in Britain than in the United States.[82] Commenting on this manifesto, *The New Statesman* contends that Kinnock is "playing the George Bush 'read my lips' game"; he proposes to fight "the election on the Tories' terms. . . promising financial discipline" and "no *significant* increases in direct taxation"[83] In its 1983 program, Labour stated that at its heart is a "partnership with the trade unions." In 1990, however, the party proclaimed, "We will create a new and vigorous partnership between government and both sides of industry."[84] Following the Liberal Democrats' 1990 national conference, the left-wing magazine noted that the centrist third party is now "to the left of Labour. . . [although] it might still seem strange to claim the former Liberals are outflanking the former socialists. Just ask, though, which party proposes more change likely to upset the privileged and powerful in Britain today?"[85] Noting these developments, the *Financial Times* editorialized that Labour's "acceptance of the market, of many of the Conservative Government's reforms of labour relations, of most of its privatizations, and of limited room to increase public spending are all homage, however unwilling, to the Prime Minister" (i.e., to Margaret Thatcher).[86] A June 1990 survey of British business executives, while finding them still dubious of Labour because of "their experience of the 1970s," concludes that the party's recent efforts "to present a more responsible image to business" have been successful in that "the Conservatives can no longer rely on fear of a Labour government to rally business support."[87]

Labour's shift to the right, in the context of the collapse of communism and the end of the cold war, has led to a revival of a pro-American foreign policy. According to Sarah Baxter: "The Labour Party is even beginning to present itself, rather daringly, as the preferred ally of a Republican president. Mrs. Thatcher's tirades against Europe and foot-dragging on disarmament have, the theory runs, irreparably soured her relations with the White House. Britain under Atlee was the US's number one cold war ally; Britain under Kinnock is the ideal partner for more temperate times."[88] But under the more accommodating John Major, these generalizations may not hold.

A small Commonwealth oppositionist social democratic party, the New Democrats (NDP) of Canada, has followed Labour's lead. Ed Broadbent, then leader of the party, noted in 1989: "The serious debate about the future is not about the desirability of a market economy. For most thoughtful people that debate is now closed. . . . We New Democrats believe in the marketplace, including private investment decisions, reduced tariffs, private property, the free disposal of assets, the right to make a profit, decentralized decision making. . . . As the world evolves so must our policies."[89]

The NDP, always much stronger in provincial than in national elections, won a majority of the seats in Canada's wealthiest and most populous province, Ontario, in September 1990, albeit with 38 percent of the vote. Although the party campaigned on the need for more expenditures on welfare and higher taxes on corporations, the leaders are not radical.[90] An article in the conservative and business oriented *Globe and Mail* noted: "the Ontario NDP is led by people who have trouble talking about economic socialism without coughing. . . . What they believe is that they can administer free-market capitalism more humanely than the free-market capitalists."[91] The social democratic Premier Bob Rae "pledged to consult with business leaders and to run a fiscally responsible government." In reply to fears that he would be antibusiness, he said: "Nobody knows better than working people that their jobs depend on a healthy economy."[92] He backtracked on a policy of public ownership of utilities in approving the sale of Canada's largest natural gas distribution company to a British firm. Rae noted that the decision "sends a signal to those considering investment in Ontario that 'we're ready to do business in the province . . . that we're practical people.'" Admitting that he had advocated nationalization of the company, he said he had changed his mind after taking office because "the cost was simply too high."[93] The realities of the marketplace have forced the NDP "to drop a campaign promise on rent controls and seek a system that will please landlords as well as tenants." This refers to a preelection commitment to eliminate "bonuses to landlords for capital or financing costs."[94]

The major social democratic movement in French Canada, the nationalist

Parti Quebecois (PQ), held office provincially from 1976 to 1985. Its record in government resembles that of the French Socialist Party. Initially it introduced a variety of social democratic measures, including nationalization of a few industries, increase in the minimum wage, and improvements in state medical-care provisions. But faced with problems of growing inflation and unemployment, the Quebec social democrats retreated. They "began to question the efficiency of nationalized industries as early as 1978, and more recent economic thinking builds more on the role of the private sector." In the early 1980s they cut public expenditures sharply, including the real income of state employees, which led to bitter struggles with the government workers and their unions.[95] Since losing office, the PQ has further deemphasized the statist elements in its ideology.

Asia: Japan and Israel

This review of socialist ideological moderation in the 1980s concludes by turning to the two economically developed and democratic Asian polities, Japan and Israel. The Japanese Socialist Party (JSP), which had dwelt in a Marxist and neutralist electoral ghetto without formulating policies to challenge the long governing Liberal Democrats, (LDP) finally, as a result of scandals by the governing party, wakened in 1989 to the challenge of gaining power. Its first woman party leader, Takako Doi, emphasizes a determination to break through the "inertia of eternal opposition" by reaching out "to all segments of the population."[96] Another party official, Sukio Iwatare, states in astonishment, "We're discussing compromise," a concept he finds alien to a once dogmatic Marxist party "accustomed to being irrelevant." Doi notes that her party is not "interested in nationalizing Japan's private industries."[97] She "no longer talks about dismantling Japan's military forces, abandoning its 29-year-old security treaty with the United States, or shutting down the nuclear power plants that supply Japan with a third of its electricity."[98] An analysis of party policy in the *Japan Economic Journal* comments that under Doi the "JSP supports the capitalist economy, no longer seeks the nationalization of corporations, and supports free trade," and is softening its position on regulation.[99] *The Economist*'s Tokyo correspondent reports that "most Socialists agree that state controlled economies have failed miserably."[100] As a result, according to political scientist Masataka Kosaka, "few Japanese... believe that Japan would go socialist under the Socialist party. For the first time Japan is relaxed about the prospect of socialist rule."[101] Foreign business experts agree that Japanese "businesses don't ... fear a Socialist government." Chris Russell, the head of equities analysis at a leading securities firm operating in Tokyo, even argues that "the Socialist Party of Japan is to the right of many right-wing parties in other countries" and "the policies of a Socialist government wouldn't be that dramatically different from that of LDP."[102]

At the other end of Asia, a similar outcome has occurred in Israel: the transformation of a committed socialist movement with personal and ideological roots in Eastern Europe and Russia into one that accepts the need for a market economy as the foundation of a strong national economy and an increased standard of living for the large depressed sector. Long predating the establishment of the state of Israel in 1948, a predominantly collectivist society had emerged, "spearheaded by individuals and institutions... deeply committed to a socialist-Zionist ideology... the trade-union movement [the Histadrut], the left-of-center political parties, and the Kibbutz [collective farm] movement."[103] From its origins in an immigrant settler society, the Histadrut has been not only a union, encompassing close to 90 percent of the employed labor force, but also the "nation's largest employer, owning factories, construction companies,... transportation, farming, banking, publishing, cooperatives and medical services."[104] Hevrat Ovdim, the Histadrut holding company, employs 22 percent of the labor force. Its largest unit, Koor, a massive conglomerate listed by *Fortune* among the 500 largest corporations in the world, was responsible in 1987 for "10 percent of Israel's $35 billion GNP, and for 12 percent of Israel's industrial exports."[105]

Socialist parties dominated the government from its inception in 1948 until 1977, and extended public ownership to various areas, including airlines, shipping, railroads, airplane manufacturing, communications, utilities, and chemicals. Considering all forms of nonprofit business—producers' cooperatives, Histadrut, and government—Israel has had the most socialized economy outside of the communist world.

As Israel absorbed immigrant populations uncommitted to socialism, and developed economically with a steadily expanding private sector, many of its socialist institutions showed themselves to be either relatively (compared with independently owned companies) or absolutely (operating at a loss) inefficient. Enthusiasm for nonprofit enterprise declined. The socialists lost control of the government in the 1977 elections and have not regained a majority since, although the Labor Party was part of a coalition government with the right-wing Likud Party from 1986 to 1990.

Most Israeli academic economists, although supportive of the left for its dovish foreign policy, now press the Labor Party to accept free-market policies. During the 1980s, many of the nonprofit institutions, such as the different companies owned by Koor and the various state enterprises, have been identified as candidates for privatization.

Although the Labor Party and the Histadrut seek to preserve the kibbutzim, they increasingly accept the need to sell off much of the publicly and worker-owned sectors.[106] The state-owned industries up for sale include the national airline El Al, Bezak Telecommunications, Israel Chemicals, and Zim Cables. Labor Party leader Shimon Peres, who was first the prime minister and then finance minister in the 1986–90 coalition government, argued, while in the latter office, that his first priority was to encourage investment and to create jobs: "Tackling social problems is secondary." His economic advisers told him that to do this he must reduce the budget "by cutting down social expenditure," advice he accepted. Among other changes proposed by Labor's leader were abolition of free schooling and of subsidies on eggs and poultry, cuts in social insurance payments and family allowances, and the end of government housing mortgages for young couples.[107] His closest adviser, former deputy finance minister Yosi Beilin, is described by the *Jerusalem Post* as "a socialist,... [who] strongly advocates privatization. Not only that: he lists the failure to expose all firms in the country... to the tender mercies of unbridled competition as one reason for the lack of economic growth in Israel."[108]

The Histadrut has recognized the need to follow similar policies in the worker-owned economy. Koor—faced with bankruptcy because it retained many unprofitable units, resisted discharging unnecessary workers, and agreed to wage increases unjustified by profits—has decided that it must sell out to private, inevitably foreign, investors.[109] The conglomerate has been in the process of shutting or selling off close to two dozen companies. Basically, Koor, like many social democratic and communist governments, is involved, in the words of one of its officials, in "a transition to a business basis of thinking." The secretary general of the Histadrut, Yisrael Kesar, has noted the similarities between the problems facing his organization and the economies of Eastern Europe in calling for *perestroika* for the Histadrut, with the end of "financial aid for failing operations."[110] Israeli socialists, like their compeers elsewhere, publicly accept the rules of the market.

Europe

The greatest triumph for the socialists' historic internationalist values is the emergence of a united Europe, in whose Parliament they are the largest party. They and the Italian communists have seen the cause of the European Community as their own. Yet as Regis Debray, leading French intellectual and official adviser to Mitterrand on foreign affairs from 1983 to 1989, notes: "The freeing up of capital movements across borders in the liberal Europe of 1992 will substantially reduce tax revenues from capital gains, further increasing reliance on taxes from wages, while further diminishing the state's role in the redistribution of income."[111] And the European social charter explicitly acknowledges as a legally protected right "the freedom not to join a trade union."[112]

Sources of Socialist Politics

Why have socialist parties in the developed world pursued the course of moderation? Why have they taken the road back to capitalism? There is obviously no simple or authoritative answer, but some insight may be found in briefly considering the adjustments that have been made to economic and electoral necessities. The shift was particularly evident in the mid-1970s, with the end of the long-period of steady growth, full employment, and low inflation. The oil shock precipitated sharp price increases and recession throughout the developed world and undermined the belief in Keynesian policies, economic planning, and higher taxes to finance a continuing expansion of the welfare state.[113] Ironically, the classic economic assumption that profits are necessary for investment and economic growth has helped to lead once radical parties and unions to accept limits on wages. As Marxist student of social democracy Adam Przeworski emphasizes, social democrats now consciously seek to "protect profits from the demands of the masses because radical redistributive policies are not in the interest of wage-earners."[114] American socialist theoretician Michael Harrington also concludes that "the French example suggests that the Left *should avoid trying to redistribute income by means of the wage system.* That, as Mitterrand and company learned to their sorrow, acts as a disincentive to hiring people and, all other things being equal, leads to an increase in unemployment."[115] As noted, postwar experience has convinced the socialists that state enterprise is inefficient, that competition stimulates innovation. They also now acknowledge that extensions of the comprehensive welfare programs are overly costly and result in economic deficits and inflation, and that high taxes slow down economic growth.

Economic rationality is not the only cause of the policy changes. Electoral concerns are clearly also relevant.[116] Worldwide structural trends, particularly in industrialized societies, have worked against the traditional left. The proportion of the work force in manual and factory labor has been declining steadily, while the segment employed in positions requiring better education and scientific, technological, and writing skills has been increasing.[117] The latter categories contribute to the support of largely noneconomic or postmaterialist reformist causes (the environment, abortion, equality for women, racial minorities, etc.) and "liberated" lifestyles, while as relatively well-to-do people they resent high taxes and state interference in the economy.[118]

Analyses of the changing values of mass electorates, from the data of the European Values Study, document these assumptions. They indicate that opinion change in the 1970s and 1980s "has been resolutely in the direction of free competition and a positive reevaluation of individual economic status [achievement]. Conversely, opinions in favour of resource redistribution, social egalitarianism, and state intervention to this effect weakened." But while "leftist" materialist values declined, "the opposite holds for the 'cultural' dimension capturing changes in morality, religiosity, family and socialization values, [and] gender relations."[119] Support for traditional leftist economic and welfare beliefs remains associated with economic class, although the relationship has declined across all age cohorts, while the increased commitment to postmaterialist social values is to be found more heavily among the younger and better educated.[120] The left parties, therefore, must look for issues that appeal to the younger middle-class sectors to make up for their declining working-class base.

The changes do not mean that they have lost popular support or are being replaced by other parties. On the electoral level, as Dennis Kavanaugh and Wolfgang Merkel have documented, looking at the voting trends throughout Europe for social democratic parties from 1945 to 1989, their proportion overall has not fallen. It has remained amazingly stable.[121]

In noting this common pattern, I am not suggesting that there are no national differences in the support for these parties or that they have the same policies. Some—particularly those in southern Europe, France, Greece, Italy, and Spain—have gained votes since the mid-1970s. Others— particularly in Belgium, Germany, Ireland, and the Scandinavian countries—have declined. A number have been able to form majority governments and will continue to do so. These include France, Greece, Austria, Sweden, and Spain in Europe; and Australia, Britain, Jamaica, and New Zealand in the Commonwealth. The other parties—ranging from Ireland to Canada to those in Italy, Portugal, the Benelux countries, Germany, Denmark, Iceland, Finland, Switzerland, Chile, and Japan—operate in multiparty systems, which do not offer prospects of national office except in coalition with nonsocialist parties. The factors differentiating their levels of support are too diverse to deal with here. They include the nature of their historic class structures, the number and intensity of other politically related social cleavages (e.g., religion and linguistic-cultural differences), and not least the impact of diverse electoral systems.

Their politics also vary. Sweden leads the others by far in the scope of its welfare programs; Australia is at the low end among countries governed by social democrats. Austria has the largest publicly owned business sector; there is much less state ownership in Germany, and very little in Sweden. What I would reiterate is that regardless of how committed different democratic socialist parties have been to intervention in the economy and redistributionist tax and welfare programs, all have moved toward classical liberalism during the 1980s—toward more free market competitive economic policies, emphasizing productivity gains rather than income transfers.

The development was presciently summed up in 1974 by veteran Austro-Marxist Josef Hindels, who identified the emergence of "Social Democracy without Socialism." By this he meant a party intent on "modernising" the capitalist system, but one that "surrendered the imaginative vision of socialism and a new society."[122]

THE THIRD WORLD LEFT FOLLOWS SUIT

Recent developments in Third World countries resemble those in Eastern and Western Europe: movement away from statism toward acceptance of the market economy and, verbally at least, of party pluralism.[123] Some of the sources of these changes reflect events in the industrialized nations, including direct influence from the experiences and statements of socialists and communists in the First and Second Worlds. Leaders and economists from both have told Third World leftists that government ownership does not work and should be dropped. In some cases, they have explicitly said that capitalism and the free market are the preferred routes to economic success.

But more important is experience, based on the failure of state and collectivist enterprises in industry and agriculture—enterprises often financed by borrowing abroad, prompted by a resistance to foreign investment and a belief in import protectionist policies. As James Henry notes, most "African countries have discovered statist solutions can discourage growth."[124] Third World countries generally rejected any advice that they encourage outside investment—seen as subjecting them to foreign control—in favor of loans for domestic investments. As a result, many are deeply in debt because of shifts in world market demand. Foreign investments, unlike loans, are sharply reduced or wiped out by downward swings in the business cycle, such as have occurred in the past decade.

Third World politicians could note that the successfully developing nations are those that put more emphasis on the market: the so-called Asian NICs, as well as Chile and Botswana. The changes in Latin America are particularly noteworthy. Linda Robinson observes "an astonishing about face in Latin American attitudes. The generation now in power was raised on 'dependency theory' literature that expounded the dangers of reliance on overseas capital. But these books are now gathering dust," as the major countries privatize and encourage foreign investment under populist leadership.[125] Developments in Cuba, once a model for Latin American leftists, have contributed to the loss of faith in socialism. As a leading Colombian radical, Clara Lopez Obregon, notes, the Cuban system is a "resounding failure" in economic terms. Former Castroite Colombian novelist Pinto Apuleyo Mendoza believes that "socialism as a system is a failure," and now supports "Latin America's hot new ideology: free market economics."[126]

Latin America and the Caribbean

The Spanish socialists and events in Eastern Europe appear to have had an impact on the Latin American left. Three years ago I was in Argentina, where Peronist leaders told me that Gonzalez, on a tour of the continent, had been telling leftist party leaders that their historic emphases on statist and redistributionist policies should be dropped. He argued that everything the state touches turns to ashes. Left-of-center parties and leaders from Argentina to Mexico have been following his advice and combating hyperinflation and low growth rates by creating freer markets, encouraging foreign investment, privatizing state-owned industry, and cutting back on the size of the public sector.[127]

The Peronist president of Argentina, Carlos Menem, is a case in point. As reported by Shirley Christian, he has rejected "the traditional Peronist concept whereby the state was the motor of the economy. . . . Equating himself to Mikhail S. Gorbachev. . . for the dramatic turnabout he started, Mr.

Menem has said Argentina's economic collapse. . . necessitated the embrace of radical, free-market ideas."[128] Openly espousing "modern capitalism," he is selling off publicly owned corporations, following a tighter money policy, and simplifying the tax system.[129] Flora Lewis notes that he is "privatizing at breakneck speed" and hopes "to privatize everything but basic government tasks."[130] The top personal income tax rate has been reduced from 45 to 36 percent, while the maximum corporate levy has been cut from 33 to 20 percent. Foreign investment and import restriction laws have been greatly liberalized. A leading Argentinian social scientist reports that "Menem is seen as a new Felipe Gonzalez who. . . administers the economy in ways acceptable to the capitalists."[131]

Similar developments are occurring elsewhere in the region. In Brazil, the left generally went along with privatization during the 1989 presidential election. At a discussion among the economic advisers of the different candidates, those "from the two most leftist parties present surprised everyone with their views."[132] Economist Cesar Maia, a deputy of the populist Democratic Labor Party (PDT) and an adviser to presidential candidate Leonel Brizola, commented: "the Left has to be conscious that the origin of the modern society is the minimal state."[133] Similar sentiments were expressed by Vladimir Palmeiry, a deputy of the Workers' Party (PT), whose candidate Luis Inacio da Silva ("Lula") made the runoff as the left candidate. *The Economist* noted that his party "has given up calling for socialization of the means of production, and even sounds hazy about maintaining the loss-making enterprises in which the trade unions have most of their strength."[134] In neighboring Venezuela, the governing social democratic party, Accion Democratica, long affiliated with the Socialist International, announced in 1990 that "most of the 400-odd public companies would quickly be sold to private investors. Those companies are blamed for most of the nation's $35 billion foreign debt."[135] Teodoro Pelkoff, leader of the more left-wing Movement Toward Socialism, also advocates privatising "a lot of state companies" and making others "joint venture[s] with private companies."[136]

More significant, perhaps, are the pronouncements by leading Chilean leftists that the post-Pinochet Christian Democrat–Socialist coalition, while drastically changing the political system, should essentially continue the seemingly successful high-growth, free-market policies of its authoritarian predecessor.[137] The Socialists have approved freeing Chile's central bank from government control.[138] Their ministers have been "busy courting foreign investors, preaching labour moderation and recommending private investment in the remaining state companies."[139] Alejandro Foxley, finance minister and a leader of the Christian Democratic left, has announced: "We'll maintain the basic features of the open economy: low uniform tariffs, the current [free] exchange rate policy, rather liberal rules on foreign investment."[140] He expects a "return to 'voluntary credit markets'" by the end of 1990.[141] Jorge Arrate, the secretary general of the Socialist Party, notes "a universal movement to reassess the content of liberal [antistatist] democracy." Ricardo

Lagos, minister of education, comments that the party has to be humble about its traditional beliefs, willing to change them, given the way "the world has changed." He particularly emphasizes the effect of the events in Eastern Europe: "Consider the impact on socialist ideology of a Lech Walesa—a union leader questioning the socialist world."[142] And writing from Santiago, Tom Wicker reported that "most Chilean socialists—Mr. Lagos, for example—no longer press for centralized government but instead support an open economy, private enterprise and democracy."[143]

In Mexico, President Carlos Salinas of the PRI, a populist party, has attacked the tradition of big paternalistic government stemming from the Revolution of 1910, supported by his party for many decades. In a speech in late October 1989, he said: "The reality is that in Mexico, a larger state has resulted in less capacity to respond to the social demands of our fellow citizens. The state concerned itself more with administering its properties than with meeting pressing social needs."[144] And he has put the nationalized "banking system... , airlines, mines, steel mills and the telephone company on the block; permitted imports to surge to pressure Mexico producers to become more efficient, liberalized foreign investment regulations; overhauled the tax system, and cut the deficit." The top corporate and personal income tax rates, as well as import taxes, have been cut significantly. On May Day 1990, Salinas told the country's workers and unions that their tasks are to "increase productivity, lower costs and help win markets." His ministers have been "receiving invitations from the new leaders of Eastern Europe to deliver tutorials on how to dismantle state-dominated economies." Not surprisingly, his approach, like that of Gonzalez, is popularly referred to as Thatcherismo.[145] According to Mexican political analyst Lorenzo Meyer, those to the left of the PRI, faced with the international discrediting of socialism, have been "trying to redefine themselves in the image of say, a Felipe Gonzalez–type of socialist—against corporate elitism, but in favor of open markets."[146]

Similar policies have been pursued by the moderate left or populist parties in countries as disparate as Bolivia, Costa Rica, Peru, and Uruguay. The Uruguayan Socialists, as a major third party to the left of the populists, have been almost unique among significant radical parties in continuing to advocate statist redistributive policies. But a party convention in November 1990 openly debated "whether to drop Marx, Engels and Lenin." Party leader Tabare Vasquez, preparing for a possible change in party doctrine, emphasizes that "Socialism implies more than Marxism," that it must not be "dogmatic, nor... closed to discussion."[147]

The stories can be matched in the most important democratic Caribbean states, Jamaica and the Dominican Republic. In the former, socialist Prime Minister Michael Manley, a strong admirer of Fidel Castro in the 1970s, returned to office in 1989 "as an advocate of free markets, privatization, global economic integration and competition." Howard French reports that he has replaced many of his leftist "social programs and promises of the past with a call to hard work," and "fiscal conservatism."[148] In the Dominican Republic, former President Juan Bosch, "kept out of office for years with United States' assistance because of his socialist leanings, spent his entire campaign this year [1990]... extolling capitalism." As French notes, the "ideological gap" between the two Caribbean leftists and "their conservative rivals has become all but imperceptible."

At a meeting of Latin American and Caribbean Leftist Parties and Organizations in July 1990, the most extreme left parties, including Trotskyites, communists, and diverse liberation fronts, moved to the right. Most "participants favored full-fledged political pluralism," and while "a few were firm believers in state control,... most preferred a more decentralized mode."[149]

Africa and Asia

The African pattern is similar. One of the continent's most enduring socialist heads of state, Kenneth Kaunda of Zambia, now acknowledges that his twenty-five-year-old government made "a gigantic error" in trying to build a welfare state, by controlling prices, foreign trade, and investment in a poor country. As he notes, "We subsidized consumption instead of production."[150] In nearby Zimbabwe, Robert Mugabe, long committed to Marxism and socialism, "has promised to liberalize trade... as part of a phased program to reduce state controls on the economy."[151] The Ghanaian government, which in the past owned 235 enterprises, is now trying to divest itself of them under its structural adjustment program (SAP).[152] Once socialist Togo also boasts of "structural adjustment programmes." President Gnassingbe Eyadema has cut the state budget drastically and liquidated or privatized many firms. The state-created steel company has been doing well since it was taken over by an American entrepreneur in 1985.[153] In Benin, President Mathieu Kerekou is "freeing up a heavily state-controlled economy," and has renounced Marxism-Leninism.[154] Gabon has followed a similar course, as its leader, Omar Bongo, has lost effective power. Julius Nyerere, head until 1990 of the ruling Marxist Revolutionary Party in impoverished Tanzania, proclaims that his country could learn an economic "lesson or two" from Eastern Europe; and the government, under his successor, President Ali Hassan Mwinyi, is now committed to a free market system.[155]

Given development in sub-Saharan Africa and Eastern Europe, it should not be surprising that the heavily socialist program of the African National Congress was drastically revised in the fall of 1990. Like socialist parties elsewhere, the South African ANC "has muted its long standing calls for nationalization of industries and redistribution of wealth. Instead, it is talking more of relying upon economic growth to deliver a more equitable share of South Africa's resources to the country's black majority."[156] Soviet economists in private discussions have strongly advised Mandela and other leaders to follow such a course, to rely on the market.

North of the Sahara, Egypt, heavily statist under Gamal Abdul Nasser in the early 1950s, with considerable government ownership and economic regulation, shifted slightly toward a market system under Anwar Sadat in the 1970s, and somewhat more so under Hosni Mubarak in the 1980s. Algeria's long-time one-party socialist regime has moved to privatization, a freer market economy, and political pluralism. And in India, the social democratic Congress Party dropped its commitments to a statist economy before losing office in 1989. It has upheld the efforts of its successor in power, a coalition that includes socialists, to "actively encourage foreign investments by allowing foreign companies to hold 51 percent equity in priority industries," as well as "sharp reductions in tariffs on raw materials, capital goods and components."[157]

Third World Communism

Cuba and North Korea apart, the Third World communist regimes have been moving in the same direction. Facing a major crisis in national morale, including "widespread disillusionment within the Vietnamese army," the Hanoi-led communists voice suspicion of "some of the best known of Americans who, often at great risk to themselves, were at the forefront of anti-war activities."[158] Since 1986, when the Vietnamese Constitution was "amended to guarantee the rights of private property," the public sector has been significantly dismantled and replaced by a burgeoning private one. The government "drew on the talents of leading American lawyers in drafting and passing one of the most liberal foreign investment acts in Asia."[159] An economic adviser to the regime, discussing the market oriented policies, boasts that "Eastern Europe is trying to do what we've already done."[160] *Doi moi* is the Vietnamese equivalent of *perestroika*.[161] It constitutes the "most radical changes" toward a full market economy in the communist world, "affecting industry and agriculture."[162] According to the *Wall Street Journal*, economic conditions in Ho Chi Minh City (Saigon) have reverted to what they were when the communists took over. The paper quotes a leading economist, Le Dang Doanh, that "Vietnam doesn't suffer so much from the sickness of capitalism as from the lack of capitalism."[163] Noting the effects of rent control on his capital city, Foreign Minister Nguyen Co Tach of Vietnam said: "The Americans could not destroy Hanoi, but we have destroyed our city with very low rents. We realized it was stupid and that we must change policy."[164]

In Cambodia, the pro-Vietnam communist government now encourages "private enterprise and open markets . . . on the ground that they are more efficient than state-owned industry."[165] It has "dropped much of the Communist ideology" and "introduced an essentially free-market system."[166] Even the murderous Khmer Rouge, as *The Economist* notes, have been "reading the newspapers." Their spokesman at the peace talks among the different national factions, Khieu Samphan, states (pretends?) they now believe in a "liberal economy."[167] Laos also has "openly returned to capitalist economics. . . . Laotian peasant farmers once again till lands that are their own, and commerce in this virtually unindustrialized country has largely returned to private ownership."[168]

Prior to its electoral defeat, the Sandinista regime in Nicaragua, exposed to a steady economic decline and Soviet advice, adopted a "market-oriented" program described invidiously and exaggeratedly by Fidel Castro as "the most right-wing policy in Latin America." The Sandinista Directorate formally approved "an austerity program so conventional and market-oriented that it has been compared to the methods of the International Monetary Fund. The measures... ranged from deep cuts in spending to new incentives for private business."[169]

The leaders of the Afghan People's Democratic Party, including President Najibullah, repudiate Marxism. A major party spokesperson, Farid Mazdak, explains its former admittedly erroneous politics as reflecting the pressures of "a time when Marxism-Leninism was quite in fashion in underdeveloped countries."[170] The South Yemen rulers, prior to uniting with pro-Western North Yemen, "knocked down the statues of Marx and Lenin and references to the Party embedded in the facades of buildings."[171] In Ethiopia also, an unpopular Third World communist regime is drastically changing its economic policies and ideology. President Mengistu Haile Mariam "announced in March [1990] that his government was abandoning Marxism-Leninism."[172] He is moving toward a free market system in which there will be no limit on capital investment in the private sector, with a wide degree of privatization of industry, construction, and agriculture.[173] To the south, in Mozambique, the once Soviet aligned Liberation Front (Frelimo) has announced a new program including support for "a free-market economy, renunciation of Marxism-Leninism, more religious freedom, private schools and free elections."[174]

AMERICAN EXCEPTIONALISM REVERSED

The American left's abstention from the shift rightward is ironic in the context of the old and persistent question of why the United States has been the only industrialized society without a viable socialist or labor party. Why has it been politically "exceptional?"[175] All over the industrialized world we have seen the labor, socialist, and social democratic parties (as well as many communist and Third World leftist ones) give up their Marxism, drop their emphases on being working-class movements, and increasingly adopt a populist reformist stance closer to the traditional American model.

But the provider of that model, the Democratic Party, has been moving in the opposite direction. While the party is not socialist, and the United States, under Republican leadership, remains much less committed to the welfare state both on policy and public opinion levels than other economically developed states, the Democrats adhere more closely to redistributionist, progressive tax, and antibusiness orientations than many social democratic parties.[176] And protectionist doctrines fostered by trade unions have made headway among congressional Democrats. The party's policies on the cultural quality of life, "permissiveness," affirmative action for minorities and women, and foreign issues date from the 1960s, and have alienated many traditional Democrats, particularly the less educated and more religious partisans, while its congressional majority now advocates higher and more progressive tax measures.

Although neoliberal economic doctrines, which focus on market forces, have received public endorsement from some Democratic politicians, including congressional backing during the later Carter and early Reagan years of measures to reduce economic regulations and taxes, the party's record suggests that in recent years it has moved left. Unlike most European Social Democrats, the Democrats continue to press for income redistribution. While the British Labour Party's 1990 program supports tenants' "right to buy" publicly owned council housing, Senator Barbara Mikulski, the chair of the subcommittee dealing with housing and her Democratic majority have resisted "transferring public housing to private [tenant] ownership" as proposed by Housing and Urban Development Secretary Jack Kemp.[177] The trend has been documented statistically by the Americans for Democratic Action (ADA), which has kept score on the ideological behavior of members of Congress. The ADA data indicate a steady increase in liberal voting among Democrats since the 1970s. The late 1980s was the most liberal period since the ADA began keeping records in 1963. The southern states particularly contributed to these changes.

TABLE 9.1
Democratic Congressional Voting Record:
Average Percent Liberal, 1971–89

Congress	Years	House	Senate
92 and 93	1971–74	53.5	59
94 and 95	1975–78	54.5	56
96 and 97	1979–82	59	59
98 and 99	1983–86	69	70
100 and 101	1987–89	75	73

Source: These data were compiled for me from the ADA files by Hilary Weinstein of the Progressive Policy Institute. I am grateful to her for this work.

In discussing the ideological changes among Democrats, I refer to a large segment, perhaps the bulk of the party's leadership in national office, most of the delegates to national conventions, and its most prominent intelligentsia, not the voters. Opinion polls indicate that the latter are much more conservative or traditional than the party's leadership. Comparison by many polls of responses to issue questions by the delegates to the 1980, 1984, and 1988 conventions with those of the party's rank and file point up wide gaps—with the median Democrat, like the average voter, being much more in the center politically than the delegates and national nominees.

Other than by support for a more redistributive tax system and calling in its 1988 platform for national planning ("targeted economic development"), the left orientation of the Democratic Party is most substantially expressed in its commitment to affirmative action for minorities and women in the form of special preferences or quotas that redistribute economic and educational resources in order to ensure equal opportunity. The debate over these issues, down to the Civil Rights Bill of 1990, has increasingly been between the Democrats and Republicans, the former seeking to apply the "socialist" principle of equality of results, the latter placing stress on the traditional American emphasis on meritocracy—equal opportunity in a competitive race.

With the exception of Jimmy Carter during his first campaign, Democratic nominees from George McGovern in 1972 to Michael Dukakis in 1988 have been linked in the public mind with advocacy of a strong state in the domestic economic and welfare areas, a soft foreign and defense policy, and social permissiveness with respect to drugs, crime, family values, and sexual behavior. Many traditional blue collar and ethnic Democrats, while still somewhat supportive of New Deal type programs, disdain the social and foreign policies associated with the party's left.

Rejecting these policies, however, is not the same thing as opposing the Democratic Party. Since the American electorate continues to place self-interest above ideology, most also support programs designed to safeguard people like themselves by providing health care, subsidizing college education, protecting the elderly, and guaranteeing jobs. To secure these objectives, they vote Democratic for Congress.

Congress is the place where cleavages are fought out. Members perform services, act as ombudspeople, and represent interests. They appeal narrowly rather than broadly. And the Democrats, with their links to mass groups and popularly based interest organizations, are in a better position to fulfill these functions. Following former House Speaker Tip O'Neill's maxim that in America "all politics is local," Democratic candidates have successfully presented themselves as advocates of whatever interests are dominant in their areas.

Why Is America Exceptional?

To understand why the recent history of party ideologies, of programmatic shifts and stances, is so different between the left in the United States and in most of the other industrialized democracies, it is necessary to appreciate the source of the initial American political exceptionalism—the absence of significant socialist movements. The evidence and arguments presented by a large number of scholars suggest that socialist class politics, as it developed in Europe, was less an outgrowth of capitalist social relations than of preindustrial feudal society, which explicitly structured the social hierarchy according to fixed, almost hereditary, social classes. Consequently, the emerging working class reacted to the political world in class terms. Conversely, in America the purest bourgeois society has treated class as an economic construct. Social classes have been of limited visibility compared with the situation in Europe.[178] Hence, class conscious politics has been limited in scope. Walter Dean Burnham has aptly summarized this overall thesis: "No feudalism, no socialism: with these four words one can summarize the basic sociocultural realities that underlie American electoral politics in the industrial era."[179]

It should be noted, of course, that Marx was right in assuming that occupation position would be a major determinant of political orientation and class organization in industrial society. In all democratic nations, including the United States, there has been a correlation between socioeconomic status and political beliefs and voting.[180] The less privileged have supported parties that have stood for greater equality and welfare protection, through government intervention, against the strains of a free enterprise economy.

As noted earlier, this pattern has changed in recent decades. The growth in the proportion of population enrolled in higher education and subsequently employed in scientific-technical, professional, and service occupations has created a sizable privileged stratum responsive to noneconomic reform causes—environmentalism, feminism, gay and minority rights, peace—and a more permissive morality, particularly as affecting familial and sexual issues. These concerns have produced new bases for political cleavage and have given rise to a variety of single-issue protest movements. Those with postgraduate education are most liberal in their views, most involved in the "movements," and most Democratic in voting behavior. Since the United States has the largest proportion of the population who are college graduates and continue on to postgraduate education, there is a greater base for New Left or new liberal politics in America than elsewhere. The record would seem to sustain the assumption. As the French political scientist Jean-François Revel pointed out in 1971: "one of the most striking features of the past decade is that the only new revolutionary stirrings in the world have had their origin in the United States. . . . I mean the complex of new oppositional phenomena designated by the term 'dissent.'"[181]

A critical intelligentsia, based on the new middle class, emerged in the 1950s with the formation of the "reform" movement in the Democratic Party, and constituted the beginning of what was subsequently labeled the New Politics. The 1960s witnessed the full flowering of the New Politics in the form of opposition to the Vietnam War, struggles for civil rights, women's and gays' liberation, and environmentalist movements, as well as the emergence of new lifestyles.

As Revel has stressed, the new American style of activism, single-issue movements, and radical cultural politics spread during the 1960s to other parts of the developed world that were also entering the stage of post-industrialism. Campus-based protest occurred in all the European countries. Sizable left-wing tendencies rooted in the new middle-class groups challenged the moderate union-based leadership of the socialist parties. But these developments were "imitations of the American prototype, or extensions of it, and subsequent to it. European dissenters, who represent the only force which has been able to rouse both the Left and the Right, the East and the West, from their academic torpor, are the disciples of the American movements."[182]

These events were stimulated and reinforce by the civil rights struggles which, from the Supreme Court's school desegregation decision in 1954, led to a continuing series of organized efforts to widen education, economic, and political rights for blacks, other ethnic minorities, gays, and women. These issues helped to radicalize well-educated whites and to mobilize blacks and others in support of the more liberal or left forces within the Democratic Party, while pressing socially conservative, less affluent whites within the party to vote Republican. Blacks, who constitute more than 20 percent of identified Democrats, back Jesse Jackson and his Rainbow Coalition, a group which—race issues apart—strongly supports income redistribution and heavy state involvement in the economy. A number of black members of Congress are openly socialist. America's inability to resolve the issue of racial equality has left it, in its third century as an independent state, more deeply divided over rights for underprivileged strata than most other industrialized nations.

Thus if the first American exceptionalism is linked to the differences between the American pure bourgeois, classically liberal (antistatist) character and the more Tory statist and fixed class systems of postfeudal Europe, the second is tied to America's lead in economic development and higher education and to the need of its polity to confront for the first time a mass-based demand for "equality of results" in ethnic and gender terms supported by the intelligentsia.

Why Are the Democrats Different?

To explain why the Democrats have not followed the lead of left groups like British Labour or the German Social Democrats in accepting pressures to move right requires a comparison of institutional and intellectual frameworks. There are, I believe, four elements distinguishing American responses from others. First is the greater importance of social movements in the United States compared with other stable democracies, reflecting the dissimilarities in electoral systems. Second is the difference in governmental structures, with parliamentary countries maintaining a centralized system with set party policies and legislative discipline compared with America's division of powers and absence of a system of party discipline. Third is the difference in economic views held by the left in countries with parties and trade unions having socialist and corporatist-derived backgrounds compared with those of American liberals and trade unionists, who have never advocated a national economic policy or corporatist (trade-off) agreement among business, labor, and government.[183] Fourth is the variation in response to the crisis of left ideologies by intellectuals in countries that have had powerful socialist and/or communist movements compared with that in one like the United States, where the large left intellectual community has never known an electorally significant domestic socialist or Marxist movement.

Institutional Factors. A peculiarity of the American polity has been the relative ease with which social movements, as distinct from parties, have arisen and had considerable impact. If we contrast the American political system with that of the affluent European nations with respect to the frequency and importance of major movements, the United States is clearly in the lead.[184] Social movements are the equivalent of minor parties in the American context. They arise because it is impossible to create stable third parties in a system whose main election involves a nationwide contest to choose an individual head of government. Parliamentary systems encourage minor parties, since various value and interest groups may elect Members in ecologically separated constituencies. The extra-electoral American movements, not being part of the normal partisan political game, are all the more likely to be more extreme programmatically. They are not subject to the party discipline needed to win the support of the electorate. Rather, they try to force the leaders of the two major parties to respond to their demands. And given the weakness of national party organization, the movements stemming from the 1960s continue to influence both parties, pressing the Republicans to the right (antiabortion, hard line on crime, less state intervention in the economy), and, as noted, the Democrats to the left.

In parliamentary countries, the party leadership usually stays in power internally even after being defeated in elections. Whether in control of government or not, they can evaluate the electoral consequences of their policies and take action to change those that appear to have failed. Most of these parties have polling and research staffs that continue indefinitely, are unaffected by election outcomes, produce research monographs, and recommend policy adjustments in response to analyses of long-term trends. Because of the separation of the executive and the legislature, parties in the United States have always been looser, less disciplined, and less bureaucratic than in parliamentary systems. And various changes in party rules and the expansion of the primary system, which occurred in the late 1960s and the 1970s, have made the national parties, particularly the Democrats, weaker than ever.[185]

Given the shifts in leadership after each electoral defeat, and national nominations and conventions not controlled or even seriously influenced by party institutions, no one can think or speak for the party when it does not control the White House. Pollsters, researchers, and key policy advisers change from election to election. Candidates first seek to be nominated and then look for money and preprimary activist support, much of which, in the case of Democratic presidential hopefuls, comes from the left. Party activists no longer concerned with patronage jobs do not ask how we can win or what went wrong in the last election; they support those closest to them ideologically. As Christopher Matthews, the Washington Bureau chief of the *San Francisco Examiner*, notes: "To win the early caucuses and primaries, a candidate needs to appeal to those passionate Democratic activists who get involved in presidential picking. Most of these people run the gamut from center-left to far-left. The people who show up at Democratic caucuses, who man the storefront in the early primary states, have little time for moderates, much less conservatives."[186] Hence the national Democratic Party, which compared with European socialist parties scarcely exists as an organization, cannot draw lessons or make policy changes binding on those who will run its next presidential campaign or represent it in Congress.

The antistatist, individualistic, and competitive orientations of Americans do not encourage thinking by trade unions or other interest groups about what is good for the nation, the economy, or their party. Should any group be asked or forced to sacrifice for the benefit of the whole, for increased productivity? The goal, in Samuel Gompers's words, is always "more." American trade unions, unlike the more "solidaristic" European socialist and Catholic ones, are as competitive and as uninterested in the national welfare as business is. Such syndicalist orientations could function well in an expanding autarkic economy in which foreign trade is of small importance. They are ineffective guides for a nation engaged in international competition.

The reluctance of American trade unions to consider policies that could bring short-term income reduction to workers (in order to improve the larger competitive position of the economy) may diminish in response to the steadily worsening position of labor organizations. Their proportion of the employed labor force keeps declining, and is now at 16 percent. Their ability to secure majorities in union representation elections is also falling off. More serious is their inability to win major strikes, more problematic than at any time since the 1920s. There were fewer labor walkouts in 1988 than in any of the previous forty years. Unions need friends in the national administration more than ever. This fact may give the Democrats more leeway with them.

The contrast between the behavior of unions in America and those linked to social democratic labor parties elsewhere also reflects the dissimilarities in the organizational structures of the parties they support. Unions in Australia, Great Britain, and much of Europe reluctantly accept restrictions on their freedom of action or wage restraint policies dictated by the disciplined parties they endorse. In America, it is not possible for a party to force unions (or other groups) to accept policies that apparently challenge their self-interest.

The need to impose some structure on the national party so leaders can enforce electorally fruitful policies is more difficult to satisfy. The lack of organization reinforces itself. Each presidential nominee has an interest in recruiting segments of the party to his campaign, hence does not seek to control future developments. As a recent example, in 1988 the Dukakis forces agreed to changes in the delegate selection rules which will give Jesse Jackson many more delegates in 1992 if he runs and secures the same percentage of votes he received four years earlier.

The Influence of the Intelligentsia. In America, as noted, the highly educated cohorts became the backbone of the Democratic Party left. Student and intellectual protests against the Vietnam War and in support of civil rights were the catalysts in the emergence of a New Politics. But the intelligentsia, a growing mass stratum, has been electorally more influential in setting the national, particularly the left segment's agenda, thus contributing much to the second American political exceptionalism.

Support for the left by American intellectuals is not a new phenomenon. They have been on the antiestablishment side for the past century.[187] They have fostered what Lionel Trilling called the "adversary culture," opposed to bourgeois and national patriotic values. They have been the strongest supporters of the relatively small far left tendencies, including in the past various radical third parties. Although such parties have almost disappeared, the most recent opinion survey of academics, taken in 1989, shows that 57 percent call themselves liberal compared with 11–20 percent among the electorate as a whole. Among those at the highest level institutions, research universities, 67 percent of the elite faculty are liberals.[188]

A striking aspect of the new exceptionalism is the judgment that Marxism is alive and relatively well in American intellectualdom. As Garry Abrams notes, "American universities may be one of the last bastions of intellectual Marxism, at least in the developed world."[189] Oxford political theorist John Gray also concludes that "the academic institutions of capitalist America will be the last redoubt of Marxist theorizing."[190] Gerald Marzorati, senior editor of *Harper's*, emphasizes that the American academic radicals have dropped "liberalism, with its notions of tolerance," in favor of "a mix of neo-Marxism and semiotics, . . . a continental language, precisely that being abandoned" by the younger European intellectuals, who have resuscitated classical liberalism, the emphasis on individual rights, the market, and pragmatism. Ironically, these overseas "writers and thinkers seem to harbor none of the easy anti-Americanism of their intellectual forefathers and of America's academic radicals."[191] Writing in the *New York Review of Books* on the attitudes and writings of American elite scientists, Cambridge University Nobel laureate M. F. Perutz notes, "Marxism may be discredited in Eastern Europe, but it still seems to flourish at Harvard."[192] Commenting in a similar way on the differences between American and Soviet literary analysts, Robert Alter, a leading student of comparative literature, points out: "Literature in our own academic circles is regularly dismissed, castigated as an instrument of ideologies of oppression." But after a trip to Moscow, he "came away with the sense that there are still people in the world for whom literature matters urgently."[193] Richard Flacks, a prominent radical sociologist, wrote in 1988: "If there was an Establishment sociology twenty years ago, we helped do it in, and so, for good or ill, the field is to a great extent ours."[194] And leftist historian Jonathan Wiener noted in 1989 that "radical history in the age of Reagan occupied the strongest position it has ever held in American universities."[195] The ideological left is also strong in Hollywood and among creative personnel in television.[196]

There are numerous fellow travelers of the intellectuals among the intelligentsia, the well-educated consumers of university research and intellectual creativity. As noted, those who have had some postgraduate education are the most left-disposed segment in the electorate. These groups vote more than any other stratum, and predominantly for liberal candidates in the primaries, thus helping to keep the Democrats on the left. German Social Democratic theorist Richard Lowenthal points up the role of "intellectual doctrinaires" in the "organization reform of the Democratic party . . . which produced the McGovern candidacy and its failure." He emphasizes "the contrast between the results of an inner-party democracy influenced by strong contingents of ideological activists and the requirements of success in a democratic election."[197] Postindustrial leftists, often self-identified radicals, have been elected to office in communities with concentrations of such people—for example, Ann Arbor, Amherst, Austin, Berkeley, Boulder, Burlington (Vermont), Cambridge, Hyde Park (Chicago), Ithaca, Madison, Manhattan, Santa Cruz, and Santa Monica.[198]

This pattern has been prevalent abroad in recent years, where the intellectuals, intelligentsia, and students form the largest base of support for Green, ecologically concerned, political parties and tendencies in many countries.[199] Still, the bulk of the intellectuals in Europe and Japan have dropped their former allegiance to Marxism. British intellectuals and academics have backed center-left parties. Swedish professors have supported nonsocialist groups. French intellectuals turned very anti-Marxist and were anti-Soviet hard-liners during the 1970s and 1980s.[200] Japanese academics have also moved to the right.[201] Their behavior in part stems from their past links to strong socialist, labor, and (in Italy and France) communist parties. Socialism as a Utopia clearly has failed, in both its authoritarian and democratic forms. Many intellectuals previously involved with left politics have turned away. An analyst of Swedish society, Ron Eyerman, in explaining why Swedish (unlike American) intellectuals have not been "an alienated stratum with an independent tradition vis-à-vis the state," points out that Swedish intellectualdom, even when on the left, "found itself at the center, rather than the margins, of society." Intellectuals there could take part in the large labor and social democratic movements. The "alienated intelligentsia that did exist was limited to the arena of high culture," not academe.[202]

The American situation has been quite different. Except for economists and other policy-oriented experts, few academics and other intellectuals have had a direct involvement in partisan politics. Leftist politics, particularly since World War II, has been too small a matter to count, and trade unions disdain intellectuals. There has been little application of radical theory to policy. As a consequence, Gray emphasizes, the American "academic class... uses the rhetoric and theorizing of the radical intelligentsia of Europe a decade or a generation ago to legitimate its estrangement from its own culture." American academic Marxism, he says, is "politically irrelevant and marginal" and "compensates for its manifest political nullity by seeking hegemony within academic institutions."[203] Leftist ideologies, therefore, have been academic in both senses of the word. As noted, they remain important in the university world, and a larger segment of the American intelligentsia appear inclined to support leftist ideologies than do their compeers in most European countries.[204] And through their numbers and position in the media and university worlds, they have considerable influence on the political agenda of Democratic Party activists.

Is change likely in America? If European politics now increasingly resembles the historic United States pattern, will the United States, after the growing ideological and cultural cleavage of the 1960s and 1970s, move back (or forward) toward a new decline of ideology? Such a change would require shifts among the intelligentsia. They were stimulated and radicalized during the 1960s and early 1970s by communist and other leftist triumphs in the Third World. Given the weakness of radicalism within the United States and the evident failure of the major communist systems in the Soviet Union and China, the alienation of American intellectuals from their own society found an emotional outlet in enthusiasm for revolutionary anti-American movements in Asia, Africa, and Latin America. The American intellectual left, however, is now faced with the collapse not only of traditional leftist dogmas in Eastern and Western Europe but also the repudiation of socialist or Marxist-Leninist commitments, and movement toward nominal acceptance of market economics and party pluralism, in the less developed countries as well.

There are no socialist Third World models to inspire leftist intelligentsia, including particularly Indochina and Nicaragua, whose Marxist movements once strongly appealed to American liberals and leftists.[205] Now, however, those regimes and parties have openly acknowledged the failings of statism in the economy.

Although few among left-leaning American intelligentsia have been sympathetic to the Soviet Union in recent decades, the effective rejection of Marxist doctrine there should have an impact on liberal orientations here, much as it has affected socialists in other countries. Gennadi Gerasimov, a major government spokesperson, has described the "ideological quarrel" in his country and governing party as "between those who read too much Karl Marx ... and those others who are more pragmatic."[206] In an article published with the express approval of then Foreign Minister Eduard Shevardnadze in the summer of 1988 in *International Affairs* (a publication of the Soviet Foreign Ministry), Andrei Kozyrev, a high official in the Ministry, wrote that most developing countries "suffer not so much from capitalism as from a lack of it."[207] At a conference of senior Soviet economists in November 1989, a leading economic policy maker, Leonid Abalkin, director of the Soviet Academy of Sciences' Institute of the Economy and then a deputy prime minister, noted that the private market is "the most democratic form of regulating economic activity." He advocated the introduction of an open stock market and the use of (Friedmanite) monetary policy rather than government regulation to affect demand.[208] The 452-page detailed programmatic analysis of the Soviet economy, issued the second week of September 1990, under Mikhail Gorbachev's sponsorship, explicitly states: "Mankind has not succeeded in creating anything more efficient than a market economy."[209] Equally important is the emergence within the Soviet Communist Part of criticisms placing the blame for Stalinism and economic failure on Marx and Lenin. Even more astonishing is that at a conference on the party and *perestroika* at the Higher Party School in Moscow, the Marxist-Leninist fathers were ignored, while statements by Max Weber and Talcott Parsons were invoked to justify reform.[210] A Soviet think tank and extremely successful publisher, Humanus, has scheduled the translation of the works of Durkheim, Parsons, and Weber.

Some indication that the changes among the left abroad are affecting radical intellectuals in the United States may be found in a magazine published by a leading Democratic activist, Stanley Sheinbaum, who has worked closely with socialists here and in Europe. The *New Perspectives Quarterly* proclaims in the introduction to a symposium on "The Triumph of Capitalism": "The great ideological contest of our century is over. The once maligned market has, after all, turned out to be materialist man's best friend." And the editors call attention to the fact that the "Soviet ideology chief has said... 'we must now admit that our concepts of public property have proven untenable,'" that socialism has lost out in the "race for economic development."[211]

More striking, perhaps, is the public change of view of a major socialist economist, Robert Heilbroner, who holds the Norman Thomas chair at the New School for Social Research. He states unequivocally, "the contest between capitalism and socialism is over: capitalism has won."[212] And he notes: "For the first time in this century—and for the first time in my life—I would argue that socialism has no plausible economic framework. Only half a century ago, the great question was how rapidly the transformation from capitalism to socialism would take place. . . . Now the great question of the last years of this century must be posed the other way."[213]

He goes on to emphasize that capitalism's success is not just political but also economic, that the evidence shows the market to be successful. This is even true in "the periphery. Look at the fantastically successful Asian countries like Korea, Singapore, Taiwan and Thailand."[214] Heilbroner points out that he is not alone among American socialists, that "America's most renowned socialist figure, Michael Harrington, . . . in his last book [he died in 1989], *Socialism, Past and Future*" was only able "to rescue out of all the

conventional definitions of socialism . . . the importance of continuous, voluntaristic pressure for social justice. For better or worse that is what remains
of socialism today."[215]

Possibilities for a Democratic shift to the right are countered by the civil
rights issue. Inequalities linked to race and other birthright attributes offend
the universalistic norms of intellectualdom and others, and well-organized
pressure groups stimulate these sensibilities. Faced by growing crime rates
and a highly visible population of homeless and beggars, the liberally disposed among the educated affluent support a symbolic politics of redistribution, while the minorities they back advocate such politics. Together they
constitute a major portion of those who vote in Democratic primaries. But
numerous polls show that most Americans oppose affirmative-action quotas
and object to tax increases intended to enlarge the scope of the welfare state,
with the exception of government-provided health services.

CONCLUSION

Similarities in policy changes among the socialist parties worldwide are so
prevalent as to suggest that the Socialist International resembles the Comintern of Lenin and Stalin in its ability to command conformity from member
parties. As should be obvious, nothing is further from the truth. The International has no power over affiliates. It is largely a discussion body. Still, as
Neil Kinnock has said, "the same broad attitudes . . . [have been] adopted,
not only by the democratic socialists and social democratic parties, . . . but
also amongst the reform wing of the old Communist parties." These involve
"a general realization that you need the combination of the market and the
socially responsible community."[216] Commenting on the democratic socialists
of Eastern Europe, *The Economist* notes that they also have begun to question whether "there really was a 'middle road'" between communism and
capitalism. Like their compeers in the West, they "accept the goal of an enterprise economy."[217]

Social democrats the world over have been convinced, as Sven Steinmo
puts it, that "they should adjust their program to the experiences history
provides. . . . Social Democrats (no matter what the official title of their
party) will not bring about 'socialism,' but this does not necessarily imply
that they are 'doomed to failure.' They have simply changed their minds."[218]
Basically, as Adam Przeworski concludes, social democrats now "struggle to
make capitalism more efficient and humane."[219] And, as Regis Debray points
out, if the socialist leaders were to "tell the truth" about their role today,
they would say it is "to carry out the politics of the Right, but more intelligently and in a more rational manner."[220] What produces the parallelism is responses to common experiences and exposures to like analyses and advice
from most economists, as well as, in recent years, the breakdown in the communist system.

The "realization" Kinnock speaks of is based on fact. State-owned industries have proved less efficient than private concerns. Competition has shown itself to be a much greater stimulant to change and economic growth than are private or public monopolies. Incentives, differential rewards, and profits make for a greater commitment to work by employees, as well as more reliable and attractive products from entrepreneurs. There is clearly a threshold beyond which taxes act as deterrents for both labor and capital. Redistributive tax policies designed to benefit the underprivileged, no matter how moral they may seem, are dysfunctional if they slow down investment and productivity. These realities of market economics are now largely accepted by many communists and socialists, though seemingly less so by American Democrats.

In line with this, a recent comparative study of tax policies finds that the effective corporate tax rate in socialist Sweden is much lower than in Republican-led America. The Reagan-Bush Republicans have been able to modify, but not reverse, the policies of previous governments. As Steinmo documents, "When all taxes are considered..., the United States relies substantially more heavily on 'redistributive' individual and corporate income taxes and property inheritance and wealth taxes than either Britain or Sweden."[221] The United States "taxes capital gains more heavily than any of its democratic counterparts."[222] The 1986 Democratic Congress made capital gains taxable like ordinary income, and party legislative leaders reject Bush's arguments that a reduction will encourage investments. They prefer to emphasize that such a change would violate tax progressivity.[223] Most social democratic parties would agree with Bush.

It is important to reiterate that since the United States has never been governed by a social democratic party, judgments about the Democratic Party's leftward course and the rightward one of socialist movements elsewhere do not imply that the American organization is becoming as committed to statism as its foreign left-to-center brethren have been. Although the Democrats are operating within a more antistatist, Protestant sectarian, moralistic, and individualistic polity than Euro-Commonwealth nations with their Tory–Social Democratic, established church, and group-centered values and institutions, the Democratic Party, though *not* the American public, is moving from the nation's historically dominant traditions toward more European left orientations. Meanwhile, the European social democrats are shifting toward more classically liberal, less state-centered, and more individual-rights oriented concerns. While the transatlantic lefts appear to be approaching each other ideologically on many issues, these changes, as we have seen, involve the Democrats moving to the left, away from the electorally rewarding center, and the social democrats going to the right, toward the center of their national politics.[224] This is the conundrum I am trying to explain.

Some of the influences that have historically stimulated economic growth, and thus the failure of socialism, in the United States—the emphases on the values of individualism and laissez-faire, and the lack of communalism—now enable the American left to ignore national needs and follow the logic of their ideology: to favor higher taxes, redistributive and nationalist economic programs, and permissive cultural politics and morality. Some would, of course, suggest that these emphases, particularly as related to economic and welfare needs, are a response to the increase in income inequality and the growth of poverty, notably reflected in the rise in the number of homeless during the Reagan era.[225] While there can be no doubt about these trends, the comparative record suggests somewhat similar patterns elsewhere. Unemployment has been much higher in most developed countries, such as Australia, Belgium, Britain, Canada, France, Germany, Italy, and Spain, than in the United States.[226] According to *Forbes*, the proportion of the very wealthy has also been greater in other developed countries; for example, Canada, Germany, Japan, and Sweden have many more multibillionaire families, with two billion dollars or more, per capita, than the United States. *Fortune*'s report on the same subject adds Britain, the Netherlands, Switzerland, and Taiwan to those who top the United States in this respect.[227] Europe, Canada, and Japan are also characterized by a greater concentration of economic power in fewer corporate hands.[228] In Sweden, after almost half a century of Social Democratic government, the distribution of wealth "was still heavily skewed: a 1981 survey showed that 89 percent of households owned no shares; while less than 0.3 percent of households owned half of all the shares held by individuals."[229] An article in *Barron's* notes that "a few big investors basically control the bulk of Swedish firms."[230] More recently, the Social Democratic government has encouraged the increased concentration of financial resources through merging all the private banks into four units and having them unite "with the country's insurance companies to create even bigger financial powerhouses."[231] As of 1980–81, the latest year for which comparable figures are available, the distribution of disposable household income was significantly more unequal in Sweden than in the United States.[232]

Those who seek to strengthen the structure of the American left party and make it more effective—the Democratic Leadership Council led by Senators Sam Nunn and Charles Robb, the California State Committee when chaired by former Governor Jerry Brown, and the "old school" party leaders headed by Robert Strauss—find themselves up against an institutionalized and activist egalitarianism. In Christopher Matthews's words, the new party strengtheners pine for a party that is "a bit less democratic but a great deal more united."[233] Robb calls for the party's "disenthralling itself from the spell of the new activist elite," and seeks the reassertion of "the primacy of the national party over individual agendas of particular constituencies."[234] As Strauss puts it: "We need a candidate who looks like he can run the show. Leadership and toughness are what . . . [we're] looking for." Another party leader, Bob Beckel, who managed Mondale's campaign, states: "We party leaders need to start guiding the process and stop being dominated by it."[235] What they hope for is an organization capable of performing the major functions that define parties elsewhere, such as nominating electable candidates and drawing up programs with maximum voter appeal. In other words, they would like the Democratic Party to become like the Social Democrats of other Western countries, ironically to end American political exceptionalism by moving their party to the right.

The seemingly universal shift abroad to support of capitalism and the free market, however, may also be of short duration. As strong advocates of such systems, Joseph Schumpeter and, more recently, Irving Kristol, have noted, they do not have the same pretensions to solve major human problems that socialism and communism once had. Capitalism, the free market, is not a utopian ideology even when limited to economic considerations.[236] At best it holds out the promise of a lottery, but, like all such awards, the jackpots go to a relatively small minority of players. Hence there must be many "losers," some of whom will be receptive to reformist or antisystem movements. The distribution of rewards must be greatly unequal, and, as Tocqueville pointed out a century and a half ago, the idea of equality presses the underprivileged to support redistributionist parties and policies.

At the center of free market ideology is an emphasis on self-interest—in invidious terms, on greed. The argument has been put from Adam Smith to Milton Friedman that the uninhibited pursuit of personal or institutional gain will result in a steadily growing economy from which all will benefit, regardless of status or wealth. But as we know, not only are there individual variations in achievement or failure, but countries have differed substantially in economic performance. And the business cycle, which seems inherent in market economies, not only fosters growth, it implies downswings as well—periods of increased unemployment and/or high rates of inflation.

Renewed disdain for capitalism is also inherent in the market situation's emphasis on mundane rationality, not on ideals. As Kristol argues, the "real trouble [with capitalism] is not sociological or economic at all. It is that the 'middling' nature of a bourgeois society falls short of corresponding adequately to the full range of man's spiritual nature, which makes more than middling demands upon the universe, and demands more than middling answers. This weakness of bourgeois society has been highlighted by its intellectual critics from the very beginning."[237] Capitalism fails to generate effective community values. Its failures have placed it at odds with many religious communities. The Roman Catholic Church offers a striking current example as it presents a collectivist, corporatist, solidaristic, familial model of social relations. The present pope, John Paul II, though playing a major role in bringing communism down in his native Poland, is a declared opponent of capitalism, which he sees as a system based on selfishness resulting in inequality and poverty. In viewing the free market negatively, he follows a Catholic tradition at least half a millennium old which has fostered communitarianism (i.e., noblesse oblige) or welfare state values.

Capitalism, which does not promise to eliminate poverty, racism, sexism, pollution, or war, cannot appeal in idealistic terms to the young. And as Aristotle emphasized 2,500 years ago, the young, and, it may be added, intellectuals, look for total solutions. Hence, new movements, new ideologies, and even old ones that hold out reformist and utopian promises will appear. Communitarian concerns will relegitimate the state in the role of social actor to reduce, if not eliminate, social, sexual, and racial—even more than economic—inequalities. To these may be added environmental concerns. Not surprisingly, such issues have begun to take priority among left-wing parties, both old (i.e., social democratic) and others, such as the Greens and the new social liberals. Classic free market liberals resist such policies as requiring interference with the market and free competition.

The struggle between the left, the advocates of change, and the right, perceived as defenders of the status quo, is not over. In the once communist-dominated countries, the terms *left* and *liberal* are now used to describe free market and democratic tendencies that seek to reduce the power of the state bureaucracies; the words *right* and *conservative* refer to groups that defend state controls. Ironically, this is the way these ideological concepts were first used during much of the nineteenth century. In the West, following the rise of socialist movements, left came to mean greater emphasis on communitarianism and equality, on the state as an instrument of reform. The right, linked to defensive establishments, has, particularly since World War II, been identified with opposition to governmental intervention. Even if socialism is not a dirty word, the contest between these two orientations has not ended. Political history—conflict—will continue.

NOTES

1. For a systemic overview, see Salvador Clotas, "Las Transformaciones del Socialismo en los Anos Setenta-Ochenta," *Leviatan*, Autumn 1989, pp. 95–106.

2. Quoted in Flora Lewis, "Triumph's Challenge," *New York Times*, May 29, 1990, p. A15. For a comprehensive discussion of the reasons why there can be no third way, see Ralf Dahrendorf, "Mostly About the Strange Death of Socialism and the Mirage of a 'Third Way,'" in his *Reflections on the Revolution in Europe* (New York: Times Books, 1990), pp. 42–77.

3. For an analysis of the variations in socialist and working-class political behavior before World War I, see Seymour Martin Lipset, "Radicalism or Reformism: The Sources of Working-Class Politics," in Lipset, *Consensus and Conflict: Essays in Political Sociology* (New Brunswick, N.J.: Transaction Books, 1985), pp. 219–52.

4. Radhakvishnan Nayar, "A Vacuous Optimism," *Times Literary Supplement*, May 18–24, 1990, p. 526.

5. Eric Hobsbawm, "Lost Horizons," *New Statesman and Society*, September 14, 1990, pp. 16, 18.

6. An early analysis of the changes in the Social Democratic parties may be found in the writings of Otto Kirchheimer in the 1950s and 1960s. See F. Burin and K. L. Shell, eds., *Politics, Law, and Social Change: Selected Essays of Otto Kirchheimer* (New York: Columbia University Press, 1969); see also Seymour Martin Lipset, *Revolution and Counterrevolution: Change and Persistence in Social Structures* (New Brunswick: Transaction Books, 1988 paperback edition, first edition published in 1970), pp. 267–304. Robert Tucker concludes that "radical movements that survive and flourish for long *without* remaking the world . . . undergo eventually a process of

deradicalization." They come *"to terms with the existing order."* Tucker, *The Marxian Revolutionary Idea* (New York: Norton, 1969), pp. 185–86. Ralf Dahrendorf notes that "right-wing social democrats are the most consistent conservatives in contemporary politics. . . . [They] manage not only with a minimum of programs, but even with a minimum of government." Dahrendorf, *Life Chances: Approaches to Social and Political Theory* (Chicago: University of Chicago Press, 1979), p. 106. Ralph Miliband argues that social democrats and trade union leaders are inherently moderated by working within "bourgeois democracy," which presses them to collaborate with their adversaries. Miliband, *Divided Societies: Class Struggle in Contemporary Capitalism* (Oxford: Clarendon Press, 1989), pp. 74–78.

7. Peter Beilharz, "The Australian Left: Beyond Labourism," in Ralph Miliband, John Saville, Marcel Liebman, and Leo Panitch, eds., *Socialist Register 1985/1986* (London: Merlin Press, 1986), pp. 213–16; "Terrible Twins," *The Economist*, October 29, 1989, p. 73; Edna Carew, *Keating* (London: Unwin Hyman, 1989).

8. "Bob Hawke of Australia: A Controversial Prime Minister Speaks Out," *Firing Line*, April 12, 1989, p. 5.

9. Ibid., pp. 3, 4.

10. Ibid., pp. 2, 8.

11. "Australia: Private Hatred," *The Economist*, September 1, 1990, pp. 32, 34; "Australian Government to Sell Stake in Airlines," *Financial Times*, September 7, 1990, p. 4.

12. "Australia Off the Dole," *The Economist*, September 29, 1990, p. 38.

13. "A Labour Government Sets Things Right," *The Economist*, June 1, 1985, p. 17. For an insightful viewpoint by the finance minister from 1984 to 1988, see Roger Douglas, "The Politics of Successful Structural Reform," *Wall Street Journal*, January 17, 1990, p. A20.

14. John Warnock, "Lambs to the Slaughter," *Canadian Forum*, November 1989, p. 13.

15. Ibid., p. 13. See also Tim W. Ferguson, "New Zealand's Unfinished Economic Experiment," *Wall Street Journal*, December 1, 1989, p. A20.

16. Del Hayward, "NZ Pact with Unions Limits Wage Rise Demands to 2%," *Financial Times*, September 18, 1990, p. 7.

17. "A Labour Government," p. 18.

18. Warnock, "Lambs to the Slaughter," p. 12.

19. Tom Gallagher and Allan M. Williams, "Introduction," in Gallagher and Williams, eds., *Southern European Socialism* (Manchester: Manchester University Press, 1989), p. 3. The economically "conservative" character of socialist policy in these countries is spelled out in the various essays in this book.

20. Allan M. Williams, "Socialist Economic Policies: Never Off the Drawing Board?" in Gallagher and Williams, eds., *Southern European Socialism*, pp. 189–91.

21. Christos Lyrintzis, "PASOK in Power: The Loss of the 'Third Road to Socialism,'" in Gallagher and Williams, eds., *Southern European Socialism*, pp. 42–43. See also James Petras, "The Contradictions of Greek Socialism," *New Left Review*, May–June 1987, pp. 3–27, and Louis Lefeber, "The Socialist Experience in Greece," *International Journal of Political Economy*, Winter 1989–90, pp. 32–55.

22. Stephen Hellman, "Politics Italian Style," *Current History*, November 1988, pp. 367, 394.

23. Spencer M. DiScala, *Renewing Italian Socialism: Nenni to Craxi* (New York: Oxford University Press, 1988), pp. 221–22.

24. Ibid., pp. 213–14.

25. "Italian Socialists Pass Communists at Polls," *New York Times*, June 1, 1989, p. A12.

26. Alan Riding, "Italy's Battered Communists Reinvent Themselves Again," *New York Times*, March 25, 1989, p. A8; see also Jeffrey Godmin, "Europe's Extremes," *American Enterprise*, July–August 1990, p. 40.

27. Daniel Singer, "Achille's Gamble," *The Nation*, April 24, 1989, p. 545; Alan Riding, "Italy's Communists Try Not To Be Ideologues," *New York Times*, May 7, 1989, IV, p. 3.

28. Clyde Haberman, "Chinese Upheaval Shakes Italy's Communists," *New York Times*, June 9, 1989, p. A13.

29. "Meanwhile, Elsewhere in Europe," *The Economist*, November 18, 1989, p. 58; Clyde Haberman, "Italy Communists Will Change Name," *New York Times*, November 26, 1989, p. Y9.

30. Jennifer Parmalee, "Italian Communist Chief Reshaping Party Image," *Washington Post*, May 16, 1989, p. A12.

31. For an overall view see Donald Share, "Dilemmas of Social Democracy in the 1980s: The Spanish Socialist Workers Party in Comparative Perspective," *Comparative Political Studies*, October 1988, pp. 408–35.

32. Quoted in Gallagher and Williams, "Introduction," p. 3 (emphasis added).

33. "Leader of the Pack," *The Economist*, March 11, 1989, Survey Spain.

34. "As Gonzalez Glides Rightward," *The Economist*, February 11, 1989, p. 43.

35. "The Next Transition," *The Economist*, March 11, 1989, Survey Spain.

36. Alan Riding, "The Spanish Victory: A Mandate for the Socialists," *New York Times*, October 31, 1989, p. A3.

37. William Randolph Hearst, Jr., "American Trade and Aid," *San Francisco Examiner*, November 5, 1989, p. A25.

38. Michael Harrington, *The Next Left: The History of a Future* (New York: Holt, 1987), p. 116. See also pp. 116–40 for an excellent account of the changes.

39. Ibid., p. 139.

40. "Very Soft Left," *The Economist*, July 9, 1989, p. 42. See also Howard LaFranchi, "Socialist Party Searches for Identity," *Christian Science Monitor*, March 5, 1990, p. 4, and David Bell, "Parti Games," *New Statesman and Society*, March 16, 1990, p. 21.

41. Julius W. Friend, *Seven Years in France: François Mitterrand and the Unintended Revolution, 1981–1988* (Boulder: Westview Press, 1989), p. 11.

42. Quoted in Suzanne Berger, "French Business from Transition to Transition," in George Ross, Stanley Hoffmann and Sylvia Malzacher, eds., *The Mitterrand Experiment: Continuity and Change in Modern France* (New York: Oxford University Press, 1987), p. 192.

43. "France's Fifth Republic: Sure-Footed," *The Economist*, October 1, 1988, p. 20.

44. Bell, "Parti Games," p. 21.

45. Dennis L. Bark and David R. Gress, *From Shadow to Substance: 1945–1963* (Oxford: Basil Blackwell, 1989), p. 445; Adolf Sturmthal, *Left of Center: European Labor Since World War II* (Urbana: University of Illinois Press, 1983), pp. 54, 59–66; Andrei S. Markovits, *The Politics of West German Trade Unions* (Cambridge: Cambridge University Press, 1986), pp. 91–93.

46. Russell V. Dalton, *Politics in West Germany* (Glenview, Ill.: Scott, Foresman, 1989), pp. 260, 286; Gerard Blumenthal, "The Social Democratic Party," in H. G.

Peter Wallach and George K. Romoser, eds., *West German Politics in the Mid-eighties: Crisis and Conformity* (New York: Praeger, 1989), p. 84. The German trade union federation, the DGB, also drastically modified its commitment to statism in its 1983 Dusseldorf Program, which revealed "an awareness that the scope and quality of investments represented a key ingredient for the success and failure of a modern economy." The document "mentioned planning as only a small part of an overall framework for an otherwise competitive market economy." Markovits, *The Politics*, p. 103.

47. Quoted in Adam Przeworski, *Capitalism and Social Democracy* (Cambridge: Cambridge University Press, 1985), p. 43.

48. Klaus von Beyme, "Policy-making in the Federal Republic of Germany: A Systematic Introduction," in Klaus von Beyme and Manfred G. Schmidt, eds., *Policy and Politics in the Federal Republic of Germany* (London: Gower, 1985), pp. 9–10.

49. SPD paper, "The Future of the Social Welfare State," reprinted in Peter J. Katzenstein, *Policy and Politics in West Germany* (Philadelphia: Temple University Press, 1987), pp. 204–5. See also Markovits, *The Politics*, p. 428.

50. David Goodhart, "SPD Agrees to Programme Under Shadow of German Question," *Financial Times*, December 21, 1989, p. 2.

51. *Basic Policy Programme of the Social Democratic Party of Germany* (Bonn: SPD National Executive Committee, 1990), pp. 40–41.

52. "SPD Debate over Lafontaine Reform Continues," Foreign Broadcast Information Service, Federal Republic of Germany, February 7, 1989, pp. 19–20.

53. Peter J. Katzenstein, *Corporatism and Change: Austria, Switzerland, and the Politics of Industry* (Ithaca: Cornell University Press, 1984), pp. 49–51, 65.

54. "Austria: The Shadow of the Past," *The Economist*, February 25, 1989, Austria Survey, p. 7.

55. Peter J. Katzenstein, *Small States in World Markets: Industrial Planning in Europe* (Ithaca: Cornell University Press, 1985), pp. 88–89.

56. Wolfgang C. Mueller, "Privatizing in a Corporatist Economy: The Politics of Privatization in Austria," *West European Politics*, October 1988, pp. 108–13.

57. Clifford Stevens, "Austria Begins Denationalization Policy to Stem Losses, Finance New Investment," *Wall Street Journal*, October 27, 1986, p. 35; Diana Federman and Clifford Stevens, "Austria Looks West for Help in Rejuvenating Economy," *Wall Street Journal*, May 20, 1987, p. 30; "Austrian Privatization," *New York Times*, November 17, 1988, p. D21; "Austria," *The Economist*, Austria Survey, pp. 8–9, 14.

58. *The Economist*, Austria Survey, p. 15.

59. Jonas Pontusson, "The Triumph of Pragmatism: Nationalization and Privatization in Sweden," *West European Politics*, October 1988, pp. 129, 133–36.

60. Harrington, *The Next Left*, pp. 130–31, emphasis in the original. See also Sven Steinmo, "Social Democracy vs. Socialism: Goal Adaptation in Social Democratic Sweden," *Politics and Society*, December 1988, p. 434.

61. Harrington, *The Next Left*, p. 161. See also Jonas Pontusson, "Radicalization and Retreat in Swedish Social Democracy," *New Left Review*, September–October 1987, pp. 17–22.

62. Steven Greenhouse, "Sweden's Social Democrats Veer Toward Free Market and Lower Taxes," *New York Times*, October 27, 1989, p. A3. See also Henry Milner, *Sweden Social Democracy in Practice* (New York: Oxford University Press, 1989), p. 211.

63. Quoted in "Mensheviksson," *The Economist*, April 1, 1989, pp. 42–44. See also Steinmo, "Social Democracy," p. 434.

64. For a profile of Feldt, his ideology, and influence in the party, see Robert Taylor, "The Acceptable Face of Socialism," *Financial Times*, June 16, 1988, IV, p. 4.

65. Greenhouse, "Sweden's Social Democrats."

66. Steinmo, "Social Democracy," pp. 407, 411. See also "The Swedish Economy Survey," *The Economist*, March 3, 1990, Survey, pp. 10, 16, 18.

67. L. Gordon Crovitz, "Sweden's Crackup: Eastern Europeans Learn There's No Middle Way," *Barron's*, July 23, 1990, p. 10.

68. "Sweden's Nice Reform, Nasty Burden," *The Economist*, November 11, 1989, pp. 59–60.

69. "Sweden Says Tax Overhaul Will Worsen Inflation Rate," *Wall Street Journal*, November 14, 1989, p. A19.

70. Robert Taylor, "Sweden's Climate Becomes More Austere," *Financial Times*, October 22, 1990, p. 4.

71. Tony Spybey, "Heart of Palme," *Times Higher Education Supplement*, October 19, 1990, p. 32.

72. Steven Prokesch, "Non-Socialists Lead in Norwegian Vote," *New York Times*, September 12, 1989, p. A3.

73. William M. Lafferty, "The Political Transformation of a Social Democratic State: As the World Moves In, Norway Moves Right," *West European Politics*, January 1990, pp. 98–99; for comparable developments in the Netherlands, see Rudy B. Andeweg, "Less Than Nothing? Hidden Privatisation of the Pseudo-Private Sector: The Dutch Case," *West European Politics*, October 1988, pp. 117–28.

74. Seymour Martin Lipset, *Political Man: The Social Bases of Politics* (Baltimore: Johns Hopkins University Press, 1981 expanded edition), pp. 54–55.

75. Gøsta Esping-Andersen, *Politics Against Markets: The Social Democratic Road to Power* (Princeton: Princeton University Press, 1985), pp. 196, 215.

76. "Labour Does Its Best," *The Economist*, May 13, 1989, p. 20.

77. "To the Boats for the Tories?" *The Economist*, March 17, 1990, p. 13.

78. "Modern Times, Labour-Style," *The Economist*, May 13, 1989, p. 61.

79. David Marquand, "Don't Be a Chip Off the Old Blockers," *The Guardian*, June 12, 1989, p. 16. See also Marquand, "Keep Right On," *The New Statesman and Society*, June 21, 1989, pp. 20–21.

80. Quoted in Jeff Greenfield, "Challenging the Liturgy," *The West Side Spirit*, May 28, 1989, p. 13. See also Hobsbawm, "Lost Horizons," p. 16.

81. Quoted in Craig R. Whitney, "Is He a Match for Thatcher?" *New York Times Magazine*, July 15, 1990, p. 36.

82. Karel Williams, John Williams, and Colin Haslam, "No Job for the Social Scapegoat," *The Times Higher Education Supplement*, August 17, 1990, p. 11.

83. "Tax Evasion," *The New Statesman and Society*, June 1, 1990, p. 4.

84. "On Second Thoughts," *The Economist*, September 29, 1990, p. 64.

85. "Editorial Trading Places," *The New Statesman and Society*, September 21, 1990, p. 4.

86. "Labour and the Economy," *Financial Times*, May 21, 1990, p. 14.

87. Charles Leadbeater, "Business Still Cautious of Labour," *Financial Times*, July 15, 1990, p. 6.

88. Sarah Baxter, "Them and US," *The New Statesman and Society*, August 17, 1990, p. 6.

89. Quoted in Charlotte Gray, "Designer Socialism," *Saturday Night*, August 1989, p. 8.

90. Seymour Martin Lipset, "Anti-Incumbancy: In Canada Too?" *American Enterprise*, November–December 1990, pp. 22–23.

91. Michael Valpy, "Brushing Away Chaff from Election Thinking," *The Globe and Mail*, September 6, 1990, p. A5.

92. Barry Brown, "Ontario's New Leader Hits Trade Pact," *Washington Times*, September 10, 1990, p. A10.

93. Richard Mackie, "Ontario Approves Consumers' Gas Sale," *The Globe and Mail*, November 8, 1990, p. B1.

94. Richard Mackie, "NDP Won't Keep Promise on No-Loophole Rent Controls," *The Globe and Mail*, November 8, 1990, p. 1.

95. John Fitzmaurice, *Quebec and Canada: Past, Present and Future* (London: C. Hurst and Company, 1985), pp. 198–200.

96. "Doi Says JSP Will Shift Gears to Fulfill Campaign Promises," *Japan Times*, August 13, 1989, p. 1.

97. Steven R. Weisman, "After Victory, Japan Leftists Face Scrutiny," *New York Times*, July 30, 1989, p. 9.

98. David E. Sanger, "Japan's Opposition Tailors Itself to the Mainstream," *New York Times*, July 21, 1989, p. A3.

99. Sumio Kido, "JSP Battling Image as Party of Idealists," *Japan Economic Journal*, August 12, 1989, p. 6; "JSP Leaders Want to Drop Goal of Socialist Revolution," *Japan Times Weekly International Edition*, March 26–April 1, 1990, p. 2.

100. "How Doi Might Do It," *The Economist*, July 29, 1989, p. 30.

101. Sanger, "Japan's Opposition."

102. Susan Moffat, "Maybe Japan Doesn't Really Need Political Leadership," *Japan Times*, August 14, 1989, p. 17.

103. Alan Arian, *Ideological Change in Israel* (Cleveland: Press of Case Western Reserve University, 1968), p. 6.

104. Ibid., p. 61.

105. Benjamin Rubin, "Koor: Israel's Economic Crisis of Faith," *Midstream*, November 1989, pp. 3–4.

106. Ralph Mandel, "Israel," *American Jewish Year Book 1989* (New York: American Jewish Committee, 1989), p. 414; Judy Maltz, "No to Koor Write-Off Plan," *Jerusalem Post International Edition*, December 23, 1989, p. 5.

107. N. D. Gross, "Hostile Reception for Peres Budget," *Jerusalem Post International Edition*, December 30, 1989, pp. 1–2.

108. "The Socialist Who Pushes Privatization," *Jerusalem Post International Edition*, June 16, 1990, p. 20.

109. "Koor on the Block," *Jerusalem Post International Edition*, January 20, 1990, p. 24.

110. Rubin, "Koor," p. 7.

111. Regis Debray, "What's Left of the Left?" *New Perspectives Quarterly*, Spring 1990, p. 27.

112. "On Second Thoughts," p. 64.

113. Leo Panitch, "The Impasse of Social Democratic Politics," in Ralph Miliband, John Saville, Marcel Liebman, and Leo Panitch, eds., *The Socialist Register*, 1985/6 (London: Merlin Press, 1986), pp. 54–56.

114. Przeworski, *Capitalism and Social Democracy*, p. 43.

115. Harrington, *The Next Left*, p. 151, emphasis in the original. Another systematic comparative analyst of the movement, Anton Pelinka, also noted that "the influence of Social Democratic parties on the state... and on society... attenuates social conflicts, mitigating the contradiction between labor and capital" by enhancing "the probability of a cooperative stance on the part of the unions." Anton Pelinka, *Social Democratic Parties in Europe* (New York: Praeger, 1983), p. 103.

116. For an excellent study of the ways the strongest social democratic party adapted its program to electoral needs, see Diane Sainsbury, *Swedish Social Democratic Ideology and Electoral Politics, 1944–1948* (Stockholm: Almqvist and Wiksell, 1980).

117. Adam Przeworski and John Sprague, *Paper Stones: A History of Electoral Socialism* (Chicago: University of Chicago Press, 1986), pp. 31–45; Eric Hobsbawm, *Politics for a Rational Left* (London: Verso, 1989), pp. 10–22.

118. Ronald Inglehart, *Culture Shift in Advanced Industrial Society* (Princeton: Princeton University Press, 1990), pp. 258–64, 318–21.

119. R. Lesthaegh and G. Moors, "Rationality, Cohorts and Reproduction," Interuniversity Programme in Demography Working Paper, 1990–1 (Brussels: Centrum Sociologie, Vrije Universitet, 1990), pp. 119–22.

120. Inglehart, *Culture Shift*, pp. 77–92.

121. Dennis Kavanaugh, "Introduction to European Politics and policies," in Gerald A. Dorfman and Peter J. Duignan, eds., *Politics in Western Europe* (Stanford: Hoover Institution Press, 1988), pp. 12–13; Wolfgang Merkel, "After the Gold Age: Is Social Democracy Doomed to Decline?" Paper presented to the conference "The Crisis of Socialism in Eastern and Western Europe," University of North Carolina at Chapel Hill, April 6–8, 1990.

122. Summarized in Melanie A. Sully, *Continuity and Change in Austrian Socialism: The Eternal Quest for a Third Way* (New York: Columbia University Press, 1982), p. 211.

123. Stephen Fidler, "Developing Nations Increase Reliance on Private Sector," *Financial Times*, September 11, 1990, p. 1.

124. James S. Henry, "Growing Nowhere," *New Republic*, August 20 and 27, 1990, p. 21.

125. Linda Robinson, "Latin America's Colossal Sale, Big Three Look to Privatization Prosperity," *San Francisco Chronicle*, "Briefing," June 20, 1990, p. 2.

126. James Brooke, "Castro Loses His Appeal to the Latin Left," *New York Times*, August 19, 1990, p. 2E.

127. Annetta Miller, "Perestroika Goes South," *Newsweek*, November 6, 1989, p. 53; Robinson, "Latin America's Colossal Sale," pp. 1, 4.

128. Shirley Christian, "Argentina's President Takes Helm of Peronists After Rival's Setback," *New York Times*, August 15, 1990, p. A6.

129. Gary Mead, "Tough Match for Argentina," *Financial Times*, July 12, 1990, p. 11; Tom Wicker, "The Long Road Back," *New York Times*, August 30, 1990, p. A23.

130. Flora Lewis, "Menem Confounds," *New York Times*, May 19, 1990, p. 23; Thomas Kamm, "Argentina Kicks Off Privatization Drive," *Wall Street Journal*, June 26, 1990, p. A12; John Barham, "Menem's Deepest Cut of All," *Financial Times*, September 18, 1990, p. 8.

131. Torcuato S. DiTella, "Menem's Argentina," *Government and Opposition*, Winter 1990, pp. 85–97.

132. Alexandre Burke Makler, "External Debt and Market Liberalization in Bra-

zil: A New Look at Dependent Development and the Patrimonialist State," senior honors thesis, Political Economy of Industrial Societies Group Major Program, University of California, Berkeley, May 1990, p. 11.

133. Quoted in Makler, "External Debt," p. 11.

134. "Brazil Middlemen," *The Economist*, November 25, 1989, p. 88.

135. "After 32 Years of Democracy, Fears of a Coup in Venezuela," *New York Times*, August 10, 1990, p. A3.

136. James Brooke, "Venezuela Isn't Exactly Wild for Another Boom," *New York Times*, September 3, 1990, p. E3.

137. Shirley Christian, "How Chile Is Devising a Democracy," *New York Times*, December 17, 1989, p. E2.

138. Shirley Christian, "Chile Is Getting Independent Central Bank," *New York Times*, December 11, 1989, p. C1.

139. "Allende's Ghost," *The Economist*, September 8, 1990, p. 50.

140. Thomas Kamon, "Chileans Set to Vote Today in the Shadow of Pinochet," *Wall Street Journal*, December 14, 1989, p. A12.

141. Tom Wicker, "Breaking the Cycle," *New York Times*, August 23, 1990, p. A19. The communists, an electorally important party before Pinochet, were insignificant in the 1990 election. See Samuel Silva, "'The Mummies of Marxism' Gasp for Breath in Chile," *Wall Street Journal*, September 21, 1990, p. A15.

142. Shirley Christian, "Chile Will Vote Freely This Week, Thanks in Part to Allende's Followers," *New York Times*, December 11, 1989, p. A3.

143. Tom Wicker, "Conflict to Consensus," *New York Times*, August 20, 1990, p. A19.

144. Marjorie Miller, "Salinas, Amid Jeers, Defends His Economic Program," *Los Angeles Times*, November 2, 1989, p. A8.

145. Larry Rohter, "Stop the World, Mexico Is Getting On," *New York Times*, June 3, 1990, p. 1F. All told, Mexico is privatizing 770 companies. Gary Hector, "Why Mexico Is Looking Better," *Fortune*, January 15, 1990, pp. 136–37.

146. Quoted in David Asman, "Is Mexico's New Market Economy Here to Stay?" *Wall Street Journal*, June 1, 1990, p. A10.

147. Shirley Christian, "In Uruguay, Two Leaders and Two Ideologies," *New York Times*, August 29, 1990, p. A5.

148. Howard W. French, "Jamaican Leader to Meet Bush Today," *New York Times*, May 3, 1990, p. A8, "In the Caribbean, It's Still the Age of Patriarchs," *New York Times*, News of the Week, May 27, 1990, p. 2E.

149. Sam Seibert with Michael Kepp, "The Left Tries to Get It Right," *Newsweek*, July 16, 1990, p. 39.

150. Angus Deming, "Kaunda's Fall from Grace," *Newsweek*, July 16, 1990, p. 37.

151. "Zimbabwean Business Confidence Increases," *Financial Times*, May 23, 1990, p. 6; Julian Berger, "Zimbabwe Belatedly Loosens Government Economic Control," *Financial Times*, July 6, 1990, p. 6; "Zimbabwe's Economy Breaking Free," *The Economist*, August 25, 1990, p. 36.

152. William Keeling, "Ghana Paying the Price for Its Political Principles," *Financial Times*, August 22, 1990, p. 6.

153. "Togo's Takeaway Economy," *The Economist*, June 16, 1989, p. 48; William Keeling, "Liberal Steps Fall Short," *Financial Times*, October 9, 1990, p. 10.

154. "Benin's Second Chance." *International Herald Tribune*, July 6, 1990, p. 6.

155. Michaels, "Continental Shift," p. 35; Roger Thurow, "Decades After Nation-

alization Drive, Tanzanian Business Clan's Hopes Revive," *Wall Street Journal*, July 23, 1990, p. A4; Neil Henry, "Nyerere Bows Out with Tanzania in Deep Decline," *Washington Post*, September 26, 1990, pp. A27–A28.

156. Christopher S. Wren, "Mandela Group Softens Its Socialism," *New York Times*, October 4, 1990, p. A3.

157. David Houaego, "Delhi Considering Radical Easing of Investment Curbs," *Financial Times*, June 29, 1990, p. 6; Sanjoy Hazarika, "As India Opens Its Economy, Some Cling to Socialist Ideals," *New York Times*, August 4, 1990, p. Y3.

158. George C. Wilson, "Vietnam Appears to Fear a Democracy Movement in Prospect," *Washington Post*, July 19, 1990, p. A28.

159. Leonard I. Weinglass, "Asia's Latest Economic Miracle Is Vietnam," *New York Times*, January 20, 1990, p. A18.

160. Barry Wain, "Hanoi Embraces Once-Reviled Capitalism," *Wall Street Journal*, May 1, 1990, p. A16.

161. Charles P. Wallace, "Vietnam Becoming Less Soviet, More Asian, More Prosperous," *San Francisco Chronicle*, February 22, 1990, p. A19.

162. Emily MacFarquhar, "Hanoi's Hasty Pudding: Beset by Hunger and Hyperinflation, Vietnam Suddenly Discovers Capitalism Turning Ho Chi Min's Communism on Its Head," *U.S. News and World Report*, July 23, 1990, p. 38.

163. Barry Wain, "Vietnam's Economic Reform Is Still a Delicate Planting," *Wall Street Journal*, May 24, 1989, p. A10.

164. Stuart Butler, "Razing the Liberal Plantation," *National Review*, November 10, 1989, p. 27. A Swedish economist, Assar Lindbeck, has recently made a similar comment with respect to his own country. "Rent control seems in many cases to be the most effective way of destroying a city—except for bombing." Quoted in Crovitz, "Sweden's Crackup," p. 10.

165. Robert Pear, "Phnom Penh, Eye on West, Tries to Shed Image as Hanoi Puppet," *New York Times*, January 8, 1990, p. 6. See also Michael J. Horowitz, "Toward a New Cambodian Policy," *American Spectator*, June 1990, pp. 24–26.

166. Steven Erlanger, "Reports from Phnom Penh Indicate New Instability," *New York Times*, June 24, 1990, p. Y9; Sidney Jones, "War and Human Rights in Cambodia," *New York Review of Books*, July 19, 1990, p. 18.

167. "Cambodia No Will, No Way," *The Economist*, March 3, 1990, p. 30.

168. Henry Kamm, "Communist Laos Mixes Strict Political Dogma with Capitalist Economics," *New York Times*, January 27, 1990, p. 4Y; Jimmy St. Goar, "A Whiff of Economic Freedom in Laos," *Wall Street Journal*, March 21, 1990, p. A20; Stan Sesser, "A Reporter at Large: Forgotten Country (Laos)," *New Yorker*, August 20, 1990, pp. 39–68.

169. Mark A. Uhlig, "Cuba Loses Allure for Nicaraguans," *New York Times*, January 18, 1990, pp. A1, A10.

170. John F. Burns, "Leaders in Kabul Seek a New Image," *New York Times*, May 5, 1990, p. 6.

171. "Asides," *Wall Street Journal*, May 22, 1990, p. A14.

172. Jane Perlez, "Ethiopia's Long War Draws Closer to the Capital," *New York Times*, July 21, 1990, p. 5.

173. Associated Press, "Ethiopia Rulers Discard Communism," *The Gazette* (Montreal), March 6, 1990, p. A10.

174. "Mozambique War's End," *The Economist*, September 1, 1990, p. 40.

175. For a detailed review of the literature on the subject, see Seymour Martin

Lipset's "Why No Socialism in the United States?" in Seweryn Bialer and Sophia Sluzar, eds., *Sources of Contemporary Radicalism*, vol. 1 (Boulder: Westview Press, 1977), pp. 31–149, 346–63.

176. Tom Kenworthy, "Gephardt's New Campaign: Rallying His Party," *Washington Post National Weekly Edition*, May 7–13, 1990, p. 14.

177. "On Second Thoughts," p. 64; Gwen Ifill, "Kemp Assails Senate Funding Curbs," *Washington Post*, September 29, 1990, p. A6.

178. See Lipset, "Why No Socialism in the United States?" pp. 50–58; and Lipset, *Consensus and Conflict*, pp. 221–25.

179. Walter Dean Burnham, "The United States: The Politics of Heterogeneity," in Richard Rose, ed., *Electoral Behavior* (New York: Free Press, 1974), p. 718. A related thesis suggests that the absence of a significant socialist movement in the United States is to be explained in part by the vitality of the classically liberal, antistatist, and individualistic values, which linked to the ideology of the American Revolution, have been much stronger here than elsewhere. Conversely, socialist movements are the other side of the Tory-statist tradition and greater collectivity and noblesse oblige orientations to be found in countries with a monarchical and aristocratic background. See H. G. Wells, *The Future in America* (New York: Harper and Brothers, 1906), pp. 72–76; Louis Hartz, *The Founding of New Societies* (New York: Harcourt, Brace and World, 1964), p. 35; Seymour Martin Lipset, *Continental Divide: The Values and Institutions of the United States and Canada* (New York: Routledge, 1990), pp. 26–29, 149–50.

180. Lipset, *Political Man*, p. 234.

181. Jean François Revel, *Without Marx or Jesus* (Garden City: Doubleday, 1971), p. 6.

182. Ibid., pp. 6–7.

183. For a review of the literature on corporatism and social democracy, see Milner, *Sweden*, pp. 23–31.

184. Lipset, *Consensus and Conflict*, pp. 296–99.

185. Nelson W. Polsby, *Consequences of Party Reform* (New York: Oxford University Press, 1983); Byron E. Shafer, *Quiet Revolution: The Struggle for the Democratic Party and the Shaping of Post-Reform Politics* (New York: Russell Sage Foundation, 1983).

186. Christopher Matthews, "Democrats Look for a Heavyweight," *San Francisco Examiner*, January 12, 1990, p. A25.

187. Richard Hofstadter, *Anti-Intellectualism in American Life* (New York: Knopf, 1963), p. 29; Seymour Martin Lipset and Richard E. Dobson, "The Intellectual as Critic and Rebel: With Special Reference to the United States and the Soviet Union," *Daedalus*, Summer 1972, pp. 138–47. See also "Text of a Pre-Inauguration Memo from Moynihan on Problems Nixon Would Face," *New York Times*, March 11, 1970, pp. 1, 30.

188. Carolyn J. Mooney, "Professors Are Upbeat About Profession But Uneasy About Students, Standards," *The Chronicle of Higher Education*, November 8, 1989, p. A20. For earlier survey data, see Everett Carll Ladd, Jr., and Seymour Martin Lipset, *The Divided Academy: Professors and Politics* (New York: Norton, 1976).

189. Garry Abrams, "After the Wall: As New Era Emerges U.S. Political Thinkers Ponder Fate of Marxism," *Los Angeles Times*, December 6, 1989, pp. E1, E6; Tony Judt, "The Rediscovery of Central Europe," *Daedalus*, Winter 1990, p. 34. For conservative views, see Peter Shaw, *The War Against the Intellect: Episodes in the De-*

cline of Discourse (Iowa City: University of Iowa Press, 1989); Paul Hollander, *The Survival of the Adversary Culture* (New Brunswick: Transaction Books, 1988); and Roger Kimball, *Tenured Radicals: How Politics Has Corrupted Higher Education* (New York: Harper and Row, 1990). For radical ones, see Bertell Ollmann and Edward Vernoff, eds., *The Left Academy: Marxist Scholarship on American Campuses* (New York: McGraw-Hill, 1982); Jonathan M. Wiener, "Radical Historians and the Crisis in American History, 1959–1980," *Journal of American History*, September 1989, pp. 399–434; Michael Burawoy, "Introduction: The Resurgence of Marxism in American Sociology," *American Journal of Sociology* 88 (Supplement 1982), pp. S1–S30; and Richard Flacks, *Making History: The Radical Tradition in American Life* (New York: Columbia University Press, 1988), pp. 185–86, 190–91.

190. John Gray, "Fashion, Fantasy or Fiasco?" *Times Literary Supplement*, February 24–March 2, 1989, p. 183.

191. Gerald Marzorati, "Europe Is Reclaiming the Language of Liberalism," *International Herald Tribune*, July 11, 1990, p. 4.

192. M. F. Perutz, "High on Science," *New York Review of Books*, August 16, 1990, p. 15.

193. Robert Alter, "Tyrants and Butterflies," *New Republic*, October 15, 1990, p. 43.

194. Richard Flacks, "The Sociology Liberation Movement: Some Legacies and Lessons," *Critical Sociology*, Summer 1988, p. 17.

195. Wiener, "Radical Historians," p. 434.

196. In 1985, a majority of the media elite identified themselves as on the left. S. Robert Lichter, Stanley Rothman, and Linda S. Lichter, *The Media Elite: America's New Power Brokers* (Washington, D.C.: Adler and Adler, 1986), p. 28.

197. See Richard Lowenthal, "The Future of the 'Social Democratic Consensus,'" *Dissent*, Winter 1982, p. 101.

198. Hollander, *The Survival*, pp. 16–18.

199. Lipset, *Consensus and Conflict*, pp. 194–205.

200. For a description of the way change occurred, see Tony Judt, *Marxism and the French Left* (New York: Oxford University Press, 1986). See also Mark Kesselman, "Lyrical Illusions or a Socialism of Governance: Whither French Socialism?" in Ralph Miliband, John Saville, Marcel Liebman, and Leo Panitch, eds., *Socialist Register 1985/86* (London: Merlin Press, 1986), pp. 240–42.

201. Masakazu Yamazaki, "The Intellectual Community of the Showa Era," *Daedalus*, Summer 1990, pp. 260–62.

202. Ron Eyerman, "Intellectuals and the State: A Framework for Analysis, with Special Reference to the United States and Sweden," unpublished paper, University of Lund, 1990, p. 18.

203. Gray, "Fashion, Fantasy, or Fiasco?" pp. 183–84.

204. A striking example is John Kenneth Galbraith, who, at a conference in July 1990 on economic reforms in Eastern Europe, railed against the "primitive ideology" of rapid movement toward market economics. He made "a veiled attack on the privatization programs planned by some East European governments." "East Europe Warned Over Fast Economic Change," *Financial Times*, July 6, 1990, p.2. See his critique of developments in Eastern Europe in "The Rush to Capitalism," *New York Review of Books*, October 25, 1990, pp. 51–52.

205. For review, see Marguerite Michaels, "Continental Shift," *Time*, May 21,

1990, pp. 34–36. See also Werner Thomas, "Die Guerilleros in Latinamerika Kampfen gegen die Zeit," *Die Zeit*, July 10, 1990, p. 2.

206. "The New Soviet Man: An Interview with Gerasimov," *National Review*, August 20, 1990, p. 31.

207. Andrey V. Kozyrev, "Why Soviet Foreign Policy Went Sour," *New York Times*, January 7, 1989, p. 27. He also noted that the Soviet Union's direct and indirect involvement in Third World "regional conflicts leads to colossal losses by increasing general international tensions, justifying the arms race and hindering the establishment of mutually advantageous ties with the West."

208. Peter Passell, "Soviet Deputy Prime Minister Is Seeking a Safe Path Through a Time of Change," *New York Times*, January 1, 1990, p. A23. The argument has been reiterated more recently by Gorbachev's personal economic adviser, Nikolai Y. Petrakev, who in an interview on June 8, 1990, "supported a decree already drafted to rapidly denationalize state-owned industry by creating a stock market and selling shares to the public." Bill Keller, "Speedup Change, Soviet Aide Urges," *New York Times*, June 10, 1990, p. 12Y. For the text of an earlier interview with Petrakev along the same lines, see "Can the Russians Really Reform?" *Fortune*, May 7, 1990, pp. 117–22.

209. Michael Dobbs, "A Plan for Two-Year Revolution," *Washington Post*, September 14, 1990, p. 1.

210. S. Frederick Starr, "Pooped Party," *New Republic*, December 4, 1989, p. 20.

211. "The Triumph of Capitalism," *New Perspectives Quarterly*, Fall 1989, p. 4.

212. Robert Heilbroner, "The Triumph of Capitalism," *New Yorker*, January 23, 1989, p. 98.

213. Robert Heilbroner, "The Triumph of Capitalism," *New Perspectives Quarterly*, Fall 1989, p. 4.

214. Ibid., p. 7.

215. Ibid., p. 10. See Michael Harrington, *Socialism: Past and Future* (New York: Arcade Publishing, 1989), pp. 248–78.

216. Patrick Wintour, "Kinnock Seeking Strategy to Speed Reform in East," *The Guardian*, December 21, 1989, p. 6.

217. "Eastern Europe Moves Right: No Halfway House," *The Economist*, March 24, 1990, pp. 21, 22.

218. Steinmo, "Social Democracy," p. 438.

219. Przeworski, *Capitalism and Social Democracy*, p. 206.

220. Debray, "What's Left of the Left," p. 27.

221. Sven Steinmo, "Political Institutions and Tax Policy in the United States, Sweden and Britain," *World Politics*, July 1989, p. 504.

222. Ibid., p. 509.

223. Henry Aaron, "The Impossible Dream Comes True: The New Tax Reform Act," *Brookings Review*, Winter 1987, p. 6; Committee on Ways and Means, U.S. House of Representatives, *Tax Progressivity and Income Distribution*. Prepared for the use of the Committee on Ways and Means by its majority staff (Washington, D.C.: U.S. Government Printing Office, 1990), pp. 53–55.

224. Evidence bearing on the difference in the dominant orientation toward the state between the United States and other countries may be found in Robert Y. Shapiro and John T. Young, "Public Opinion Toward Social Welfare Policies: The United States in Comparative Perspective," *Research in Micropolitics*, vol. 3 (Greenwich,

Conn.: JAI Press, 1990), pp. 143–86; and "America: A Unique Outlook?" *American Enterprise*, March–April 1990, pp. 113–20.

225. Lipset, *Continental Divide*, p. 39; Kevin Philips, *The Politics of Rich and Poor: Wealth and the American Electorate in the Reagan Aftermath* (New York: Random House, 1990).

226. Douglas Webber, "Social Democracy and the Re-emergence of Mass Unemployment in Western Europe," in William E. Patterson and Alastair H. Thomas, eds., *The Future of Social Democracy* (Oxford: Clarendon Press, 1986), pp. 36–49; "Economic and Financial Indicators," *The Economist*, July 21, 1990, p. 101. Conversely, the United States and Canada have experienced a much greater increase in the number of new jobs created between 1973 and 1986 than Japan and Europe. Angus Maddison, *The World Economy in the 20th Century* (Paris: Development Centre of the OECD, 1989), p. 132.

227. "The World's Billionaires," *Forbes*, July 23, 1990, pp. 189, 255; Julianne Slovak, "The Billionaires Rank by New Worth," *Fortune*, September 11, 1989, pp. 73–133.

228. Lipset, *Continental Divide*, pp. 129–34.

229. Alastair H. Thomas, "Social Democracy in Scandinavia: Can Dominance be Regained?" in Patterson and Thomas, eds., *The Future of Social Democracy*, p. 203.

230. Crovitz, "Sweden's Crackup," p. 10.

231. John Burton, "Insurance Against Hard Times Ahead," *Financial Times*, November 2, 1990, p. 25.

232. Peter Stein, "Sweden: Failure of the Welfare State," *Journal of Economic Growth* 2:4 (1989), p. 38.

233. Matthews, "Democrats," p. A25.

234. Charles S. Robb, *New Directions, Enduring Values* (Washington, D.C.: Democratic Leadership Council, 1988), p. 34.

235. Matthews, "Democrats," p. A25.

236. Joseph Schumpeter, *Capitalism, Socialism and Democracy* (London: Allen and Unwin, 1976), esp. pp. 131–63, 421–25; Irving Kristol, *Two Cheers for Capitalism* (New York: Basic Books, 1978), esp. pp. 153–187, 255–70.

237. Kristol, *Two Cheers*, pp. 186–87.

Contributors

DAVID CALLEO holds the Dean Acheson Chair at the School for Advanced International Studies at the Johns Hopkins University and is Director of its European Studies Program. His major books have been *America and the World Political Economy* (with Benjamin Rowland), *The German Problem Reconsidered*, *The Imperious Economy*, and *Beyond American Hegemony*.

DANIEL CHIROT is Professor of International Studies and Sociology at the University of Washington. He has written *Social Change in a Peripheral Society*, *Social Change in the Twentieth Century*, and *Social Change in the Modern Era*.

BRUCE CUMINGS is Professor of East Asian and International History at the University of Chicago. He is the author of *The Origins of the Korean War*, a two-volume work, and of numerous studies about the political economy of East Asia. The first of his volumes on the Korean War won the American Historical Association's John K. Fairbank Award.

STEPHEN E. HANSON is Assistant Professor of Political Science at the University of Washington. He is completing a book on *Time and Industrialization in the USSR*.

KEN JOWITT is Professor of Political Science at the University of California at Berkeley. He is the author of *Revolutionary Breakthroughs and National Development*, *Images of Detente and the Soviet Political Order*, and *The Leninist Response to National Dependency*.

NICHOLAS R. LARDY is Professor of International Studies at the University of Washington. He is the author of *Economic Growth and Distribution in China*, *Agricultural Prices in China*, *Agriculture in China's Modern Economic Development*, *China's Entry into the World Economy*, and other studies about the economy of modern China.

SEYMOUR MARTIN LIPSET holds the Hazel chair of Public Policy at George Mason University and is a Senior Fellow at the Hoover Institution of Stanford University. He is a past president of the American Political Science Association. His best known books are *Union Democracy*, *Political Man*, *The First New Nation*, *Consensus and Conflict*, and *Continental Divide*.

ELIZABETH J. PERRY is Professor of Political Science at the University of California at Berkeley. She is the author of *Rebels and Revolutionaries in North China* and *Shanghai on Strike: The Politics of Chinese Labor.*

W. W. ROSTOW is Professor Emeritus of Economics and History at the University of Texas in Austin. He is the past chairman of the Policy Planning Council of the Department of State, a past special assistant to Presidents John Kennedy and Lyndon Johnson, and the author of some thirty books. His most influential work is *The Stages of Economic Growth: A Non-Communist Manifesto,* and his most recent book is *Theories of Economic Growth from David Hume to the Present.*

Index